The Climate Planner

The Climate Planner is about overcoming the objections to climate change mitigation and adaption that urban planners face at a local level. It shows how to draft climate plans that encounter less resistance because they involve the public, stakeholders, and decisionmakers in a way that builds trust, creates consensus, and leads to implementation. Although focused on the local level, this book discusses climate basics such as carbon dioxide levels in the atmosphere, the Intergovernmental Panel on Climate Change, the Paris Agreement of 2015, worldwide energy generation forecasts, and other items of global concern in order to familiarize urban planners and citizen planners with key concepts that they will need to know in order to be able to host climate conversations at the local level. The many case studies from around the United States of America show how communities have encountered pushback and bridged the implementation gap, the gap between plan and reality, thanks to a commitment to substantive public engagement. The book is written for urban planners, local activists, journalists, elected or appointed representatives, and the average citizen worried about climate breakdown and interested in working to reshape the built environment.

Jason King, AICP, is an urban planner who has directed multi-disciplinary teams around the U.S. and the world, and has served as the project director and prime author on over 200 plans for cities, towns, neighborhoods, and corridors. From the first plan he worked on for the Tarautao Islands of Thailand, to the multiple plans he authored in Coastal Louisiana, Southeast Florida, and the American Southwest, Jason's work has focused on social, economic, and climate change resilience. He is a Principal at Dover, Kohl & Partners.

"*The Climate Planner* is a very accessible and pragmatic book that helps readers navigate the challenging political landscape of climate change and find solutions. At the same time, the book is holistic and marries the disciplines of climate science, effective communication theory, and local climate planning to achieve the local cohesiveness required for climate action plan implementation. *The Climate Planner* empowers citizens, urban planners, and local elected leaders with solutions. The material is well-timed and opportune. I believe this book will become a classic in the field of planning."

—**Diana Peña**, *founding partner, Able City, U.S.A.*

"Jason King provides us with real and practical solutions to the climate crisis. *The Climate Planner* is a great resource for anyone seeking to affect change in their communities. Offering the latest data and research in climate change and sustainability planning, *The Climate Planner* also provides a local perspective from cities and communities from across the world. Readers will come away empowered to fight for a better future, to answer the call to make a difference during these perilous times."

—**Carlos Gallinar**, *former planning director for El Paso and Principal at Gallinar Planning & Development, LLC, U.S.A.*

The Climate Planner

Overcoming Pushback Against Local Mitigation and Adaptation Plans

Jason King

NEW YORK AND LONDON

First published 2022
by Routledge
605 Third Avenue, New York, NY 10158

and by Routledge
2 Park Square, Milton Park, Abingdon, Oxon OX14 4RN

Routledge is an imprint of the Taylor & Francis Group, an informa business

© 2022 Jason King

The right of Jason King to be identified as author of this work has been asserted by him in accordance with sections 77 and 78 of the Copyright, Designs and Patents Act 1988.

All rights reserved. No part of this book may be reprinted or reproduced or utilized in any form or by any electronic, mechanical, or other means, now known or hereafter invented, including photocopying and recording, or in any information storage or retrieval system, without permission in writing from the publishers.

Trademark notice: Product or corporate names may be trademarks or registered trademarks, and are used only for identification and explanation without intent to infringe.

Library of Congress Cataloging-in-Publication Data
Names: King, Jason (City planner), author.
Title: The climate planner: overcoming pushback against local mitigation and adaptation plans / Jason King.
Description: New York, NY: Routledge, 2022. |
Includes bibliographical references and index.
Identifiers: LCCN 2021006618 (print) | LCCN 2021006619 (ebook) |
ISBN 9781032020235 (hardback) | ISBN 9781032020204 (paperback) |
ISBN 9781003181514 (ebook)
Subjects: LCSH: City planning–Environmental aspects. | Urban ecology. |
Climatic changes–Effect of human beings on.
Classification: LCC HT166 .K5557 2022 (print) |
LCC HT166 (ebook) | DDC 307.1/216–dc23
LC record available at https://lccn.loc.gov/2021006618
LC ebook record available at https://lccn.loc.gov/2021006619

ISBN: 9781032020235 (hbk)
ISBN: 9781032020204 (pbk)
ISBN: 9781003181514 (ebk)

DOI: 10.4324/9781003181514

Typeset in Adobe Garamond Pro
by Newgen Publishing UK

Illustrations by Pamela Stacy King

Contents

Acknowledgements vii

Introduction 1

PART 1   WHY ARE WE DOING THIS? LOCAL PLANNING AND THE CALL 9

1   Climate Planning Objection 1: "Climate change is a lie. It can't be proven. The climate change myth is a political maneuver." 15

2   Climate Planning Objection 2: "We don't have the will. We don't have the money." 55

3   Climate Planning Objection 3: "Climate change is not that bad. It's only a few degrees. It's just an attention-getter. Scientists are using the issue to get their research funded." 89

4   Climate Planning Objection 4: "All change brings both good and bad. Besides, the climate change cure would probably be worse than the disease." 107

5   Climate Planning Objection 5: "We have bigger problems than climate change and other priorities." 127

6   Climate Planning Objection 6: "Retreat is not an option. Everywhere in the world is prone to some kind of natural disaster. We need to take a stand." 145

7   Climate Planning Objection 7: "It's a lost fight. It's too late." 179

8   Climate Planning Objection 8: "Someone will fix this. Some new technological invention will save us." 191

9   Climate Planning Objection 9: "The future can't be predicted. Climate models are unreliable." 217

10 Climate Planning Objection 10: "I'll be dead when this happens." 231

v

vi ■ *Contents*

PART 2   CREATING CLIMATE PLANS...241

11   Drafting the Plan: The Main Stages 243
12   Co-authoring the Plan with the Public 247
13   Dealing With Setbacks...275

PART 3   TWO AMERICAN CITIES IN 2050 281

14   Miami and Southeast Florida...285
15   El Paso, Texas 297

Conclusion: The Way Forward 315
Index 319

Acknowledgements

I want to thank the many communities that have hosted me and my planning team over the years. Our job has always been to help local people develop their ideas into plans and then turn those plans into action. When we do our best work, people are more informed and more likely to choose to help future generations. Although this book does not necessarily reflect the opinions of the firm or my colleagues, it could not have been written without the experiences I gained working with the people at Dover, Kohl & Partners, especially my wife and co-worker, Pamela Stacy King, who has always been a source of inspiration and support.

Introduction

The stakes are high when it comes to climate planning. Our world is in trouble. We're beginning to suffer flooding, sea-level rise, heat waves, drought, forest fires, food insecurity, water insecurity, and population displacement like never before. Climate change is no longer something we plan for in the future. The situation is worse than we are comfortable talking about and it's going to take everyone to fix this problem.

Big, important climate initiatives require the efforts of many people at every scale and leading others, even working with others, can be difficult. At the same time, after hearing *the call*, the call to do something to make the world a better place, one finds recognition and comradery as part of a group engaged in important work that no solitary endeavor can offer. This book is about overcoming the objections to climate change mitigation and adaptation that we face at a local level. I describe case studies in which communities I have worked with encountered pushback and then I relate lessons applicable to other places. Change is not made without inconvenience, even from worse to better.

At the international level, new technologies, treaties, standards, and regulations will be essential to lessen the coming harm. At the national level, investments need to be made in solar and wind power, advanced power grids, carbon capture and storage, biofuels, electric vehicles, better insulated buildings and other carbon-saving efforts. But it's hard for the average person to know how to help at those scales. Most people do not have offices in Washington D.C. or at the United Nations. Viewed globally, climate change feels as out of one's control as thermonuclear war or worldwide pandemic. Viewed locally, however, many communities are making real progress and there are productive and meaningful ways for the average person to engage.

As federal and state commitment oscillates up and down, the municipality (the county, city, or town), the smallest government unit, can be the most important when it comes to fighting climate change. Climate is in many ways a world problem solved at the local level. At the local level we work on mitigation efforts which incentivize solar and wind power and necessitate LEED (*Leadership in Energy and Environmental Design*) requirements on new buildings. We work to conserve and

DOI: 10.4324/9781003181514-1

2 ■ *Introduction*

reuse water. We protect forests and build urban tree canopies. We plan walkable, bikeable communities connected by transit which emit less carbon pollution.

On the local level we must also adapt our communities. First, we develop hazard mitigation programs to identify vulnerabilities and then we work to defend areas with infrastructure such as pumping systems and new levees, retrofit places by elevating buildings and streets, and help relocate people away from indefensible locations. At the federal and state level, regulations are created, and funding is allocated, but it is local government's job to implement those initiatives.

Although focused at the local level, this book discusses climate basics like carbon dioxide levels in the atmosphere, the Intergovernmental Panel on Climate Change (IPCC), the Paris Agreement of 2015, worldwide energy generation forecasts, and other items of global concern in order to familiarize urban planners and citizen planners with key concepts they'll need to know in order to host climate conversations on the local level. The greatest power an individual possesses in the offensive against devastating climate change may just be their ability to talk about it knowledgeably. Every person who talks about climate is doing a public service.

We'll also discuss how to draft climate plans that encounter less resistance because they involve the public, stakeholders, and decisionmakers in a way that builds trust, creates consensus, and leads to implementation. The plan-making process itself can strengthen bonds among neighbors which, in turn, allow communities to bounce back faster after disasters. Urban planners call this "social resilience." I have been leading urban planning efforts across the country for many years and I can see that the plans that made a measurable difference – the plans that bridged the *implementation gap*, the gap between plan and reality – owe much of their success to the specific public process we used, and we will discuss ways to achieve the maximum level of public involvement on climate plans.

We'll discuss cities that are the most vulnerable to climate change as case studies. They include desert communities and low-lying coastal communities, and we will imagine how they will fare in 2050 and 2100 if they continue to work to mitigate and adapt. Using advanced computer modeling programs, this book will describe how even the most vulnerable communities have a fighting chance under even the worst forecasts if they begin now and stay committed. We will avoid framing the problem as a climate apocalypse with a debilitating narrative of doom and gloom. We no longer need a terrifying wake-up call; people are awake. We need to set goals for 2050 and 2100 and plan a road map for action.

Our intended audience is anyone worried about climate breakdown and working to reshape the built environment. Of course, we need to recognize that the *built environment* now might just include what we used to call the *natural environment*. The book is written for students, urban planners, local activists, journalists, elected or appointed representatives, and the average citizen. This is a book about specific actions we can take.

On another level, this book describes *the call* to improve any part of the world and the journey a person, their team, and their community must make to work

Introduction ■ 3

collectively and effectively. The book is about winning and losing, and finding and re-finding will and courage. In this way, the book is applicable to more than just climate planning.

Topics Covered

In **Part 1** of this book, we will discuss the ten most common objections to drafting and implementing climate plans. I provide a summary of global warming and climate change myths and then discuss Science's response. Local planners need to be able to contend with these myths even if they are outside one's professional area of expertise. Though, for instance, it may be the UN's job to set up the United Nations Framework Convention on Climate Change, the US Federal government's role to fund research by the National Oceanic and Atmospheric Administration, and the job of the UN and US to work together to increase fuel efficacy standards, regulate utilities, and administer carbon pricing, I have found that I can't make progress locally unless I can speak about the national and international conversation.

I can't recommend that a town incentivize solar roofs without finding myself in a discussion about the coal policies of China and India, and so this book talks a little about China and India. When I recommend adding electric car charging stations to a city's parking garages, I often hear how upset people are about the unfairness they believe is built into international carbon reduction treaties and so this book will spend a few moments talking about those treaties. There's a lot of anxiety in America when it comes to policies imported from Europe, and so we'll talk about the IPCC and the Paris Agreement.

It takes more than a single snappy retort to change a person's mind or to redirect a community when it comes to climate because there is no one reason for denying or ignoring climate change. There will never be an *ah-ha* moment after we correct a person's misconception. All strong opinions are tied up in messy psychodynamic concepts like political perspective and social identity. Our worldview is more tribally based than objective and tribes are always both for something and against something. Reason rarely convinces people to abandon an idea because it wasn't reason which put the idea into them in the first place. It takes an inclusive planning process, an invitation to join a new group, many repeat conversations, and an actionable plan people can place their confidence in to make progress. The "Notes From the Field" sections of the book include anecdotes and short case studies in which objections were successfully overcome (more often than not).

These sections can be unashamedly discursive and you can be excused for wondering how the Tea Party's fear of zombies in St. Lucie County, Florida really has anything to do with the climate challenge at hand, or how the author's young son's firm belief that vegetarians cannot eat pretzels connects to global carbon emissions. I would argue that unless we understand the social context behind how climate policy is decided and the emotional context climate planners find themselves

4 ■ *Introduction*

working in, we aren't being clear enough on the factors at play, and the perceptual difficulties we encounter when it comes to the job of climate planning. And I have included these stories for a third reason: I thought you might think these quick diversions interesting and enjoy them.

Our social identities, the identities we bring to public meetings and municipal planning processes, come from membership in a social group.[1] People often respond to concepts like climate change based on how they think the group would want them to respond. We must learn how to engage whole groups and the "Notes From the Field" sections explore some approaches. In some ways these sections are an urban planning travelogue. We'll go to noteworthy places and meet interesting people working on climate issues.

People react to what they hear based on their own self-interest, their own needs, and their own desires. People have a hard time accepting anything that requires them to change how they live their lives. However, the same instincts that make a person deny or ignore climate change can be flipped when we offer a sense of belonging and the satisfaction of contributing to a shared project. This is one aspect of what I refer to repeatedly as *the call*. Climate, like any other collective challenge, can bring us together. Climate can give people a sense of shared purpose. If you can give people that, then this work gets a lot easier.

In **Part 2** of the book, we discuss a variety of climate plan types in detail and look at the necessary steps for creating a climate plan which can survive pushback. Some readers may want to start with this section if it is time to draft a climate plan or write a Request for Proposal (RFP) to seek outside help.

Chapter 11 examines the main steps in drafting a climate plan. Local jurisdictions occur where streets and homes are flooded, where infrastructure is installed, where potable water is supplied, and where building permits are issued. When storms and droughts occur, citizens look to their local governments for answers and solutions. Urban planners must be able to fix the current problems, look ahead to future challenges, and know the mitigation and adaptation techniques which will help their community.

This phase involves learning about how the world will change in the future. It is a journey into the unfamiliar because the future will be different from the present. Caring about the future often puts us out of step with the average person and can make planners the target of negativity, especially when it comes to a highly politicized topic like climate change. Get ready. Reshaping our hometowns requires collective power: we must organize people, deal with the negativity, and lead, nonetheless.

The next step is to co-author the plan with the public, and this is covered in **Chapter 12**. In this phase, we plan. A plan for climate change mitigation and adaptation recognizes the threat of climate change and describes the role a community can play in reducing the impacts while guiding the community to take effective action to prepare for disasters. We must make clear to the public that we can mitigate and adapt or suffer.

When creating plans, the more hands on the plan the better. Everyone is familiar with the old adage: "If you want to move fast, go alone, but if you want to go far, you need to bring others." To be successful, public outreach can't be limited to a single meeting advertisement with an open-ended invitation to attend. Public outreach needs to be a long-term commitment to meeting people where they are, building trust, and constantly working to make it easier for people to engage. Today this happens both in-person and virtually, on the internet.

Outreach must also involve populations that are historically underrepresented in public meetings. This can be difficult and time-consuming, but if we can involve the entire public and all the decisionmakers substantively, then when we're done it is much more likely (though never guaranteed) that everyone in the community will take a piece of the plan and work to make it a reality.

At this stage we must handle the pushback of a public skeptical of government spending, and especially skeptical of spending in a way that they might believe will only benefit future generations. In this stage we must describe the problem in a way that helps people to care about the future, even if it is a future they may not see. Graphics, maps, and visualizations are essential to describing the climate problem as an event that is occurring today and will only get worse if action isn't taken.

When asked: "Will the plan work?" I often, after more than 15 years of working as an urban planner, reply: "Plans don't work, people do," because no plan will implement itself. It is people we must convince and inspire. A climate plan must understand the motivations, missions, and fears of the public, elected officials, and agencies that would be responsible for implementation. The plan must help these people accomplish their goals.

Once a plan is created, it must be brought to the community and its elected officials to adopt. Formal adoption by a community is essential, but equally essential is informal adoption by informal local leaders. Once adopted (in every sense) we need to work toward plan implementation. Successful climate plans show demonstrably reduced Greenhouse Gas (GHG) emissions year after year. Successful plans are part of a community's Capital Improvements Plan (CIP), the plans that fund adaptation infrastructure. In this chapter we will discuss why so many climate plans sit on the proverbial shelf collecting dust while others are on the desks of municipal staff, guiding decisions.

The final step is to deal with setbacks, and this is covered in **Chapter 13**. Once a plan is adopted, a period of intense, focused action working under the administration that approved the plan typically follows. In time, however, other administrations will have other priorities and they may even be ideologically hostile to climate planning. Remember to stay calm and work with the opposition (or wait them out) without losing your job or your influence in the community. Rebrand the effort and stay politically correct. Seek outside validation from non-profits or at the state level and keep at it, in different ways, quietly adding teeth to your community's climate policies through revisions to the land development regulations and zoning.

6 ■ *Introduction*

In **Part 3**, we use advanced land use modeling tools to imagine Miami, Florida and El Paso, Texas in the year 2050. Part science and part speculative science fiction, predictions about the future provide a kind of storytelling that can help us discuss what to do today. Out of necessity, arid cities and low-lying coastal cities began discussing climate change and its environmental impacts relatively early compared to other places. While they are the most vulnerable geographically, they are less vulnerable in the sense that they will not be blindsided by the problem and are already accustomed to contending with pushback.

We'll look at Miami and Southeast Florida as an example of a low-lying coastal city. Cities facing similar physical challenges include, especially, New York, New Orleans, and Virginia Beach in the United States; Dhaka, Jakarta, Bangkok, Shanghai, and Guangzhou in Asia; Mumbai and Kolkata in India; Lagos, Brazzaville, and Dakar in Africa; and Venice and Alexandria on the Mediterranean. There are many more. Planning for low-lying coastal cities in the era of climate change is unfortunately becoming a major new sphere in the world of urban planning. The actions taken by Miami and Southeast Florida, the proverbial canary in the coal mine given their acute vulnerabilities, are especially useful to study.

In 2016, *Rolling Stone* magazine shocked Miami with an article entitled "Goodbye Miami,"[2] and a description of a future dystopia which sounded to most local climate planners like an unlikely worst-case scenario. What's a more likely future? What will happen to Southeast Florida as hurricanes become more destructive? Can a region which is used to growing fast grow its way out its problems? Will the region be able to replenish its beaches as the waters rise or will beach tourism disappear? Will neighborhoods remain livable as water levels rise under homes and swamp septic tanks and building foundations? Will weeks of uninterrupted inundation make life impossible?

Let's also consider El Paso, Texas, a desert city. Over 500 million people live in the world's desert regions in cities like Phoenix, Las Vegas, San Antonio, Salt Lake City, Riyadh, Tripoli, and Cairo. These communities face declining water supplies and a rapidly growing population. They may be living on borrowed time as temperatures rise and available water is used up or turns salty. Deserts may see temperatures rise 5 to 7 degrees Celsius (9 to 13 degrees Fahrenheit) by the end of the century, and rainfall drop 10 to 20%, according to a United Nations Environment Programme Report.[3] In 2012, the City of El Paso adopted a Comprehensive Plan with a Sustainability Element. After nearly ten years of implementation El Paso has made significant progress. But will it be enough?

In 2018, Beto O'Rourke, a Democratic presidential candidate, talked about how he and his young son worried El Paso would be "uninhabitable" if the world continued "on its current trajectory" unless "something dramatically and fundamentally changes."[4] We can look at El Paso in 2050 based on the city's adopted climate plans and use modeling software to examine the current trend and possible scenarios. What is the current trajectory? What are possible headlines from the future? Will there be a Day Zero when El Paso runs out of water? Might El Paso become a solar energy powerhouse? How many days will temperatures rise over 100°F per year? How many climate refugees could El Paso see? Will in-migration help or hurt the city? Will El Paso be uninhabitable if, despite whatever actions the city might take, the world doesn't change fundamentally?

The book's **Conclusion**, "The Way Forward," provides a brief summary and some encouragement. What tools do we have right now that can help solve the climate problem? What new tools do we need? Climate planning is a misunderstood, undervalued, and politically hot topic for urban planners, admittedly, but at some point in our profession's history just about every discipline within the field of planning faced intense pushback. From environmental protection to equitable housing, everything we're working on today was once fraught with difficulties and grave professional danger. If you are an urban planner now you will be a climate planner soon. Be bold. It is the only way forward.

Notes

1 Turner, J. and Oakes, P. (1986). The significance of the social identity concept for social psychology with reference to individualism, interactionism and social influence. *British Journal of Social Psychology*, Volume 25 (3), pp. 237–252.

2 Goodell, J. (2013). Goodbye Miami. *Rolling Stone*, June. Retrieved from: www.rollingstone.com

3 United Nations Environment Programme (2006). *Global Deserts Outlook*. Retrieved from: https://wedocs.unep.org/handle/20.500.11822/9581

4 CNN (2019). Climate crisis town hall with Beto O'Rourke (D), presidential candidate. Aired September 4. Retrieved from: http://transcripts.cnn.com/TRANSCRIPTS/1909/04/se.09.html

WHY ARE WE DOING THIS?

1

Local Planning and the Call

Introduction to Part 1
Why Are We Doing This? Local Planning and the Call

Climate plans come in many forms and those are discussed in Chapter 2, but every climate plan involves two parts: **mitigation** and **adaptation**. Mitigation initiatives aim to reduce or prevent greenhouse gas emissions and involve actions like installing solar panels on government buildings or instituting a bicycle-sharing system to reduce the carbon pollution of automobile use. Climate adaptation initiatives prepare a community for the unavoidable impacts of climate change, such as sea level rise or extreme weather events. Initiatives might include raising sea walls, updating building codes, or water recycling efforts.

Significant, meaningful action means collective action, and collective action begins at the community level. As important as individual action may be, the carbon pollution problem can only be mitigated when we reinvent our systems at the level of the city, region, nation, and planet, and this will take a lot of people. Likewise, no one individual can afford to adapt even a small town to shrinking water supplies or surging seas – the cost would be too great. It takes the entire town, every time. The enormity of the problem has a silver lining: communities that work together to create new climate plans or add big new commitments to their existing plans often find themselves participating in a transformative process that transcends the old battle lines drawn by longstanding, unsolvable issues or tensions.

The call to action in movies takes the form of the hero's quest in which a character has an idea, leaves his village, has an adventure, returns to his home, mobilizes the community, and leads them to defend their home using the wisdom the hero has gained. The call we discuss in this book is just like that, except we needn't go anywhere physically; the journey is an inner one. The heroic quest is one you take to find out what you believe. It is also a quest for identity in which people don't know quite who they are at the beginning but, by the end, they know.

At the level of the individual or household, some people vote for candidates who make climate a major agenda item and change their lifestyles to lower their carbon footprint using energy and water more wisely. Some switch to renewable energy providers for their home or add solar panels to their roof. Many people purchase hybrid or electric vehicles. Others participate in local climate conferences or marches and post alarming articles on Facebook. They donate to climate action groups and may even enroll the offices where they work in carbon offset programs. We all know people who go even farther and eat vegan (for purely environmental reasons), use public transportation or their bike for their daily commute (even when a car would be more convenient), and are never without their Nalgene water bottles and bamboo utensils in order to lower the amount of waste they produce. The people I know who do all of these things typically reach a point in their journey in which they feel they are not doing enough. The logical next step for them is to work at the community level.

DOI: 10.4324/9781003181514-2

Why Are We Doing This? ■ 11

At the same time, many people feel they don't have the extra time to reorder their life or extra income to donate to a cause. They don't have the money needed to turn their homes into renewable powerplants or upgrade their car. They do what they can but are still left feeling powerless. The best cure for that sense of personal powerlessness is participation in a municipal effort because by participating in any way, even virtually on the internet, these people are introduced to their community's professional planners and staff members, people paid to work on the issues that residents can't find the time to work on, and there is comfort in that. A city plan puts more than just two hands to work; a plan can mobilize a thousand people. Over a long enough a period, a good plan can task a hundred thousand. Mayors, commissioners, and presidents are temporary, but plans last.

A citizen's work isn't over after plan adoption, however. Once the plan is adopted, it can be a full-time commitment to stay involved, stay aware of upcoming issues, hold elected and appointed officials to plan goals, and keep others attending meetings and voicing their concerns. The call to action isn't a single moment, like in a movie; it is many moments, and a continual discipline. It is a lifestyle. A municipality of 25,000, or even 250,000, may only have a handful of gadflies and fewer than a hundred fully engaged citizens who make local affairs their personal mission, but, from what I have seen, a single individual, community activist, senior staff member, or elected official, can keep a community on track.

This kind of work can be frustrating. This kind of work has its ups and downs. The people I know who are engaged at the community level must take breaks for months, years, or even whole administrations. If you swim against the stream, you know the current's strength. And, let's face it, public meetings are an ordeal every time. However, there's just about nothing better than the feeling of having made a difference. I, myself, have felt the deep satisfaction at having made a difference, and I have seen other people feel it too.

It's no secret that most people who participate in local government are older. Older people have more time and, often, fewer resources, and participating in local government is free. Older people also find personal fulfillment in participation. Everyone wants to be needed by someone. Everyone needs to feel important. Older people who have fewer hopes for themselves can hope for their community. They can sometimes even re-find the fervor of youth. In my experience, the older people in a community are as likely to be an agent for positive change as the younger. Enlist their help.

It's a lot easier to mobilize a community and keep them engaged, than one would think. Once people feel they've made a bit of a difference they usually go back for more and continue to participate locally. Working toward a goal helps people escape, for a little while, preoccupations with the problems in their lives. Life never feels empty at a City Council meeting just before the adoption of a plan that involved a community effort. People who act locally know what's in it for them. Frankly, the actual issue they are working on can feel secondary. The philosopher Soren

12 ■ *Why Are We Doing This?*

Kierkegaard suggested that the passionate state is the highest state for people. People want to be tasked. They want to feel important. It just takes a plan.

That's Not How Things Work in My Town

In other places, there are no indications at all of a latent desire to save the planet which simply needs an outlet. There is no observable call. For many citizen-planners there is zero discussion of climate locally and it is hard to imagine that there ever will be one. Let me suggest that because these are the places where the most progress is to be made the greatest sense of achievement is possible. In my opinion, these can be enviable places to work because there's no expectations to disappoint. I'll talk a lot about places like this in the "Notes From the Field" sections. These are the kinds of places I usually work.

How much can a person further the climate conversation in places like Cambridge, Massachusetts where their first climate plan was adopted in 2002, they have implemented highly technical building efficiency requirements and greenhouse gas emission targets, they have an 18-person Climate Protection Action Committee which includes MIT and Harvard professors, and the committee meets every month to discuss such minutia as the climate change theming of the local Mermaid Parade?[1] Cambridge has achieved an enviable (and arguably sufficient) amount of local awareness. Citywide, it has plenty of climate-related *umph*. What's even left to do?

There's a lot to do in Lubbock, Texas. There's a lot to do in Mobile, Alabama. It will be a while before the people working on climate in those cities have to worry that they are redundant.

Whether your town is one that wants to participate in the climate struggle or couldn't care less, your job is the same: Educate and build public support for new climate initiatives. There are opportunities to do this in every community. Let's give one example of a relatively easy step that can be taken everywhere. Across the country I have seen small towns update the portion of their building codes related to *mitigation* and *resilience* (even if those terms are not used) after a natural disaster. In every case, the new local code exceeded the life-safety provisions in the standard building codes. Standardized building codes were often designed as a one-size-fit-all at the federal or state level. For this reason, new regulations could only be invented at the local level because only local people understand their local climate challenges (even if their regulations never mention *climate* and stick to the term *natural disasters*). The citizen-planners who improve health and safety codes save lives. It's okay to begin your climate planning after a disaster and begin it without ever discussing climate. Start with the codes.

Leading a Discussion on Climate

At City Council, for better or worse, you are dealing with *real* people. When it comes to speed bumps, bike lanes, potholes, fence permits, parking lot lighting, and even trickier issues like taxes, up-zonings, and traffic, you are dealing with *real*, physical, observable, and understandable issues that the average person can weigh in on. It isn't rocket science; city planning is ultimately about streets, public spaces, and buildings and everyone has enough experience with those things to participate. However, for these same reasons it can be incredibly difficult to bring the findings and recommendations of the global science community to the local forum.

Around the country, I have observed members of the public take their three allotted minutes at the microphone to talk to elected leaders about climate change on all variety of topics. Slowly, these people are introducing terms and educating. I have observed that planning staff reports increasingly discuss the root cause of new flooding problems, unexpected storm damages, and even increasingly hot days. These reports are changing public sentiment.

Abraham Lincoln stated that with public sentiment anything can be done and without it, nothing. Specifically, in a speech on the spread of slavery in Ottawa, Illinois, in 1858, Lincoln said,

> In this, and like communities, public sentiment is everything. With public sentiment, nothing can fail; without it nothing can succeed. Consequently, he who molds public sentiment, goes deeper than he who enacts statutes or pronounces decisions. He makes statutes and decisions possible or impossible to be executed.

Local government provides us with the ability to shape public sentiment. What follows are common objections, potential replies to those objections, and stories which describe how planning teams I've worked with have dealt with objections to climate planning. It isn't easy. You may have loud negativity hurled angrily at you while you are in front of a room filled with people who aren't sure what to think and are watching your reaction very closely. Listen to the objections and, I recommend, be as respectful as possible. Most importantly, listen. Understanding the objections will improve your efficacy. Let me describe the objections I hear all the time.

Note

1 City of Cambridge Climate Protection Action Committee Agenda (2019). Wednesday, March 14. Retrieved from: www.cambridgema.gov/-/media/Files/CDD/Climate/climatecommittee/2019/CPACagenda031419_processed.pdf

Chapter 1

Climate Planning Objection 1

"Climate change is a lie. It can't be proven. The climate change myth is a political maneuver."

We need to put aside what we believe the climate conversation to be because in most of America it is not the same conversation that we read in *The New York Times*, *The Guardian*, or urban planning publications. There's still a lot of skepticism in the world and it's helpful to put ourselves in the skeptic's place for a moment.

As an attendee at a public meeting involving climate change how can one tell that the presenter isn't simply seeking attention? How do we know they aren't alarmists? There's a long tradition of fortune-tellers, false prophets, Chicken-Littles, and fear-festers. Reckless fearmongering for the purposes of attention-getting comes naturally to people. Often, they don't even know they're doing it. At the very least, there is no one who does not exaggerate. For these reasons, the crowd is slow to trust.

Remember the Y2K scare? The world feared computers would stop working at the stroke of midnight on December 31, 1999 because instead of allowing four digits for the year, many computer programs only allowed two digits. We were told computing would stop and havoc would ensue. Nothing happened. At that same time *millennialism*, the end-of-the-world fear, took other forms. As a young man, I met Sheik Nazim Al-Haqqani in Northern Cyprus, the Sufi Muslim sheikh who got the world's attention when he predicted the Last Judgment would occur in the year 2000.

DOI: 10.4324/9781003181514-3

15

16 ■ *Why Are We Doing This?*

A lot of people, like Jerry Falwell, the American pastor, and Edgar Cayce, the psychic, seemed pretty sure that 2000 would be the big year. Nothing happened. People remember this. You might think that climate change and millennialism have nothing in common. One is based in science and the other in some kind of misplaced religiosity, but many of the people I talk to see them as the same thing. They remember being worried – very worried – and then watching as nothing happened.

On December 21, 2012 when the Mayan calendar purportedly foretold that the world was to end, I looked out the blinds to make sure the world was still there. I probably don't need to tell you that the world didn't end in 2012. My wife held the stone souvenir calendar we bought at Chichén Itzá, the ancient Mayan city in the Yucatán in Mexico, and asked, "Do we need to get a new one of these?"

At the same time, despite all the Cassandras and wolf-criers, world-shattering events like the worldwide economic meltdown of 2008 seem never to be predicted. The 2020 COVID-19 pandemic took everyone by surprise. The science community warned that pandemic was possible but many diseases, like Ebola, were described by the histrionic media as a world emergency well before they reached that scale. You can't blame people for feeling that the future is unknowable. "Man's most valuable trait is a judicious sense of what not to believe," wrote Euripides. There is such thing as healthy skepticism. It is simply being misapplied.

Science Has Yet to be Fooled

The most effective climate presenters I have seen establish credibility by deferring to science. This is tricky, because climate science remains abstract and unless you are a scientist directly involved in climate data gathering, you must rely on information you have no personal experience of. Although climate science feels less and less abstract every year as the effects of climate change become observable, the melting of far off ice sheets that I read about in Greenland, disappearing permafrost in Siberia I saw on Facebook, the collapse of the Akkadian Empire due to their climate crisis 4,000 years ago I saw on the History Channel, and sinking Pacific Islands featured on CNN will not sway the average person in Fayetteville if they have been told not believe any of that by someone they trust; like their state senator.

When reporting the science, I think the place to start is with changes that have already been observed. **The world is roughly 1.8 degrees Fahrenheit warmer and the worldwide sea level is approximately 8 inches higher than in 1900 and the rate of warming and rate of rise are accelerating**. These are simplified numbers that I use in presentations but every percentage of a degree and portion of an inch matter and therefore, so do citations.[1]

In my work in the U.S. I tend not to talk in terms of Celsius and centimeters and use Fahrenheit and inches. An increase of 1.8°F translates to 1°C. A rise of 8 inches rise translates to 20.32 centimeters. When we talk about the size of California's fires in hectares instead of acres, we lose the people in our audience. I also try, wherever possible, to quote the Intergovernmental Panel on Climate Change (IPCC) and not media interpretations of IPCC reports in order to stay on scientifically firm ground.

Since the last National Climate Assessment was published, 2014 became the warmest year on record globally, 2015 surpassed 2014 by a wide margin, and 2016 surpassed 2015. The period from 2016 to 2020 ranked as the hottest years in human history. Sixteen of the warmest years on record for the globe occurred in the last 17 years.[2]

Sea level rise is closely linked to increasing global temperatures. So, even if uncertainties remain about just how much sea level may rise this century, it is virtually certain that sea level rise will one day pose a deadly challenge to coastal communities and ecosystems. We have already begun to see increased and even permanent inundation, more frequent and extreme coastal flooding, erosion of coastal landforms, and saltwater intrusion within coastal rivers and aquifers. Climate change is happening today.

Intergovernmental Panel on Climate Change (IPCC) and World Temperatures

The scientific community has unanimously agreed that the world is warming, and nearly unanimously agreed that humans are the cause.[3] The Intergovernmental Panel on Climate Change (IPCC) is the United Nations body for assessing the science related to climate change. It was created in 1988 by the World Meteorological Organization (WMO) and the United Nations Environmental Programme (UNEP), and thousands of scientists from all over the world contribute to the work of the IPCC.

The IPCC's Comprehensive Assessment Reports summarize tens of thousands of scientific papers published each year. The IPCC's Sixth Assessment Report is scheduled to be completed in 2022. The Fifth Assessment Report (ARS5), completed in 2014, concluded that "Warming of the climate system is unequivocal"[4] and "it is extremely likely (95 to 100% probability) that human influence was the dominant cause of global warming."[5]

Many changes linked to the rise of world temperatures, including long-lasting heatwaves, record-breaking wildfires, declining sea ice and glaciers, wetter hurricanes, floods, and drought, have hit sooner than predicted just a decade ago according to the *United in Science* report.[6] The report, coordinated by the World Meteorological Organization, projects a rise in average global temperatures of between 2.9°C and 3.4°C by 2100, a shift likely to bring catastrophic change across the globe.

"The IPCC, let me tell you about the IPCC," was something I heard in the hallway after a presentation in El Paso, Texas by a stooped older man who was well known at public meetings, I could tell, by the reaction of the staff planners walking with me. They, quite literally, ran away. The man gave me a hard, flinty look, and had a lot to say. Nothing I had read in the *New York Times* prepared me for it.

18 ■ *Why Are We Doing This?*

To the man's point, it is important to note that the IPCC has admitted that papers it has endorsed have overstated the effects of climate change. A paragraph in the Fourth Assessment Report (ARS4) included a projection that Himalayan glaciers could disappear by 2035, for instance. The IPCC has since said that this is unlikely. You may hear about the problems with the "Hockey Stick Graph" and other overstatements made in IPCC endorsed papers. I heard about those things in El Paso that day as the man rambled acidly about, and I quote, "the IPCC fraudsters." What a great phrase. Admittedly, as climate science increasingly becomes a topic of popular non-fiction (and fiction) the number of overstatements will grow, and events will be predicted which will not come to pass.

There have been inconsistencies in IPCC predictions, but that's because climate change has been studied for a long time and when it comes to predictions, there has been trial and error. However, for every erroneous claim which made the news there were many others refuting that same claim, published concurrently, which didn't. Science has yet to be fooled.

In 1979 the first major study of global warming, *Carbon Dioxide and the Climate: A Scientific Assessment*, was published by the National Academy of Sciences[7] and I always think two things when I hear the year 1979. First, we've been studying climate and carbon for longer than I thought and, second, as a practical matter, that's not a lot of time considering all the education and policy changes that have followed at the international, federal, state, and local levels.

Others see it differently, I know. It has been pointed out to me by my *greener* peers that the scientist Joseph Fourier warned us in 1824. US Senator George Perkins Marsh warned us about climate change in 1847. We knew and we should have listened, absolutely. We're a foolish species – I find myself conceding. I got it. But I still take comfort in the idea that so much education and policy has happened in just over 40 years. Imagine the changes we'll see in the next 40 years.

"Prove it!" I had shouted at me in 2010 at a meeting in which I discussed the advantages to the planet of the LEED-rated Children's Museum we were proposing in Montgomery, Alabama. LEED (Leadership in Energy and Environmental Design) is a green building rating system which provides a framework for highly efficient green buildings. The meeting participant wasn't exactly asking me to prove climate change then and there; they were simply asserting their belief that it was unprovable.

"Prove it!" I had shouted at me on a bus tour I was co-leading for municipal planners in 2019, outside Carmel, Indiana as I talked about climate change in relation to one of the sites we had toured: the astonishingly well done new, walkable community called West Clay.

"What do you mean: prove it?" I asked the tour participant in pained astonishment.

Climate deniers make me nervous. Deniers pounce on any overstatement or erroneous prediction people like me make as proof of incompetence or deception. Unlike Galileo, who faced deniers in his own time when he announced the world was round, I have never had to contend with the Roman Inquisition or had a showdown

Climate Planning Objection 1 ■ 19

with a Pope, but I have had iPhones held in my face, recording everything I said, and had my statements used out of context in strange "investigative" videos. It's happened many times but the times I won't forget were in Martin County, Florida; San Marcos, Texas; and Ramapo County, New York. These are three very different places, but the passion and rancor of a certain few were the same.

"I'm not a scientist. I can't prove it. The best I can do is relate what science is telling us," I have said.

"You are arrogant, so absolutely arrogant, to believe that humans can do something that would affect this great big world," was said to me in Ramapo County. I had only touched on the idea that walking more and driving less would be good for the climate. I had only just begun to present.

"Mmmmmm ... okay," I said. What else can you say? The person continued to talk, and I gave her the dutiful absorption one expects from a planning consultant. I kept in mind that we all have mental maps of the world that cognitive psychologists call *schema* and this person, an older and otherwise very nice woman originally from Austria with a strong accent despite many years living in New York, had an entirely different mental map of the world. With two different mental maps of the world we were almost, literally, from two different planets.

"See for yourself," I have said to skeptical crowds. I have found it useful in my presentations to suggest that the audience simply look up the average historical temperatures in their hometowns. An internet search will take people in many directions, but they will eventually find the National Weather Service or the National Oceanic and Atmospheric Administration (NOAA), the United States' top climate science agency. Temperatures are listed in a straightforward way and without commentary on NOAA's site.

Sometimes NOAA isn't a source of information people are willing to trust. That's okay; there are other sources. President Thomas Jefferson, for instance, also recorded the temperatures every day at Monticello, his mountaintop estate, for 20 years. "Check his numbers," I said once in Henrico County, Virginia, not far from Monticello. I have found that people who are skeptical when it comes to federal agencies like NOAA tend to take Thomas Jefferson very seriously.

Jefferson was a devoted follower of phenology, the science of keeping track of seasonal changes: the first day buds appeared on trees, the first Robin to appear in spring, and so forth. Even as president, Jefferson found the time to pursue this hobby. When modern climatologists report, for instance, that cherry trees in Montana are blooming before cold snaps have concluded three weeks earlier than former times and this causes bloom damage and lower crop yields, they are making the same kind of observations Jefferson devoted a large portion of his life to. At the time I am writing this the Monticello website makes it easy to see what Jefferson recorded each day and then check his record against the day's current temperature.[8] Looking at Jefferson's own numbers we can see a warming trend.

At night, alone, and awake, we've all had the experience of observing strange health symptoms and wondering if we're in real trouble. The cause is usually just

20 ■ *Why Are We Doing This?*

something we ate, or stress, but we know that when the thermometer says our body temperature is well over 98.6°F, our doctor, our family members, and even our employer, will all agree that we should take the day off.

"The world is warming. It has an awful fever. See for yourself," I say.

Change Takes Time

When we look back in history, we see that it can take an absurdly long time to change public sentiment. The campaign to end smoking provides one of the best examples of this. In 1950 the world's most prestigious medical journals had demonstrated a clear association between smoking and lung cancer but their findings had no effect because people simply loved smoking too much to quit.[9] The number of people smoking rose quickly in the 1950s and it wasn't until 1964 that the United States Surgeon General's report on smoking and health demonstrated the relationship between smoking and cancer.[10] As scientific evidence mounted in the 1980s, rapacious tobacco companies claimed the studies linking smoking and lung disease lacked credibility. Billions were spent in deceptive campaigns to make people act against their own best interests. The people who wanted to continue to smoke looked around, saw others smoking, and decided that the experts were alarmists. Worldwide, smoking continued to grow in popularity despite the fact the message was out: Smoking will kill you.

Things have changed. Cigarette smoking rates dropped from 42% of people in the United States to 14% between 1965 and 2017 according to the American Lung Association.[11] The problem isn't gone; smoking is still the number one cause of preventable death in the United States. However, information became available, many people worked hard to educate (like the staff and volunteers at the American Lung Association), and attitudes changed. Climate pollution and the individual decisions we all make which contribute to the problem will likely follow a similar trajectory. However, the smoking analogy makes one thing clear: It will take time.

Climate Change Denial and Agnosticism

While debate in the media and in society rages on concerning man-made global warming, there is no longer debate in the mainstream scientific community. It is accepted that the world is warming and there is near universal acceptance that people are the cause. This fact is as well established as the link between smoking and lung cancer. The conversation has moved on from "Is this really happening?" to "What do we do?" When it comes to taking action, I find that today inertia and complacency are bigger problems than skepticism.

Even the websites of the large oil companies ExxonMobil, Chevron, Southern Company, and British Petroleum don't deny climate change. Their websites all

Climate Planning Objection 1 ■ 21

tout, paradoxically, their commitment to the environment, detailing their efforts to "cut emissions" and help the world achieve a "2 degrees Celsius" climate goal,[12] describing "Greenhouse Gas reduction targets" and the donations they make to places like Houston, Texas, which was devastated by climate-related catastrophe.[13] Their websites show pictures of windfarms stretching into the distance and gleaming solar arrays.[14] And while their websites never say the words "climate change" the implication is clear: "We know. We know. We're working on it." Maybe this is just for the benefit of shareholders,[15] maybe energy companies aren't serious about action and just wasn't to be seen as doing something, but admission is the first step.

Many former climate change deniers on the national stage now acknowledge global heating is caused by human activity and they have shifted their energies to arguing that the market and technical innovation – rather than government action or international treaties curbing emissions – are the best way to handle the problem.[16] However, working as a local planner you find that in most of America skepticism is still real. This could be due to inertia. The politicians and energy companies that worked so hard to convince everyone that climate heating couldn't be proven may have moved on, they may even tacitly acknowledge the problem now, but the public has not moved on.

In public meetings we quite often hear, "It's a lie, it can't be proven, and scientists just want funding." Words like this constitute *denial tropes*, planted in the community by vested interests. The word *trope* comes from the Greek word *tropos*, which means "to turn."[17] Tropes are words, expressions, or ideas that are used to change minds, to *turn* people against things. Tropes exist in movies as plot conventions. *David versus Goliath* is a trope at the heart of many films, and, more to the point, so is the *con man trope*. When scientists are being framed as con men it triggers everything we have learned from movies about con artists who work to gain the confidence of naive people and then part them from their money. If a person states a trope, they're showing that they made the trope their reality. It does not matter how well documented it may be that the trope was used to implant fear, the fear itself is valid. Calling people *duped* will not help the spirit of cooperation. Communication begins with understanding.

Why are these tropes so persuasive? Climate change is a global problem which requires a collective response and when we're not sure what to think or do we look around to see what others think and how they act. We're always trying to stay in synch with the people around us.[18] For this reason, the social norm, the rules of group-beliefs and group-conduct are different among different groups. While Americans once got all their news and social cues from established newspapers or the old three TV news networks (ABC, CBS, and NBC), today fake news, essentially political propaganda from both sides, proliferates on cable stations and social media and people can live blithely in inward-focused bubbles.

The right wing, at least at this time in history, is against responding to climate change. The reasons for this may have to do with the vested interests which support them. Or maybe American Conservatives are people who will always root

22 ■ *Why Are We Doing This?*

for Goliath. Or maybe the essence of Conservatism is suspicion when it comes to change. I don't really know. That's a topic best left to political experts to explain. The bottom line is that the old way of getting information, from people around us and media sources we trust – a highly effective shortcut which works most of the time – is simply misleading people on the topic of climate change.

I am no expert, but it does seem that propaganda wars aren't a new phenomenon in America. I realized this reading *Scandalmonger* (2000) by William Safire and *Alexander Hamilton* (2004) by Ron Chernow. Thanks to the benefit of time, we can all see that media wars like the one between Alexander Hamilton's Federalists, who wanted a strong central government run by educated property owners, and Thomas Jefferson's Democratic-Republicans, who wanted power to stay with the states and farmers, are nothing new. The same thing is happening today, though it involves a lot more people, and the same kind of propaganda battles will continue into the future.

I recommend that you read Fox News, *The Federalist*, and Britain's *Telegraph* occasionally (or the *New York Times* and *Slate* if you lean right politically). There are a lot of media bubbles out there and getting a glimpse outside your own can be eye opening. It helps us in our conversations with the public, and those conversations are important because it is possible to build trust with those who are still unconvinced about climate change. It's even possible to win over the zealous. When a zealous and, ultimately, irresponsible perspective is voiced, I find myself nodding with recognition because *I heard that one*. I read it on a libertarian website like Reason.com or saw it in a Fox News clip featuring Tucker Carlson. My initial head-bobbing simply shows that I am familiar with the trope, but it is often mistaken for agreement. This is important. This buys me time. I may just get a chance to speak when the person is finished.

When it's my turn, I say, "I understand that perspective," and I may go on to repeat the more convincing aspects of the denial argument myself; "but, objectively speaking …," I say, and then I proceed to give an impartial analysis as best I can and here's the thing: I find that I am often listened to. I find that the person I am talking to wants to find common ground. Maybe it's just human nature, but I find that they want to extend me the courtesy I showed them. I often hear my argument being repeated right back to me by the person I am talking to. Those conversations are rewarding. When they involve the members of a County Commissioner or City Council these exchanges might change public policy. Polite conversation may be something we need to relearn in this era. I am teaching myself.

When it comes to national politics people can be tribal, standing behind big banners and repeating talking points, but at the local level it is different. We all know better than Washington politics (both sides) and a short, respectful conversation with people working on a local plan reveals this. Get ready, though, thanks to all the fake news the urban planner's world – the world of public meetings and discussions about the future – has gotten weird. Let me tell you a story about just how bizarre and difficult things can get.

Figure 1 The Deering Estate in Miami, Florida

Notes From the Field
Engaging Southeast Florida in Climate Planning

In 2012, our team went head-to-head with a climate-planning backlash funded, in part, by Koch Industries – the energy and manufacturing conglomerate. While we

24 ■ *Why Are We Doing This?*

were trying to plan Southeast Florida for climate change (as well as economic prosperity, equitable transportation, and environmental protection) we had to fight an extremely well-funded effort to systematically dismantle our plan coalition and stop the plan.

The plan, *Seven50* (*Seven Counties, 50 Years*), is a blueprint for growing a more prosperous and resilient Southeast Florida during the next 50 years and beyond, and combating climate change is a core principle of the plan. I was the project director for Dover, Kohl & Partners and our firm led the multi-disciplinary consultant team charged with mapping a strategy to achieve the best possible quality of life for the southeasternmost counties along Florida's Atlantic Coast: Monroe, Miami-Dade, Broward, Palm Beach, Martin, St. Lucie, and Indian River. Between 2012 and 2014 *Seven50* was my primary professional focus. Today, I still work to help implement the plan.

The *Seven50* Plan was the result of a partnership between two Regional Planning Councils (RPCs), the South Florida RPC and the Treasure Coast RPC, which together secured a competitive grant of US$4.25 million from the US Department of Housing and Urban Development's Sustainable Communities Initiative. We worked especially close with Marcela Camblor, the project director for the regional planning councils, as well as with the RPC directors.

At the heart of *Seven50* was an effort to persuade the four northern counties of Southeast Florida to join the three southern counties and sign the *Southeast Florida Regional Climate Change Compact*. The *Compact* is a nationally recognized resolution to coordinate climate mitigation and adaptation activities across county lines.[19] The *Compact* made clear the threat climate change posed to our region and pushed state and local officials to update land use laws, transportation systems, and infrastructure.

The planning effort also sought to get the region speaking with a single voice in order to petition state and federal agencies for climate mitigation and adaptation funding. The region didn't think of itself as one entity, and locally, at that time, the term *Southeast Florida* was not yet commonly used. South Florida and Treasure Coast were the regional names everyone used to distinguish the two areas, and *Seven50* proposed a new geography to both reflect contemporary trends in the economy and to combine our efforts when it came to the climate challenge.[20] Southeast Florida was home to more than 6.3 million people at the time, more than 25% of the population in the state of Florida, a state that is always close in presidential elections and key to every candidate's ambitions. Imagine the influence such a region could have on national climate policy.

My team and I roamed the entire region for two years, a region larger than the state of New Jersey.[21] I visited several dozen municipalities I had never been to after a decade of living not too far away. We brought the latest data on sea level rise to every meeting and used an extensive public process that utilized both hands-on live events and interactive online tools. Our work seemed so common sense to me. I had no inkling that we'd face such resistance.

NOAA and Global Sea Level Rise

In coastal areas, the majority of climate adaptation planning at the local level takes the form of preparing for sea level rise and this was a primary *Seven50* task. In the United States, almost 40% of the population lives in coastal areas with high population densities that are vulnerable to sea rise.[22] Sea level rise means flooding, shoreline erosion, and more hazardous storms. Strategies range from reinforcing the coast to retreating from areas we can't expect to defend. There are a few points from NOAA one needs to know to plan for rising seas and these points were foundational to our work in Southeast Florida.

- **Sea level rise is a documented phenomenon.** The average rate of global sea level rise over the past two and half decades has been about a tenth of an inch per year (3.1 mm), or an inch every 12 years, but the rate is accelerating. Remember, this is a global average and sea level rise at specific locations may be more or less than the global average due to local factors.
- **Flooding events are increasing.** In many locations along the US coastline, nuisance flooding is now three to ten times more frequent than it was 50 years ago. Every segment of the Southeast Florida coastline, for instance, has seen increased nuisance flooding in the last ten years.
- **There is an agreed-on range when it comes to sea level rise.** Scientists are very confident that global mean sea level will rise at least 8 inches (0.2 meters), but most believe it will rise no more than 6.6 feet (2 meters) by 2100, depending on the energy decisions we make. Locally, climate planners usually have a shorthand number that they use to talk about sea level rise and in Florida: we tell people to prepare for 2 feet of rise by 2060.

Beginning a Regional Planning Effort

The *Seven50* project officially began on June 27, 2012, with our opening summit, the first of four summits, held in Old School Square in Delray Beach, Palm Beach County. Delray Beach is a small coastal city which became one of the region's most successful "Main Street" towns after a series of redevelopment projects along Atlantic Avenue in the early 1990s. Delray Beach is a model community when it comes to urban revival and mixed-use place-making and we picked it as a summit location because of the inspiration it has given urban planners in Florida. Over 600 people attended the summit. Every presentation we made was filmed. We had the entire region's attention, and I was astounded to realize very quickly that many of the people I was talking to had never heard of climate change, sea level rise, or the threat to Florida's coast.

Really? I thought. You've never heard of this?

I sat at a table of participants in the balcony of the barn-like Fieldhouse at Old School Square. We had more attendees than we had planned for and I had to set

26 ■ *Why Are We Doing This?*

up five extra tables quickly on the catwalk balcony above the main gymnasium floor. Down below me, on the main floor, were over a dozen tables and each had a multi-colored flag that read either *Economy, Climate, Development, Environment, Culture,* or *Leadership.* The flags stood for the elements of the plan and the volunteer work groups people could join in order to participate in the project. We had all just finished listening to a series of speakers on a variety of topics when I began to work with my tables.

"I didn't understand the map they showed," a middle-aged woman in glasses said to me of a map that was only flashed as part of one presenter's PowerPoint. The presenter, Bill Spikowski of Spikowski Planning Associates, may have assumed that everyone was already familiar with the maps which showed sea level rise and potential coastal inundation. Or maybe Spikowski was aware of the pushback he risked if he dwelt on that slide too long and so he moved quickly to a less controversial topic.

"Will the Everglades flood?" she asked. "Is that what I saw? Isn't the Everglades already a swamp?"

"Everything could flood," I said. "Or could flood periodically with storm surges and high tides. And, yes, the Everglades is a swamp, but in the future, it could be open water. That would be terrible for the plants and animals there. And us." As one of the main organizers of the day's sessions I realized that we really should have spent more time on the topic of coastal flooding. I thought everyone already knew.

"Even Delray? We just built a wall down there." She pointed toward the shore that was less than a mile away. "The water is rising?"

"Yes," I said. "The water is rising." I wanted to move quickly into the exercise and pass out the survey materials. We had so much to do and I had to guide more than 30 people sitting at five tables. At my other tables they were already digging into the green folders with the table facilitator instructions and looking around for their facilitator, but I felt that I couldn't end my conversation with the woman from Delray yet.

"We're planning for between 9 inches and 4 feet of rise by 2060," I felt compelled to say. "But the rate of rise is the biggest concern. If it rises slowly, we can adapt by building seawalls, lifting buildings, and lifting streets. In places where it is really bad, people can move away. If it rises quickly, it will be a problem, it could even be a disaster, and the seas have risen fast before."

"I didn't know," the woman said placing the glasses that hung around her neck to her face. She was signaling to me that she was eager to get started on the tasks.

Really? I thought again. You've never heard? Some part of me felt that it was time to climb some high steeple, ring the bell, and call out: "Hey, haven't you heard? The seas are rising! You all know this, right?" I remember that woman clearly, because, again, as improbable as it seems, as far as I could tell she had never heard of sea level rise.

As I worked my five tables and watched over 600 people complete table exercises on the gymnasium floor, I was amazed to find that the responsibility of planning for the next 50 years didn't overwhelm the participants. The crowd appeared

Climate Planning Objection 1 ■ 27

comfortable – as if planning for the next 50 years was a routine event. There was a mistake happening under those flags, though, I had begun to suspect. Participants discussed climate change under the green flag labeled *Climate*, when, in fact, everyone should have been discussing climate. Climate change affected everything. At least we didn't consign the topic to *Environment* with its myriad possible topics and hardened supporters and detractors. I could see people arguing. I could see people standing at the head of tables with their hands on their waists or wagging fingers as they gave sermons.

While my five improvised tables didn't have a workgroup flag the rest did and each workgroup flag had an icon. *Leadership*, for instance, showed a muscular man atop a mountain with a flag in hand. No one sat at either of the two leadership tables and this was another ominous portent I didn't understand at the time.

Later in the project I learned that there were people, many people in fact, who saw our plan as little more than high-handed interference in local matters, and some creative iconoclast had labeled the icon in the *Leadership* flag as the *New Soviet Man*, the ideal person posited by the Communist Party of the Soviet Union. He's a superman who is healthy, educated (in a sense), and enthusiastic to spread the communist revolution. Let me suggest that when leading projects intended to bring people together, don't use flags with the simple, strong, confident iconography of 1920s authoritarian propaganda. I had drawn the image of the muscular man with some help from a graphic artist and never thought it would present a problem. However, this was just the beginning, and I quickly found that everything in the project had two meanings.

The problem of double meanings was due to the fact that some areas in our region were very urban, such as the southern cities of Miami and Fort Lauderdale, and other locations were rural, such as the western portions of Palm Beach, Martin, St. Lucie, and Indian River counties in the north. In general, there was a rural–urban, north–south, divide.

This rural divide exists in many places, even in Australia, I came to learn from Peter Richards of Deicke Richards, an urban planning firm based in Queensland, as he observed our project. He told me how urban and progressive Sydney had a strained relationship with rural and conservative Queensland that was very similar to Florida's north–south divide.

"I'm watching all this, and I'm thinking: I guess you just decided to ignore the massive alarm bells that must be ringing in your heads," Richards said. He watched me for recognition. Again, he was from conservative Queensland. He saw no recognition in my eyes. "Yeah, I can picture someone from Sydney coming up and trying the same thing."

The spilt was arguably much worse in Florida, Richards conjectured with the cool objectivity and swift insight of a man from the other side of the planet, because Florida was a swing state. In American politics, the term *swing state* refers to any state that could reasonably be won by either the Democratic or Republican presidential candidate. Florida is also a battleground state, a state both political parties

28 ■ *Why Are We Doing This?*

invest heavily in, because in 2000 Florida proved that it could determine presidential elections. Our regional plan naively attempted to fuse together two ideologically distinct places whose differences were being exasperated by the national politics of the 2012 US presidential election as President Barack Obama, the African American Democratic nominee and incumbent, ran against Governor Mitt Romney of Massachusetts, the Republican nominee.

Nevertheless, the first summit concluded successfully, and our team created a website to discuss the results of the exercises and engage participants in similar exercises online. We hosted a series of workgroup meetings around the region and reached another 800 people in just a few months.

Our *Seven50* Executive Committee met regularly, and we reported on the progress of the project to the Committee. Our Executive Committee involved mayors, county commissioners, college presidents, school board members, Department of Transportation representatives, business development board heads, and representatives from the farming, medical, housing, real estate, and legal industries. We also continued to travel the region and present during County Commission and City Council meetings and in presentations and workshops with organizations interested in regional cooperation. I met many thoughtful community leaders and elected officials who were thinking hard about how to live in a warmer and more turbulent future.

We brought the flags and table activities around with us wherever we went. The flagship vehicle of our travelling roadshow was my wife's packed MINI Cooper with its *OBAMA'08* bumper sticker. I remember when the Director of one of the Regional Planning Councils saw that sticker and winced. He knew what was coming, too.

Then the opposition organized. Unrest began in Indian River County, the extreme northern part of Southeast Florida, when Commissioner Bob Solari, a local Tea Party commissioner, scheduled a vote to opt the county out of our partnership in December 2012.

"Why is Solari doing this?" I asked Michael Busha, Executive Director of the Treasure Coast Regional Planning Council. He had been working with the northern counties for decades.

"If this project wasn't federally funded, I don't think we'd be having this conversation," Busha said. The opposition to *Seven50*, he said, "was about the anger and angst people feel over how the federal government has been behaving these last couple of years. *Seven50* provides a perfect venue to speak out against much larger issues that are upsetting people around the country."

"Issues like …?" I asked.

"Everything related to Obama," he said.

The federal program which funded *Seven50*, itself, was an issue. In 2009, well before *Seven50* had begun, the Obama administration had created the Office of Sustainable Communities and tasked the Department of Housing and Urban Development (HUD) to lead the preparation of regional plans. The regional plans were to integrate housing, land use, economic development, workforce

Climate Planning Objection 1 ■ **29**

development, transportation investment, and infrastructure investment into a long-term vision. The Sustainable Communities program proposed a comprehensive, multi-disciplinary approach to regional planning. But HUD was probably the least popular federal department among Republicans at the time.[23] Resistance to planning for *sustainability*, a term associated with the Democratic Party, had begun in Washington and many people in our rural counties found the regional planning initiative to be imperious and infuriating.[24]

Hundreds of people attended the Commission meeting in Indian River to fight *Seven50*. Speakers presented for five hours during the public comment period and their comments ranged from concerns that *Seven50* was a plot to rob them of property and liberty, to diatribes involving the United Nations and its secret plan to establish one world government. Thomas Jefferson's "Tree of Liberty" quote was cited a few times. Attendees spent the three minutes allocated to them talking about how our plans and renderings were, to quote one participant, "herding people into public housing in mega towers." They discussed how President Obama was a secret Muslim with a plan to institute Sharia Law.[25] They mentioned the strong man on our Leadership flag quite a bit. In a photo taken of the event I saw a cardboard sign with a picture of the Leadership flag and the words: "This is what fascism looks like." I had to admit that they were right, the flag's bold icon was what fascism looks like, but they were wrong about our project.

Many of the speakers were from groups like the American Coalition 4 Property Rights (AC4PR), the Taxpayer's Association of Indian River County, and the Republican Liberty Caucus of Southeast Florida. It is interesting to go back today and see how the most vocal critic of *Seven50*, AC4PR, a group whose website called *Seven50* a perpetuator of the "global warming lie"[26] became inactive less than six months after the 2012 presidential election. This could be because the group lost funding shortly after the election was decided, but we will never know. We will also never know why they used the "4" in their name, a convention usually reserved for carvings in picnic tables like "Ralph loves Dolores 4 Eva." I suppose they thought it made them look hip. I suppose I am still bitter.

Commissioner Peter O'Bryan, of Indian River, a member of our *Seven50* Executive Committee, argued at the Commission meeting that his county should stay in the *Seven50* partnership.

"Look, forget Solari," O'Bryan said with an ill-hidden disdain for Solari, his fellow commissioner. "I am part of this *Seven50* effort. And you know that I am not a Democrat. You know that I don't care one bit for Obama." O'Bryan argued with a straightforward, hard-headed Irish articulacy that *Seven50* was a voluntary and advisory plan with no regulatory component. He argued that the plan's only value was as a repository of useful ideas. "This isn't about Obama Communism," he scoffed. Nevertheless, Indian River County voted overwhelmingly to withdraw from the coalition.

Commissioner Solari then took his show on the road and he and his band of Tea Party activists packed local government meetings in the northern counties

30 ■ *Why Are We Doing This?*

and waved tiny American flags, cheered each other, and jeered elected officials. Political organizations like the Tea Party, funded in part by the political wing of Koch Industries, helped fund Solari and his activists.[27] David and Charles Koch were the sibling inheritors of the second largest privately owned company in the U.S. and the Kochs spent a small portion of their US$80-billion wealth on the Tea Party, Political Action Committees (PACs), and libertarian think tanks which, among other things, spread misinformation concerning climate change.

Our work continued, though. It included television and radio appearances, more travelling roadshows across the region, several Planning Directors' Forums, a conference for emerging young leaders, and presentations to every chamber of commerce, non-profit organization, senior center, homeowners' association, and college classroom that wanted to listen and discuss. A local news station even asked me to do an interview in which I stood atop a rip rap wall on Miami Beach's South Point Park to explain sea level rise basics for viewers who, Christina Vazquez, the interviewer, told me, "had never heard of sea level rise."

"Really? You think there are people living in Miami who have never heard?" I asked the interviewer. She did. Sighing, I answered my first interview question with the words, "The world is warming, and the water is rising." Appearing on local news[28] and talking about sea level rise was as close to ringing the church bell in warning as I was going to get, and I was thankful that the project afforded me that opportunity. Before the project ended, I was interviewed by the *New York Times* and National Public Radio, but that spot on the local TV channel, the place most people still get their news, felt like the most important interview I'd get to do.

During the travelling roadshow workgroup meetings, we talked about more than just sea level rise, and covered more than just the basics. We forecasted that the region's daily tonnage of greenhouse gas emissions could conservatively be expected to rise 67% by 2060. We discussed how cities produce dramatically fewer greenhouse gasses per person than suburbs and talked about how the region could build in a way that emitted fewer carbon emissions. We talked about the need to densify the region in select places to pay for resilience infrastructure. We asked the public to help us identify optimal places for denser, walkable centers at key intersections.

We planned a mix of residential, commercial, and workplace uses within walking distance to reduce car trips. We showed apartment buildings, townhomes, offices, retail, and commercial buildings integrated into a walkable urban fabric. We contrasted this vision with the conventional approach to development which plunked down single-use, car-dependent pods. Everything we drew was accessible from sidewalks and bike paths. At densities just slightly higher than suburbia, excellent mass transit was feasible. Our renderings showed streetcars and trains. We designed places of two to six stories of height. In a phrase, we showed *smart growth*.

AC4PR saw a different agenda in the work. They described our work on their website as: "Housing choice – LOST. Unlimited travel by car – LOST. Private property rights – LOST. Low density character of county – LOST."[29]

Climate Planning Objection 1 ■ 31

Our team started to change course in reaction to the criticism. During our next round of presentations my team members began to describe the urban living which we talked about as a way of housing "newcomers" to the region, younger people and older people, especially, who preferred less expensive living at higher densities. Our plans were for others, our team stressed. This was in part because our speakers wanted to make it clear that no one would be forced from their single-family homes.

The speakers also made this point, I believe, because they themselves typically owned suburban homes on large lots and wanted to avoid hypocrisy. The team described transit as a way to get cars off the road to reduce traffic for SUV drivers like themselves. AC4PR may have heard this message but it didn't temper their rhetoric. They wrote, "*Seven50* will re-engineer your life and the way you live, if not tomorrow then certainly in your children's and grandchildren's time."[30]

Is it hypocritical for planners to plan urban lifestyles for future generations that the planners themselves didn't choose? Or is it good planning? Doesn't planning compact, defendable centers simply acknowledge that the future will be different from the present? Whatever the case, we were doing our best to tailor our message to our increasingly hostile audience.

Summits Two and Three

Our second summit was entitled *A Look Ahead, Trend and Opportunities* and held on January 24, 2013 at Miami-Dade College's Downtown Miami Campus. It was attended by more than 300 people. We hung a map of the region that was 30 feet long and 10 feet high to greet participants. Everyone was encouraged to draw their ideas on the map and those ideas ranged from big ideas, like new routes for regional rail, to small ideas, like edible gardens. People used green markers to color farms they wanted to see protected and placed orange dots that represented new population centers located far from the shore. At the conclusion of the exercise there were no angry protests or big red Xs written on the map. The map made it look like we had a cohesive region with a common vision for the future. This was probably because we were meeting at a college campus in the heart of urban Miami.

When we arrived to our third summit, however, it was again clear that we didn't have one unified region. *The Future in Focus Summit* was held June 21–23, 2013, at the West Palm Beach Convention Center, a place within driving distance to many rural communities. The convention center didn't require a trip on the MetroRail like Miami Dade College and offered plenty of parking. We were immediately greeted by two dozen protestors with signs like, "Liberty or Death. YOURS!" and "Stop the Global Takeover!"

I left my wife's MINI Cooper with the Obama sticker at the beginning of the parking lot after saying something to her to the effect of: "Park here, Dear. I don't want to see our family car flipped over and set on fire." I crossed the parking lot that was about the size of a New England state and approached one group too

32 ■ *Why Are We Doing This?*

pre-occupied with talking to each other to notice me arrive. I smiled, shook the activists' hands, and accepted their printed literature.

"You should join our group," said a woman who looked like a schoolteacher in an old movie with perfectly straight bangs, neatly rounded hair that hung just above her shoulders, enormous oval glasses that came to points at the ends, a high-collared plaid buttoned shirt with the top one diligently fastened, and a mauve cardigan sweater. I describe her in detail because she'll become important to this narrative a little later. She didn't realize that I was one of *Seven50*'s leaders.

"Thanks, but I'm not sure that would make sense," I said. Nevertheless, she handed me a paddleboard sign that had a red X across the project name, *Seven50*. I accepted it with startled submissiveness. I still have that sign.

When I entered the convention center I learned that Solari's group had arranged a counter-summit. They had rented multiple event spaces directly in front of our spaces on the convention center's long, steel-and-glass hallway. The thousands of people who would attend our three-day summit would be presented an alternative option before they even reached our front door. On the counter-conference's posters I saw that Solari's group had booked the noted climate change denier, John L. Casey, author of *Cold Sun*.[31] He was famous (in his way). We didn't have anyone famous.

The two conventions began and when I wasn't presenting, on a session panel, helping others get ready for their sessions, or dealing with all the audio-visual idiosyncrasies of improvised conventions, I attended the counter-summit. The first time I walked the long hallway I could see that its organizers had booked the convention hall's largest spaces (presumably at great cost), but that the spaces had just a few people in them. Even their main space had only a dozen attendees.

I took a seat up front among the counter-summit attendees. Three of the attendees were slightly hunched in wheelchairs. One was an ex-army veteran with silver-white hair under a cap embroidered with the name of an airborne division. Several women wore orthopedic shoes and the very dark, oversized lenses that kept out direct sunlight.

The schoolteacher-looking woman who had encouraged me to join their group in the parking lot was at the podium reading a quote from Abraham Lincoln which transitioned into a homily on American independence that she read from a tidily stapled stack of papers. She occasionally looked up with the patient, expressionless stare that primary school teachers give misbehaving students, though the audience behaved quite well. I read from the printed agenda placed on my seat that the schoolteacher headed the AC4PR. This was my first introduction to the organization.

The schoolteacher began to talk about how the "*Seven50* group" would enforce "demographic and density quotas" that would bring crime and drugs to suburban communities, put family businesses out of business through the use of "hurricane building codes" and "carbon-free zoning," take people's land with eminent domain, build "stack-and-pack high-rises" of "federalized living spaces," take away cars, and punish people for being "independent free thinkers and self-sufficient capitalists." She called my team "radical lefties," "Russian Communists," and "Chinese

Climate Planning Objection 1 ■ 33

Communists." She looked at her audience coldly and stated, flatly, "*Seven50* means control of the seven Florida counties within 50 years."

Whoa. I didn't understand what I was hearing. I looked around and worked to see it from her perspective. The people around me were all senior citizens. I tried to understand the apprehension and even fear that some people, especially older people, felt about the future. I get more fearful and downright crankier every year I get older too. Urban planners see that kind of thing at every zoning hearing.

"I remember John F. Kennedy, that great American president," the schoolteacher said, "and our fight with Communism. Same thing." She proceeded to talk a lot about Kennedy.

If one remembers when John F. Kennedy was inaugurated, then they remember an Earth with half as many people as today. Half. The solutions we need today must be different from the ones that worked in the past if only because there are so many more people on the planet. When Kennedy was elected, there were 190 million people in the U.S. and 3.2 billion in the world according to the 1960 U.S. census. Today there are 327 million people in the U.S. and 7.5 billion in the world according to the 2020 U.S. census. We can expect another billion people worldwide by 2030 and we can expect the population to nearly double again by 2100 to 11.5 billion. Every generation will require new solutions.

I continued to listen to the Upset Schoolteacher. I understand the head-in-the-sand attitude towards climate change. In many ways, it's too awful to think about. I don't like to think about it. Most of the people I know in Southeast Florida are climate ostriches. Understandably. Already the sea level in Florida is 8 inches higher than it was 70 years ago, the rate of acceleration is picking up, and Florida's seas are rising an inch every three years.[32] I expected to hear a lot of climate skepticism, and, let's call it, *ostrichism*, at the counter-conference, but the Upset Schoolteacher didn't appear to have a skeptical bone in her body. She really seemed to believe all kinds of zany things would happen and that the world would unravel if we attempted any new solutions. She really seemed to believe that sustainability would be used as a reason to enslave future generations. It was Red Menace, the communists-are-coming-to-get-you stuff, from the 1950s and 1960s. The same communism scare was used to fight Medicare in 1965, Social Security in 1935, and probably the national parks and public schools at other times in history.

"The U.S. is ready for another revolution," the Upset Schoolteacher said. "The stars and stripes versus the hammer and sickle."

I reached for sympathy and understanding and not blame or disgust, but it all sounded like disturbed rantings to me. The woman had so much energy. It had to be a little exhausting to be so paranoid, I thought.

"I'm ready for Liberty. Are you?" she asked. "I am ready to push back on the U.N. like it is King George. Are you?"

That didn't make sense. It was compelling though. Although I didn't understand it, I wanted to hear more. I was fascinated. Unfortunately, I was due back to my own conference to give a presentation (an *overly* rational presentation I was beginning to

34 ■ *Why Are We Doing This?*

feel considering the competition) on the results of the previous summits and traveling workshops. As an urban planner, I often feel that it is my job to inform boards, commissions, and councils – and not to motivate. The Upset Schoolteacher was telling a far more interesting story about world domination. She was motivating. I decided to stay and listen until the very last moment.

"If human activity is causing climate change then almost anything could be justified in terms of government response," she said.

Good quote. I wrote it down. I wrote a lot of what she said down. I still have that notebook. I mean, the thinking was bad; it was the same slippery slope argument we always hear: *If you do X, then Y is inevitable* – even though X is sensible and Y will never happen in a million years, but her lines were snappy and memorable.

"The Progressives are coming for each and every one of us."

As I listened, I couldn't help but wonder: Who was paying for this? I understood the skepticism that could be traced to the political power of the fossil fuel industry; it bought them time before regulations required expensive conversions to renewable power sources and it bought them time to acquire alternative energy producers and keep profits high, but who would fund this woman? Who would want to be associated with her weird paranoias? *Seven50*'s sponsors, the U.S. Department of Transportation, U.S. Environmental Protection Agency, and the U.S. Department of Housing and Urban Development, all wanted to be identified at the beginning of every one of my presentations. The Upset Schoolteacher made no such references. Her funders seemed to want to remain anonymous.

Suddenly, she looked directly at me as if speaking to me. I felt like a naughty fifth grader. She pointed right at me as she continued to speak of conspiracy and secret plots. "Propagandists," she said. "Agents of Evil," she said with an unflinching stare. I could feel my already tenuous hold on patience and understanding melting away.

What would I say if she called on me, I wondered? Ideas formed.

"So, if I am part of a U.N. conspiracy, can I expect a free trip to the Hague?" I could have asked. "I mean, who do I talk to about that?" But no, as a professional, I couldn't say anything snarky, though it seemed like the only genuine and self-respecting response to such weirdness.

"Let me tell you," she raised her voice. "This is what I would say to the organizers of that *other* conference …." She was looking right at me. Yep, she knew who I was. Other people noticed that she was talking directly to me and they were looking at me, too. One man backed his chair away from mine (or so I imagined). It may have been my nametag. The alternative conference didn't have nametags. Why hadn't I taken off my nametag? It said "Conference Organizer" right on my nametag!

"This is what I would say to the organizers of that *other* conference …" she continued. "GO BACK TO MIAMI!" The crowd applauded. I stood up. Everyone watched me. But I just left. Unfortunately for the purposes of an exciting narrative I didn't seize the opportunity to respond to the Upset Schoolteacher. I just went back to my conference.

Climate Planning Objection 1 ■ 35

I was relieved to be among my own people. Then a strange thing happened. For the first time, I heard how much the tone of our conference sounded like the counter-conference. The green activists from Tropical Audubon and the Environmental Law Center (two groups I have immense respect for), along with a few of the urban planning consultants on our team, talked about how *they* (on the other side) were motivated by money and political power despite *their* pretense of caring about America, and how it was *our* job to save civilization from climate change, the greatest threat it has ever faced. I heard the same "we must fight them" language and the same "good-against-evil" narratives.

I didn't think that the Upset Schoolteacher was motivated by money even if someone was paying her. There are easier ways to make money. She was motivated by something more sincere and more strong. She cared about America.

A few of our speakers felt it necessary to demonize single-family homes, highways, driving kids to school (instead of walking or biking them to school, presumably), shopping as weekend recreation, and omnivorous diets. *They* (again, the people on the other side) weren't interested in commuter trains, our speakers said, *they* wanted highway expansions. But I knew the speakers. They lived in suburban houses and drove just about everywhere. Maybe a few biked recreationally on weekends, and recycled (I had to suppose), and perhaps one or two had solar panels atop their homes, but our speakers were exaggerating small differences and widening the gap between us all.

This isn't to say there was some moral equivalency between the arguments in the two conferences. Our speakers weren't as slanderous and libelous – or, to be fair, as imaginative or riveting – but as residents of the planet Earth we are all in this climate fight together and we're all guilty. If only there were evil people somewhere, insidiously committing evil deeds and all we had to do was separate them and destroy them. There isn't. The car that took me to the conference was powered by oil. In his 1961 novel *The Winter of Our Discontent*, John Steinbeck suggested that a crime is something someone else commits. One of the things that makes me optimistic about the climate change fight is that we're all at fault and all in it together.

When our session was over, I left the presenter's table and began to walk back to the other conference when I was stopped by one of the members of my team, an urban planner like myself, who asked, "Why are you even bothering with those people? Do they even listen to themselves? Do they really think every scientist around the world is part of some giant conspiracy?"

"I don't know," I said, and I went back.

In the shared hallway between dueling conferences the counter-conference attendees stood on the edges by the windows. I saw wizened older people with silver spectacles, some slightly hunched or leaning on walking canes, speaking to each other out from under the wedge of baseball caps that covered bare heads. Our conference attendees were more likely to be younger and sporting ironed shirts and professional blazers. The two groups never looked at each other and seemed to inhabit

36 ■ *Why Are We Doing This?*

separate but parallel universes. I felt that I was the only person who could observe them both at the same time.

I listened to multiple presentations and when it was my turn to present, I talked about how in industrial societies everyone is contributing to carbon pollution and everyone has a strong reason to avoid the conversation. "The keenest sorrow is to recognize ourselves as the sole cause of all our adversities," wrote the ancient Greek dramatist Sophocles. Mass action will not come out of us-against-them narratives; they don't foster the spirit of compromise and excitement for innovation that we will need. Instead of vilifying and scapegoating, the conference was supposed to be about greater awareness and a discussion of viable alternatives. This became my message. It could be summarized by the words: "We're all in this together." Insipid, I know, but important.

The first time I heard that the Koch brothers were funding the opposition to *Seven50* I thought: Oh, no. Not because of the power and clout of the nefarious two, but because I didn't think that such a powerful enemy narrative was going to help us all work together. During the conference I'd heard the Koch brothers and fossil fuel companies described as modern-day pharaohs whose activities were causing the Biblical plagues of our time: wildfires, floods, droughts, and storms. Maybe. But while I don't think irresponsible plutocrats should get away with their crimes, I doubted that pointing fingers at them would get us anywhere. And I am absolutely sure that pointing fingers at the political targets of national politics isn't the job of local planners.

Toward the end of the second day of the dueling summits, counter-summit attendees began to appear at our presentations. They joined sessions in which we discussed topics like Everglades restoration in the era of sea level rise, the economic return of investments in local arts, reinforcing coastlines and retreating from others, converting municipal vehicle fleets to electric power, and the gridlock on our highways and need for more transit options.

Our speakers were all local and before they spoke, I urged them to tell the crowd where they lived – from the congenial little town of Stuart to colossal Downtown Miami – and I recommended that they say a few words about themselves. The audience tends to side with people living lives they recognize. I think skeptical audiences look at the speakers and size *them* up, as much as their message. We conducted group visioning exercises and I facilitated the tables that had the counter-conference attendees because I worried that they might become problems. At my tables I had Tea Partiers from St. Lucie County, evangelicals from Indian River, Deep Ecologists from the University of Miami, Greens, Libertarians, and former campaigners for Obama and Romney.

I listened to people who were blatantly dismissive of suggestions that there could possibly be any connection between carbon emissions and global warming. Everyone deferred to Science, or at least, their own version of the science, and we couldn't talk about global warming without canned speeches erupting. I did my best to move the tables to other topics. We talked about the algae blooms caused by the pesticides and herbicides dumped by sugar companies south of Lake Okeechobee into our rivers. We talked about hurricanes, rising insurance rates, and rising drinking water rates. I could typically find something that everyone at my table was either for or against. When I felt I had earned a little trust by listening, I related some of the issues we had been discussing back to the problem of the world's changing climate.

I could see that the views of the Upset Schoolteacher weren't reflective of most of the other counter-conference attendees. No one asked if our team was part of a U.N. conspiracy. If anything, our presentations had sparked reasonable concerns. I remember being asked about possible tax increases, the noise express trains might generate as they travelled through neighborhoods, and whether high apartment buildings at the end of one's street might allow people with telescopes to peek into single-story bathrooms.

We moved into day three and the counter-conference ended a day early. Maybe it was due to a lack of attendance. I never had a chance to talk to John L. Casey, author of *Cold Sun*. I had overheard one of the counter-conference attendees explain to another with reverence and respect that Casey was an astronaut. I've always wanted to talk to an astronaut. I have since come to realize that he was never an astronaut and I'm glad I didn't have the opportunity to force my way into a conversation between him and his readers with my questions about the commercial possibilities for space travel (I have always wanted to go), or what toilets were like on the International Space Station. Imagine the awkwardness I would have added to an already strained couple of days.

"The Parkinson's convention is over," one of the planners I worked with said.

"They ended the conference early because they decided that they'll be more effective disrupting us," another of my colleagues told me as I arrived for a presentation I was to give. I took the podium and looked out on all the new faces sitting in the filled rows and standing along the walls. My audience was mostly people from the counter-conference and I greeted them with gratitude. "Thank you for joining us." I meant it. It was a lot of work to prepare the summit, I wanted as large an audience as we could get, and there was only so much value in preaching to the choir.

The Seven50 *Scenario Modeler*

"Choose your future," I said, and I presented the online scenario modeler we had developed to help people imagine different versions of 2050. I loaded the modeler, which was co-developed with the firm MetroQuest, and showed the audience how it worked. It is worth pausing a moment here and discussing the model in detail. Local planning efforts need more online interactive modelers.

First, the modeler asked users to prioritize what they wanted to see in the future from a list that included contrasting options like "More transit within walking distance" and "Larger homes on bigger lots." Then it asked multiple-choice questions related to growth management and economic development. When I finished answering the questions in front of my audience a future scenario appeared which

38 ■ *Why Are We Doing This?*

most closely correlated to my answers. The scenario was called *Region in Motion*. Every scenario showed sea level rise; it was shown as an inescapable part of our future, but the Region in Motion scenario showed densification around transit stops that were bulwarked with levee infrastructure.

This is what the scenarios were called.

- **Trend. Stay the Course.** This scenario reflected no changes in land use, climate, transportation, or economic development policy. Generally, it could be described as a continuation of development trends that resulted in low-density sprawl which created high levels of carbon pollution. This scenario imagined only a couple compact, walkable centers connected by transit that could be defended with resilience infrastructure. This scenario showed 2 feet of sea level rise by 2060 and vast expanses of the region inundated periodically by unchecked tidal flooding.
- **Suburban Expansion.** In this case, growth would be planned according to suburban principles, with large lot platting, extremely high carbon emission rates, low farmland protection, and new highways through pristine Everglade lands. New development was placed beyond our current urban boundaries and subject to continual flooding unmitigated by adaptation infrastructure.
- **Strategic Upgrades.** This approach involved targeted infill within existing metropolitan areas and a mix of land uses and building types. Commuter Rail and Bus Rapid Transit would connect major destinations. Historic metro centers would continue to see population increases and areas for reinforcement, retrofit, and retreat were identified.
- **Region in Motion.** This scenario focused all development into historic metropolitan centers or into new metro areas on higher ground, away from the shore. It connected the centers with rail and used streetcars, busses, and biking trails to connect people to the centers without needing to drive. This scenario optimized energy and water efficiency. With its emphasis on urban infill, this scenario did the best at providing areas that could be lifted, pumped, and bulwarked against sea level rise.

In another part of the modeler, each scenario was evaluated based on the following indicators so that participants were able to weigh the relative value of their policy choices, side by side:

- Farmland consumption
- Infrastructure cost (transportation, water, sewer, and utilities)
- Single family homes vs. more affordable condominiums, apartments, and townhouses
- Range of transportation choices
- Walkability of communities (walk to work, school, stores, transit, parks)
- Average housing and transportation costs as a percentage of household income
- Climate resilience investment

Climate Planning Objection 1 ■ 39

I talked about the conversations we'd had with the public and with policymakers which became the basis of the four scenarios and showed the audience how they could vote on the scenario they preferred. As I present, I try to imagine myself as a member of the audience and I think about the questions they may be asking: Is this speaker approaching me with openness and friendliness? Is he or she honest? Are they knowledgeable? Does this person appear to share my concerns and worldview?

Halfway through my presentation I projected an image of 80-story towers in China that marched up and down hills and let the audience gaze on the slide in silence.

"No one we have talked to yet wants Southeast Florida to look like the megacities of China," I said. "No one we talked to believes the efficiencies that this kind of living might offer are worth the trade." The next slide showed a *New York Times* article that read *China's Great Uprooting: Moving 250 Million into Cities.*[33] I placed a big red X through the image. "People want Transit Oriented Development," I explained, and I discussed City Place in West Palm Beach, and Sunset Drive in South Miami, two of the region's most walkable and visited places. "But no one wants to be China." I know that I was grossly oversimplifying the diverse landscape of modern China, but a quick discussion of China seemed necessary after the allegation that I was a Chinese Communist. "That's not a future option in our scenario modeler because that's not an acceptable outcome."

People nodded. It's amazing how much encouragement a speaker can find when just two or three heads nod. I suspected that in the minds of some of my audience members, especially members of older generations, any talk of density is associated with Communist central planning in Eastern Europe with its high-density housing and public transit. I once saw Soviet apartment blocks outside of Tblisi, in the Republic of Georgia. Awful. Our job in Tblisi was to take those down and re-plan at a more human scale.

"Urban planning has a lot of *past* in its past," I said. "A lot of excesses, mistakes, and lessons learned. Still, forced migrations are not what we are talking about."

Hands went up. I had asked the audience to hold questions, but I allowed a few anyway. The first few were about how the model worked. Then came a question that was a little different.

"How do you know that you aren't an unwitting agent?" asked an older man in a white T-shirt, camouflage shorts, and large work boots.

"Excuse me?"

"Do you even know ..." I couldn't hear the rest, as the man's voice was wobbly and weak.

"I suppose I don't," I responded.

"You seem earnest enough, but let me tell you ...," he continued to talk but I continued to have a hard time understanding him.

"Alright," I said. He appeared to be done. "Thank you." I continued. I planned to talk to the man after the presentation to hear what I'd missed and respond a little.

40 ■ *Why Are We Doing This?*

When it came to sea level rise, I spent a lot of time that summit, as opposed to the first summit, explaining climate resilience. Back then, everyone used the word *resilience* and not *resiliency* – sorry, but as an English Major I must pause here to note that I consider *resiliency* a needless variant of the noun *resilience* – though I must admit that today the word *resiliency* is more common. Using the model, I went back and forth between images which showed Southeast Florida in 2045, 2060, and 2110 and showed everything from increased nuisance flooding to catastrophic inundation.

"When will we see rise like that?" I was asked by a person standing close to the podium. The woman in a professional navy suit was one of the presenters at the counter-conference and when she had entered the room and sat close to the stage I expected an interjection at some point.

"The slides list approximate dates, though the timeline is a really anyone's guess," I said.

"So, setting the far-off future to the side for a moment, will the people in this room see any of that?" she asked.

"We'll see between 9 inches and 4 feet by 2060," I said. "We'd hardly notice 9 inches, but 4 feet would be a disaster." I was oversimplifying, but she nodded, and to my surprise didn't ask anything further. Presentations on science must be simple, brief, and consistent. I repeated variations of, "between 9 inches and 4 feet by 2060" several times. Climate presentations must also repeat, repeat, repeat in order to leave people with a message they can take home with them.

"Any other questions?"

"I don't believe any of this," I heard from a mustachioed man with his arms crossed tightly in front of him.

"Technically, that's not a question. Does anyone have a question?" Of course, I didn't say that. "Tell me more," I said instead. The question-and-answer session following my presentation was long and involved more answers from the audience than questions, but when asked questions I tried to respond to everything as honestly as possible.

By the end of the project, several thousand people had used the online modeler and 73% had chosen the *Region in Motion* scenario, the smart growth scenario with an emphasis on defending, adapting, and retreating. Despite the attention-grabbing opinions of extremists, I think it is safe to conclude that the average person wants what the urban planner wants. It might not feel that way at times, but if the urban planner's ideas are not clearly in the public interest and expressing values shared by the majority, our profession would cease to exist.

Commissioner Solari continued to travel our region like Paul Revere to warn people of the threat posed by regional planning. He continued to give speeches on liberty, at one point describing seat belts and building codes as a "coercive arm of the state" and at another point describing how our planners were using a mind control method called *Delphi mind control*. According to Solari, our plan was to destroy the American way of life.[34]

The Planning Team: Often its Own Worst Enemy

In June 2013, Solari's effort was handed a secret weapon by our team. Andres Duany, the Cuban-born Miami starchitect and founder of the New Urbanism movement in town planning, gave a presentation to the City of Vero Beach which, in short, didn't go well. His firm, Duany Plater-Zyberk (DPZ), was part of our multi-disciplinary team, and the brilliant and imperious Duany had a secret plan to win over Solari's Tea Party.

It isn't an exaggeration to call Duany brilliant. Anyone who has ever worked with him or has read his writings agrees. It also isn't an overstatement to call his plan secret. As project director for the Consultant Team I had asked Duany to go through his presentation with us beforehand so we could give him some pointers on how to navigate the crowd he'd be facing, but receiving pointers really isn't on brand for him.

"I have never gone through a presentation before an event with anyone, and I, simply, do not see the need," Duany told me while on speakerphone.

"I want you to present, but …," I said.

"Of course you do."

"Andres," I said into the phone while I sat at the head of a conference room full of people (including our client) who were all nervous about letting Andres present. "Let me tell you about these people. They …"

"Why don't we simply tell them that they are right?" he said.

Ha! Ha! Ha! My team and I laughed. We're all fans of Andres and wanted to stay on his good side. *Aahahaha!* Laughing diffuses tension.

"No," he said flatly. "I am serious."

Duany is often compared to Howard Roark, the renegade architect in Ayn Rand's 1943 libertarian novel *The Fountainhead*. Duany fights government land use and building code regulation which raise the cost of construction and he is at odds with restrictive environmental planning like wetlands regulations which, he has said, makes great cities like Charleston, South Carolina impossible to build today. He's against many laws and environmental protections that mainstream urban planners are in favor of. Maybe he could win over the libertarian opposition, I thought.

He didn't. Duany gave a two-hour presentation in Vero Beach and when he was done the opposition felt it had proof that our team's ultimate goal was nothing less than tyranny. If you Google the words *Seven50* and *Duany* you can still watch his presentation, which was ultimately about America's proud tradition of urban planning. Beginning with Pierre L'Enfant's plan for Washington DC, Duany's message was: We are a nation of people who have done great things together in the past and we can do great things in the future. But the presentation also included familiar Duany-themes including a comment on the "efficiency" of "fascism" when it came to urban planning.

Duany asserted that great projects can't be built today in a world where there's so much public discussion and NIMBYism (Not In My Backyard hostility to development).

42 ■ *Why Are We Doing This?*

He described NIMBYs (and there were over 100 in the room the day he presented) as "petty" and "ill-informed." He talked about the power once enjoyed by rulers like Baron Haussmann and Napoleon III during their reinvention of Paris.

Maybe tyranny is better organized than freedom, but you can't actually say that. Tyranny has too many other, let's call them, *downsides*. The Tea Partiers had come to the meeting looking for signs of heavy-handed big government plans, socialist authoritarianism, and fascism, and it didn't take a lot of selective hearing to find just what they were looking for in his presentation.

While you're on Google, you can also watch a film made for the American Coalition 4 Property Rights entitled "Tyranny in Florida: Seven50 Exposed," which quite convincingly depicts Duany as an openly evil, mustache-twirling villain. The professional-grade special effects wouldn't look out of place on a television network and our team assumed at the time that it was Koch-related monies that paid for the film. As Duany speaks, the film's driving violins and military drums provide a Wagneresque soundtrack we could describe as "The evil army struggles toward world domination." When Duany says, "The idea that you actually secede from this plan, instead of effecting those agencies [the agencies which sponsored the plan: US HUD, DOT, and EPA] is not the way to change the world. They'll crush you," and the words "WE WILL CRUSH YOU" appear over and over. That kind of thing.

I have a lot of respect for Andres Duany and DPZ and I know that the failure of his Vero Beach presentation affected him deeply. In other presentations during the *Seven50* project he and his partner, Elizabeth Plater-Zyberk, offered thought-provoking discussions that reflected a lifetime of thinking about Southeast Florida. In our second summit I believe that Duany taught lifelong Florida residents things they never knew about the region's urban design. But his Vero Beach presentation was a major setback for the project.

The Coalition Dissolves

In every movie the bad guy wins at first. I know, I know, I am already on the record saying that I am against us-versus-them narratives (and I am) and so I point this out only as a student of film. In the movies, things always go seriously wrong before you get to the happy ending.

When St. Lucie County scheduled a hearing to discuss leaving the Partnership in November 2013, I attended and took the podium and microphone to present to the County Commission. I found myself in front of more than 300 angry people – most of whom wore the newly adopted red shirts of the anti-*Seven50* cause. Police stood along the back wall of the commission chambers. I had a feeling these people had all seen the film with Duany and were hoping he'd make an appearance, and so I was not only an Agent of Evil, but also a disappointment. The Upset Schoolteacher from the summit sat up front, just as I had done for her presentation at her group's counter-conference.

Signs were bouncing up and down throughout the room. I saw one with Duany's face photoshopped into a kind of Russian-style military uniform like Stalin wore. My favorite was hand-drawn and read, "Have one doubt, they call it treason. Roberta Flack. 1969." Thoughtful. Truly. Most of the signs simply read, "Agenda 21 is COMING" or something equally tedious and misinformed.

At the time, I had heard of Agenda 21 but never researched it, figuring that it was no more applicable to my work than the 9/11 Truth movement or moon landing conspiracy theory. I soon learned, however, that Agenda 21 was key to understanding what was going on. From the eighteenth-century Illuminati panic to the more recent QAnon fears, conspiracy theory is a political force we can't deny. Agenda 21 is the most pertinent current theory for urban planners and worth a quick discussion. Let's pause the St. Lucie County Commission story and leave me at the podium waiting to speak, hands clasped behind my back, miserably, while we discuss Agenda 21 further.

Agenda 21

Agenda 21 is a non-binding voluntary action plan of the United Nations drafted during the U.N. Conference on Environment and Development (UNCED) held in Rio de Janeiro, Brazil, in 1992. The Agenda 21 document is a rambling 300-pages about sustainability and while there are many good ideas within it, it also contains many controversial proposals about wealth redistribution. I have always been surprised that the U.S. signed it.

A fictional novel titled *Agenda 21* written by Glenn Beck and Harriet Parke popularized the Agenda 21 conspiracy theory in 2012. The novel borrowed heavily from George Orwell's novel *1984* with its vision of totalitarian government, brainwashing propaganda, hunger, disease, scarcity, and mass incarceration. In *Agenda 21*, an authoritarian American government takes power using a mandate to save the planet from carbon pollution and in the "Afterword" of the book Beck, at that time one of the nation's leading misleaders, wrote, "If the United Nations ... and naïve local governments get their way, it [the dystopian setting of his book] may start to look familiar, very quickly."[35]

In the book, common terms used by urban planners are given a new meaning. Beck lists the nine Secret Principles of Agenda 21 and lists alarm words people should listen for, because, he writes, they will clue attentive persons to the fact that whatever policy, initiative, or plan is being discussed, the discussion is *in fact* part of the worldwide Agenda 21 conspiracy.

The *Agenda 21* Secret Principles are:

1. To move citizens off private land and into high-density urban housing
2. Create vast wilderness spaces inhabited by large carnivores
3. Reduce traffic congestion and slash fuel use by eliminating cars and creating "walkable" cities

44 ■ *Why Are We Doing This?*

4. Support chosen private businesses with public funds to be used for "sustainable development"
5. Make policy decisions that favor the greater good over individuals
6. Drastically reduce the use of power, water, and anything that creates "carbon pollution"
7. Use bureaucracies to make sweeping decisions outside of democratic processes
8. Increase taxes, fees, and regulations
9. Implement policies meant to incentivize a reduced population (i.e., "one child per family" type laws).[36]

You have to admit that some of those items sound like good ideas – not the ones concerning forced migrations, large carnivores, and reproductive rights, of course – but some of the others. Beck's evil genius is to be found in his ability to subvert the common understandings of these ideas. In Beck's mythology, *equity* and *equitable* are alarm words because they *in fact* refer to how wealthy countries like America must transfer their resources to developing countries. *Reforested* in fact means there should be no private ownership of land. Large populations must be moved so that land can be *rewilded* to restore predator habitats. *Sustainable Development* really means that Mother Earth will only have a chance to survive if we shrink the economy, put land into government hands, and overly regulate the use of our natural resources.

Urban planners often define *sustainable development* with the following phrase: "Sustainable development is development that meets the needs of the present without compromising the ability of future generations to meet their own needs." In *Agenda 21*, Beck argues,

> If you can't do anything that might "compromise" the ability of future generations to meet their (unknown) needs, then there's really not all that much that you can do. Want to cut down some trees to clear the way for a new home? Sorry, those trees help cleanse the air of CO_2 – future generations need them. Want to put a fence around your yard? Sorry, that might prevent the free flow of wild animals and have unintended consequences in the future … And on and on it goes.[37]

Many people fear that sustainable development is, to quote Beck in *Agenda 21*, "Just a way of saying centralized control over all of human life on Planet Earth."[38]

In Beck's closing words he tells his readers that they are not radicals or conspiracy theorists because the official 2012 GOP platform gives credence to the Agenda 21 fear when it states, "We strongly reject the U.N. Agenda 21 as erosive of American sovereignty, and we oppose any form of U.N. Global Tax."[39] Like any competent conspiracy theorist, Beck is successful at taking real world items and weaving them into elaborate myths. I wish I had known about Agenda 21 and Beck's book before the St. Lucy County Commission meeting. It would have helped me understand what my audience was hearing as I talked. Because I was baffled.

Climate Planning Objection 1 ■ 45

While I waited at the podium to make my presentation to the hostile crowd two commissioners gave speeches that applauded the attendees for taking such an interest in local government. Then the Commission announced that public comment would be heard before our presentation, before we'd said anything about *Seven50* or about the planning process. At a commissioner's request, I left the podium and left the first slide of my presentation glowing on the screen. "Thanks for Attending!" was written ingratiatingly in bold letters.

The names of people who submitted cards to speak were called and I sat with my back to the motley crowd composed of almost entirely retiree-age people as they hooted and hollered for each other. I gave my full attention to the speakers despite their dismissal of all connections between carbon emissions and global warming and their reckless and unsubstantiated allegations against me, including a lot of talk on the "false science" in the presentations I had given during the previous summit. I did appreciate when the comments were about my team and our project because most weren't. Every conspiracy theory the internet could provide was voiced including concerns over fluorinated water and inoculations, Flat Earth Movement stuff, Birther Movement stuff, and one headscratcher of a theory I had never heard before involving zombies.

By making public comment the first agenda item it was easier for members of the crowd to make their accusations or give their rant, and then leave before we could reply. I wasn't surprised. Municipalities are too often run as if the goal were to make happy the maximum number of people who show up on County Commission night.

I was accused of working for the U.N. and of being a "ringmaster" for a "communist circus" (presumably this was a reference to our summit). I was part of a government cover-up – quite a few cover-ups in fact – though I had no idea what thing we were covering up. It was never stated. I refused to take the attacks personally. It can't be personal.

Commissioners praised the commenters with quotes like "Precaution is the soul of virtue." The Upset Schoolteacher with her perfect posture clapped for every speaker and offered antiquated phrases of encouragement like "bravo" and "absolutely brilliant." It was bizarre, nightmarish, bureaucratic, and yet full of weird humor. It was a short story by Kafka.

It is worth noting that it was my birthday that night and I still hoped to take my wife to Red Fish Grille, a Miami restaurant located on a romantic lagoon where live Spanish guitar would play. I know that building bridges between America's different generations is an important part of urban planning, but it was my birthday and I didn't want to spend it with the Upset Schoolteacher, the American Coalition 4 Property Rights, and an angry mob of senior citizens.

I was asked to return to the podium by the Commission. The room was about as quiet as Pamplona when the bulls are running, and the Commission only half-heartedly attempted to quiet the crowd with statements like "People … people … let's let this man try to defend his ideology."

46 ■ *Why Are We Doing This?*

Thanks.

I gave an overview of the project, made it clear that the regional plan was still in the process of being written, ignored a lot of rude jeering, and implored St. Lucie County to stay part of the conversation. I described how important everyone's input was to the plan. I didn't, however, shy away from presenting the realities of a changing climate with its severe storms and coastal flooding. I described how important local government was to the fight but how local government couldn't do it alone. State and federal funding was necessary, and I talked about how the plan would help get our region the attention of state and federal agencies. In closing, I listed all the things that *Seven50* had nothing to do with – including U.N. resolutions, American liberty, fluorinated water, communism, and zombies (I couldn't resist).

My presentation didn't help. St. Lucie County left *Seven50* after a vote of 4 to 1. It wasn't a surprise. Elected officials bow to the pressure of well-organized vocal minorities too often. It was an unwinnable fight. I was a little surprised, though, when one of the commissioners who voted against the plan asked to meet with my team afterward in his office. He insisted that his vote to leave wasn't the act of political cowardice it appeared to be. Our team said little to nothing as he talked, talked, and talked. Midnight came and went, and my birthday disappeared.

Just a few weeks later, Martin County, the third of our five counties, opted out of the coalition. Signs began to appear at public meetings that read *Four50* instead of *Seven50*. Clever. Truly.

The Final Summit

The final *Seven50* summit was hosted on January 15, 2014. The title of the event was "A Time to Lead," and the agenda focused on plan implementation. I made sure that the *Leadership* flag with the *New Soviet Man* stayed in my wife's car.

We had produced a 20-minute promotional video summarizing the plan and its recommendations along with attractive footage from Miami Beach, Key West, West Palm Beach, and other evocative destinations. The film showed smiling people bicycling, using transit, and eating at outdoor cafés. The film included brief statements from myself, other project consultants, and members of the Executive Committee describing their hopes for the region. Considering all the other anti-plan messages on the internet, I felt that we needed a film to present the project fairly.

We let the people appearing in the film, mostly assembled by Marcela Camblor from the regional planning council, talk about any aspect of Southeast Florida's future they wanted. The film company, First + Main, did an excellent job filming and producing the video on a small budget and with a quick turn-around. The video became the project's grand finale and is still on YouTube.

After the video, we unveiled the *Seven50 Blueprint for Regional Prosperity* with a series of presentations. *Seven50* is still today both a printed document and an

Climate Planning Objection 1 ■ 47

interactive website you can review at seven50report.org. The analogy of the "blue-print" held true; the plan has the detail of architectural construction blueprints with its detailed mapping of new development, transit, open space, and resilience investments. The plan used a highly graphic format that was accessible to the reader and encouraged creative linkages among diverse topics. Another strength of the document was its summaries of information into a practical toolkit. Illustrations of adaptation strategies for climate change translated abstract concepts into practical tools for preserving communities.

Seven50 was portrayed as a project of the Obama administration throughout the public process and many of the people who attacked the plan did so with the 2012 election in mind, but we tried to make sure that the short-term interest in national politics did not affect the long-term aspirations of the plan. The plan does contain tacked on messages about how *Seven50* will not "limit liberty" or take away "municipal sovereignty." That material was written in direct response to the angry crowds and was intended to provide political cover for upper-level plan supporters. However, I believe that the plan is as relevant today as it was when we wrote it. I believe it will remain relevant for decades.

At the end of the summit, the mayors of the four counties which remained in our coalition signed and endorsed our plan. By the end of the project the number of people the project reached (if you count media impressions such as newspaper articles or Twitter reach) was over a million in a region with a population of six million. While the efficacy of large-scale regional plans in America is always a question, Dr. Robert Burchell, one of the country's most esteemed urban planners from Rutgers University, told the audience, "The conversation itself changes the trend" and we all felt that we were changing the course of Florida history.

A *Seven50* Postscript

Commissioner Solari retired from his position on the City Council in 2019 to local fanfare and praise. Tea Partiers all over the country sent supportive messages. The Upset Schoolteacher still appears at meetings as upset as ever, fighting "social engineering" and "high density stack-and-pack, mixed use developments" at our charrettes (which she calls "charades") when we work in the northern part of the region.[40] I can't help but enjoy seeing her; I have known her from a distance for so many years and she continues to liven things up.

It has been nearly a decade since the plan was signed by the mayors of the region's largest counties, and I continue to give presentations to local municipal-ities on how to incorporate *Seven50*'s recommendations into local Comprehensive Plans. The *Seven50* document continues to be downloaded and the plan video is still viewed. The *Seven50* Plan and the coalitions created as a result of the plan have helped secure funding in the region for everything from bike trails to raised seawalls, high-speed rail to high-speed internet, local resilience officers, street trees,

48 ■ *Why Are We Doing This?*

electric charging stations, a pilot underwater tidal turbine project, and numerous other initiatives.

Notes From the Field

Resilient, Multi-modal Improvements for Florida State Road A1A in Fort Lauderdale

After Hurricane *Sandy* in October 2012 a critical stretch of Florida State Road A1A in Fort Lauderdale washed away. More than 27,000 tons of sand and US$20 million later, North Fort Lauderdale Beach Boulevard between Northeast 14th Court and Northeast 18th Street reopened. It is now safer, stronger, and more resilient with bike lanes, wide sidewalks, new flood barrier walls, and a higher elevation. The reconstruction of North Fort Lauderdale Beach Boulevard provides a model for future roadway resilience projects.

A1A runs the entire length of Florida and is the state's easternmost major north–south arterial roadway. The storm washed out the road's oceanside sidewalks and parking spaces and national news footage showed a new pay-to-park kiosk station sitting in 3 feet of sand, tilted to the side, and getting smacked by waves. Because our firm was heading the *Seven50* project at the time and bringing attention to the sea level rise issue when few others were in our state, we were asked to give input on the design of a more sustainable A1A.

I toured the site where construction workers had added steel pylons to keep the road from eroding any further. Traffic was still reduced to one lane in each direction. I watched a couple of cyclists try to bike through the construction site before being redirected by the construction workers and I pictured a facility with more space for cyclists and pedestrians. I had to assume that it wasn't just the storm that destroyed the road; higher seas and erosion were also to blame, and the roadway would have to be lifted to prevent the same damage in the future.

New designs were drafted and redrafted, and less than two years after the storm had hit (a relatively short period of time in the road-building world) a US$20 million rebuilding project was implemented which involved roughly US$6 million in multi-modal enhancements and beautification. Today, the new roadway features a landscaped median, clearly marked 5-foot-wide bike lanes each way, a 17-foot-wide beachfront promenade on the east side of the road, a protective (and decorated) wave wall on both sides of the road, new seawalls sitting atop 44-foot-deep sheet pilings on the seaward side, an updated drainage system, relocated underground utilities, and an additional 3 feet of overall height. The project also extended the beach 35 feet to provide natural flood protection.[41] Today, the new stretch of road is higher than the ocean, has walls to stop high tide and storm surge water, and provides safe spaces for pedestrians and cyclists.

Coastal Armoring

Fort Lauderdale's new stretch of A1A is an example of coastal armoring.[42] Coastal armoring involves linear protection such as levees and seawalls that fix the shoreline in its current place and take the force out of high waves. Linear protection is the most commonly used tool for protecting development along shorelines and includes a variety of elements like sandbags, rip-rap walls, beach re-nourishment, concrete seawalls, bulkheads, earthen levees, and offshore breakwaters.

Armoring is our oldest and most widespread flood protection tool. The coastline of the Netherlands is largely protected along its long length by various forms of coastal armoring dating back hundreds of years. San Francisco's Embarcadero sits atop a seawall completed in the 1920s which took more than 50 years to build. The Embarcadero is not just a wall; it is a major destination in the city for locals and tourists. Japan's coastline is armored and super levees are being considered for cities like Tokyo and Osaka. Super levees involve building up the dry-land side of a high levee to be as much as 30 times wider than the levees are tall. These types of levees are often planned with new centers of activity, even new towns, on top of them.

The disadvantage to armoring is that it is a short- to mid-term solution in an era of sea level rise. Coastal armor is engineered to accommodate a certain, fixed, storm size or a single point of sea level rise on a timeline. Armoring also requires costly annual maintenance and regular monitoring to ensure the system remains safe. An unusually large storm event can rupture levees as we saw in New Orleans after Hurricane *Katrina* in 2005, but even well-maintained levees can break.

Structural flood protection can also increase human vulnerability by giving people a false sense of security and armoring can encourage development in areas that are vulnerable to flooding. Even still, the state of Florida (and other coastal states) will need to adopt a preventive and holistic policy involving coastal roadways because today the state's armoring is occurring inconsistently, one stretch at a time, and only after major disasters.

Reconstructing State Roads with Shoreline Armoring

Many of Florida's large highways and arterial roadways are adjacent to the shore and parallel to the coastline. It would be prudent to lift the roads to act as minor levees, breaking the waves when storms hit, and raising the roadways above the inevitable future flooding line so that they can be safely travelled during evacuations. However, I have participated in many shoreline roadway upgrade projects and they rarely involve lifting the road. I have watched the public get upset when the Florida Department of Transportation (FDOT) chose temporary fixes, inexpensive, and expedient alternatives even when it was clear that the roadway needed to be reconstructed at a higher height to preserve the roadway's viability and protect the community from wave action.

50 ■ *Why Are We Doing This?*

As an urban planner working for FDOT, I have explained to the public that most roadway upgrade projects are Federal 3R Projects limited to resurfacing, restoration, and rehabilitation, and that reconstruction (*the fourth R*) was not possible under the limits of the program. FDOT can't yet use 3R funds to lift the road.

"Why not?" they ask.

"It's just not possible. Not yet," I say in a tone that suggests *maybe one day*.

Federal 3R monies were once limited to road maintenance until the Surface Transportation Assistance Act of 1982 in which Congress indicated the objective of the 3R program was both maintenance *and* enhancing safety. So, if federal guidelines require highway agencies to consider safety improvements to decrease crashes and make streets safer for pedestrians and cyclists whenever a road must be resurfaced, why not consider the long-term life of the roadway and the long-term safety of the community in the era of sea level rise? When shoreline arterial roads are simply rebuilt at great expense no higher than their original height, aren't we just kicking the proverbial can down the road?

The reconstruction of Florida State Road A1A in Fort Lauderdale in 2012 addressed sea level rise thanks in large part to the City of Ft. Lauderdale Transportation and Mobility Department. Local advocates are essential to making any state's Department of Transportation think harder about the future. Other roads, like Alton Road in Miami Beach (which was reconstructed in 2015) have also been lifted and had pump stations and new drainage facilities installed because residents demanded no less. Despite these successes, and despite a lot of discussion on the topic, I don't think an overview of South Florida's resilience efforts would lead one to conclude that we have fully transitioned from the *planning* stage to the *implementation* stage when it comes to retooling major roadways as resilience infrastructure in order to adapt to rising seas or worsening storms.

South Florida's east coast, along U.S. Route 1 (US1) and State Road A1A (SR A1A), doesn't look like Japan's National Route 1 system, the largely armored system of coastal roads that parallel the Tōmei Expressway between Tokyo and Nagoya and end, literally, in fortifications around Tokyo Bay. And there are no plans to build this kind of resilience infrastructure. Although Japan has had a longer history of massive hurricanes and surge events, South Florida must assume that our future will be just as turbulent. In South Florida there is no unified plan that I am aware of to build armored (or even elevated) coastal roads anywhere in the Long-Range Transportation Plans (LRTPs) or the street plans of the coastal municipalities. Local Metropolitan Planning Organizations and Departments of Transportation who lead the creation of these plans still feel that the cost to lift and bulwark streets is simply too high and they point to the fact that there is no dedicated funding source for accomplishing these goals.

Street segments are built higher and stronger only when not doing so means total roadway failure at the moment of completion. It is often argued by the DOT that the current generation of South Floridians simply aren't interested in paying for the resilience of future generations. That said, in the many road upgrade projects I have been involved with, the question was never asked.

Climate Planning Objection 1 ▪ 51

I did ask once. As part of the plan for Highway 44 in Crystal River, Florida, in 2020, I asked this poll question on our interactive website: "Would you be willing to pay more in taxes and fees in order to see Highway 44 elevated to be more resilient in the future as seas rise and street flooding becomes more prevalent?" Of the 123 respondents, 53% answered "Yes," 33% answered "No," and 14% answered "Maybe." In my opinion, when more than half the population in an area voices a willingness to lift streets an exploration of the idea should be required as part of the Florida Department of Transportation's analysis. I talked to DOT representatives in September 2020 about lifting the road and, they, well, laughed.

We need to keep pushing. Urban planners should understand that resilience infrastructure, including the armoring of coastal roads, can become part of the design of new projects and upgrades to existing infrastructure at any point before construction. When projects reach the top of the Long-Range Transportation Plan list they don't have to be built the way they were designed (and priced) before climate change adaptation became part of the national conversation. It isn't too late. Municipalities must appeal to their Local Metropolitan Planning Organizations and Departments of Transportation concerning projects already in the works.

Admittedly, there's more to adaptation planning than the armoring of coastal roads or any other major capital project. Adaptation includes changes to building and land development codes which incrementally lift and reinforce the landscape. These updates may be the most effective form of adaptation. However, urban planners must continue to work to add more street elevation projects, drainage and roadway improvements, new berms, shoreline and roadway stabilization, mangrove restorations, and beach re-nourishment projects to the official lists of slated projects.

In Southeast Florida, I think it's fair to say that the progress to implement the recommendations of resilience advocacy groups such as the Miami-Dade County Sea Level Rise Task Force have been too slow.[43] Plans, such as the *Resilient305 Strategy*, a 100 Resilient Cities Program pioneered by the Rockefeller Foundation, are entirely unimplemented. "Winning slowly is the same as losing," wrote Bill McKibben, author of *The End of Nature*, the first book for a general audience about climate change in 1989.[44] When I review current efforts to build a stronger coast, I can't believe more isn't happening.

We see green shoots we hope will grow. Inundation maps and vulnerability assessments have made it into Miami-Dade's Long-Range Transportation Plan, thus coordinating investment priorities with climate projections. Looking at these maps, though, it appears that the strategy is simply to let go of low-lying coastal places by making future transportation decisions based on vulnerability to inundation. Adaptation isn't considered.

Some scientists claim that large-scale adaptation of low-lying coastal places like Southeast Florida isn't possible given what's coming.[45] Maybe the flooding problem is, literally, insurmountable. Sometimes I can't help feeling that giving up and moving away is the real (though undiscussed) plan for Southeast Florida, though I know that fiscal conservativism is more to blame. When I ask the directors of our counties'

52 ■ *Why Are We Doing This?*

resilience offices about why more isn't being done, I get the feeling that the way to advance to the highest positions in climate mitigation and adaptation in cities, counties, and regional governments is to promise not to do anything expensive.

There are high-investment, high-population places that are worth saving. We know that sea level rise will be a part of Southeast Florida's future, and though the specific details of how high the waters will rise and how fast they will rise is still largely unknowable, it is the role of local urban planning to build smarter, stronger, and safer in the future. For now, we must work toward a more resilient coast one street segment at a time.

Notes

1 Specifically, global annual average temperature (as calculated from instrumental records over both land and oceans) has increased by more than 1.2°F (0.65°C) for the period 1986–2016 relative to 1901–1960; the linear regression change over the entire period from 1901–2016 is 1.8°F (1°C). Global mean sea level (GMSL) has risen by about 7–8 inches (about 16–21 cm) since 1900, with about three of those inches (about 7 cm) occurring since 1993 (very high confidence). USGCRP (2017). Climate science special report: Fourth National Climate Assessment, Volume I, Wuebbles, D.J., D.W. Fahey, K.A. Hibbard, D.J. Dokken, B.C. Stewart and T.K. Maycock (eds). U.S. Global Change Research Program, Washington D.C. Retrieved from: https://science2017.globalchange.gov/downloads/CSSR2017_FullReport.pdf

2 Dunbar, B. and National Aeronautics and Space Administration (NASA) (2017). NASA, NOAA data show 2016 warmest year on record globally. Retrieved from: www.nasa.gov/press-release/nasa-noaa-data-show-2016-warmest-year-on-record-globally

3 IPCC (2007). *Climate Change 2007: The Physical Science Basis. Contribution of Working Group I to the Fourth Assessment Report of the Intergovernmental Panel on Climate Change.* Solomon, S., D. Qin, M. Manning, Z. Chen, M. Marquis, K.B. Averyt, M. Tignor and H.L. Miller (eds). Cambridge and New York: Cambridge University Press. Retrieved from: www.ipcc.ch/report/ar4/wg1/

4 IPCC (2013). Summary for Policymakers, B. Observed changes in the climate system. In: Stocker, T.F., D. Qin, G.-K. Plattner, M. Tignor, S.K. Allen, J. Boschung, A. Nauels, Y. Xia, V. Bex and P.M. Midgley (eds), *Climate Change 2013: The Physical Science Basis. Contribution of Working Group I to the Fifth Assessment Report of the Intergovernmental Panel on Climate Change.* Cambridge and New York: Cambridge University Press, p. 4. Retrieved from: www.ipcc.ch/site/assets/uploads/2018/03/WG1AR5_Summary Volume_FINAL.pdf

5 IPCC (2013). Summary for Policymakers, D. Understanding the climate system and its recent changes. Ibid., p. 13.

6 Morton, A. (2019). Countries must triple climate emission cut targets to limit global heating to 2C. *The Guardian*, September 22. Retrieved from: www.theguardian.com/environment/2019/sep/23/countries-must-triple-climate-emissions-targets-to-limit-global-heating-to-2c

7 National Research Council (1979). *Carbon Dioxide and Climate: A Scientific Assessment.* Report of an ad hoc study group on carbon dioxide and climate. Woods Hole, Massachusetts, July 23–27. Washington, D.C.: The National Academies Press. Retrieved from: www.nap.edu/catalog/12181/carbon-dioxide-and-climate-a-scientific-assessment

8 Thomas Jefferson Foundation (n.d.). Today's Weather at Monticello. Retrieved from: www.monticello.org/weather/indexp.html

9 Doll, R. and Hill, A.B. (1950). Smoking and carcinoma of the lung: Preliminary report. September 30. *British Medical Journal*, Volume 2 (4682), pp. 739–748. Retrieved from: www.ncbi.nlm.nih.gov/pmc/articles/PMC2038856/

10 Terry, L. et al. (1964). Smoking and health: Report of the Advisory Committee to the Surgeon General of the Public Health Service, U.S. Department of Health, Education, and Welfare. Retrieved from: www.unav.edu/documents/16089811/16155256/Smoking+and+Health+the+Surgeon+General+Report+1964.pdf

11 American Lung Association. (n.d.). Retrieved from: www.lung.org/research/trends-in-lung-disease/tobacco-trends-brief/overall-tobacco-trends

12 See, for example, ExxonMobil at https://corporate.exxonmobil.com/

13 See, for example, Chevron at www.chevron.com

14 See, for example, Southern Company at www.southerncompany.com/

15 Moran, S. (2019). Most oil giants still fighting shareholder pressure to address climate. *Climate Liability News*, April 11. Retrieved from: www.climateliabilitynews.org/2019/04/11/most-oil-giants-still-fighting-shareholder-pressure-to-address-climate/

16 Iannelli, J. (2019). Rick Scott brags about his nightmarish climate change record in letter to Environmentalist. *Miami New Times*, September 10. Retrieved from: www.miaminewtimes.com/news/florida-sen-rick-scott-brags-about-his-climate-change-record-11263292

17 For a definition, see, for example, www.merriam-webster.com/dictionary/trope

18 Marshall, G. (2014). *Don't Even Think About It: Why Our Brains Are Wired to Ignore Climate Change*. New York: Bloomsbury.

19 Southeast Florida Regional Climate Change Compact Counties (2012). *A Region Responds to a Changing Climate*. Retrieved from: https://southeastfloridaclimatecompact.org/wp-content/uploads/2014/09/regional-climate-action-plan-final-ada-compliant.pdf

20 Trias, R. and Garcia-Zamor, J.C. (2015). *The Seven50 Plan and Regional Governance in Southeast Florida*. Wuhan: Scientific Research Publishing Inc.

21 The seven counties of Southeast Florida total 8,628 square miles.

22 NOAA information. Retrieved from www.climate.gov/news-features/understanding-climate/climate-change-global-sea-level. NOAA makes several references: Church, J.A. and White, N.J. (2011). Sea-level rise from the late 19th to the early 21st century. *Surveys in Geophysics*, Volume 32 (4–5), pp. 585–602; IPCC (2013). Summary for Policymakers, op. cit.; Leuliette, E. (2014). The budget of recent global sea level rise: 1995–2013. Published by the National Oceanic and Atmospheric Administration. Retrieved from: www.star.nesdis.noaa.gov/sod/lsa/SeaLevelRise/documents/NOAA_NESD; Parris, A. et al. (2012). Global sea level rise scenarios for the US National Climate Assessment, NOAA Tech Memo OAR CPO-1. Retrieved from: http://cpo.noaa.gov/sites/cpo/Reports/2012/NOAA_SLR_r3.pdf; Pelto, M.S. (2015). [Global climate] Alpine glaciers [in State of the Climate in 2014], *Bulletin of the American Meteorological Society* (BAMS), Volume 96 (7), S19–S20; Sweet, W. and Marra, J. (2014). 2014 State of nuisance tidal flooding. Published by the National Oceanic and Atmospheric Administration. Retrieved from: www1.ncdc.noaa.gov/pub/data/cmb/special-reports/sweet-marra-nuisa; Thompson, P.R. et al. (2019). Sea level variability and change [in State of the Climate in 2018]. *Bulletin of the American Meteorological Society*, Volume 99 (8), S84–S87.

23 MacGillis, A. (2017). Is anybody home at HUD? *New York Magazine*, August 21. Retrieved from: http://nymag.com/intelligencer/2017/08/ben-carson-hud-secretary.html

54 ■ *Why Are We Doing This?*

24 American Coalition 4 Property Rights. Retrieved from: www.ac4pr.org/timeline/

25 VeroNews.com (2012). County Commission votes to withdraw from Seven50 regional planning group. Retrieved from: http://veronews.com/2012/12/18/county-commission-votes-to-withdraw-from-seven50-regional-planning-group/

26 American Coalition 4 Property Rights, op. cit.

27 Mayer J. (2010). Covert operations: The billionaire brothers who are waging a war against Obama. *The New Yorker*, August 23. Retrieved from: www.newyorker.com/magazine/2010/08/30/covert-operations

28 Vazquez, C. (2014). Miami lives with impacts of climate change. Local ABC10 News. Retrieved from: www.google.com/amp/s/www.local10.com/news/2014/02/10/miami-lives-with-impacts-of-climate-change-2/%3FoutputType%3Damp

29 American Coalition 4 Property Rights. Retrieved from: www.ac4pr.org/oldhome/

30 Ibid.

31 Casey, J.L. (2011). *Cold Sun*. Victoria, B.C.: Trafford Publishing.

32 Southeast Florida Regional Compact Climate Change (2016). Integrating the unified sea level rise projection into local plans. RCAP Implementation Guidance Series. Retrieved from: https://southeastfloridaclimatecompact.org/wp-content/uploads/2017/01/SLRGuidance-Doc.pdf

33 Johnson, I. (2013). China's great uprooting: Moving 250 million into cities. *The New York Times*, June 15. Retrieved from: www.nytimes.com/2013/06/16/world/asia/chinas-great-uprooting-moving-250-million-into-cities.html

34 Fire Ant (2013). Florida Tea Partiers: Urban planners are using mind control, tyranny in sustainable development project Seven50. *Broward Palm Beach New Times*, July 10. Retrieved from: www.browardpalmbeach.com/news/florida-tea-partiers-urban-planners-are-using-mind-control-tyranny-in-sustainable-development-project-seven50-6466441

35 Beck, G. and Parke, H. (2012) *Agenda 21*. New York: Threshold Editions, p. 122.

36 Ibid., p. 285.

37 Ibid., p. 244.

38 Ibid., p. 251.

39 Ibid., p. 252.

40 Frey, P. (2019). Phyllis Frey: Vero Beach, FL implements progressive agenda. Vero Communiqué, March 25. Retrieved from: https://verocommunique.com/2019/03/25/phyllis-frey-vero-beach-fl-implements-progressive-agenda/

41 Adaptation Clearinghouse (2016). Fort Lauderdale, Florida – Highway A1A redesign project. Retrieved from: www.adaptationclearinghouse.org/resources/fdot-rebuild-of-highway-a1a-in-fort-lauderdale.html

42 *Spur* for people (2009). Strategies for managing sea level rise. *Spur*, Issue 487 (November–December). Retrieved from: www.spur.org/publications/urbanist-article/2009-11-01/strategies-managing-sea-level-rise

43 Gimenez, C. (2018). Report regarding seeking funds and establishing a reserve fund to facilitate implementation of the recommendations of the Miami-Dade County Sea Level Rise Task Force – Directive No. 160999, Agenda Item No.2(b)1, June 19.

44 McKibben, B. (2017). Bill McKibben: Winning slowly is the same as losing. *Rolling Stone*, December 1. Retrieved from: www.rollingstone.com/politics/politics-news/bill-mckibben-winning-slowly-is-the-same-as-losing-198205/

45 The World Bank made this conclusion. *Politico* Magazine (2016). Philip Stoddard, Harold Wanless, Mayor, South Miami; geologist, University of Miami. The climate doomsayers. *Politico*, March 3. Retrieved from: www.politico.com/magazine/politico50/2016/philip-stoddard-harold-wanless/

Chapter 2

Climate Planning Objection 2

"We don't have the will. We don't have the money."

Urban planning is the art of the possible and we naturally stop (or postpone) imagining a better future when we encounter a lack of political will or a lack of funding. We make our recommendations, work to organize support, and hear, inevitably: What about the schools? What about policing and emergency services? The firefighters need a larger station. What about all the many things residents are clamoring for? The senior center needs a bigger room for Zumba. There isn't money for seawalls, an upgrade to electric vehicles, or the preservation of a single tract of forested land. The aims of long-range planning too often don't feel relevant enough to people's lives. Climate plans are shelved at every level of governance.

"The oceans are rising, and the rivers are drying."

"We have more urgent issues right now."

We can't help but feel that if people truly understood the threat, they would find the will and resources. When Coronavirus (COVID-19) hit in early 2020, it was astounding to see what's possible when the world unites to solve a problem.

In March 2020, a dumbfounded planet resolved to deal with a deadly pandemic that no one understood. Stay-at-home orders were issued and adhered to in states around the U.S. and countries around the world. The U.S. Congress passed the US$2 trillion CARES Act to support families and businesses from the negative results of the lockdown – and that was just the beginning of the spending. Nearly

DOI: 10.4324/9781003181514-4

55

56 ■ *Why Are We Doing This?*

every country in the world enacted a similar system to cushion people from the economic crash. Businesses and employees figured out how to work from home and all large gatherings from conventions to sports events were cancelled everywhere.

The average person did what they could, quickly learning new ways of living that involved masks, hand sanitizer, and staying home as often as possible. We worked from home. We taught our kids across our dining room tables. And, not incidentally, global carbon emissions dropped to record lows. Then, less than one year after the complete genome sequence of the virus was made available for study by China in January 2020, several vaccines had been developed by the global medical science community. Science, government, and the public, all came together with a unity of purpose and amazing cooperation to solve a worldwide threat.

On Earth Day in April 2020, Secretary General Petteri Taalas, the head of the United Nations World Meteorological Organization, said:

> We need to show the same determination and unity against climate change as against COVID-19. We need to act together in the interests of the health and welfare of humanity not just for the coming weeks and months, but for many generations ahead.[1]

While pandemics have a more rapidly realized negative effect than environmental issues and plagues pique a sense of urgency in ways climate change cannot, many people working on climate issues began to see a silver lining in the COVID-19 tragedy. It looked as if once people fully understood the scale of the crisis the world could muster the same resolve to reduce emissions and build systems to help communities suffering from drought, floods, fires, heat waves, and rising seas. Climate action wouldn't look the same as pandemic actions; they wouldn't happen overnight, but climate actions could, cumulatively, amount to more re-investment over longer periods of time and a greater total effort. It's not the strength but the duration of our climate planning that will matter. It was encouraging to see just what was possible. Let's not forget what we saw.

Before we leave the Great Pandemic of 2019–2021, we should say that its lessons aren't just emblematic of a collective will we need to find. In 2014 an ancient virus, which had lain dormant under Siberian permafrost for at least 30,000 years, became infectious again (according to scientists). The contagion posed no danger to humans or animals, but other viruses could be unleashed as the ground becomes exposed.[2] One day there could be a very direct link between climate change and pandemic: We might all get "Cave Man Flu." Anyway, enough about pandemic, let's get back to climate change, even though I will always remember the COVID-19 period fondly in one way: It was a relief to be constantly panicking about a different end to civilization than climate change.

At the local level, the funding to fight climate change comes from numerous sources – from taxes used to build public infrastructure like renewable energy plants, resilient streets, and resilient public spaces to new regulations drafted to improve the environmental performance of buildings and transportation systems. Increasingly, in my work, I hear, "We don't have the money" or "Resilience can't be a priority right now," or "Our department doesn't have the funding for this" more often than outright denial that climate change is a problem. We'll need to find the money.

The U.S. has never been entirely comfortable with taxes. Let's blame King George III. Before 1776, the American colonies were subject to taxation by the United Kingdom. This became a cause for rebellion, and that rebellion gave the U.S. its independence. Culturally, Americans have continued to be more wary of taxes than other advanced countries. We identify with cultural heroes like Henry David Thoreau, who went to jail for refusing to pay personal taxes because they would be used to help fund the Mexican–American War in 1846. Today taxes are routinely presented as at odds with personal independence and this isn't a new idea or limited to one political party. Ralph Waldo Emerson, a nonpolitical and quintessential American, would have agreed.

However, as a practical matter, federal, state, and local governments already collect enormous sums and the focus of that public investment is continually shifting to solve the problems of the day. While we must recognize a cultural anti-tax philosophy, we should also acknowledge that the public treasury is substantial. Let's discuss how those monies are generated and how they can be used to mitigate and adapt to climate.

Paying for Resilience

The U.S. has separate federal, state, and local governments with taxes imposed on each level in the form of income taxes, payroll taxes, property taxes, special assessments, sales taxes, certain fees, capital gains taxes, redevelopment trust funds, and fees. Property taxes are based on the fair market value of properties and range depending on the state. Sales taxes are imposed by most states and many local municipalities. They are collected at the time of sale and remitted back to state and local government. Every time you buy something locally, you'll notice a line that says "Tax" on your receipt because an additional charge of between 5 and 15% has been added, and much of that money stays in the municipality or state. Most local projects related to climate mitigation and adaptation are funded through property taxes, sales taxes, and utility usage fees, although infrastructure projects, which can include everything from stormwater system upgrades to sea walls, can receive state and federal funding as well.

Property taxes are levied on real estate and based on an appraisal of the monetary value of each property. Property taxes have existed for a long time in the U.S. They may have first been collected from the Pilgrims at Plymouth in 1620 to build a fort. Today, property taxes are the main tax supporting local education, police, fire protection, government, roads, and infrastructure like sewers, bridges, street trees, and street lights. Taxes used on resilience projects must appear in the municipality's

58 ■ *Why Are We Doing This?*

approved Capital Improvement Plan (CIP). CIPs are used to build resilience infrastructure like lifting streets and building coastal barriers. How urban planners can be more successful at getting their projects into the CIP is discussed later in this section.

By the beginning of World War II only New York and New Orleans had **local sales taxes**.[3] Today, in many jurisdictions in the U.S there are multiple levels of government which impose a sales tax. For example, sales tax in Chicago (specifically in Cook County, Illinois) is set at 10.25%, consisting of a 6.25% portion for the state, 1.25% for the city, 1.75% county and 1% regional transportation authority.[4] Some portion of the county sales taxes have gone toward the city's urban heat reduction strategies, the planting of trees, and the redesigning of the roofs of public buildings to reflect heat. The Chicago Climate Action Plan (CCAP) outlines 26 actions to reduce greenhouse gases and nine actions to prepare for climate change. The city has set a goal of reducing greenhouse gases 80% below 1990 levels by 2050.[5] Thanks to county sales taxes they have a source of revenue to help meet their goals.

Special assessment taxes rely on a special enhancement, a benefit, for its justification. The most universally known special assessments are charges levied against properties when sewer lines are installed or streets are paved. However, special assessment tax levies can be used for other purposes including rainwater storage to deal with more frequent flooding due to rainfall (using permeable pavements or underground storage tanks, for example), and installing better flood defenses such as sea walls and increased pumping capacity.

In Miami Beach, a Community Redevelopment Agency (CRA) which I helped create in 2020, has resilience infrastructure such as raised streets, sea walls, and dike-in-dune shoreline armoring at the top of its projects list. Resilience is a new goal for CRAs. A CRA is a special district in which future increases in property values are placed into a **redevelopment trust fund** to support economic development projects and programs within that district. The main purpose of CRA is to benefit the entire community by building wealth, eliminating blight, and addressing the quality and inclusiveness of growth. There are more than 220 CRAs in Florida and many will need to retool their project lists to combat climate change if they want to avoid the blight they are charged with reducing.

Fees can also be levied. A Board of County Commissioners, for instance, can impose a Public Infrastructure Fee (PIF) to pay for a specific government program or service. In St. John's County, Florida, a 1,600-acre, mixed-use development in the northern part of the county known as "The Pavilion at Durbin Park" uses a half-cent fee to fund transportation improvements and that fee will disappear once all the infrastructure is paid off.[6] This fee could be said to be a kind of climate resilience project to the degree that the infrastructure supports transportation choices that provide alternatives to single-rider automobiles.

Boulder, Colorado, uses a kind of local "carbon tax" approved by voters in 2006.[7] Boulder's Climate Action Plan (CAP) tax on electricity customers is used to fund renewable energy, energy efficiency, and transportation. Boulder customers who subscribe to wind-generated power through the local Xcel Energy Windsource Program are not taxed on that portion of their electricity usage. CAP tax funds have been used to provide rebates on solar installations and fund Eco Pass (bus pass) subsidies in that city.

Investing in Resilience and Requiring Resilience

When it comes to climate, the cost of inaction will be greater than the cost of action, but that's never been a particularly persuasive argument at the level of local government where it's the next administration and next city council that will pay the cost of inaction. There is funding for sustainability and resilience, though, and as a community's values begin to change the funding slowly appears.

Climate plans help change values. Climate plans also help make municipalities eligible for additional state and federal funds. Adopting a climate plan can help a local community compete for monies they already pay to state and federal governments. I find this argument especially persuasive with local governments. Let's discuss climate plans that were implemented through reapportioned local monies, federal and state grants, and upgraded regulations.

Investing in resilience in Montgomery, Alabama

I am a big proponent of tree planting campaigns and I am delighted when places like Montgomery, Alabama begin planting trees in their downtown according to local plans. Trees and plants have a new public purpose: They are *emissions sinks*, the opposite of *emissions sources*, and absorb carbon dioxide from the atmosphere. In 2014, 11% of U.S. greenhouse gas emissions were offset by sinks resulting from land use and forestry practices.[8] One major sink has been the net growth of forests in America. Much less land is used for grazing than, say, 200 years ago. We see sinks created even by our urban forests, and the trees, shrubs, and groundcover that are located in-between our buildings.

Streets in flood zones should be lifted and rainwater should be stored under them. All streets have regular repair and reconstruction schedules which involve state funding. New public spaces should also be lifted to retain rainwater onsite, re-use that same water if possible, offer high levels of shade to fight the urban heat island effect, and generate their own electricity through innovative technologies. These improvements may raise the cost of public infrastructure, but as a percentage of the total project budget (given the tremendous amounts that must be bonded to build anything locally) resilient elements and green improvements are very small.

When Montgomery, Alabama rebuilt Trenholm Court, a public housing community my firm helped design, they included the lifting of streets and public spaces, in addition to the provision of affordable housing. That project was funded by a 9% low-income tax credit from the Alabama Housing Finance Authority, Montgomery Housing Authority funds, city funds, and loan sources. The new neighborhood is

60 ■ *Why Are We Doing This?*

called Columbus Square and when the rains come and the Alabama River, its tributaries, and its wetlands flood (as they are prone to do), the residents of Columbus Square are less likely to face water damage in their new homes.

We must put in place policies that raise the environmental and resilience standards on both new private development and on public projects. All buildings, streets, and public spaces will need to be upgraded in time. There is usually very little cost to raising the environmental performance standard one notch higher when it comes time for upgrades.

Requiring Resilience in Las Cruces, New Mexico

Adopting new building standards, like elevated building and roadway heights, or even requirements for green roofs (vegetative or solar, for instance), will also cost little compared to an overall project budget on any major project. We often hear from the development community that the city's environmental regulations are making development more expensive and there is undoubtedly some truth to that, but it is important to note that in municipalities where environmental regulations have been in place for some time, the cost of green development is factored into the selling price of land. Land is likely to sell for lower prices in places where development costs are high in order to account for the added cost of development.

In my own experience working on new communities in Las Cruces, New Mexico I watched the New Mexico State Land Office adjust the price of public land leased or sold to a developer based on the cost of the public benefit the developer was being asked to provide by the municipality. I worked on Mesa Vista, a walkable, mixed-use community with a comparatively low carbon footprint and an affordable housing component. The traditional neighborhood protected twice as much of the arroyo and natural lands as was required by the land development code and turned those arroyos into a natural amenity with trails and vistas of the mesa (views of the Organ Mountains, specifically) that were open to the public. Again, the cost of buying that tract of public land was reduced to account for the cost of implementing the city's vision as described in its Comprehensive Plan, *Elevate Las Cruces*.

Requiring Resilience in Somerville, Massachusetts

The world has seen a rise in sustainable building in the last few decades and while part of the trend is thanks to customers asking for more sustainable structures, I think that most of the achievement can be attributed to higher-standard building regulations at the municipal level. Somerville, Massachusetts provides an example.

Somerville is a city just five miles from Downtown Boston and when Somerville approved its new zoning ordinance in 2019 the ordinance raised the environmental standard for new construction higher than neighboring communities, including the City of Boston, and the development community pushed back.[9]

Climate Planning Objection 2 ▪ 61

Our firm was tasked with the plan for Assembly Square, a new neighborhood rising from a former brownfield site in Somerville. The optimal use for the vacant properties on the site (otherwise known as the "highest and best use" as defined by real estate appraisers looking to maximize the value off the site) was identified to be life science complexes. These involve medical, pharmaceutical, and technological research labs, administrative offices, and campuses and provide high-paying jobs and tremendous tax revenue for municipalities. The prospective developers of the life science buildings told us that Somerville had raised their environmental standards too high and that this would cost the city. We were told that Somerville was still an untested market for the life sciences and that developers would simply build in Cambridge, Brookline, Quincy, or one of the other emerging life science markets in farther-flung Watertown and South Boston. Somerville had gone too far, they said.

Specifically, the new zoning ordinance required development projects over 50,000 square feet to achieve LEED Platinum certification. Earlier drafts of the ordinance established the requirements at LEED Gold to match sustainability standards in Boston and Cambridge but the city's planning director, George Proakis, and its mayor, Mayor Joseph Curtatone, wanted to aim higher.

While there are many building certification standards, the LEED v4.1 BD+C guidelines, the latest version of the standards developed by the U.S. Green Building Council, provide the best-known framework for green building and construction based on a wide variety of factors including the land's proximity to public transit and bicycle facilities, water efficiency, light pollution, rainwater management, and renewable energy.

"No one can build an all-electric building on this site," we were told by a representative from Grey Star Real Estate, the owner of a property that the company hoped to sell to a life science developer. Life science laboratories are especially energy-consumptive and Grey Star Real Estate felt that nothing short of an all-electric building, powered by solar panels, would produce enough points to meet the city's LEED Platinum requirement. "Other labs can build enormous solar farms next door, but we can't," Grey Star Real Estate said. "The city surprised everyone with this."

"No, they didn't," an urban planner on our team said. He explained to Grey Star that in November 2018 Somerville had adopted its Climate Forward plan and that the plan's goal was to reduce emissions from buildings, among other actions. It made sense, my teammate said, that the code update which followed the Climate Forward Plan would mean higher LEED standards as a condition of awarding a building permit.

"Well, from our perspective, our property is no longer competitive," Grey Star said.

"All the cities around Boston have committed to becoming carbon neutral; isn't it simply a matter of time before they all raise the standard?" I asked.

"Not if they are smart," was the response from Grey Star's representative.

62 ■ *Why Are We Doing This?*

It is understandable for a property owner to want to maximize the value of their property and do everything they can, including fighting regulations that could limit the value of their land. However, LEED designers don't look at certification in terms of winners and losers; they see certification and the dilemma of greenhouse gas emissions as a complex and interesting problem which is entirely solvable. I have yet to come across a case in which the only route to certification involves a single, impossible, or even wholly impractical solution like a solar farm in the middle of a dense city.

One year after our conversation with Grey Star the development of Life Science buildings in Somerville's Assembly Square has not been slowed by the new regulations. The latest large project is called the XMBLY Business Campus and it includes two 26-story towers and over 1 million square feet of life science offices for pharmaceutical and technology companies in addition to 500 luxury residential units with restaurants on the ground floor. The XMBLY project alone would mean over 4,000 construction and permanent jobs for the city[10] and millions in annual municipal tax revenue.

The communities which have climate change mitigation and adaptation within their locally approved plans are the ones that will see the biggest gains in resilience. Raise the standard. How green can you make your plans and codes? There will be a cost to both the public and private sectors, but the cost is less than you think, and the cost is worth it.

Is There Anything More We Can Do?

So much of this book is about raising the level of discourse on resilience and sustainability from, well, zero, to something more than zero, or about making the first steps when it comes to new regulations or new capital improvements, and so it is interesting to consider Somerville, Massachusetts, again, because it is a city in which the climate conversation is quite advanced.

In 2015, Somerville mayor Joseph Curtatone committed to the Compact of Mayors, a global coalition of city leaders dedicated to reducing their greenhouse gas (GHG) emissions and making their communities more resilient to climate change.[11] Following that commitment, Mayor Curtatone pledged to make Somerville carbon neutral, or having a net-zero release of GHG emissions, by 2050. What followed was a series of plans to achieve carbon neutrality and adaptation goals including the city's Greenhouse Gas (GHG) Inventory (2016), Carbon Neutral Pathways Assessment (2017), the Somerville Climate Change Vulnerability Assessment (2017), and the Somerville Climate Forward Plan (2018). The plans envision net zero and resilient new building standards, adapting buildings to flooding and heat, improving energy performance in existing buildings, improving equitable low carbon mobility – including improving bus reliability and expanding bicycle infrastructure, transitioning the city's fleet to electric vehicles – updating stormwater management to consider new flooding events caused by the Mystic River, expanding the urban canopy with resilient trees, and reducing waste. What more can they do?

Climate solutions must be home-grown because many of the climate initiatives that work in one place don't work in others given the availability of solar, wind, and geothermal energy and local climatic variation in elements like soils, precipitation, and tides. At the same time, cities like Somerville still look up to cities like San Francisco, Portland, Seattle, and Vancouver in one way: plan implementation. The west coast cities are ahead when it comes to leading by example, advocating at the state level for carbon neutrality and the de-carbonization of electricity, and creating a culture of climate action. And so that's the job of plans like the Assembly Square Neighborhood Plan. We must make climate preparedness a goal for leadership on every level, from the City Council and the Planning Commission, to the residential building managers and local business owners. Our job is to educate locally on resilience with our public process and in plan implementation, and in this way, we push community climate action regionally and globally, and not just locally.

The Assembly Square Neighborhood Plan will be the first neighborhood plan for Somerville since the adoption of the Somerville Climate Forward Plan, and the first plan to incorporate the Climate Forward recommendations. We can imagine a neighborhood that is net zero. We can imagine a neighborhood in which people could walk to daily needs despite a hotter world and the potential for regular flooding. No matter where we work, there's still a lot we can do.

We'll Adapt When There's No Other Option

"Adapting to global warming is cheaper than preventing it," is often heard in climate discussions at the international, federal, state, and local level. Let's discuss the international level because local planners can't guide the public conversation unless they can comment on activities at every level.

Less than a decade ago the projections for decarbonizing the world economy were a lot scarier, but the evolution of cheap solar has largely changed the math. Just as the title suggests, Roy Scranton's book, *Learning to Die in the Anthropocene* wasn't optimistic.[12] The core of the book was written in 2014 before the arrival of cheap solar and the book posited that "global decarbonization was irreconcilable with global capitalism" because "basic economic stability depends on cheap, efficient energy" and "decarbonizing the global economy without a replacement energy source would mean turning off approximately 80% of our power, causing a worldwide economic meltdown."[13]

Scranton wasn't working for the fossil fuel industry or running for a Senate Republican seat, he was deeply concerned about the environment and he describes his politics as "left-leaning" in the book. Nevertheless, he saw no viable solutions. Scranton wrote that even worldwide decarbonization *with* replacement energy looked so "unpalatable" that "any politician who honestly and frankly worked to

64 ■ *Why Are We Doing This?*

detach her nation's economy from oil and coal would not survive" in any kind of democratic government. "The rigorous austerity necessary for such an effort would," he said, "mean either economic depression or poverty for most of her constituency, a massive redistribution of wealth, or both."[14]

Compare Scranton's perspective to the widespread articles in 2019 describing the global "collapse" in the number of new coal-fired power plants.[15] Construction of coal plants has fallen 84% since 2015. A report from the NGO-backed Global Energy Monitor reported that the decline of coal has been caused by the falling costs of renewable energy. In the electricity market, major financial institutions have also blacklisted coal producers, and political action to cut carbon emissions is growing. Mitigating global warming by stopping the output of carbon may prove cheaper than paying to adapt to warming.

In the world of medicine, doctors talk about suicide-by-lifestyle. Smoking, drinking to excess, sedentary jobs, and diets high in sugars and fats lead to problems of the heart, liver, and other organs. The idea that "adapting to global warming is cheaper than preventing it" sounds a lot like "when it becomes necessary, I'll just get an organ transplant." An organ transplant is a highly risky, costly, and desperate act which in many cases could be avoided with relatively small lifestyle changes. To continue the analogy, just as the cost of solar has gotten cheaper, these days we all have access to fresh fruits, vegetables, and healthy snacks like never before. Today we understand the need to consume less sugar, quit smoking, take exercise, and reduce alcohol use and there are many support systems to help people with food and alcohol addiction issues. By mitigating, by working to decrease fossil fuel use, we are working to get the world used to another kind of safe, healthy living.

Why Should the U.S. Lead?

If you've spent any time debating the challenge of climate change, you've likely come across a common excuse for inaction. It goes something like: "The U.S. might be able to cut emissions, but that won't solve climate change because China and India won't do the same." I've heard this objection many times. "China plans to build a new coal-fired power station every week until 2030. Why should we do anything if they won't?"[16]

When I hear this, I hear people saying that they are afraid that life, which is hard enough (no matter how well off a person may be financially), will get harder if we collectively decide to take serious action on the climate crisis. I also think that people's innate sense of fairness leads them to feel that if things don't get equally hard for everyone then they shouldn't be asked to bother. This trope about China and India is a bit out of date, however.

Recent reports cite how, in China and India, which have accounted for 85% of new coal power capacity since 2005, the number of permits for new coal plants has dropped to record lows.[17] China pledged to eliminate its carbon emissions by

2060.[18] Students in India's leading educational institutions pledged to do the same later in life when they attain positions of power.[19] The entire geo-political energy story is complicated, but, suffice to say, we can now respond, "China and India are beginning to do their part, and so should we."

Whether coal plant retirements will be enough is a question. According to the IPCC, keeping global warming to manageable levels requires a 70% reduction in coal power generation by 2030, and a total phase-out by 2050. That's a tall order in countries where coal is cheap and the standard of living (including essentials like access to electricity) can be low. However, at least in developing nations, there is no good reason for inaction now that we understand that the shift to renewable energy is expected to have a negligible impact on global economic growth.

A U.S., Department of Energy report entitled "Revolution Now: The Future Arrives for Four Clean Energy Technologies" (2013) described the dramatic cost reductions in onshore wind power, Polysilicon photovoltaic modules (solar panels), LED lighting, and electric vehicles. Although these four technologies still represent a small percentage of their total market when it comes to electricity, vehicles, and lighting, they are growing rapidly.[20] Utility-scale wind power and solar, electric vehicles, and LED lights finally make economic sense. The economist Paul Krugman put it this way:

> So is the climate threat solved? Well, it should be. The science is solid; the technology is there; the economics look far more favorable than anyone expected. All that stands in the way of saving the planet is a combination of ignorance, prejudice and vested interests.[21]

"Climate mitigation and adaptation monies could be better spent," is something we also hear. Bjørn Lomborg, author of best-selling and controversial book, *The Skeptical Environmentalist* (2001), argued that many of the costly measures and actions adopted by scientists and policymakers to meet the challenges of global warming will ultimately have a minimal impact on the world's rising temperature. Lomborg admits climate change is real but argues that other human problems such as indoor air pollution, malnutrition, or water sanitation are problems that can be solved at far less cost.[22] The common response globally to Lomborg's argument has been, simply, "Let's solve those things too. It isn't an either/or situation."

Local Capital Improvement Plans (CIPs)

While we need to understand the discussion at the international and federal levels well enough to participate in *big picture* conversations, our work focuses on the local level. On the local level, pushback to climate mitigation and adaptation may come from the mayor or manager's office when it comes time to add to the Capital Improvement Plan (CIP). Capital improvements are the purchases municipalities

66 ■ Why Are We Doing This?

make. The CIP identifies capital projects and equipment purchases, prioritizes the projects, provides a timetable for completion, and provides options for financing.

The CIP implements the goals of the City Council, School District, Parks and Recreation Department, and other local government entities. Typical CIP projects include items like public building renovations, fire station replacements, and the construction of new schools. In a mid-size municipality, a CIP can include hundreds of millions of dollars in investment over a five-year planning period. For climate planners, mitigation projects might include LEED-rated public building design and wind and solar generators. New climate adaptation projects might include shoreline levees, rip-rap walls, and built-beaches in low-lying places, or, in mountainous areas, the repair of roadways, culverts, and retaining walls which prevent surging rainwater from flooding communities.

Climate plans are generally implemented through a combination of regulations, partnerships with the private sector, city expenditures, and capital investments. Unlike land development regulation reform or development review, however, capital investments are generally planned, designed, funded, and constructed entirely outside of the Planning Department's sphere of influence. Given this reality, it can take a bit of creativity and persistence to ensure that the climate plan influences and informs the CIP.

The CIP also includes General Obligation (G.O.) bond referendum items. A bond referendum is a voting process that gives voters the power to decide if a municipality should be authorized to raise funds through the sale of G.O. bonds. A G.O. bond is a long-term borrowing tool (typically 20 years) in which a municipality pledges its full faith and credit (specifically, its taxing power) to repay the debt over a specified term. Generally, G.O. bonds are the least costly financing option available to municipalities for potential bond projects. CIP projects often include stadiums and ballparks, new recreation centers, golf courses, new schools, and school additions. After many years of urban planning, I count my true successes by the number of plans that resulted in G.O. bonds.

The main reason it is difficult to add climate adaptation projects on to the CIP is that many municipalities feel they barely have enough in the municipal budget for the maintenance of its existing infrastructure. In some cases, a municipality may not even have the bonding capacity to secure a loan for new infrastructure. It can be especially difficult to convince voters who are not in communities facing dramatic climate trauma like flooding, wildfires, or hurricanes to invest in resilience. Many communities believe they simply won't find the political will to secure loans to pay for sustainability or resilience.

Urban planners need to understand their community's CIP planning process in order to be effective. Planners must know when CIP meetings occur. Those meetings typically only involve municipal financial services, infrastructure services, and city leadership. Planners must become part of those meetings, learn how to build bond package recommendations, learn to convene departments to discuss the urgency of climate planning through forums and roundtables, and commit to coordinating with city leadership on an ongoing basis.

Municipalities can create a separate Capital Planning Office to prioritize projects, allocate resources to projects, and identify which projects to initiate, reprioritize, or terminate. This Office can provide a more objective approach to capital planning which otherwise is conducted ad hoc by individual departments working in isolation. A Capital Planning Office is more apt to recognize emerging public needs, like the need to adapt to a changing climate. The Office is also more likely to recognize the diminishing returns of novel new purchases for the Police Department, for instance, over the municipality's first investments in climate mitigation or adaptation. A well-drafted CIP which talks about climate goals in addition to other public benefits like traffic congestion reductions and environmental restoration can allow municipalities to compete for millions of dollars in federal funding when it comes to items like electric streetcars, bus rapid transit, and multi-modal major arterials. Municipalities can even amend their charter to require that the CIP be consistent with the municipality's climate plan, though charter amendments are rare.

The CIP can be used to pair climate planning work with ongoing municipal initiatives. The CIP includes projects that are entirely compatible with climate planning including drainage, roadway, water utility, and sewer system improvements. These requests are typically made by the municipal Public Works Department and can be augmented to think further ahead and with climate considerations in mind. The CIP also includes investments recommended by the Police and Fire departments, and emergency management and climate planning can often be developed in tandem with these departments. Climate planners must look for opportunities to add resilience to every project that makes its way to the top of the CIP. Resilience measures could include adding solar arrays to public buildings, underground water storage and wind turbines to city parks, electric vehicles to a city's fleet, additional height to roadways in coastal areas, and developing new sewer districts to low-lying neighborhoods likely to flood.

It's the People, Not the Plan, Which Changes the World

It's helpful to think of the CIP in terms of the plan's authors instead of the paper plan. "The plan won't implement itself," we often say. "Plans don't *work* or *not work*; it is people who work." Urban planners need to know their elected officials and their motivations, understand the agencies that would be responsible for climate plan implementation and their missions, and understand how climate planning can help further those same goals and missions. When the "ask" comes for climate projects to be added to the CIP or to departmental budgets the climate projects should be in sync with all the other goals the elected officials and department heads have discussed.

Sometimes it is the personal relationship and rapport the municipal planner has established with elected officials, the Public Works Department, or CIP staff that gets climate mitigation and adaptation projects on the CIP. In other cases,

68 ■ *Why Are We Doing This?*

it is because of a mutual understanding of joint goals. Climate plans need to discuss a municipality's various departments, not just new projects. The plan should describe departments, non-governmental organizations, non-profit agencies, and local charitable organizations, along with the missions of each, and how each can contribute to climate mitigation and adaptation as an expression of their own goals and values. The plan should also end with a clear implementation matrix which identifies the responsible agency, timeframe, and funding source.

Getting to know elected officials, department heads, and local organizations is helped by the charrette process described in this chapter. The charrette brings everyone to the table at the same time, requires them to leave their offices and, to some degree, their officialdom, and get to know the urban planners and the public constituency that is championing climate planning. During the charrette we can avoid the trap of discussing climate change mitigation and adaptation costs without providing the crucial context of the cost of inaction. In the charrette, climate planners can get elected officials and department heads to make promises.

Resilience Grants

In 2013, Boulder County, Colorado, experienced a rainstorm approximately twice as large as any storm in its 120-year weather record. The storm damaged hundreds of homes and commercial buildings and caused approximately US$150 million in damage to county transportation infrastructure. The county decided that it needed a Resilience Study to prevent damage of that magnitude in the future.[23]

Boulder County's Department of Community Planning and Permitting secured funding for a Resilience Study from two grant sources: Grant-funded through the Community Development Block Grant-Disaster Recovery (CDBG-DR) funds, and federal funds from Housing and Urban Development (HUD), administered through the state's Department of Local Affairs (DOLA). Grant funding totaled US$181,000. The county commissioned the engineering firm, ATKINS, which drafted a resilience study that included policies, programs, projects, procedures, and 173 potential resilience actions.[24]

One novel aspect of the resilience study was how it helped make the case for additional resilience funding by estimating the cost of inaction including the cost of potential flooding on the existing building stock, the cost of transportation impacts, and the overall impact to local economic productivity. In total, the study found that climate-related damages and disruptions could cost the community over US$120 million every year. Planners need to remember to include the "cost of inaction" in their Request for Proposals for climate plans or in their own workplan for studies they plan to complete in-house. The cost argument helped make the case for restricting the amount of construction that occurs in flood zones because that one act was found to be the greatest contributor of damages and costs.

The Community Development Block Grant (CDBG), one of the longest-running programs of the U.S. Department of Housing and Urban Development,

Climate Planning Objection 2 ■ 69

funds local community development activities with the stated goal of providing affordable housing, anti-poverty programs, and infrastructure development. CDBG, like other block grant programs, differ from categorical grants made for specific purposes, in that they are subject to less federal oversight and are largely used at the discretion of the state and local governments and their subgrantees.[25] CDBG monies are typically used for public infrastructure and so CDBG is a logical source of resilience funding.[26] In the case of Boulder County, they accessed CDBG monies specifically earmarked for flood recovery. If you are in the U.S., your community probably receives CDBG funding. How is it spent?

The second source of funding for the resilience study was the State's Department of Local Affairs (DOLA). Every U.S. state has a comparable department which is responsible for tasks like local government assistance, property taxation, property assessment appeals, affordable housing, and housing construction regulation. If your state has a similar state agency then it is worth asking if the agency is awarding resilience grants.

Boulder's Resilience Study helped the city qualify for additional Federal Emergency Management Agency (FEMA) grants which were matched with state sales tax funds. The Resilience Plan recommended infrastructure improvements like the reconstruction of road walls where flood water overtopped roadways and spilled into urbanized areas. The plan links resilience projects with internal policies related to development review and updates to the county's land use and zoning regulations.

People think that their local government isn't working on climate issues because there's some countervailing force from vested interests. This is rarely the case, in my experience. Local government is simply busy on other issues and has other spending priorities. We need to make sure climate is part of the conversation.

Notes From the Field

Preaching Common Sense, Humility, and Politeness on Climate Issues in San Francisco

Shaun Bourgeois and I go way back. We met in our early 20s at the American University in Cairo and, as Philosophy majors we're members of a tiny, oddball group that thinks life's big questions are worth serious time and thought. I like to think we're both independent thinkers, but his views tend toward the political right, sometimes the extreme right, and my views tend toward the left and sometimes the extreme left. This has yet to get in the way of our friendship and working relationship.

Shaun is a real estate finance and economic development specialist, and we team whenever we can. The economist on a multi-disciplinary planning team should have gone to Harvard and be a Republican (or at least hold a few views that a Republican would recognize) because it balances out the rest of the team with our state college diplomas and Obama-Hillary-Bernie MacBook decals.

"I just don't see any evidence that we are at a climate tipping point," Shaun said as he showed me a graphic entitled "600 Million Years of CO_2 Data Reveals Current CO_2 Starvation." The graphic depicted how in every era before today's (an era some call the Anthropocene, though Shaun's graphic stuck to the non-politicized official

Figure 2 Golden Gate Bridge

name, the Holocene) the world's CO_2 concentrations were far higher. In the Pre-Cambrian and Cambrian periods, for instance, 600 to 500 years ago, the parts per million of CO_2 was nearly off the charts. "Between the axis of the earth, the clouds, the Sun itself, and the Earth's orbit," he said, "there are just so many factors that are more powerful than CO_2 moving from .014% of the atmosphere's composition to .028% that it's hard to get worked up about it."

I agreed with him that the concept of a "tipping point" no longer generates a sense of urgency in me. If there is a tipping point – a point at which our atmosphere and oceans have absorbed so much heat that climate change spins completely out of control – is that kind of thing knowable? And is the concept even helpful? My experience with big tasks is that they should involve many deadlines – none of them too fixed.

"But," he replied, "I do recognize backdoor efforts to get people to clamor at once for some transnational effort to give up sovereignty for their own good."

Hmmm, I couldn't agree with that one entirely, but I could see his point. One can imagine a single-issue extremist climate government demanding overly disruptive, ill-considered, politically driven knee-jerk responses. Looking back at human history, authoritarianism seems like a sadly normal state of human affairs and worse reasons than *we need to save the planet* have been given for tyranny.

"I'm not sure I'd fit into the kind of utopia these people are seeking to create," he wrote.

Like a lot of people, Shaun sees the climate change debate as the old "Socialist versus Capitalist" fight in a different format, and he's a steadfast capitalist. Shaun and I have conversations like this all the time and so, in 2019, I invited him to join me and present on climate change at an American Planning Association Conference in San Francisco.

"San Francisco? They're going burn me alive as a heretic," he said.

"Yep," I replied. "They probably will."

Despite not exactly feeling comfortable with the venue or audience Shaun agreed and joined me and another speaker on the podium in front of more than 200 urban planners. For my portion of the session, I gave a presentation entitled "Handling Climate Change Adaptation Pushback" which became the basis of this book, and I have to imagine that the audience expected more of the same from the next speaker on our panel.

Shaun's first slide read, "What does *handling climate change adaptation pushback* mean?" His next slide read, "Burn the heretics?" He advanced slides that asked, "Ignore them?", "Wait them out?", "Argue?" and, finally, "Listen?"

"Understand," he said to the crowd, "you want to make changes that require resources that must either be new or repurposed to fight climate change and, in some cases, not everyone wants to do that." He then asked the audience a series of questions like, "Is climate-change-related pushback of a different nature than pushbacks of other types?" and "In a world of limited resources, are cost-arguments surprising?", and "If all climate change deniers disappeared overnight, would adaptation pushbacks still exist?"

72 ■ *Why Are We Doing This?*

Philosophy majors ask questions. I don't do that enough anymore, I thought. The audience was silent and listening. Cell phones and tablets were down. The audience knew what I was going to say the moment I began presenting but they were never sure what Shaun was going to say (or ask) next.

"Let's look at New Orleans," Shaun continued. A picture of Jackson Square appeared behind him. Shaun grew up in New Orleans. He's lived around the world and could have set up his practice, Deadalus Advisory Services, in any city with a major airport, but he picked New Orleans (problems and all) to work and raise his family because for him New Orleans is home.

He showed historic maps and talked about how New Orleans was a highly strategic location in the eighteenth century, the closet point of solid land to the mouth of the Mississippi River, and the central byway for travel into the North American continent. He described how it was inevitable that one of the European powers would settle there and fortify it. He talked about how the city had always seen flooding and how efforts to protect the city from the river with levees and pumps created conditions for wider damage. The river was channelized, new silt could no longer resupply the shifting earth, and oil and gas companies made highways through the marsh.

"The end result is that there's a lot less *there*, there." He talked about how South Louisiana was losing land that was washing away into the Gulf of Mexico. He said that his biggest concern was subsidence, and discussed how subsidence, the gradual caving in or sinking of an area of land, was visible in cracking foundations and hole-ridden roads. He showed what looked like an earthquake fault line on the road in front of his house. I recognized the crack from when I visited him years before and I was amazed that it still hadn't been fixed. "Maybe building on a swamp wasn't such a great idea," he said.

The audience laughed. And then the audience (and I swear I saw this) leaned forward – all at once. They could sense he was approaching the end and they didn't want to miss a thing. Shaun asked the audience: "What parts of city, county, and state budgets would you suggest be cut to fund climate change adaptations? None? Well then, what taxes should be raised and on whom?" He talked about how 400 years of bad decisions and profligate spending had only served to get his region into greater trouble. "I mean, how are we to trust?"

When Shaun asked, "How are we to trust?" I thought about the millions of government-averse Americans who will refuse to accept higher taxes and restrictions on their lifestyles without revolting politically. And when I hear Shaun, a respected friend, speak for them, I understand a little better. Shaun echoed the words of a lot of people I know who say they can't trust political movements led by "liberal, coastal elites" who think so little of Americans living in "flyover country." Listening to Shaun it seemed to me that the climate change fight would probably swing back and forth like any other political pendulum. And, as he's a friend, I saw the back and forth as okay, as fair.

In closing, Shaun asked the urban planners to be cognizant of trade-offs. In a world of limited resources and time we must recognize that prioritizing climate change meant deprioritizing something else, something that for many would be more local and more urgent. He asked the crowd to create hierarchies, to rank their wish lists from the most needed items to the least, and to focus on the most needed. "Be prepared to horse-trade," he said, "and I strongly recommend that you link your issues to needs other than climate change."

Shaun's final point was in keeping with the theme he'd established at the beginning. I'd summarize his recommendation to the audience as: *Listen.* "And be humble and polite," Shaun finished with his slight but unmistakable New Orleans accent.

Let's keep in mind that many of urban planning's big plans, from the car-only vision presented by the Futurama Exhibit of the 1939 World's Fair to the mass clearings of urban renewal in the 1950s and 1960s, have done tremendous damage. Remember that the best-known urban planner in America was Jane Jacobs and she was absolutely furious with the profession. Plan with humility.

When we talk about *saving the world* it's easy to ignore the costs to individual people our proposals imply. We forget that people have other, much more urgent priorities like the sinking street in front of their houses. We need to recommend cost-effective strategies tailored to the communities where we work. We also tend to ignore the fact that there's not much trust when it comes to big government initiatives. Big government initiatives created the problems in the first place more often than we'd like to admit. We must always consider the smallest, least invasive, approach when it comes to people's lives.

Notes From the Field

Funding Protective Levees in Jean Lafitte, Louisiana

Jean Lafitte, Louisiana, just south of New Orleans, is a place that both Shaun and I hold dear. The question for Jean Lafitte is less about whether the town will be swamped by sea level rise than when. And when that day comes, will enough of the place's people, culture, and history remain? Jean Lafitte will not disappear entirely. Its inhabitants are fighters. And they have, literally, a fighter for mayor.

I first met Mayor Timmy Kerner when our team interviewed for the Jean Lafitte Comprehensive Plan project in April 2011. We needed the project because the Great Recession of 2008 to 2010 had taken its toll on salaries, staffing, and job security. I had done my research and knew that the town was outside the boundaries of the levee system built by the U.S. Army Corps of Engineers around the greater New Orleans area, had hardly any hurricane storm surge protection, and had limited flood protection. I also knew that in 2007 Jean Lafitte had been left out of the plan for new levees even though the center of Jean Lafitte was only 22 miles south of New Orleans' center.

Exclusion from the levee plan didn't just mean that the town would lack protection; it was worse than that. Jean Lafitte's natural defenses, the coastal marsh, had been scored by oil and gas canals, and starved of replenishing sediment by the

74 ■ *Why Are We Doing This?*

channelization of the Mississippi River. All around Jean Lafitte planned *diversions*, cuts in the existing levee systems, would create powerful new Mississippi tributaries where water would rush out and allow sediment-rich waters to flow and build land, but those same diversions threatened to wipe out Jean Lafitte.

The floods caused by the diversions would simulate the geological processes that created the Mississippi Delta in the first place, and over the course of years and decades the flow would patch the holes in the marsh's Swiss cheese fabric. However, in the short term, the mid-Barataria Diversion just west of Jean Lafitte would send water flowing at volumes greater than the continent's largest rivers. This would likely kill off giant populations of oysters, shrimp, blue crab, and dozens of species of fish that local fishermen and women relied on for their livelihoods. Worse still, computer modelling suggested that diversion waters would blend with wind-driven high tides and storm surges, effectively bounce off the northern levee walls, join with pumping discharges from the New Orleans metropolis, and wash Jean Lafitte away.

The problem was compounded by sea level rise. NOAA projected that by 2100 water in the Gulf of Mexico could rise as much as 4.3 feet along the Southern Louisiana landscape. The land has an average elevation of only about 3 feet. If that happens, everything outside the protective levees — most of Southeast Louisiana — would be underwater.[27]

I never learned what the other urban planning firms that we competed against for the project said about the levee situation. Many urban planners are against what they see as artificially extending the life of places like Jean Lafitte at great public expense. Of course, if that were my position I wouldn't have applied for the job. I believe every community has the right to fight to exist. I live in Miami, after all.

"We need to get Jean Lafitte in the levee system," I said directly to Mayor Kerner during the question-and-answer portion of the interview. Listening to our hosts during the interview I quickly learned to say *Gene* Lafitte instead of a French pronunciation.

"You think that's possible?" Mayor Kerner asked me, addressing our team directly for the first time. The long-time mayor was dressed casually in a white shirt and jeans. He had been a boxer when he was a young man and still had a hefty-strong body.

"Yes, Mayor," I said. "It's possible." We had already presented our team's experience and commitment to maximum public involvement. I was joined by Victor Dover, founding partner of our firm, and a team of transportation and economic specialists.

"Hmmm," Mayor Kerner said. That was it. That question was the only one he asked during the interview which was conducted by the Center of Planning Excellence (CPEX) of Baton Rouge, a non-profit organization that coordinates urban, rural, and regional planning efforts in Louisiana.

A few days later I got the call that we were hired. We were strongly urged, however, to add two local sub-consultants: David Waggoner of Waggoner & Ball Architects, a national proponent of the *living with water* approach that uses natural systems

Climate Planning Objection 2 ■ 75

to deal with flooding; and the Shaw Group, the mayor's favored levee engineer. I welcomed the opportunity to work with these experts.

Our first team meeting was in November 2011 in Jean Lafitte's Multi-Purpose Center as we prepared our presentation for our public hands-on design session. The mayor wasn't present, but the engineer from the Shaw Group explained the mayor's big idea for the town. He showed us a plan for a ring levee that, when complete, would be one of the longest in the world. It would involve over 65 miles of levee designed at 16 feet high to survive 100-year storms, and include multiple floodgates, sluice gates, and roadway gates. The price tag was US$1.2 billion.

That's not possible, I thought. No one would fund that kind of project to protect just 1,900 residents. It would cost more than US$630,000 per resident.

David Waggoner was blunt. "Louisiana …," he said with a subtle New Orleans accent (*Looo-see-ana*), "… is poor." He looked up at the luminous levee plan projecting on the wall from the engineers' projector. "That thing makes no sense."

"Let me ask you then, what do you think we should do?" responded the engineer from the Shaw Group with the thickest Louisiana accent I had ever heard. It sounded like, *"Le' me ax you den, whadda you tink we to do?"*

Waggoner didn't respond but Aaron Chang, one of his associates, did.

"We need to let the big muddy river do what it does," Chang said without any trace of an accent. "We need to stop building walls and let the delta rebuild the delta. Let the sediment flow and it will rebuild land. Sure, it will absolutely destroy some places, and some livelihoods, but all of that would likely die out as erosion continues."

The engineer from the Shaw Group let out an audible scoffing sound that was a combination of bafflement and scorn. The big man knew the bayou; he had talked over lunch in his Cajun English about fishing and hunting, about the fish camp he owned, and about teaching his kids to work a Winchester Rifle. Chang, the associate from Waggonner & Ball, was a stylish, thin, black-clad architect, and a recent transplant to New Orleans. It felt natural to side with the engineer from the Shaw Group, the local boy. I didn't want to consign Jean Lafitte to some kind of sacrifice zone in favor of a theoretical ecological restoration process, but the levee didn't make sense either.

Would we present the ring levee to the public? Would we present it as a project we endorsed? If we did, we'd have to build our entire Comprehensive Plan and all its mitigation and adaptation concepts around the daring assumption that the levee would be built. If we didn't endorse the project then what would I say to the mayor? I felt like I made a promise during the interview to push for a levee though I didn't realize the magnitude of that promise. I didn't realize that he planned to protect every square foot of the entire sprawling town.

The easiest thing to do was to assume that nothing we said really mattered. Mayor Kerner had been pushing for levees for decades and under his leadership Jean Lafitte was on a journey that wouldn't be altered. At the same time, I think local plans prepared by experts in accordance with sound planning principles

76 ■ *Why Are We Doing This?*

do matter. There was no document in Jean Lafitte that a resident could pick up and say, "This is our plan." After big storms when residents were trying to decide whether to replace their furniture for the second time and their carpet for a fifth, what did they see when they looked into the future? Opportunities are lost when people don't know how to pitch in and help. One person alone can't save a town.

Our team decided that we didn't need a unified position concerning the levee at that time. We didn't know each other yet. We didn't know the public. We left our internal meeting to go meet with the mayor.

Our team toured Jean Lafitte in two all-terrain golf carts and I sat next to the mayor as he drove us around the historic fishing community with its moss-covered cypress trees, beautiful (though invasive) water hyacinths in the estuaries, and egrets in the marsh. We motored up an old levee embankment that protected one side of the town from waves. From atop that hill we could see signs that the town had been hit hard by storms and flooding. We saw the remains of cars and pontoon boats clinging to the shore, spilling sandbags, homes with blue tarpaulin roofs, and businesses that were still boarded. From atop the grassy, earthen levee we could see the ghost forests, the forests without leaves because the dry land had become wet and the trees were choking on sea water. We could see the Lafitte Skiff, an iconic fan-tailed wooden fishing boat, which stood on concrete piers like a waiting ark.

Jean Lafitte is a narrow ridge of land roughly 12 miles long and, on average, 1 mile across. Without taking major action it would suffer the same fate as Isle De Jean Charles in Terrebonne Parish, Louisiana, explained the engineer from the Shaw Group. Isle De Jean Charles was once 11 miles long and 5 across but had shrunk over the years to a mere 1 miles long and a quarter a mile across. The engineer talked about how the people of Isle De Jean Charles were in conversation with the United States Department of Housing and Urban Development to evacuate and resettle the community elsewhere.[28] No part of Isle De Jean Charles would be saved.

The mayor talked about how the town's problems had been made worse by the loss of wetland due to the channelization of the Mississippi, and the exploration and drilling for oil. We could see the wide bayou rivers with latte-colored water that coursed through what were once dense wetlands with live oaks and bald cypresses. The mayor talked about how the people of Lafitte had lived off the water for generations. He talked about trapping and skinning muskrats as a young man. People fished, crabbed, oystered, and built and repaired boats. They also worked the offshore oil rigs, somewhat paradoxically.

"We can save it," he said. "We just need to get in the state levee plan."

"You don't think that maybe you're a little too far out to defend?" I asked the mayor as we stood high on the embankment with the warm wind passing all around us.

He didn't say anything.

Since 2007, the Coastal Protection and Restoration Authority of Louisiana has completed or funded construction of a total of 135 projects, resulting in over 36,000 acres of land benefited, 282 miles of levee improvements, and over 60 miles of barrier islands and berms constructed or under construction according to the

Climate Planning Objection 2 ■ 77

Authority's 2017 Coastal Master Plan.[29] That is significant. However, the amount of land that the authority couldn't save, the land that had disappeared, far exceeded what they could save. In 100 years, Louisiana's coast has lost 1,900 square miles of land due to saltwater intrusion and subsidence.[30] How far could the coastal protection plan be stretched?

We left the levee and continued to tour the town. We saw run-down wooden shotgun-style homes, some lifted in the air on stilts, and large country estate houses on "lily-pad" mounds with steep gradients to avoid flooding. The town was home to poverty but also wealth.

Mayor Kerner knew the names of every resident we passed. Though he seemed a naturally quiet, almost timid, man, I watched him stride across the street and shake hands on several occasions. One resident, a tall, heavy-set man with a patchy grey and yellow beard, greeted Kerner by saying, "I'm still here, Timmy."

"I respect it. I respect it," the mayor said with an accent like the engineer's (*Ah respek it. Ah respek it*).

The man the mayor talked to nodded with pride. I couldn't help but wonder if chronic exposure to natural disasters may have resulted in a kind of pathological psychological resilience in Jean Lafitte. The man seemed to look up to the mayor as the captain of a ship that they were both prepared to go down with. Shared trauma can strengthen a sense of community, for good or ill.

Mayor Kerner took us to a town cemetery where Jean Lafitte's families – families like his – had scrubbed algae off the white box graves for centuries. Jean Lafitte is only 2 feet above sea level on average and had been flooded by storm surge several times. In 2005, Hurricane *Katrina* swamped the town and the storm's 120-mile-per-hour winds stripped roofs off houses. A month later, Hurricane *Rita* flooded the town along with much of lower Jefferson Parish and even dislodged the whitewashed tombs from the graveyards. The mayor told us about how residents in Lafitte had found skulls in their backyard gardens among the debris. More than 150 houses had to be demolished in Jefferson Parish after *Rita*.

Then came Hurricane *Gustav* in 2008, which swamped the entire area. Hurricane *Ike* followed later that same season. Just months before we had arrived Tropical Storm *Lee* has flooded dozens of homes. Kerner showed me a photograph of a resident sitting on a porch couch during Tropical Storm *Lee*. His hands were behind his head nonchalantly and he wore no shoes – just muddy socks. It was a nice house, wide, and tall, with terrific fanlight windows. In the picture, the seething flood waters had risen within 6 inches of the man's feet and the house looked like it could float away. The man was nonchalant. More than that, he was smiling.

Jean Lafitte was changing, but as I looked at aerial photos and historic maps I could see that Jean Lafitte had seen nothing but change in its history. It looked absolutely nothing like the community of 200 years ago when the town's namesake pirate, Jean Lafitte, used to hide with his men in the swamp they called Bayou Barataria. Lafitte and his comrades helped General Andrew Jackson defend New Orleans from the British in the final battle of the War of 1812. Pirates fought alongside the soldiers

78 ■ *Why Are We Doing This?*

who once hunted them; it's a poignant image. In 1930, there were more than 50 miles of marshes, ridges, and barrier islands between the Lafitte Area and the Gulf of Mexico. Today, there are only the skeletal remains of a once-viable natural protection system which hid the pirates and buffered them from storms.

After our tour I met with Mayor Kerner in his office. There was a black-clad pirate mannequin with a tricorn hat standing just behind him. The mannequin had a sword in its leather belt and its plastic hand reached outward from a frilled swashbuckler shirt to just above the mayor's head. I couldn't help but want to shout, "Look out!"

"That's Jean," Mayor Kerner said (he said, *Gene*, of course).

"Ah."

The mayor had shelves of model fishing trawlers and pirogue canoes, a collection of bobblehead dolls, baseball caps, assorted plastic pirate items, and framed pictures of deceased family and friends. Mayor Kerner told me he envisioned a museum for all the items. He thought his town could become a major tourism destination and employ residents who had lost their jobs to cheap seafood imports from Asia. He pointed to one photo and told me that the person in it was his father. The jolly-looking old man had been the town's first mayor when it was incorporated in 1974.

"Okay," I said, "we'll talk about tourism in the plan document, but about that levee …"

"Let me tell you about the levee," Mayor Kerner interrupted.

The issue of securing levees was always on his mind and everything else felt like a prelude to the moment he began talking about them. He told me that securing the funding to build levees was a campaign promise he'd made 20 years before. At the time of our discussion in 2011, Kerner had been mayor for 19 of his 51 years. He said that levees were his "mission in life."

"And we're gonna get'em," he told me. "When people say 'you need to leave' I say, 'Make sure the next time you say that that, you're out of my reach.'" He said this so quietly I could hardly hear the words. He said it like a man who meant it.

"Got it," I said. Or if I didn't, I thought it.

"You'd better," he warned.

Wow. The soft-spoken, bulky man was a big teddy bear except when it came to levees.

When the time for the big public hands-on session finally arrived on Saturday, November 12, 2011, no one came. My team from Miami, CPEX staff from Baton Rouge, and the other consultants from as far away as New York City and Washington State, all found ourselves alone in the town's Multi-Purpose Center. The tables around us were set with base maps and facilitator folders. All around the room were GIS analysis maps on easels. We even had coffee and donuts on a back table. Thirty minutes after the scheduled start time people began to trickle in but no more than a dozen. We were told that everyone in town was at a high school football game. When our event was over, the hum of the projector was the only sound when Mayor Kerner said, "I'll fix this." He got on the phone and we re-held the event three nights later and had nearly 100 attendees.

Climate Planning Objection 2 ▪ **79**

The fact that the mayor could rally so many people together for our charrette demonstrated how Jean Lafitte possessed social resilience. The people who attended the charrette based on one call from Kerner were the same ones he had led to build sandbag walls to protect City Hall. They were the same people who searched with him on recreational watercraft for stranded families along flooded streets after a big storm.

My presentation introduced the project we called *Jean Lafitte Tomorrow* and the complete team: Dover, Kohl & Partners, the Center for Planning Excellence, the Shaw Group, Waggoner & Ball Architects, Hall Planning & Engineering, EcoNorthwest, Street Plans Collaborative, and CSRS Engineering. It was an impressive team for such a small project. I think that the attendees could tell that I wanted to give Jean Lafitte everything we had. We talked about the history of the town and the history of resilience planning in Louisiana. I showed the Shaw Group's levee plan as part of the presentation but didn't say anything about the concept except "You are all familiar with it." I explained the hands-on exercises and we convened in small groups.

"What should the town look like a generation from now?" I asked the audience once they were sitting in their seats. The people at my table were all local and they described how they had built a Safe House Emergency Operations Center recently. They told me that a new town hall pavilion and an arts center were planned. They talked about how the town was slowly becoming a place for day-trippers looking to escape New Orleans for a little peace and quiet. No one talked about retreat. They all affirmed their commitment to the place, but their stories of storms and loss communicated worry, fear, and sadness.

We conducted an exercise using cards that asked, "What is one word that comes to mind about Jean Lafitte today?" and "What is one word that comes to mind about Jean Lafitte in the future?" The most common response for today was "home" and the most common response for the future was some version of "more visitors."

During the charrette, the multi-day open house and design session that we conducted, we worked on what we called "Comprehensive Resilience." This involved policies and investments that were as much focused on building the local economy with its disappearing fishery jobs as building up the land. People visited the studio when we held stakeholder and technical meetings, and I met people who had been hardened and numbed by the collapse of the local seafood industry and all the storms and flooding. Adversity had sharpened their feeling of alienation from the mainland. Adversity had also strengthened their power of resistance. There would be no point in saying: *You all need to leave while you still can*. None.

Our team searched for answers to the town's problems that didn't rely on a billion-dollar levee, even though the Shaw Group often put the levee up on the screen. Their slide showed a system that looked no less ambitious to me than the Great Wall of China. The caption on the slide read: "THE SOLUTION: Lafitte Area 100-Year Flood Protection Ring Levee System."

CPEX had arranged for a delegation from the Louisiana Flood Protection Authority to visit Jean Lafitte to meet with our team and discuss including Jean

80 ■ *Why Are We Doing This?*

Lafitte in the New Orleans system. The delegation's senior-most person, a tall, grey-haired engineer with thick glasses, began the conversation by talking about New Orleans.

"New Orleans is still pretty beat down from *Katrina*," he said. "The Lower Ninth Ward still has just a few homes." We understood that this was his way of beginning the negotiation. He was saying, in effect: "Things are bad in New Orleans and you are all so far from New Orleans down here." The delegation had a lot on their hands. They were representatives of the world's most expensive, and most ambitious, climate-change-adaptation plan, Louisiana's 50-year, US$50 billion Coastal Master Plan.

I showed the delegation plans and renderings we'd done for Rosethorn Park, a waterfront park that could host fish market stalls for local fishermen and women to sell directly to visitors. Our team proposed outdoor dining pavilions, a music stage, and a dance floor. We showed Fleming Canal, Goose Bayou, and Lower Lafitte with fishing cabins assembled like villages on elevated platforms all connected by a bike trail. My wife, Pamela Stacy King, is a senior planner in our firm and she had planned several years' worth of public and private investment in detail – down to the street and even individual lot.

Renderings by James Dougherty, our Director of Design, drew from the local architectural vernacular and showed Creole cottages with classical proportions, bungalows with big porches, and Main Street buildings designed in a local style. Our team's work suggested that people could live and work in beautiful places like Bayou Barataria without making it ugly. We talked about how this was critically important if the town was seeking to become a destination for tourism.

We urged the delegation to see the town for what it could be instead of what it was. I suppose it sounded like we were arguing for the levees on behalf of Jean Lafitte. The delegation listened without interrupting, but without asking questions either. Mayor Kerner intentionally didn't attend the meeting, probably hoping that our outsider objectivity would convince the delegation to extend the wall in a way his repeated efforts had failed to.

"Now, what do you really think about the mayor's levee idea?" a member of the Authority asked me.

Before I had a chance to answer another member of the Authority said, "I know you're not from here, but this place is always flooded. It's hard to imagine a way of fixing that."

I was tempted to say we hadn't given the mayor's levee much thought. I could have said that we were focusing on economic development in the town whose population and jobs were disappearing, and we were only capable of working on one impossible problem from hell at a time. But that would have been insincere. I had thought a lot about the levee.

"I'm from a place that's always flooded too," I said as a resident of Miami Beach. "I'm not giving up on it. And I think it's too early to give up on Jean Lafitte." I then argued against the cold cost–benefit formula used to determine which communities

Climate Planning Objection 2 ■ 81

got levees and which were left out. My team joined in. Although in 2011 there wasn't a single hotel or bed and breakfast in the area, we argued that because the town was just a short drive from New Orleans, Jean Lafitte could be a place that city dwellers could escape to, breathe fresh air, enjoy barefoot summer weekends, celebrate local culture, and walk and bike the bayou. The town just needed a little economic priming. We talked about how our team included people from all over the country and how we saw Jean Lafitte as a place which could draw people from around the world.

The Authority listened to us politely but stayed ominously silent. They could have talked about how over 35% of the New Orleans Metropolitan Area sits below sea level. They could have told us that the entire coastline of Louisiana was being swallowed by the sea with 2,000 square miles gone.[31] The state loses a football field of land every single hour. They could have told us that Louisiana had to pick its battles, but, instead, they were silent. At the conclusion of the meeting they shook our hands and went back north. When Mayor Kerner asked how it went I didn't know how to reply.

"They listened," was all I said.

During the week-long charrette we ate a lot of jambalaya and gumbo at local restaurants. I met waitresses and restaurant patrons with accents so thick I had no idea what they were saying to me. They were welcoming and polite, but they might as well have been addressing me in Dutch. The primitive cabins of the fish camp where we stayed (the place was called *Bayou Fuel* with a decided denial of pretense) lacked warm water and heat and that tried our patience. My wife didn't like staying in a room that held ten bunkbeds lacking mattresses though it was just the two of us, and she wasn't as enamored by the fiberglass trophy fish décor as I, but she was absolutely infuriated by the cold water.

I had my morning coffee gazing out at the marsh with its undulating, low-rise, mangrove coast. I had my coffee outside so I didn't have to listen to my wife reacquaint herself with the freezing shower. The bayou's water flowed under the aquatic trees that shaded oyster beds, shrimp, and young amberjack, mullet, pompano, and sheepshead fishes. It was one of the world's most productive ecosystems and it smelt like it: Swamp gas, decay, and sulphur. Even still, the fish camp continued to show me astounding sunrises.

I watched oyster farmers work the water with rakes, harvesting their submerged plots like the vegetable farmers of the land. The dragonflies that feasted on the mosquitos rammed into me, surprised that I was there. Even after her shower my wife stayed inside those mornings to avoid the clouds of mosquitos. Jean Lafitte didn't spray for bugs like in Miami. It was probably better for the ecosystem. It was definitely better for me – the morning I remember best was the one in which my wife realized we had run out of creamer for the cheap instant coffee supplied by Bayou Fuel. She hated that coffee, but it kept her from driving 14 hours home and working the charrette remotely. She had her moment of realization – a moment that, for me, rang louder than the shotgun blasts of the early morning duck hunters. I stayed outside.

82 ■ *Why Are We Doing This?*

As I drank my coffee and swiped at mosquitos the last morning of the charrette, I watched duck hunters unload their shotguns and camouflage vests out of the back of a Chevrolet Silverado 3500 pickup. They looked like a military unit. They were headed into the cypress tree forests. It was still possible to live a life of wilderness and freedom in Jean Lafitte. Then I went in, put on my pressed suit, and went to the Multi-Purpose Center to meet with the community one last time.

By the end of the week, we had developed six principles for the plan:

1. Assess opportunities and threats
2. Enhance local assets
3. Focus on the heart of town
4. Diversify mobility options
5. Build stronger and safer
6. Live with water

When it came time for the final presentation after a week of listening, drawing, and discussing, we didn't show the billion-dollar ring levee because I had come to conclusion that the promise of a ring levee around the entire town was a false hope. I am an optimist (perhaps by professional necessity), but I couldn't show the slide produced by the Shaw Group that read "THE SOLUTION."

Over the course of the week, however, we had learned that Mayor Kerner was consolidating city services near Town Hall in an area known as Lafitte. The town of Jean Lafitte comprised three unique historic towns: Lafitte, Barataria, and Crown Pointe. Single-family homes stretched between the centers along six linear miles. The mayor's policy of consolidating city services replaced a different policy pursued by his father, the previous mayor. His father had spread public buildings and services throughout Jean Lafitte in the interest of fairness. However, under Mayor Kerner, the new Safe House Emergency Operations Center had been built within sight of Town Hall, and Town Hall was planned to be the nucleus for all the town's other investments. Our team then took the idea of focusing development in Lafitte, the heart of town, even further, and in ways the mayor hadn't considered.

I worked with James Dougherty on a plan and visualization of what we began to call the *Heart of Town*. The first slide showed a hand-drawn birds-eye-view of the existing town hall, post office, police station, and baseball fields. We showed St. Anthony Catholic Church which sponsored the Blessing of the Fleet Festival at the beginning of every shrimp season.

"This is the physical and spiritual heart of Jean Lafitte," I said as Dougherty's watercolor rendering glowed behind me on the projector screen. In the next image, the cabins my wife had planned (presumably with warm water) appeared. Then came the arts center, a new fisheries market, a wetlands education center, and an auditorium. The change-over-time sequence showed new homes along a new grid of streets that formed behind the deep lots on the town's primary corridor, Jean Lafitte Boulevard. Dozens of townhomes and apartment buildings mixed with hotels and

Climate Planning Objection 2 ■ 83

restaurants. It was safe to assume that one of the buildings my wife had drawn would contain a Starbucks.

Next, the town's civic lots, big lawns around the post office and Town Hall, filled with buildings. St. Anthony Catholic Church, a humble single-story structure, gained a new face and three-story steeple. In the final slide a levee appeared around Lafitte. The levee we proposed only needed to be one square mile to accommodate enough new structures, streets, and public spaces to grow a walkable town. With just one square mile of protection, the town's population could double.

"Retreat to the heart of town," I said. It was the first time I'd said the words, but they became my new strategy. It sounded a lot better than the bloodless term, *strategic retreat*. In addition to the area around Town Hall we identified two other compactly defined centers as places for secondary consideration. In my mind, though, bulwarking Lafitte was sufficient. Kerner could continue his effort to build a town too valuable to be left behind, but with a focus on Lafitte because it provided a realistically defendable area.

We should say at this point that it was a *relatively* defendable area in the short- and mid-term. The long-term looked bleak. At the same time, most community plans focus on what is possible within the lifespans of plan participants and their families. As part of my presentation, I pointed out that new strategies would be needed as the climate changed, information changed, and values changed. Jean Lafitte, one of the poorest communities in the country, was thus given the same strategy as the wealthiest cities of the world, like Miami Beach in Florida or Santa Monica in California, namely: Build a town center too valuable to abandon.

The question remained: How long could the little town last? But we didn't need to answer that question. We advised the town to work to keep the investment coming, both public and private, in the hope that the place (or some kernel of it) would one day become too important to sacrifice in the eyes of the state and nation. We also urged safety in the new era of stronger storms including lifting buildings higher than FEMA standards, avoiding development in floodplains, maintaining evacuation times, and investing in emergency evacuation vehicles, early warning systems, pumps, and rip-rap walls. Admittedly, Jean Lafitte Boulevard, the single road to the mainland, would have to be lifted and would one day need to become a bridge between the bulwarked centers.

During the question-and-answer session, a person in the audience assured me that if the road was ever submerged, they would raft in. The reduced levee we proposed could be paid for locally, participants suggested. Federal and state aid would help, but by refocusing Mayor Kerner's Lafitte Area Independent Levee District with its small property tax, the *heart of the town* concept had a chance. After the presentation, the Mayor said he was pleased by our work. He said he'd prioritize the newly dubbed *Heart of Town*.

"I'm still working to protect every square inch of Jean Lafitte, too, though," he said.

84 ■ *Why Are We Doing This?*

Given the slow, expensive, and controversial process of building levees, I had worried during the charrette that even if Jean Lafitte was included in the New Orleans levee system the town would not live to see New Orleans build it a levee. I bet the mayor did too, though maybe he didn't admit this because publicly he was too committed to protecting every resident, every home, every cemetery, and every cypress forest. He had already begun a retreat to a defensible center, however, by locating public investment in one location and by narrowing the area that needed to be protected with levees. Our plan simply continued the idea that Mayor Kerner had begun to implement already. The best ideas come from locals.

Early the next year, I returned to Jean Lafitte for plan adoption. I remember walking into the Town Council chamber for the vote. It had just rained – hard – and off the concrete pathway that led to the front door of the chamber the ground looked solid, but I knew it would melt under the pressure of my step. I suppose Jean Lafitte didn't look different from anywhere that had seen a lot of rain – soggy with mud and wet grass – but I couldn't help but picture a disintegrating landscape around me. From where I stood, I could see the bend in the river where water flowed quickly, limiting the build-up of replenishing sentiment. I pictured the river rise to its hind legs and walk across the land, kicking over everything in its path. I pictured the slow-motion disaster of climate change. Protecting the multi-generational fishing community would require constant and profound human intervention. Was it possible to ever really commit in the way that was needed? I continued down the path and opened the doors to the Council chamber.

The plan was adopted unanimously by Mayor Kerner and the Town Council. The name of the plan remained *Jean Lafitte Tomorrow* to give people confidence that Jean Lafitte would still be there tomorrow. The mayor was happy. People cheered. People don't usually cheer the adoption of a municipal plan. What to think? I looked around that little Town Hall at all the people as they clapped. I knew a few names now. I felt a befuddling mix of worry, fear, and hope. Suffice to say, I clapped too.

I had become convinced that some portion of Jean Lafitte would always remain. I needed to believe that. The surviving area would include the town hall, cemetery, church, school, many new buildings, and several neighborhoods for people who would relocate from the farther flung areas of the town. The Blessing of the Fleet, the tradition of building pirogues, the pirate stories, and the strange, decidedly un-French pronunciation of the town's name would all survive.

We learned later that our presentation to the Louisiana Flood Protection Authority had helped Jean Lafitte's case because the Louisiana Flood Protection Authority extended their levee plan to include Jean Lafitte. How much our team had helped the town make the list of places to protect is impossible to know, because anything we said had to have been eclipsed by the mayor's years of persistence. However, I do think that professional planning experts from out of town can persuade in ways locals cannot. Our plan document was also beautiful and inspiring, and that had to help.

Hundreds of millions of dollars were allocated by the Authority for Jean Lafitte's levees, though nothing close to the US$1.2 billion the mayor's ring levee system required. "Work Starts on Protective Levee for Jean Lafitte" read the headline in the New Orleans newspaper, *The Advocate*, in 2014. Lafitte's *Heart of Town* is now protected by a new levee which was completed in 2018. Three miles of floodwall protection now ties into the pre-existing levee embankment, providing risk reduction to more than 453 acres.

Our *Retreat to the Heart of Town* strategy for Jean Lafitte is not applicable everywhere. Across the world, adaptation will involve retreat from areas that are too dangerous to inhabit. When, in 2016, the U.S. Department of Housing and Urban Development made history with a US$48 million grant to relocate the residents of Isle de Jean Charles, an area that had lost 98% of its land to the sea, it was the right thing to do. We'll have to do much more of that. However, Isle de Jean Charles is 80 miles from Jean Lafitte, more southerly, westerly, and farther out into the Gulf of Mexico. We have to draw a line somewhere.

Just like the residents of Isle de Jean Charles, there are many people living outside of Jean Lafitte's *Heart of Town* that will have to retreat, and the cost burden will fall on the residents and government. Hopefully, some portion of those people can retreat to the bulwarked part of Lafitte. At least temporarily. As climate change research continues it is getting harder and harder to imagine that coastal Louisiana will remain habitable in the long-term. However, the fight gives people meaning. It's a wonderful place with amazing people. Truly. And working to save Jean Lafitte is one hell of *a call*.

Jean Lafitte Tomorrow remains the town's plan nearly ten years later. Mayor Kerner continues to make Jean Lafitte a place too valuable to abandon, lobbying successfully for funds that come predominately from federal, state, and parish grants. I am told that Kerner still carries a copy of our plan to meetings across the state to help make the case for his town. I'm told that a copy of the plan sits under glass in the Town's new history museum. To date, the new levees have withstood several tropical storms and one major hurricane.

Notes

1 World Meteorological Organization (2020). Earth Day highlights Climate Action. Press Release Number: 22042020, April 22. Retrieved from: https://public.wmo.int/en/media/press-release/earth-day-highlights-climate-action
2 Morelle, R. (2014). 30,000-year-old giant virus comes back to life. *BBC World News*, March 4. Retrieved from: www.bbc.com/news/science-environment-26387276
3 Chicago Climate Action Plan (2008). Retrieved from: www.chicago.gov/city/en/progs/env/climateaction.html
4 Illinois Revenue (n.d.).Tax rate database. Retrieved from: www2.illinois.gov/rev/research/taxrates/Pages/default.aspx
5 Chicago Climate Action Plan, op. cit.

86 ■ *Why Are We Doing This?*

6 Campbell, E. (2018). 2nd "tax" on recieps confuses customers at new Walmart. News4jax, November 9. Retrieved from: www.news4jax.com/news/2018/11/10/2nd-tax-on-receipts-confuses-customers-at-new-walmart/

7 City of Boulder Climate Initiatives (n.d.). Boulder's Climate Action Plan. Retrieved from: https://bouldercolorado.gov/climate/climate-action-plan-cap-tax

8 U.S. Environmental Protection Agency (2016). Inventory of U.S. greenhouse gas emissions and sinks: 1990–2014. EPA 430-R-16002. Retrieved from: www.epa.gov/climatechange/ghgemissions/usinventoryreport.html

9 Levine, E. (2021). Following Somerville's LEED: How the city is working towards green construction. *Scout Somerville*, March 10. Retrieved from: https://scoutsomerville.com/leed-platinum/

10 *Boston Real Estate Times* (2020). BioMed Realty to acquire Somerville property. *Boston Real Estate Times*, June 15. Retrieved from: https://bostonrealestatetimes.com/biomed-realty-to-acquire-somerville-property/

11 City of Somerville (2015). Mayor Curtatone signs on to compact of mayors to address climate change. Retrieved from: www.somervillema.gov/news/mayor-curtatone-signs-compact-mayors-address-climate-change

12 Scranton, R. (2016). *Learning to Die in the Anthropocene: Reflections on the End of a Civilization*. San Francisco: City Lights Publishers.

13 Ibid., pp. 171–172.

14 Ibid., p. 46.

15 Carrington, D. (2019). Global "collapse" in number of new coal-fired power plants. *The Guardian*, March 27. Retrieved from: www.theguardian.com/environment/2019/mar/28/global-collapse-in-number-of-new-coal-fired-power-plants

16 Booker, C. (2010). The woolly world of Chris Huhne. *The Telegraph*, May 29. Retrieved from: www.telegraph.co.uk/comment/columnists/christopherbooker/7783317/The-woolly-world-of-Chris-Huhne.html

17 Shearer, C., Mathew-Shaw, N., Myllyvirta, L., Yu, A. and Nace, T. (2019). Boom and bust 2019: Tracking the global coal plant pipeline. Global Energy Monitor/Sierra Club/Greenpeace, March. Retrieved from: https://endcoal.org/wp-content/uploads/2019/03/BoomAndBust_2019_r6.pdf

18 Myers, S.L. (2020). China's pledge to be carbon neutral by 2060: What it means. *New York Times*, September 23. Retrieved from: www.nytimes.com/2020/09/23/world/asia/china-climate-change.html

19 *South Asia Monitor* (2020). Students in India to take carbon-neutrality pledge to commemorate Paris Agreement. *South Asia Monitor*, December 9. Retrieved from: https://southasiamonitor.org/open-forum/students-india-take-carbon-neutrality-pledge-commemorate-paris-agreement

20 Tillemann, L. (2013). Revolution now: The future arrives for four clean energy technologies. U.S. Department of Energy, September 17. Retrieved from: www.energy.gov/sites/prod/files/2013/09/f2/Revolution%20Now%20--%20The%20Future%20Arrives%20for%20Four%20Clean%20Energy%20Technologies.pdf

21 Krugman, P. (2014). Salvation gets cheap. *The New York Times*, April 17. Retrieved from: www.nytimes.com/2014/04/18/opinion/krugman-salvation-gets-cheap.html

22 Lomborg, B. (2001). *The Skeptical Environmentalist: Measuring the Real State of the World*. Cambridge: Cambridge University Press.

23 Boulder County (2019). Floodplain management and transportation system resiliency study and action plan. Retrieved from: www.bouldercounty.org/transportation/floodplain-management/floodplain-management-and-transportation-system- resiliency-study-and-action-plan/

24 Ibid.

25 U.S. Department of Housing and Urban Development (HUD) Exchange (n.d.). CDBG: Community Development Block Grant Programmes. Retrieved from: www.hudexchange.info/programs/cdbg/

26 HUD Exchange (n.d.). CDBG activity expenditure reports. Retrieved from: www.hudexchange.info/

27 Marshall, B. (2013). New research: Louisiana coast faces highest rate of sea-level rise worldwide. *The Lens*, February 21. Retrieved from: https://thelensnola.org/2013/02/21/new-research-louisiana-coast-faces-highest-rate-of-sea-level-rise-on-the-planet/

28 Jarvie, J. (2019). On a sinking Louisiana island, many aren't ready to leave. *Los Angeles Times*, April 23. Retrieved from: www.latimes.com/nation/la-na-jean-charles-sinking-louisiana-island-20190423-htmlstory.html

29 Coastal Protection and Restoration Authority of Louisiana (2017). Louisiana's Comprehensive Master Plan for a Sustainable Coast. Retrieved from: http://coastal.la.gov/wp-content/uploads/2017/04/2017-Coastal-Master-Plan_Web-Book_CFinal-with-Effective-Date-06092017.pdf

30 Ibid.

31 Marshall, B. (2014). Losing ground: Southeast Louisiana is disappearing, quickly. *The Lens*, August 28. Retrieved from: www.scientificamerican.com/article/losing-ground-southeast-louisiana-is-disappearing-quickly/

Chapter 3

Climate Planning Objection 3

"Climate change is not that bad. It's only a few degrees. It's just an attention-getter. Scientists are using the issue to get their research funded."

We often hear climate change dismissed with statements like, "It's just a few degrees. It isn't the end of the world." How could that be? I've never read an article on climate change that concluded: *It's no big deal.*

Perhaps this optimism comes from the fact that climate change is more than a challenge, it is a terror. Climate change is now taught in my children's Elementary School and when my kids bring the topic up, I automatically say, "It will be alright. It's something to live with but it is not the end of the world. I don't want you to worry." I say this because I don't want their lives to be filled with worry. If you view the statement "It's just a few degrees" as something said to avert anxiety, panic, and fear, then you can sympathize with the person saying it.

"It will be alright."

Unfortunately, though, just 1°C – the difference between 0 and 1°C, for instance, is the difference between ice and water, between freezing and melting; 1 degree means calamity. During the last ice age the Earth was just 6°C cooler

DOI: 10.4324/9781003181514-5

89

90 ■ *Why Are We Doing This?*

than it is today. We're on track to warm the planet between 2 and 4°C by 2100, accelerating glacial melt, sea-level rise, and other changes. The world has already warmed 0.8°C (1.5°F) since 1880 and we're starting to see intense droughts, heat waves, wildfires, flooding, and storms.[1] On any given day, it seems that some part of the manmade world is either on fire or underwater.

Life begins on the other side of despair, suggested Jean-Paul Sartre. "There must be a bright side," we hear as people try to move away from despair. For example, we hear that higher latitudes, like Siberia, may become productive due to warming. It is suggested that the cold, desolate portions of the U.S., like enormous Montana, which has the same population as the tiny state of Rhode Island, will one day have a pleasant year-round climate. It's nice to picture Missoula, Montana – a place I like a great deal despite its punishing cold – as a verdant paradise of year-round food and homegrown wines with a climate 3°C warmer than today. But Missoula can never be a fair-weather paradise: It hardly ever rains, the city receives just 2 inches of average precipitation during its wettest month, and it is far more likely that it will become as parched as the Serengeti.

We hear that underpopulated rustbelt cities like Detroit, which are located on the abundant water supply of the Great Lakes, will become new centers for people. This may be true, though that kind of mass migration would require breathtaking hardship elsewhere and no one wants to see the same hardship that Detroit felt when people left after decades of economic decline. Working in Detroit and seeing all those abandoned buildings, I felt that I was in an archeological dig site viewing the remnants of a civilization that had disappeared.

It's also cherry picking to look at the bright side, and only the bright side, and choose the argument that makes one's point while ignoring the many arguments which do not. It's cherry picking to talk about what's possible – Montana with pleasant Mediterranean-like summers and a regenerated Detroit – without talking about what's likely. Making the point that some areas may become more temperate climatically and concluding *that's good* ignores the fact that so many more places on Earth would become absolutely unlivable.

Unfortunately, the soil in Siberia, Montana, and all the Earth's arctic areas is usually poor and the terrain of the world's underpopulated places is typically mountainous. The amount of sunlight reaching those places also won't change. Sunlight is governed by the tilt of the Earth[2] and those areas won't be any more farmable. Unlivable places will remain largely unlivable and livable places will become unable to support people. There will be no new Edens. No new Genesis. There will be parched Earth and abandoned cities like in the Book of Jeremiah. In places of mass in-migration there will be overcrowding, slums, and savage competition for natural resources.

"Maybe after a couple decades of heating the water, it will be warm enough to swim in," my friend, an urban planner in Rhode Island, joked wryly about the state's Narragansett Bay. "I mean, there has to be some upside."

Climate Planning Objection 3 ■ 91

There isn't one. Some suggest that warmer winters would mean fewer deaths, and while that may be true in some places, deaths attributable to heatwaves already far outnumber deaths due to winter.[3] We hear how some plants will thrive if there is more carbon dioxide in the air (it's often pointed out that some greenhouses use machines to actually add carbon dioxide) though that effect will be eclipsed by decreases in water available for farming[4] and plants need water more than just about anything. The pecan farmers I met in drought-ridden West Texas will attest that climate change has not been kind to their crops.

We hear that a world with less ice at the poles will enjoy some economic advantages. Maybe. But while the opening of a year-round ice-free Arctic passage between the Atlantic and Pacific would confer some commercial benefits, this isn't balanced out by the melting of Greenland, the inevitable coastal flooding, and the fact that as the world warms there may be a lot less food to trade. The port cities that would benefit from quicker routes to commercial centers around the world will be facing intense and frequent flooding.

At a 2005 full-moon party on the beach in Islamorada, in the Florida Keys, Marlene Conaway, the Director of Planning for Monroe County (and my boss at the time), said, "Who knows? There will probably be benefits. There must be a silver lining," as she talked about global warming.

Perhaps it was the Rum Runner in my hand, but I said, "No, that's not true." All my co-workers in the circle looked at me. My boss was the kind of person you might prompt conversationally if she was in the right mood, but no one attempted back-and-forth dialogue, and you certainly never challenged Marlene Conaway.

"Why do you say that, Jason?" she asked frostily.

I started to talk about the coral of Thailand I had studied and how coral lived at the *threshold of survivability*. "So does human civilization," I concluded flatly and a bit self-righteously. I put my straw back in my mouth (along with my foot) and sipped my fruity cocktail. No heads nodded in agreement. Marlene looked at the moon. I looked at the moon. I came to my senses and quietly snuck away.

Looking back, I think that Marlene, like a lot of people staring into the face of such disaster, must, instinctively, try to find the silver lining and this seems like a normal human reaction. In the Florida Keys, 300 miles of road needed to be raised to stay ahead of sea levels, costing as much as US$7 million each mile or US$2 billion in total. The county's road budget is a mere US$25 million.[5] In the Keys, it is an impossible situation with no silver lining and Marlene Conaway probably knew that better than any of us but on a clear, warm night under swaying palm trees she couldn't help but fantasize.

The unfortunate, unavoidable fact is that the negative impacts of global warming on agriculture, human health, sea-level rise, environmental systems, and economic systems will far outweigh the positive. At the same time, the people looking to move past despair have their point: Life is never as unendurable and impossible as

92 ■ *Why Are We Doing This?*

it logically ought to be. And, though it's no excuse for inaction, sometimes silver linings do occur which we never could have imagined.

Looking For Attention, Or Money

"It's just an attention-getter," we hear.

"I am just relating what scientists are telling us," we retort.

"Scientists are using the issue to fund research," is the response we hear across the country, as if read from the same widely distributed script. "Scientists are people and people are bad sources of information. They tend to withhold, distort, and use information to accomplish hidden purposes. They are just out for money."

What do we say next?

At a 2019 sustainability conference I attended in El Paso, Texas, the speaker, Collin Leyden, a Regulatory and Legislative Affairs manager at the Environmental Defense Fund, was asked a simple question after his presentation: "Where do you get your funding?"

"Private and public sources," he answered quickly before taking the next question. Climate presenters are asked this question often and it seems prudent to answer quickly and not ask, "Why do you ask?"

Climate scientists and environmental advocates are often accused of distorting evidence and facts for money. When the innuendo that a climate scientist is corrupt appears in the media it is usually a kind of retaliation after a famous global-warming skeptic was found to have received millions from fossil fuel companies. Thankfully, climate scientists rarely succumb to the temptation to make far more money working for those same fossil fuel companies. However, the accusation of corruption has its power because people do act in their self-interest, and one's self-interest does cloud a person's objectivity. Scientists are only human, subject to the same cognitive biases, the same whims of ego, as the rest of us.

At the same time, anyone who has known someone working in science and has followed their career knows that it's a hard job and tough path. It seems to me that climate scientists are far more likely to be driven by the idea that they will discover something that no one knows, the chance to understand our world, and the chance to make the world a better place, than by the research grants (which are tiny), employment (which is extremely competitive and requires advanced education and enormous debt), politics (have scientists ever really been listened to the way they deserve?), and fame (which might exist among one's peers, just as it does in any profession, but hardly ever translates to the kind of fame that impresses non-scientists).

Lately when I think of working scientists I picture Winter Beckles, a friend of the family working on his PhD in evolutionary biology and studying how the native Green Anoles lizards (*Anolis carolinensis*) in Miami are moving higher and higher up local vegetation as the species competes with the non-native, and far more abundant, Brown Anole (*Anolis segrei*) from the Caribbean. And that's it. And he's not the first person to study this. He's one of many scientists jockeying in a crowded field to observe something new and relevant in a personal struggle to survive which has a strong resemblance to the green lizard's own plight. I can't help but feel that if Beckles, with all his charisma, drive, and attention to detail, applied himself to any other field here in Miami, a place of tremendous prosperity and opportunity, he'd become wealthy. Are there any wealthy scientists?

Many scientists and climate planners are compelled by the urgency of the situation to work to identify an undiscussed aspect of the climate equation, study it, and discuss the grim and, still, unpalatable topic. They don't have to. Similarly, my own work as an urban planner gives me a great deal of flexibility to work on any aspect of the city planning equation: Economic development, transportation, affordable housing, real estate development, urban design, and so on. I could choose to ignore climate change, the most important planning issue of our time. Many of my peers do.

At a presentation in Miami Beach in 2015 I found myself admitting to the crowd, "I don't want to be the global warming person. I want to be the walkable urbanism person. Cafés, sidewalks, and street trees. Everyone loves that stuff. But we need to talk about climate."

It's All Just Politics

The scientific ideal involves the search for more and more data and the discipline to make conclusions based on the data alone (or, more often than not, the self-control to refuse to make conclusions at all). The public saw this when the COVID-19 pandemic hit the world with blinding speed in early 2020. People demanded answers on how the virus worked and what they could ingest to protect themselves. Hydroxychloroquine? Vitamin D? Household bleach? And scientists refused to speculate. They refused to *play politics*.

Nevertheless, I often heard "It's all just politics" as I worked on the regional plan for Southeast Florida. "*Sea-level rise* is a *Democrat* term." It was also commonly claimed that climate research was funded by the leftist departments of the U.S. federal government, like the Environmental Protection Agency, and left-wing foundations such as Greenpeace,[6] to help Democrats gain political advantage.

"What's happening in Washington has nothing to do with what's happening here," was my retort from the microphone at a meeting in Martin County, Florida, in 2012. "We don't need to discuss D.C.'s political antics or power struggles." I have found that it is helpful when working at the local level to share people's apathy and even disgust with Washington D.C. if you, at all, feel it yourself.

Statements like "I don't appreciate either party's divisiveness" marks the urban planner as someone whose secret politics don't have to be investigated before that person can be listened to. I have said things like, "We don't know what's going on in D.C., not really; those people will say anything, but we do understand what's

94 ■ *Why Are We Doing This?*

happening locally." We need to work to solve the most urgent issue of our time and I suggest that the way to do this is to avoid a connection to D.C. politics and instead link your work to the international effort. Let's discuss the international effort in more detail.

The Paris Agreement

The Paris Agreement is a pact within the United Nations Framework Convention on Climate Change (UNFCCC) dealing with greenhouse-gas-emissions mitigation and adaptation. It is often referred to as the "Paris Agreement of 2015" in reference to the 2015 United Nations Climate Change Conference, though member nations did not begin to sign the Paris Agreement until Earth Day, April 22, 2016 at a ceremony in New York.

The Paris Agreement is the first truly universal agreement among nations to tackle climate change. In a century from now, the Paris Agreement is likely to still be remembered. Unlike it predecessor, the 1997 Kyoto Protocol, the Paris Agreement involved big polluters like the United States, China, and India. The Paris Agreement has been ratified by 179 countries, including the U.S. (which signed but never ratified the Kyoto Protocol), China, India, members of the European Union, and all other major emitters.[7]

In response to the Paris Agreement and thanks to the falling cost of zero emissions technology, more and more countries, businesses, and local governments are implementing policies to drive the transition to cheap and clean renewable energy. In 2017 alone, around 70% of new power generation installed globally was renewable energy, with more solar photovoltaic capacity being added in 2017 than that of coal, gas, and nuclear combined.[8]

The Paris Agreement is a historic agreement because it locked countries into verifiable steps and targets they would take, and those same steps and targets form the basis of local strategies. The Paris Agreement creates an architecture to start doing the right thing and our local climate plans seek to accomplish those same goals, though at a smaller scale.

The treaty has a number of key elements including keeping global warming "well below" 2°C above pre-industrial levels and to "pursue efforts" to keep warming to 1.5°C. By just about every calculation, this commitment means global emissions must fall to zero by around 2050. The world is currently not on track to achieve the objectives of the Paris Agreement. Substantial progress has been made but more will need to be done by all countries to limit warming to below what many consider the point-of-no return.[9]

Local planners have influence over local land use including the power to preserve natural lands which convert carbon to oxygen, transportation policies which reduce automobile use, power generation and water use in communities which own their own utilities, and so forth. The main barrier to preservation, transit, clean energy, water conservation, and avoiding severe climate change impacts may simply be political will at the local level, and this is something we can do something about.

Since the United Nations signed on to the Paris Agreement, progress across the globe has been uneven and, sometimes, discouraging, but there is good news. Carbon emissions are already falling in over 30 cities. A coalition of cities known as the C40 published a 2018 analysis[10] which identified cities that have hit their "peak" emissions before 2015, meaning they have since reduced their greenhouse gas emissions by at least 10%.[11] These cities include Athens, Austin, Barcelona, Berlin, Boston, Chicago, Copenhagen, Heidelberg, Lisbon, London, Los Angeles, Madrid, Melbourne, Milan, Montréal, New Orleans, New York City, Oslo, Paris, Philadelphia, Portland, Rome, San Francisco, Stockholm, Sydney, Toronto, Vancouver, Venice, Warsaw, and Washington, D.C.

The cities achieved this goal through a variety of methods. In San Francisco's case, the power grid was decarbonized. In 2019, 77% of all electricity supplying the city came from GHG-free sources including all city-owned buildings. According to the C40, Paris added seven times the number of cycle paths, added self-service bicycle-hire, and launched several new streetcar lines. Sydney optimized energy use in buildings by implementing a wide range of programs, grants, and incentives targeting building performance and retrofitting city-owned buildings. Vancouver doubled the amount of waste it composted and began to gather landfill gas in order to reduce its landfill's emissions. The challenge for these cities will be to stick to renewable energy sources and practices despite increases in population and through successive political administrations.

Despite greenhouse gas emission commitments in the largest cities of the world, most urban planners work in "real America," "real China," and "real India," which we will define as suburban, emerging suburban, or rural municipalities where a great deal of education is still needed and political pushback is the strongest. If you don't live in New York City or Rome you may find it difficult to help your community climb down from the ledge of peak emissions. However, if you don't live in a great city, you are in the majority because most people do not live in or near one of these metropolises, and your contribution to the effort is even more critical.

It's the Sun!

"It's the Sun," I was told in Las Cruces, New Mexico, as I worked on the *Elevate Las Cruces* Comprehensive Plan in June 2019. "It's just an attention-getter. This warming trend is from the Sun."

"Right," I said from the head of the table during our Sustainability Stakeholder meeting. "It's the Sun." The bald older gentleman who made the comment shook his head as if he'd scored a point on a goalie on a soccer field. I didn't understand why. Another participant at that meeting, the campus architect at New Mexico State University, a university striving to raise the sustainability standard locally, was giving me a death glare and I didn't understand that either.

96 ■ *Why Are We Doing This?*

The campus architect explained to me later that what was meant by "it's the Sun" was the belief that solar fluctuations are the cause of warming and not greenhouse gas emissions. Science tells us that it isn't the Sun – or, at least, not the way the man meant. In the last 35 years of global warming the Sun has shown a slight cooling trend. While the Sun and climate sometimes track together, the two have been going in opposite directions in recent years.[12]

"It's probably the Sun," was said to me at a project interview in Missoula, Montana, in November 2019 when the topic of climate change arose.

"Well, I'm not a scientist, but I believe attributing temperature rise to the Sun involves an overly selective reading of data," I might have said because I'd learned my lesson in Las Cruces. "It's confirmation bias. You want to see a thing, a thing that fits with your worldview, and so you find evidence for it where evidence doesn't exist." However, I was competing to win the commission to design a new community outside Missoula and I didn't want to correct the interviewer, a property owner, local rancher, and one of the people who would decide if my team would be awarded the project.

"And if it's the Sun," the rancher continued, "well, I mean, it's a *big* Sun – I don't know that there's much we can do about the problem." The rancher got disapproving looks from the long-suffering eco-conscious urban planners around the room. There were unblinking stares over the tops of glasses, light scowls, pursed lips, and squints that said: *Really?*

I considered explaining how solar panels are compatible with grazing and how the landowner could turn his fields into power generation, but I didn't believe the man's issue with climate change adaptation was economic. I assumed that it was political. And so, instead, I changed the topic and talked about how much I respected Downtown Missoula's commitment to decrease the heat island effect by adding more trees. Who could disagree with that? Is there anyone against shade? "Because the world is getting hotter and drier," I said. "Hotter and drier" is often as much as I am able to say about climate change. It was the rancher's turn to frown.

I might have heard other myths. I might have heard, "There is no consensus," though the fact is that 97% of climate experts agree humans are causing global warming. Or "the Earth is actually cooling," though the last two decades (2000–2020) were the hottest on record.[13] There's a long list of things I might have heard. The problem isn't the Sun, it's the greenhouse effect cause by carbon dioxide in the atmosphere, but, of course, the truth is more complicated than that.

Carbon Dioxide and the Atmosphere

"Stopped," was allegedly the last word of Joseph Henry Green (1791–1863) as the English surgeon monitored his own pulse. Then he died. Admittedly, the world's vital signs are not as clear-cut. The climate has always been changing.

Carbon Dioxide (CO_2) is a greenhouse gas which is the main driver of climate change and for the last 800,000 years atmospheric CO_2 has never been over 300 parts per million. Today CO_2 levels are way over that number and it means disaster.

This tends to be how presentations on climate begin and it reflects scientific consensus accurately enough.[14] With these facts established, the presenter can then talk about any aspect of the climate catastrophe: How climate could render large portions of the world uninhabitable, displace hundreds of millions of people, and cause suffering on an unimaginable scale.

As I am writing this, an online search tells me that CO_2 levels in the atmosphere today are 408.37 parts per million (ppm) and last year it was 405.66ppm on the same day. That's an increase of 3ppm per year. A person doing the same calculation might compute that by 2050 the world will reach roughly 500ppm. That sounds bad. But is it? One can then look at world temperatures back to the Cambrian era, 500 million years ago, and compare CO_2. If I do this on my EarthViewer app[15] questions arise.

I can see that 39 million years ago the world had 731ppm and yet the world temperature was roughly the same as today. Shouldn't it have been a lot hotter? If I go back 67 million years, I see that CO_2 levels were three times higher than today and it was only 2°C warmer. Shouldn't it have been *a whole lot* hotter? If I go back 460 million years, I find that CO_2 was more than ten times higher and that the Earth was only 6°C warmer. Granted, 6°C is quite a bit, but why wasn't it ten times hotter?

If you look up these discrepancies online you might end up, as I did, reading a denier's explanation: "Talking about CO_2 levels is a futile exercise. It's like trying to predict how long it takes for a feather to fall from the Tower of Pisa using Newton's laws of motion and gravity alone."

Huh.

The problem, scientists say, is that CO_2 can't tell us the whole story. There are additional factors like land use changes, carbon soot and halocarbon emissions, and albedo variations that must be considered cumulatively to determine the net impact. One factor, for instance, is solar activity. Yes, we're back to talking about the Sun. Scientists say that while atmospheric CO_2 levels possibly topped 5,000ppm in the late Ordovician Period around 440 million years ago, the world was only 1°C warmer because solar activity can go up and down and it was down 440 million years ago.

"Well," a skeptic might ask, "if CO_2 can't tell the whole story, then why can't we use other explanations to explain warming like the Sun getting hotter, orbital variations, underground temperature variations, volcanic activity, cosmic rays, satellite microwave transmissions, CFCs, soot, ozone, and oceanic conditions like El Nino (ENSO) and the Pacific Descadal Oscillation (PDO)."

However, scientists tell us that those conditions have had no effect, a tiny effect, or even promoted cooling conditions.[16]

98 ■ *Why Are We Doing This?*

"Are you a climate scientist?" we may be asked.

The last time I found myself in this position was at a presentation in Baton Rouge, Louisiana, in 2016. And, again, I was at a planning conference preaching to the choir (or so I thought). I continued to relate the science (as I understood it) to a small crowd of attendees after a session I had spoken at. My session wasn't on climate; it was on *Gemütlichkeit*, the German experience of comfort and coziness, cheer and comradery that only occurs out of doors. This is the kind of thing I like to talk about. But I had referenced climate change in the presentation when I said that there is an even greater need to build outdoor spaces deliberately if we really expect people to be outside as the world gets warmer and drier. That statement attracted attention I wasn't seeking and I was cornered by a practiced climate denier.

"It's the Sun," the climate denier said. He was a large man of, perhaps, Asian descent. "Look at the Ordovician Period. CO_2 was higher in the late Ordovician period and the world was the same temperature."

"The Sun was much cooler during the Ordovician."

"You're an expert on the Ordovician period?"

"No. Are you?"

The bottom line is that climate reacts to whatever forces it to change at the time, and humans are now the dominant force. For this reason, the *Anthropocene* has been proposed as a name for our epoch.[17] Greenhouse gasses – mainly CO_2, but also methane and others – that were emitted by human activity are responsible for the climate's changes. When CO_2 decreased, the world got cooler (generally), and when they increased, the world got warmer (generally). The whole story is A LOT more complicated – I mean, that's nature for you – but CO_2 is the primary culprit.

When CO_2 levels jumped rapidly, the global warming that resulted was highly disruptive and sometimes caused mass extinctions. While we can't say for certain where the proverbial feather dropped from the Tower of Pisa will fall, we can say that it will, eventually, hit the ground. The timeframe can't be pinpointed but the outcome is certain. The world is warming and we're all in trouble.

Now let's discuss the Dustbowl Era because you are bound to hear about it, eventually. Another denial argument states that during the periods 1860 to 1880 and 1910 to 1940 the world warmed just as fast as in recent times. The Dustbowl Era, for instance, was caused by the unusually dry era in the summer of 1930. Then the world cooled. So, might things just get warmer for a bit and then cool down?

Science says that, yes, those were warm periods, but they only represent natural short-term variations. Science also points out that a statistical analysis of the rate of warming over these periods finds that warming from 1970 to 2001 was greater than the warming from both 1860 to 1880 and 1910 to 1940. Also, the period of warming we are in now, beginning in 2001, is even greater than all the others. Can we be sure that things won't cool off again? No. And this illustrates a point that will become inescapable as this book goes on – namely, nature is astoundingly complicated. However, Science tells us that even if it cools again, that short-term cooling will only represent a short-term variation and not the long-term trend toward warming.

How does any of this relate to our work at the local level? Local land use and transportation choices greatly effect CO_2 emissions, and land use is left to municipalities to decide and transportation choices are left to regional transportation agencies whose members represent local municipalities. What we do locally affects what happens globally and in many ways. Again, the global commitment to fighting climate change is implemented at a local level.

As we make our presentations locally, we must keep in mind that Science is being asked to provide tidy, easy-to-remember answers today because Science has become a political actor. We should be able to employ those answers, but we must also keep learning, enjoy the challenge, get comfortable being over our head in scientific conversations, and learn to tolerate ambiguity, because sometimes there aren't simple answers.

Notes From the Field

Gathering Data in the Tarutao Islands of Thailand

I had an opportunity few people do: To watch scientists study nature for its own sake. We never discussed policy and we never plotted to change a single thing about the world and in so doing I learned what Science is essentially about.

In February 2000, when I was in my early 20s, I joined a Wildlands Studies team on a kind of study abroad. The team was led by Dr. Charles Chris Carpenter, a conservation scientist with a PhD in Biological Ecology and we studied the islands of the remote Ko Tarutao Marine National Park, Satun Province, on Thailand's southwest border with Malaysia. When I joined the team, Dr. Carpenter had been conducting research in the islands since 1992. Today, he still studies the same area and has acquired nearly 30 years of data on how coral reefs and coastal habitats can change as a result of storms, shifting wind patterns, seismic events, human exploitation, and sea temperatures.

We boarded the wooden longtail boat at 7am, just after sunrise, and motored out to our first site. Tucked away in Thailand's deep south, the archipelago is composed of pristine rainforests and untouched sand beaches. On Ko Adang, the island where we camped on the beach, the only residents were monkeys. With masks and snorkels affixed to our faces, Carpenter, myself, and 11 other student-researchers jumped into the choppy water (always choppy in my memory). I immediately began flailing, twisting around, kicking with clunky fins, and spitting sea water. I had never been snorkeling before and as I gasped and struggled, I thought: I am going to drown 3 feet from the boat.

Eventually I gained control and we snorkel-swam above the sea floor to the transect tapes, rectangular areas whose length and width were marked by white tape. Then we began to float, counting fish types on a plastic board with resin pencils. Below us the coral looked like stacks of flapjack disks in one place, like the bulbous, brainy heads of aliens in others, and like the long, gnarled fingers of witches. Each formation had a name, but I didn't know the names because the coral wasn't our focus. We were there to count fish during a timed stationary-point fish census. I had learned ten or so fish shapes and their names including grunts, butterflyfish, angelfish, damselfish, eels, rays, cardinalfish, and triggerfish.

I remember staring at a shimmering world of coral ravines with the wonder of a person staring into space for the first time. I remember watching the fish, giant

Figure 3 Thai Boat

Climate Planning Objection 3 ■ 101

clams, and small forests of waving anemones with amazement and curiosity. But all that quickly faded and it became tedious work. Did that fish just double back into the square because it saw me? Should I count it twice? Did that entire school of fish just double back? Couldn't this be better done with an underwater drone like in the movies? Was that an anemonefish or a clownfish? Are clownfish anemonefish? Was that a shark? Wait, was that a SHARK?!

The work wasn't nearly as frustrating or scary for the other research students. They floated atop the water like lotus flowers on lily pads, on the sea of tranquility, the Buddhist virtues of Thailand personified. Or, at least, that's how it looked to me. I wore a white cotton shirt as I floated the reef edge to avoid sunburn while my teammates all wore long-sleeve spandex diving suits. I had cheap, clunky, plastic fins I'd rented locally that had been gnawed on by a dog (I hoped it had been a dog) and my teammates had stylish, lightweight, winged-shaped gear they'd been using for years.

On my first day in the water, I saw three Goliath Grouper, each the size of a bed pillow, with menacing toothy grins and a Box Jellyfish that Dr. Carpenter had told us possessed enough venom to kill a room full of people. I gave them both plenty of space and probably failed to count a few dozen fish.

We spent four to six hours a day underwater without headphones or conversation and then started again the next morning – one morning after another. The data would allow scientists like Dr. Carpenter to talk about the change over time in the numbers and variety of fish species. Every day, more than a dozen young people floated as inertly as jellyfish and counted Damselfish, Trumpetfish, Squirrelfish, and Sharpnose Puffer with the water warming and cooling around us for reasons it is best not to discuss. We had to stick to our posts for the full duration of the count. Maybe it was a little gross, but it is only by such means that human knowledge creeps forward.

The fish depended on the coral off the Adang-Rawi island group that was part of a national park. However, the seas had been intensively exploited both by locals and outsiders, and anchor scars were everywhere. In some places the dragnets of the fishing trawlers had torn the coral to rubble even though trawlers were not allowed in the waters. The islands supported a small population of indigenous people whose ethnicity was different from the Thai of the mainland. The sea peoples (*chao le*) – namely the Moken and Urak Lawoi – had inhabited the islands long before the national park designation and lived like shipwrecked pirates off the reefs and surrounding waters.

A healthy coral reef is a world teeming with life, and it is in the reefs that much of the seafood we eat begins. But corals live at the threshold of survivability and even slight changes to the environment can harm them. When corals are stressed by changes in conditions such as light, nutrients, temperature, or acidity they expel the symbiotic algae living in their tissues, causing their tissue to turn completely white.[18] This is called *bleaching*.

A key impact of today's climate crisis is that the seas are becoming more acidic as they absorb carbon emissions. The ocean has absorbed 20 to 30% of human-induced

102 ■ *Why Are We Doing This?*

carbon dioxide emissions since the 1980s,[19] and coral reefs are bleaching around the world. Over the last 30 to 40 years 80% of coral in the Caribbean has been destroyed. Over 50% of coral in Indonesia and the Pacific is in decline.[20] Globally about 1% of coral is dying out each year. The Great Barrier Reef off the waters of Australia is roughly the size of the coast of California and it has seen a 30% decrease.[21]

In many areas where the staghorn coral was bleached it looked like an underwater bone yard.

"Is this natural?" I asked Dr. Carpenter, back on the boat.

"No, it isn't natural," he said. He then qualified that statement by talking about the life–death–life cycles of coral, but he never implied that there was anything natural about the bleaching we had seen.

Coral can sometimes survive bleaching and bounce back because coral can seem to die and then revive like plants. But when bleaching is caused by a rise in temperature, the temperature must drop back to a normal level for the coral to recover. The Intergovernmental Panel on Climate Change special report on the impact of global warming hypothesized that if global warming reached 2°C (3.6°F) then every coral reef on the planet would begin a precipitous decline that would begin with bleaching.[22] Put all together, the coral reefs of the world are the size of Texas. Imagine all that death.

The first law of ecology is that everything is related to everything else. The fate of reef fish populations are tied to the life of the coral and reef fish populations are declining on a global scale as a result of habitat degradation, pollution, fishing, and temperature rise. Yet year after year Dr. Carpenter returns to a reef that is slowly bleaching and fish populations that are gradually lessening. During his decades, he's watched sections of reef die before his eyes and the living tissue of coral rot away. He told me he wasn't depressed by the sight. He was just doing a job.

"Have you seen trawlers looting the place?" I asked Dr. Carpenter.

"Yeah. You see the lights at night."

"What do you do about it?"

"We account for it in the research and we submit our research to Satun College."

"We need to alert someone."

"The looters probably have the consent of the police. I don't know. We're just here to study."

"These people are terrible," I said looking around for a boat with the word POACHER written across the hull to go sink.

"They are the same people who serve you guys mango lassis in the morning on Ko Lepe. That's a *chao le* island. They only loot at night. During the day they make you lassis." Dr. Carpenter never went over to Ko Lepe with the beachside cantinas we students loved so much and that seemed to be the extent of his protest. Curious, meticulous, and as coolly objective as a mountaintop statue, scientists are exasperating. The Thai have an expression: *Jai yen*. It means *cool heart*, and it refers to composed, calm, and patient people like Dr. Carpenter. Most of the researchers I've met have the same demeanor.

Climate Planning Objection 3 ■ 103

Dr. Carpenter even looked at climate change differently. For all the sadness and misery that global heating means for the world, its discovery, alone, was an astounding achievement he said. It must have been one of Science's most important discoveries, he told us one day as we blew water out of our snorkels before jumping back in to count more fish.

There is now research on any climate change question one asks from the number of butterflyfish off the Thai coast to the giga-tonnage of ice lost on the East Antarctic ice sheet. Whenever an iceberg splinters off the Antarctic ice shelf we know its size. It's usually the size of Rhode Island. As a Rhode Island native I used to bristle at the fact my state is used as a unit of measure for any sizable chunk. Now, having been away for many years and growing nostalgic, I use Rhode Island whenever I can as my unit of measure for ice chunks, water deficits, solar arrays, and other large-scale items.

Every fact informs climate science, from the number of days over 100°F on any point in the globe to the CO_2 emission savings of mass transit systems. Urban planners use this data every day and it is made possible thanks to countless scientists working with data from satellites, in labs, or in the field, like Dr. Carpenter. They've figured out how to measure just about everything. They've found within themselves the patience for a timed stationary-point fish census and the self-control to not cause a ruckus when they see looters in national parks for fear that the scientists will be expelled from the places where they study.

All successful endeavors involve detailed records. Count everything. Without knowing numbers, you can't identify problems or create strategies to overcome challenges. The data Dr. Carpenter gathered was useful to Thai marine scientists and the staff of the national parks who were responsible for managing the coral resources. People like Dr. Carpenter are counting for us all.

I tried to talk to Dr. Carpenter about the political implications of climate change, but he turned that conversation down. He was uncomfortable – in some ways he actually appeared to be physically uncomfortable – when it came to contro-versial topics. He looked down, his jaw clenched, and he mumbled under his breath. Then he shrugged with a big spasmodic heave of his shoulders as if to fling off the conversation.

In the mornings sitting in the shade before going out on the boat and talking about the day's tasks, Dr. Carpenter did like to talk. He talked about water acidity levels and fish populations. He weighed every word, always careful, but, still, he could give long lectures. I have met theatrical PhDs, histrionic attention-grabbers who routinely overstate, but in my experience they are rare. When I think of scientists, I think of Dr. Carpenter.

While in Thailand, I pitched a proposal to the Tarutao National Marine Park to allow me to create a research station out of an abandoned, teak wood Customs House on the far side of the island. If they said *yes* and a U.S. university became interested in hosting a permanent research station there, then I wouldn't have to leave the island paradise, and the faculty and students could help police the park

104 ■ *Why Are We Doing This?*

waters in ways the limited park staff, afraid of the poachers, or in league with the poachers, could not. I didn't like counting fish, but I liked snorkeling down as deep as I could go and plucking off the Crown-of-Thorns Jellyfish and Sea Urchins that ate the coral. I liked taking stands.

It was better that the marine park said no to my research station proposal, or at least, didn't say *yes*, avoiding confrontation, as the Thai are apt to do. I would eventually take what I learned to the Florida Keys and work to protect habitat and coral. More about that in a later chapter.

Most people will never be lucky enough to see coral reefs and I was lucky enough to spend so much time with them that they bored me. I will never forget the first view: Sitting on the ceiling of a watery blue room of electric colors and neon fish. I remember the way the light filtered down to the living ocean floor. I remember Thailand. I remember days when the water was calm, and I watched from a thatched pavilion as the floating researchers stayed out for five, six, seven hours, just floating, floating, and counting fish in silence. What we learn about the natural world we learn from the cool-hearted, the *jai yen*. We can trust them and their objectivity.

Notes

1 IPCC (2018). Global Warming of 1.5°C. An IPCC special report on the impacts of global warming of 1.5°C above pre-industrial levels and related global greenhouse gas emission pathways, in the context of strengthening the global response to the threat of climate change, sustainable development, and efforts to eradicate poverty. Masson-Delmotte, V., P. Zhai, H.O. Pörtner, D. Roberts, J. Skea, P.R. Shukla, A. Pirani, W. Moufouma-Okia, C. Péan, R. Pidcock, S. Connors, J.B.R. Matthews, Y. Chen, X. Zhou, M. I. Gomis, E. Lonnoy, T. Maycock, M. Tignor and T. Waterfield (eds). Retrieved from: www.ipcc.ch/sr15/

2 Mendelsohn, R., Dinar, A. and Williams, L. (2006). The distributional impact of climate change on rich and poor countries. *Environment and Development Economics*. Volume 11 (0–2), pp. 159–178.

3 Medina-Ramón M. and Schwartz, J. (2007). Temperature, temperature extremes, and mortality: A study of acclimatisation and effect modification in 50 US cities. *Occupational and Environmental Medicine*, Volume 64, pp. 827–833.

4 Solomon, S. Plattner, G-K., Knutti, R. and Friedlingstein, P. (2009). Irreversible climate change due to carbon dioxide emissions. *PNAS,* Volume 106 (6), pp. 1704–1709.

5 The Associated Press (2018). Climate change forcing Florida Keys to raise roads. *WLRN*, February 4. Retrieved from: www.wlrn.org/post/climate-change-forcing-florida-keys-raise-roads

6 Payne, H. (2015). Global warming: Follow the money. *National Review*, February 25. Retrieved from: www.nationalreview.com/2015/02/global-warming-follow-money-henry-payne/

7 United Nations (2016). Paris Agreement. United Nations Treaty Collection, July 8. Retrieved from https://treaties.un.org/pages/ViewDetails.aspx?src=TREATY&mtdsg_no=XXVII-7-d&chapter=27&clang=_en

8 Jackson, E. (2018). Enough with the fairy tales about the Paris Agreement. It's time for facts. *The Guardian*, August 15. Retrieved from: www.theguardian.com/commentis free/2018/aug/15/enough-with-the-fairy-tales-about-the-paris-agreement-its-time-for-facts

9 Ibid.

10 C40 Cities (2018). 27 C40 cities have peaked their greenhouse gas emissions. Retrieved from: https://c40-production-images.s3.amazonaws.com/other_uploads/images/1923_Peaking_emissions_Media_Pack_Extended_version.original.pdf?1536847923

11 Poon, L. (2019). Carbon emissions are already falling in 30 cities. *City Lab*, October 19. Retrieved from: www.citylab.com/environment/2019/10/c40-peak-carbon-co2-emissions-highest-cities-climate-summit/599644/

12 Usoskin, I.G., Schuessler, M., Solanki, S.K. and Mursul, K. (2005). Solar activity, cosmic rays, and Earth's temperature: A millennium-scale comparison. *Journal of Geophysical Research*, Volume 110 (A10). Retrieved from: https://agupubs.onlinelibrary.wiley.com/doi/full/10.1029/2004JA010946

13 IPCC (2018), op. cit.

14 IPCC (2018), op. cit.

15 EarthViewer 2.0, Mark E. Nielsen, PHD producer.

16 Feulner, G. (2012). The faint young Sun problem. *Review of Geophysics*, Volume 50, RG2006. Retrieved from: https://skepticalscience.com/argument.php

17 Waters, C.N. et al. (2016). The Anthropocene is functionally and stratigraphically distinct from the Holocene. *Science*, Volume 351 (6269): aad2622.

18 NOAA (n.d.). Historical Maps and Charts. NOAA Ocean Podcast: Episode 08. Retrieved from: https://oceanservice.noaa.gov/podcast/july17/nop08-historical-maps-charts.html.

19 IPCC (2019). *IPCC Special Report on the Ocean and Cryosphere in a Changing Climate.* H.-O. Pörtner, D.C. Roberts, V. Masson-Delmotte, P. Zhai, M. Tignor, E. Poloczanska, K. Mintenbeck, M. Nicolai, A. Okem, J. Petzold, B. Rama and N. Weyer (eds). Retrieved from: https://report.ipcc.ch/srocc/pdf/SROCC_FinalDraft_FullReport.pdf

20 Gardner, T. (2003). Long-term region-wide declines in Caribbean corals. *Science*, Volume 301 (5635), pp. 958–960.

21 Ibid.

22 IPCC (2018), op. cit.

Chapter 4

Climate Planning Objection 4

"All change brings both good and bad. Besides, the climate change cure would probably be worse than the disease."

"Shifting to alternative energy will destroy our economy," we hear. "If we limit carbon emissions it will halt growth, cut our gross domestic product, eliminate jobs, and hurt the economy."

"No," climate activists argue, "it will save our economy because the path we're on destroys everything."

The truth is, of course, somewhere in the middle the average person can't help but think and this creates hesitancy and inertia.

"These people want to commit economic suicide," I heard from a fellow attendee at a climate change session during a 2016 conference in Baton Rouge hosted by the Center for Planning Excellence (CPEX). Camille Manning Broome of CPEX had given a heartfelt, informative presentation about the state of climate adaptation in Louisiana. She recommended sensible, retrained growth for the state going forward. She recommended a nationwide shift to renewable energy. Adaptation alone would not save Louisiana she argued: The world had to change. That made sense to me, but not everyone heard Camille the way I had.

DOI: 10.4324/9781003181514-6

108 ■ *Why Are We Doing This?*

"If we shift to renewables and the Chinese don't, we'll eliminate our competitive advantage," a fellow attendee said outside of the session as we sipped free coffee.

"And communism takes over," I offered, unhelpfully.

"I mean, maybe, but you see what I am saying," said the attendee with a sincerity that made me regret my levity. I had been taken off guard because I was talking to an architect with a successful New Orleans practice and I was surprised to hear a climate denial argument from him. Denial comes from sources you don't expect because people hold secret opinions they don't readily express.

Talking to the architect more over lunch I learned that he had two young children in the New Orleans school system and he was concerned about the paucity of school funding that he'd witnessed as part of his school's Parent Teacher Association. This issue eclipsed his climate concerns. He talked to me a lot about Louisiana's poverty. He wanted to design for the future, but he worried that a serious national climate policy would make Louisiana even poorer.

"How would climate policy hurt Louisiana?" I asked. I really wanted to know. I don't recommend Socratic dialogues where you concede a point only to better refute it. I recommend actually working to understand fear and attempting to synthesize ideas.

The architect's argument went something like this: Thanks to fossil fuels (coal, natural gas, petroleum, and other gases) the world enjoyed an industrial revolution and an agricultural revolution. Fossil fuels employed a blue-collar workforce and created a massive middle class. Thanks to fossil fuels we have a dependable food supply, light at night, heat in the winter, refrigeration, air-conditioning, convenient transportation, and on and on. Thanks to fossil fuels places like Louisiana, which are rich in oil and gas resources, have a dependable source of income.

"Beware the person who wants to change nothing but be equally afraid of the person who wants to change everything," the architect said.

I agreed that no sane person would choose deindustrialization and a return to a pre-industrial past. I agreed that no normal person would even choose unemployment, food lines, and gasoline lines to give the planet time to heal or to (maybe) preserve the planet for future generations. These are unacceptable sacrifices.

The architect contended that no one could explain how we could cut emissions significantly without closing down virtually all of our economy and that it just wasn't worth it. This is a commonly held belief.[1]

"Don't ruin the world," the architect said with real feeling.

Don't ruin the world? Is that really what he thought the conference was recommending? My takeaway from the conference was that preventing climate heating and furthering economic development were two sides of the same coin because unless sea-level rise in Louisiana was halted the place was effectively doomed. Did he see us all as eco-fascists and end-of-the-world enthusiasts?

The necessities of life include food, shelter, clothing, *and* fuel, wrote Henry David Thoreau.[2] The world can shift its fuel sources, but life isn't possible without some kind of fuel. When it comes to changing the world, people want their standard of living to stay the same – just greener. That's what we are suggesting.

I, myself, can't help but watch the Degrowth movement, as I understand it, with apprehension. I don't think a world of simple living, post-consumerism, and post-growth[3] would be a utopia. I'd like to think the world would look like Old Mistick Village in Connecticut, which presents a recreated historic town just before the steam engine was invented with gabled wooden homes on brick streets, comfy tavern fireplaces with woodsmoke smells, picturesque orchards, fertile fields, grand sailing ships, and horse-drawn carts, but I fear that a post-growth world would look more like the tougher neighborhoods of Juarez, Mexico with their heat, poverty, sewer smells, and guns.

Working on the local level involves a great many reality checks. Many environmentalists will say that the core climate problem is capitalism – not even carbon-driven capitalism, just capitalism. Well, maybe, but here's a reality check: Being anti-capitalism won't get you far as a local planner. In America today our ideas of identity, freedom, and success are attached to capitalism. We must believe that capitalism provides the only palatable framework for a solution. Regulated capitalism. But capitalism. The people at CPEX's conference in Baton Rouge weren't suggesting anything different, as far as I could tell. "The Climate Rebellion's true target is not climate, it is …," climate deniers begin, and the list will then include things like capitalism, eurocentrism, patriarchy, class hierarchy, U.S. exceptionalism, and freedom.

We can fix the world without ruining it. Local planners must communicate the belief that, as far as we can tell, extremism won't be required to make the world greener and that the effort to decrease carbon pollution wouldn't be a quixotic gesture which only serves to make life harder.

Let's Fix the World

When we say "fix" the world we mean no more than "upgrade." In 2018 nearly 40% of U.S. electricity generation came from non-fossil fuels according to the U.S. Energy Information Administration and the percentage of energy from renewable energy sources is increasing.[4] By 2050 over half of the electricity in the U.S. is expected to be generated by solar power according to the Administration[5] and no one would accuse the U.S. Energy Information Administration of being a radical organization looking to deindustrialize the planet.

Why? Largely because wind and solar are cheap. If the cost of solar and wind technologies continues to drop, we'll pay less for energy. According to renewable energy enthusiasts, decarbonizing the U.S. electricity system would save US$1.8 trillion over the coming decades.[6] Has the ongoing shift to renewable energy ruined anyone's life?

"Spend three minutes thinking about what carbon-free means and you will never vote for a Democrat," was a commonly heard refrain during months leading to the 2020 presidential election. While outlawing oil and gas could have catastrophic effects on civilization, a dramatic reduction and replacement with renewable sources

110 ■ *Why Are We Doing This?*

would not. "We can't afford a shift to renewable energy," we heard. But that just isn't true. The reality is we can't afford not to.

Invention and innovation comes quite naturally to people. In early times there were no garbage collectors and people didn't treat household sewerage, and so human settlements suffered plague outbreaks and other terrible diseases. Our ancestors found a way to pay for basic sanitation. At the turn of the twentieth century, urban rivers were dumping grounds for raw industrial wastes and cholera outbreaks were common, and so the cities of the world found a way to regulate waste disposal. The indiscriminate spraying of toxic DDT pesticides caused widespread birth defects and the chemical was banned after the United States Environmental Protection Agency was created in the 1970s. We rarely worry about mercury and lead in our drinking water or that our food is safe to eat thanks to the work of federal agencies whose creation was vociferously fought and today every country on earth, no matter how poor or corrupt, has similar agencies and comparable environmental and health standards.

If we consider all the horrifying injuries and deaths, property and business costs in New Orleans, the Jersey shore, Houston, and the Bahamas due to recent hurricanes alone then it is clear something needs to be done. Consider the wildfires of California and Australia. While natural disasters have always been an issue, according to a 2012 study by the European non-governmental organization the DARA Group and the Climate Vulnerability Forum, climate change is already contributing to over 400,000 deaths and costing the world US$1.2 trillion each year.[7]

In order to avoid dangerous global warming, we need to reduce global greenhouse gas (GHG) emissions by about 50% by the year 2050.[8] Skeptics often make the argument that we simply don't have the technology necessary to reduce emissions this much, this quickly. Pacala and Socolow (2004) investigated this claim by examining the various technologies and policies available to reduce GHG emissions.[9] Their study identifies 15 current options which could be scaled up. Several of these are within the sphere of local government planning.

1. Improved fuel economy
2. Reduced reliance on cars
3. More efficient buildings
4. Improved power plant efficiency
5. Substituting natural gas for coal
6. Storage of carbon captured in power plants
7. Storage of carbon captured in hydrogen plants
8. Storage of carbon captured in synthetic fuels plants
9. Nuclear power
10. Wind power
11. Solar photovoltaic power
12. Renewable hydrogen
13. Biofuels
14. Forest management
15. Agricultural soils management

If we use this list as a starting point, we see the job of urban planners could be to install charging stations for those who can afford electric cars, make electric public transit available to everyone else, and build out high-speed rail at a scale where air travel stops becoming necessary for most trips. On the local level we must continue to update our building and land use codes to require LEED Buildings, allow for wind power everywhere, require solar and green roofs, and protect farms.

Comprehensive Plans and Energy

Our main tool for urban planning in the U.S. is the municipal Comprehensive Plan. The creation and update of these plans is tied to the Standard State Zoning Enabling Act (SZEA), which provided a model law for U.S. states to enable zoning regulations in their jurisdictions. It was drafted by a committee of the Department of Commerce and first issued in 1922, and it requires a community plan before updates to zoning. It is a century-old tool in need of continual refreshing and through the years many different Comprehensive Plan elements have been added to the list. The next generation of Comprehensive Plans should have resilience elements and energy elements. This book has described the kinds of goals, strategies, and action items that can be found in those elements.

Does your code allow renewable energy to be produced locally? Comprehensive Plans should set goals to enable large-scale photovoltaic farms and other renewables. Land development regulations should allow rooftop and ground-mounted photovoltaics under 15 acres in size as of right without a public hearing. Solar farms, or large-scale ground-mounted photovoltaic facilities greater than 15 acres, should be allowed with a Special or Conditional use permit. Add to your list of permitted uses within your zoning districts: "Solar farms," or, more broadly, "Utility-scale renewable energy," and add to your definitions section: "Utility-scale renewable energy generation includes solar, hydropower, geothermal, and wind but does not include propane, natural gas, or any carbon dioxide polluting source." Modern solar farms do not reflect light, generate more noise than other neighbors, create pollution, or bring down property values. Consider incentivizing solar as well. I encourage codes to allow an extra story of height on all structures that guarantee to have solar panels on their roof.

Slowly the argument "The cure is probably worse than the disease" is being replaced by the argument "The way to address climate change is not by increasing regulations and taxes." That's a positive first step. However, at the local level regulations are our primary tool for affecting change and taxes pay for the adaptation infrastructure that will be necessary.

Admittedly, adaptation infrastructure and big engineering projects can be controversial topics, but we can't fool ourselves into thinking that the way to prepare for sea-level rise, or the way to stop sea-level rise, is to be more energy efficient. We must prepare now for the sea-level rise that may be far off but is inevitable. Bulwarking our coastlines will cause environmental disruption and there will be pushback. Let's talk about the resistance we face when we propose adaptation infrastructure.

112 ■ *Why Are We Doing This?*

Notes From the Field
Reducing Risk with the Virginia Key Boulevard Levee

In August 2014 I was invited to participate in the South Florida Resilient Redesign Workshop, and it was there I realized that more than denial or skepticism, it is uncertainty and fear that generate pushback. At the height of the hurricane season, as storms swirled off the coast of Africa, I joined Miami architects and climate adaptation experts from around the world to redesign three prototypical South Florida study areas with a mix of reinforcement, retrofit, and retreat.

The Southeast Florida Regional Climate Compact, a regional consortium united by a compact to work on climate mitigation and adaptation, and representing four counties in Southeast Florida, hosted the event. The work was to become part of the region's climate action plan. The list of participants included nationally renowned designers and starchitects such as Elizabeth Plater-Zyberk of Duany Plater-Zyberk; David Waggonner of Waggonner & Ball Architects of New Orleans; the heads of Miami's architecture colleges; climate change journalists and authors; several Dutch firms and institutes including Arcadis Engineering, Deltares, BoschSlabbers, and H+N+S Landscape Architects; and the mayors and directors of the region's cities, planning agencies, and sustainability offices. It felt like we had everyone we needed to solve Southeast Florida's adaptation problems.

After a few days of opening presentations and site tours we went to work. Miami's American Institute of Architects (AIA) chapter hosted the event at its offices in Downtown Miami and supplied the teams with base maps and a range of drawing materials. I chose to design the Alton Road area in Miami Beach because my home was within the study area. I marked my home with a red circle on our base map. My home at the time was a 1930s Mediterranean Revival condominium building designed by Ralph Murray Dixon, the starchitect of another era. I was probably the only participant with a home on one of the base maps. I began to draw.

Miami Beach is the American city most likely, one day, to be underwater. The city has more people and more property at risk due to rising water than any other because as an offshore barrier island the entire city is within a coastal high hazard area. Miami Beach will face chronic inundation by 2035, according to the Union of Concerned Scientists.[10] Nearly 26,000 homes are at risk of chronic flooding by 2060. The value of the property at risk is US$16 billion. Whatever solutions we came up with to save Miami Beach during the Resilient Redesign Workshop could apply to any of the many coastal cities and towns in Florida, New Jersey, Texas, and Louisiana where communities face the most risk.[11]

Renaldo Borges, the Miami architect who sat next to me at the workshop, began to draw street elevations showing raised streets and small Art Deco-era buildings being replaced with titanic, glass-and-steel towers of the kind he was already known for designing. The City of Miami Beach's Sustainability Coordinator sat across from us and answered questions about the city's plans and the building codes. Participants who were not comfortable drawing sat next to the people who were.

A representative from the Consultant General of the Kingdom of the Netherlands worked at the end of our table with Piet Dircke, a civil engineer with the title "Global Leader" at the firm Arcadis, an international management, design, and engineering company. I stood over my map with John Englander, an oceanographer and author of the 2012 book *High Tide on Main Street*. John and I decided that in order to solve the problems in our 30-block study area we were going to need to zoom way out. I unfurled a map of the entire city.

As Englander advised me, I drew city-wide resilience infrastructure including Dutch-style dike-in-dune systems lining Miami Beach's shoreline and living shoreline breakwaters made by installing mangrove forests offshore. Then an idea occurred to me and I began to wonder if the heart of Miami could be protected from the kind of catastrophic (10-foot-plus) storm surge it saw during a 1926 hurricane by a combination of reinforced barrier islands and flood gates.

I began to draw, essentially, a levee and flood barrier system that began on the shore south of Miami's downtown, crossed Florida Bay with a canal gate, followed the Rickenbacker Causeway to Virginia Key, continued north along Virginia Key's east coast, and connected Fisher Island to Miami Beach with canal gates. It seemed to me that all of downtown, Port of Miami, Brickell, Little Haiti, and the Upper Eastside up to North Miami could effectively be bulwarked and even sealed by a combination of lifted islands, each raised 20 feet, and connecting gates. To my knowledge no one had ever drawn anything like it for Miami. The ideas I drew were big enough to attract the attention of Dircke from Arcadis.

"Ya," he said with a thick Dutch accent while nodding his head. He then showed me pictures on his tablet computer of the Maeslantkering in the Netherlands, a barrier which opens and closes on hinges and protects Rotterdam while allowing ships to pass through during normal periods. With a similar system the Port of Miami could continue its operations, and Dircke believed that this was important because Miami was a port city. That made sense. He worked on design considerations related to minimizing the impact on the ecosystem and allowing for maximum tidal flows.

"Don't think of it as a wall, think of it as a real estate project," Dircke told me. For someone not from Miami he understood the city pretty well. Large public infrastructure investments were less likely to get funded than oceanfront real estate. I widened the islands and the levee and ran a multi-way boulevard along it with space for transit riders, drivers, cyclists, and pedestrians. Thousands of new homes, workplaces, restaurants, and retail could be located on the raised islands, safe from the water that rises up through the porous limestone and threatens the city. Virginia Key alone would see over 250 additional acres and at an urban density of 80 to 100 units per acre it could be home to 20,000 to 25,000 people. All those people would be high above the water.

Everyone worked late into the night on a variety of ideas, began early the next day, and worked even later the next night. I enlisted the help of illustrators in my office to accurately model what I called the *Virginia Key Boulevard Levee*. It would

114 ■ *Why Are We Doing This?*

be a multi-billion dollar project but would protect both the Alton Road study area I was assigned to plan, my Miami Beach home, and the heart of the two million person city.

At some point during the workshop Steven Slabbers, the Dutch landscape architect, said, "Everyone asks: How will you pay for it? How will you pay for it? Let me tell you, funding follows inspiration." So, with the help of Englander, Dircke, and others, I aimed for inspiring. I pinned up my designs for comment and critique. Then came trouble.

"No, no, no," said one of the organizers from Rebuild by Design, a U.S. HUD (Housing and Urban Development) initiative that was organized after Hurricane *Sandy*. "They drew a wall in New York and it was all anyone talked about. We can't show a wall."

"I agree," said a representative from the Institute for Sustainable Communities, one of the workshop's funders.

"What about the eel grass?" asked an urban planner from Miami Beach. "Or the manatees?"

"While eel grass and manatees are important to me, I am a little more concerned about the 10-foot wall of water that might hit my house," I said before I could stop myself. Mid-sentence, I had attempted to say this with light-heartedness, but I found the tone in my voice to be deadly serious.

"So, you don't care about sea life?" the urban planner asked.

How was I to answer that?

"You are only protecting the core of the city?" asked another participant. "What about Little Haiti?" I got a cold look with a hard warning.

"It protects Little Haiti," I said. I pointed to Little Haiti on the map.

"What about over here," the woman asked pointing away from Little Haiti and to the northwest part of the city, an area that was historically a minority community.

"I am not sure we can protect everywhere," I said.

"You are going to need to."

I am all for the campaign to protect the natural environment, including manatees, and I am all for efforts to advance social equity. Absolutely. The great thing about being an urban planner is that you can work on all of these issues at the same time, but sometimes some agendas can feel a bit distracting to the job at hand.

"You're right, I will find a way to protect the northwest," I said. I would. It was important. Save everyone. No less. I didn't know how, but I liked that idea.

"Adaptation isn't about solving the problem," Miami Beach's Sustainability Coordinator said when she saw my wall. "It's just buying time."

"Buying time is okay," I said.

"We should be helping Miami let go, not dig in," said one of the architects from New Orleans who believed *living with water* – basically creating large detention basins in cities in some areas and allowing the water in, and retreating from hard-to-defend areas in other areas – needed to be the main goal of the project. The *living with water* concept was presented as the "Dutch solution" because the American

Climate Planning Objection 4 ■ 115

landscape architects learned it from some recent water plazas installed in cities in the Netherlands but as far as I could tell the Dutch solution was walls and bulwarks. The Dutch had been building those for nearly a millennium. The word "bulwark" itself is a Dutch word.

Other people defended my designs. The gist of their defense was that if the Boulevard Levee made use of all the other adaptation best practices that were being proposed around the room then the "new city" would be made environmentally palatable. That made sense to me. I immediately began to draw decentralized, renewable offshore energy generation systems that could help power the entire city during energy disruptions. I recorded in my notes that I needed to talk about inclusionary housing practices.

I kept drawing and refining the idea. Head down. Pencil sharpener humming.

"You aren't solving the main problem. The water will still rise under our feet," I was told by a person standing over my shoulder.

"We're helping to solve the immediate problem: big storms," I said. "One could wipe us out. It's like a cholera epidemic. Act fast. The slow rise is like heart disease and it will take a variety of ..."

"Levees don't work in Miami."

"There's a levee on our western border. The Southern Glades Trail on Miami's western levee protects us from ..."

"Walls won't work."

"Thanks for the input."

I drew tree-lined streets that would be high enough to avoid the saltwater intrusion that might kill trees elsewhere. An urban canopy would provide a leafy green shield for outdoor life as the world's temperatures increased and heatwaves lasted longer.

"They don't want to treat the cancer because they are worried their hair might fall out."

I looked up. It was Piet Dircke from Arcadis. "Thanks Pete."

I penciled sketches of modern-day parapets and ramparts. Lightly drawn lines of turrets and keeps appeared. I sketched chemin-de-ronde gangways, outer encircling walls, and inner holds all drawn with a contemporary style like Mies van der Rohe might have drawn. I cantilevered like James Stewart Polshek and towered like David Childs. It was beautiful. I thought.

"I'm sorry, but we're not showing that levee," said the City of Miami Beach's Sustainability Coordinator. She was ultimately the curator of the upcoming Climate Compact Summit where the ideas would be displayed. If she was against the idea then no one would ever see it. Apparently, she had been viewing my work from a distance and was simmering with opposition.

Piet Dircke whispered to me, "A lot of people are afraid of anything more than buckets," before he began to defend the idea to the group. He recommended elements which would help the region's environment, like sand motors, that were essentially beach-and-habitat-creation pumps that built land instead of diminishing it like

116 ■ *Why Are We Doing This?*

most pumping systems. But the environmentalists didn't like his ideas either. I began to see that one person's engineering achievement is another person's environmental disaster.

Throughout the pin-ups from the other teams and the lunch that followed people continued to express outright hostility to my idea. Just about every question I got was aggressive. The project was described as, or insinuated to be, a waste of public monies, a false sense of security for people who needed to begin evacuating, a vanity project, and a *climate mega-project* that would, like every other mega-project, be obsolete the moment it was constructed. Seas would continue to rise, and storms would continue to worsen. The levee would not help at all, they said.

"The people in New Orleans don't talk about the hurricane, they talk about the day the levees broke," I was told by a member of the New Orleans contingent. "People can't rely on walls."

"What would be the carbon footprint of all the construction needed to build the levee?" I was asked.

"Other countries are trying to build their way out of their problems," I responded. China, Japan, and Singapore have all built new cities on the water. Dirke had shown me several amazing projects on his tablet. Bulwarks like I had drawn had been built all along the North Sea in Europe and in many places in the United States, including Florida.

I discussed Miami Beach's own eastern beach which pushed the water back a quarter of a mile. I talked about the two miles of wall along the Miami River through Brickell and the four miles of wall from Biscayne Canal to the Little River. I discussed the Herbert Hoover Dike built on Lake Okeechobee after hurricanes in 1926 and 1928 killed thousands.[12]

"The Army Corp of Engineers doesn't build walls anymore," I was told by one of the conference organizers.

"I don't think that's true," I responded quietly through gritted teeth while picturing the expanding levee systems in Louisiana that I had worked on.

There was also outright hostility to the idea of adaptation, alone. People expressed their belief that planning to adapt in any way was tantamount to giving up on the idea of fixing the climate problem. While the 1926 hurricane that devastated the villages around Lake Okeechobee was *natural*, I was told, any storms that occurred after the widespread use of the combustion engine were *manmade*, and any major attempts to adapt were enabling.

I was asked: Wouldn't building a new barrier island system of larger islands just enable more fossil fuel use? If people believed there was a physical solution to the problem of sea-level rise and climate change, wouldn't it mean they'd never change how they lived? Would they ever stop driving and start bicycling? Stop eating meat and start eating their vegetables? Protect manatees? Throw off capitalism? Switch to solar and vote Democrat? This sounds like a ridiculous list, I know, but over the course of the event I heard some version of all of this.

Chris Bergh, director of the South Florida Nature Conservancy, approached me after one particularly mean critique. He was a big, red-bearded man with a quiet voice. During the workshops I had learned that he lived on Big Pine Key in the Florida Keys, an island which he admitted would probably be the first to go when sea-level rise began to accelerate. But he loved the island. The nature. The sea. He said he'd be the last to leave. I felt the same way about Miami Beach. He told me that he understood the impulse to fight and to "rage against nature" and not give up.

"But be careful what you build," Bergh said to me. "We need to think farther into the future. We will have to leave. We just will. We need to think about what we leave behind and its effect on the natural system." His polite thoughtfulness and the considerable amount of time he had clearly given to thinking about the problem made me realize that in Southeast Florida the climate catastrophe might be mitigated in the short- or mid-term, but not in the long-term. There was no ultimate solution; every solution would be provisional. "Be careful," he counseled, "that you don't leave the place worse than you found it when it's time to go."

"That makes sense to me," I said.

Piet Dircke didn't agree. "A time will come when Miami no longer has the luxury of foreswearing all the moral hazards of building a wall. Just build a wall."

That made sense too.

Six years have passed since the Virginia Key Boulevard Levee concept was introduced. Nothing has happened with the idea since. By contrast, New York's Rebuild By Design project gave birth to New York City's BIG U, a protective system around the low-lying topography of Lower Manhattan that would provide ten continuous miles of protection and amenities. Hundreds of millions of dollars have been pledged to build the project by U.S. HUD, and from New York City, a city I think it is fair to say is absolutely committed to green practices.

To the credit of the Virginia Key Boulevard Levee's detractors, the concept was still presented at the Climate Leadership Conference. It was never projected on the big screen, but a rendering we'd made was hung on the wall gallery-style with the other concepts from the workshop. The Virginia Boulevard Levee didn't appear in any of the printed or digital materials that followed the climate conference.

It was interesting to me how comfortable the climate conference organizers were with presenting evacuation. The *living with water* concept involved more than just urban water retention facilities; those plans included new wetland sloughs a mile wide which would swallow commercial districts and neighborhoods. It looked to me like the *living with water* idea was less about getting people to live with water, and more about getting them to give the land back to the ocean one portion at a time.

Since the climate conference, my work has taken me to Boston, a city that discarded the idea of a massive harbor barrier that would have been similar to the Virginia Key Boulevard Levee. They cited cost, interference with shipping, ecological damage from dredging, and altered currents.[13] I believe that the environmental community adopted the idea of climate change early, but that big infrastructure remains

118 ■ *Why Are We Doing This?*

at odds with that group's values and so they, alone, can never deliver real solutions. Climate adaptation will need other champions.

I presented the Virginia Key Boulevard Levee several times after the conference to municipalities, the local chapter of the Urban Land Institute and American Planning Association, two local universities, the South Florida Water Management District, and to the Army Corp of Engineers, the federal government's engineering arm. Before I began my presentation to the Corp I asked if they had a plan for Miami. I assumed they had a back-pocket plan (at least) for everywhere. The person I talked to didn't know of one.

After Hurricane *Irma* in 2017 flooded sections of Downtown Miami, Congress asked the Corp to come up with solutions to protect coastal Miami-Dade from hurricanes. In June 2020 it was announced that the Army Corp of Engineers had a provisional plan for three separate walls, six linear miles total, and 13 feet in height. The total price tag was US$4.6 billion and the federal government would pay 65% of the cost. Miami-Dade would be responsible for the rest.[14] I couldn't help but wonder if the Army Corps' idea would survive the local objections I had encountered.

The Corps' proposal differed from mine. The walls weren't very long, and they were hyper-focused on three areas of the city. There was no real estate component. No one would get rich. That was an element I always believed would be necessary to get private support. I worry that the Corps' plan also asked Miami for too much of a contribution without a corresponding gain in property taxes to justify the project to voters who were unconcerned about the distant future and only thought about now. And while the Corps' plan did involve elevating and floodproofing homes it did not attempt to build any new higher land. New, higher land seems essential to me to Miami's long-term survival.

When asked to comment on the Corps' proposal I said I was glad that the city was considering walls. At that point, it had been six years since the South Florida Resilient Redesign Workshop. But I told my contact at the Army Corps that I didn't think their proposal went far enough.

"You are only proposing six miles," I said. "In Japan, 245 miles of walls were built in Miyagi Prefecture, north of Tokyo, after a major tsunami hit the area in 2011."[15]

"This isn't Japan. We don't have the long history of these storms that they do," I was told. "Give it time."

Give it time. If there's a lesson in this book I hope it is that. When it comes to climate mitigation and adaptation our civilization is still new to the idea. Whether we actually have the time to give the problem is a worthwhile question. But in my opinion, we have no choice.

Was the Virginia Key Boulevard Levee a good idea? Was it a good idea in the short- and mid-term, at least? If slow evacuation and the deconstruction of Southeast Florida's cities needs to be the plan in the long-term (as Chris Bergh from the Nature Conservancy suggested), is a massive climate adaptation infrastructure project a good idea today? Would the wall provide a false sense of security and a reason not to evacuate when a Category 5 with a high storm surge approached? Would the wall

Climate Planning Objection 4 ■ 119

cause a major catastrophe if it failed? The idea never received the kind of public attention and feedback that might have helped answer those questions. I still can't tell if it was a bad idea or an idea whose time has simply not yet come.

I placed a short film on the Dover, Kohl & Partners YouTube channel depicting the Boulevard Levee concept.[16] Take a look and see what you think.

Notes From the Field

Risk Analysis in Miami Beach: "Wait, Where Did My House Go?"

I remember looking up at the screen behind me as I sat at the presenter's table in front of more than 100 people and finding that my house on Miami Beach was to be revegetated as part of someone else's climate plan. In 2017 I had been asked to speak at the Miami Design Preservation League's Art Deco Weekend. The theme for the weekend event was *Forty Years of Fabulous* and it commemorated Miami Beach's first Art Deco Festival in 1977. I was part of a panel asked to talk about Miami Beach's next 40 years.

Isaac Stein, a landscape architect at West 8, explained a plan and rendering he'd done for South Beach in Miami Beach with a focus on the area from 5th to 15th Streets. He proposed extending the island's western shore outward with revegetated mangroves and living breakwaters. That was fine with me, but he also recommended allowing half the island's neighborhoods to flood so that they could be revegetated.

I counted the blocks north from 5th Street and west from Washington Avenue and confirmed that my home, a two-story Mediterranean Revival building, wasn't part of the plan. Where my red barrel-tiled house once stood was an aqua pool that looked like it would be a comfy home for mussel beds and crocodiles.

"Can you put that slide back up?" I asked Stein during the question-and-answer part of the talk. He did. "You flooded my house," I said. The audience didn't make a sound as they waited for Stein's reaction. I assumed other people saw their homes flooded too.

Stein winced and explained that the graphic was simply illustrative; his plan recommended bringing back a layer of the natural landscape to protect the city from rising sea. He called it an *urban estuary* without any recognition of the contradiction inherent in that phrase. He talked quite a bit, somewhat nervously.

I could see the logic. Miami Beach is a barrier island that is routinely battered by hurricanes and floods. It was hardly even a *natural* island, most of it was built by digging up mud, piling it high, and constructing a wall around it to keep the mud in, sandcastle-style. Miami Beach is mostly fill. Perhaps the day would come when a storm would cause catastrophic damage and the western side of the island which was once mangrove in some places, and open water in others, could be allowed to revert. I had to agree that the cost to continually replace Miami Beach, or any urbanized barrier island, would be significant as the seas rose. And I do believe we need to move from the planning phase to the implementation phase with our adaptation ideas. He was boldly showing precisely how to apply the *living with water* concept, which involved allowing water back into our settlements.

But damn, my house was gone.

The Atlantic side of the island was fortified in Stein's plan by wide sand dunes and a built shoreline that would protect three blocks east of Ocean Drive. Today, the Atlantic side of the island, near Lummus Park, is 11 feet above sea level and the

Figure 4 An Art Deco Hotel on Miami Beach, Florida

Climate Planning Objection 4 ■ **121**

island slopes down to 2.5 feet on the western edge. My block was closer to the west edge. My block just missed the cut-off.

"I'm having a heard time communicating what it is like to see a recommendation like this," I said. "I mean, to see your home gone …" I was at a loss for words. I had drawn my share of plans and renderings which illustrated the same concept throughout Florida, Louisiana, Texas, and coastal Alabama. I had flooded plenty of homes in my plans and illustrations too.

Stein didn't respond. The room sat nervously.

I looked back up at the screen. I understood that barrier islands were never meant to be as heavily developed as they are today and that I, and the many other people who lived on the barrier islands, were to blame. I grew up in the Northeast where I learned that after the Pilgrims landed on a sandy spit of land on today's Cape Cod they paused for a little while but then moved inland. They could recognize that barrier islands and sandy spits were never going to be safe. Why didn't Miami Beach?

Still, Stein had erased my home. I eyeballed him.

"I was invited to present," he said as if he was afraid I was going to toss a chair at him. "And, again, it's only illustrative."

Only illustrative. How many times had I used that phrase in my own presentations?

Just a few years earlier Miami Beach had celebrated its 100th anniversary. I spoke during those festivities too, and no one that I heard speak (myself included) was talking about sea-level rise. What a difference a few years made. We'd reached the point as a community in which speakers are invited to show Miami Beach half-evacuated.

"It's an interesting concept," I said. I sat down.

The question-and-answer session continued and while I answered questions from the audience I struggled in my head to identify my principles when it came to Miami Beach, or any low-lying city. Reinforce or retreat? Build higher and pump, or allow the water in? Understand, I had two young children whom I played with on the living room carpet of that condominium which Stein had transformed, on the screen above me, into a shimmering pool of turquoise bordered by ominous dark greens. It was the first home I'd ever purchased. While I knew that as my kids got older we would need a bigger place, my plan was to retire on Miami Beach no matter what the island looked like.

I tried not to take Stein's concept personally. And I know – perhaps better than just about anyone – how often plans are not implemented. It occurred to me that I had found myself in this kind of situation once before. When I was 19 and Pledge Class President at the Phi Gamma Delta Fraternity at the University of Rhode Island, I discovered that the new campus plan proposed tearing down our enormous Georgian-style fraternity house. The master plan had identified our site for a proposed 1,000-car parking garage.

My fraternity brothers and I met with the university president. He was frank with us and communicated a sentiment he said he'd heard quite a bit. He said that many people on the campus and around the country considered the fraternity an institution that was unhelpful to academics, gender equality, and student safety.

122 ■ *Why Are We Doing This?*

The president didn't know the half of it. For one thing, our fraternity took hazing quite seriously and none of the things we did – things I still can't discuss, sworn to secrecy as I am – helped my GPA. Nevertheless, my fraternity brothers and I objected strongly to the campus plan in the campus newspaper and at multiple Greek events.

Today, the fraternity house still stands, though 25 years later the campus plan, which has been updated several times, still proposes replacing it with a parking garage.[17] I hate to look at that plan. I haven't been an active part of Greek life since leaving college, but I hope the best for my frat. Call me nostalgic, but I still hope naked snow angels are a tradition.

Let's get back to Miami Beach.

"What do you recommend?" Stein asked me after a member of the audience objected to his plan and he was beginning to feel outnumbered.

"Well, I recommend … my presentation."

I had given my presentation before Stein's and I had talked about my work on *Seven50: The Prosperity Plan for Southeast Florida* and *Plan NOBE: The Plan for North Miami Beach*. My plan, in a nutshell, was to save the island for as long as we could.

"I liked his presentation," one member of the audience said while pointing to me. I recognized this person from the public planning charrettes we had done locally. The plan for North Miami Beach was extremely controversial because it resulted in the largest historic district designation in over 30 years on Miami Beach. It created the Normandy Isle Historic District and Northshore Historic District and protected over 400 historic structures that showcased the Miami Modern architectural style. People questioned the wisdom of designating historic structures, requiring them to be preserved, on a barrier island.

Plan NOBE argues that Miami Beach is great because of its historic districts. The Deco, Streamlined Moderne, and Miami Modern (MiMo) buildings are exquisite, and Miami Beach's Art Deco District became the nation's first urban twentieth-century historic district when it was listed on the National Register of Historic Places in 1979. The island contains 14 Local Historic Districts, four National Register Districts, and over 2,600 buildings that are located in the districts, with 1,900 listed as Contributing Buildings – buildings contributing to the historic fabric and worthy of protection. Miami Beach may be the only community in the world with a statue dedicated to a preservationist: A bronze bust of Barbera Baer Capitman, a woman who stood in front of bulldozers and wouldn't let them pass, sits across from the Cardozo Hotel on Ocean Drive. Preservation is the island's shared culture.

Plan NoBe didn't ignore the threat of sea-level rise. Among other strategies, it talked about lifting the historic structures. This has been done all through history from Venice after its many years of floods, to Galveston, Texas, after the hurricane of 1900. Miami's historic buildings are all also, inevitably, remodeled from time to time, and remodeling often involves a floor-to-ceiling gutting of all interior wood in order to remove rot, keep up with new fashions, and meet new codes. Lifting the MiMo facades after a "facadectomy" (as it was called locally) would not be too great

Climate Planning Objection 4 ■ **123**

an additional cost. The "lifting" strategy didn't seem to make its way into Stein's work. He'd simply flooded all our historic districts and left the remaining buildings to rot.

Plan Nobe had introduced the idea of lifting historic structures to the community and local preservationists like Daniel Ciraldo, Executive Director of the Miami Design Preservation League, became known for the idea nationally. Ciraldo makes a distinction between *Destructive* versus *Constructive Resiliency*. According to him, sending historic structures to the landfill and replacing them with luxury glass and steel condominiums is *Destructive*, even though developers use the buzzword *resilient* in order to justify the destruction because it helps them in the permitting process. Ciraldo says replacement is destructive because it destroys buildings, displaces residents, and increases housing costs. *Constructive Resilience*, by contrast, reuses buildings (recycling them in a sense), keeps residents in place, and stabilizes housing costs.

"So, you plan to stay?" Stein asked me.

"Yes."

Every homeowner in Miami Beach that I know who thinks about climate wonders: Should I sell or should I not? And if not now, when? When will the music stop? If they are investors they think: If I keep my investment property for ten more years can I sell for a higher profit? What if it is worthless at that time? I have heard this kind of thinking called *real estate roulette* locally.

I think that over a certain age the people of Miami Beach (if not all Miamians) are committed to the city. That was my plan, at least. By the time I retire in 2050 the sea is expected to be 2 feet higher. I think that's a condition the island can manage, though it will be expensive to bulwark and pump Miami Beach and owners like myself will have to bear the cost. If the seas rise faster or higher, I will reassess of course, but my current plan is to ride out whatever comes.

I realized something as I talked to Stein. While my presentation had talked about sea-level rise and had plenty of illustrations similar to Stein's, my time horizon was only 30 to 50 years into the future, and as far as I understood Stein's work, his depiction went farther out – 100 years or maybe 200 years. I was reminded that in the field of urban planning we make recommendations for the short-term, midterm, and long-term. My work reflected the policies of the current regional and local governments and the political will of the people presently living on Miami Beach. Nothing I had proposed in my work for the region had foreclosed on the possibility that, as Stein had drawn, one day it would be time to say goodbye.

After the Deco Days event was over, I talked with Stein a bit and he conceded that maybe his effort to benefit *the city* in the abstract, and not the individual residents and business owners within it, "presented issues." I appreciated that.

As we had our conversation, a member of the audience whom I did not recognize said to Stein: "Nice presentation. Hey, I plan to stay, but I promise to turn the lights out when I leave." The older man winked at Stein and patted my arm with thanks

124 ■ *Why Are We Doing This?*

and, let's call it, a kind of *gallows comradery* that only comes with committing oneself to a place that is in serious danger.

"Which house was yours?" Stein asked. "I'll look more closely at that area."

"It's okay," I said.

Notes

1 Booker, C. (2010.) The woolly world of Chris Huhne. *The Telegraph*, May 29. Retrieved from: www.telegraph.co.uk/comment/columnists/christopherbooker/7783317/The-woolly-world-of-Chris-Huhne.html
2 Thoreau, H.D. (1992). *Walden and Resistance to Civil Government: Authoritative Texts, Thoreau's Journal, Reviews, and Essays in Criticism.* New York: Norton.
3 Demaria, F. et al. (2013). What is degrowth? From an activist slogan to a social movement. *Environmental Values*, Volume 22 (2), pp. 191–215. Retrieved from: www.jnu.ac.in/sss/cssp/What is degrowth.pdf
4 U.S. Department of Energy (2019). Annual energy outlook 2019 with projections to 2050. U.S. Energy Information Administration Office, January. Washington, DC 20585. Retrieved from: www.eia.gov/outlooks/aeo/
5 Ibid.
6 Cushman Jr, J.H. (2014). Shift to low-carbon economy could free pp $1.8 trillion, study says. *Inside Climate News*, October 9. Retrieved from: https://insideclimatechange.org
7 Fundación DARA Internacional (2012). Climate Vulnerability Monitor. Retrieved from: https://daraint.org/wp-content/uploads/2012/09/CVM2ndEd-FrontMatter.pdf
8 IPCC (2018). Global Warming of 1.5°C. An IPCC special report on the impacts of global warming of 1.5°C above pre-industrial levels and related global greenhouse gas emission pathways, in the context of strengthening the global response to the threat of climate change, sustainable development, and efforts to eradicate poverty. Masson-Delmotte, V., P. Zhai, H.O. Pörtner, D. Roberts, J. Skea, P.R. Shukla, A. Pirani, W. Moufouma-Okia, C. Péan, R. Pidcock, S. Connors, J.B.R. Matthews, Y. Chen, X. Zhou, M. I. Gomis, E. Lonnoy, T. Maycock, M. Tignor and T. Waterfield (eds). Retrieved from: www.ipcc.ch/sr15/
9 Pacala, S. and Socolow, R. (2004). Stabilization wedges: Solving the climate problem. *Science*, Volume 305 (5686), pp. 968–972.
10 Harrington, J. (2019). From Atlantic City to Key West: 21 beach towns that will soon be under water. *USA Today*, July 18. Retrieved from: www.usatoday.com/story/money/2019/07/18/atlantic-city-key-west-beach-towns-will-be-under-water-climate-change/39697819/
11 Ibid.
12 US Army Corps of Engineers (2008). Lake Okeechobee and the Okeechobee Waterway. Army Corps of Engineers South Florida Operations Office. Retrieved from: https://web.archive.org/web/20081012182022/http:/www.saj.usace.army.mil/sfoo/index.html
13 Mufson, S. (2020). Boston harbor brings ashore a new enemy: Rising seas. *Washington Post*, February 19. Retrieved from: www.washingtonpost.com/climate-solutions/2020/02/19/boston-prepares-rising-seas-climate-change/?arc404=true

14 Harris, A. (2020). Feds have $4.6 billion plan to protect Miami-Dade from hurricanes: Walls and elevation. *Miami Herald*, June 6. Retrieved from: www.miamiherald.com/news/local/environment/article243276326.html

15 Aquino, F. (2013). Crown Prince Naruhito, Princess Masako visit tsunami victims in Miyagi. *Japan Daily Press*, August 21. Retrieved from: https://web.archive.org/web/20130824135232/http://japandailypress.com/crown-prince-naruhito-princess-masako-visit-tsunami-victims-in-miyagi-2134298/

16 YouTube (2020). The Barbican: The Virginia Key Boulevard Levee Concept. Retrieved from: www.youtube.com/watch?v=69NrHX_KfKY

17 Goody, Clancy & Associates, et al. (2000). University of Rhode Island Kingston Campus master plan. Retrieved from: https://web.uri.edu/planning/files/2000-KingstonCampusMP-HI2-blank-pages-removed-8-19-13-reduced-size-for-web.pdf

Chapter 5

Climate Planning Objection 5

"We have bigger problems than climate change and other priorities."

Climate scientists have always said that climate change won't present itself like in the movie *The Day After Tomorrow* (2004), which started with a single crack in the Arctic ice shelf, moved quickly to continent-sized superstorms, a 25-foot rise in sea levels, a phalanx of tornados clobbering Los Angeles, and then, after just a few days, the end of human civilization (practically). Climate change will be slow, the world is warming rapidly, but it's only *rapid* in geological time.

Climate change hasn't felt slow. The warmest five years on record occurred from 2015 to 2020, and during that period the world saw record-breaking fires, devastating hurricanes and floods, widespread heatwaves and drought, and mass glacier loss.[1] The climate crisis feels more like the new nuke, ousting the role the atomic bomb once played in our shared nightmares. Popular TV series like *The Expanse* (2015) and films like *Tenet* (2020) imagine a world with high seas and massive storm walls, searing heat and drought, the way films like *Planet of the Apes* (1968) depicted post-atomic war wastelands. While the COVID-19 pandemic reminded us that there's a whole world of things to be afraid of, climate change still remains the world's biggest problem and most pressing priority.

The Guardian, a UK newspaper, updated its style guide in 2019 to introduce terms that more accurately describe the environmental crises facing the world. Instead of "climate change" the preferred terms are "climate emergency," "crisis,"

DOI: 10.4324/9781003181514-7

128 ■ *Why Are We Doing This?*

or "breakdown." "Global heating" is favored over "global warming." In September 2019, the BBC stated that it gets coverage of climate change "wrong too often" and told staff: "You do not need a 'denier' to balance the debate."[2]

Still, we can't expect a sudden global catastrophic event like in disaster movies to convince the world all at once. Change will be more subtle and awareness will come slowly. Where there are catastrophic wildfires people will say there have always been wildfires. Where aquifers are running dry people will say the aquifer was simply overtaxed, it wasn't climate. When it floods, skeptics will point out that 100 years ago there was a bigger flood. Every new tragedy will be dismissed as a continuing – and not new – issue.

In the less developed parts of the world, farming is becoming more difficult and clean water scarcer. Increasing famine and ecological problems have exacerbated political unrest and led to upheaval. In developed countries, that upheaval has led to multiple refugee crises.[3] The climate crisis means that the planet will gradually become less hospitable to human life, and both natural and geopolitical catastrophes will become more common and more impactful.

Local urban planners can see climate change's effects in a way that state and federal staff may not. Local planners work with Federal Emergency Management Agency (FEMA) floodmaps and can see their growing inadequacy. After major flooding event planners routinely must report that the extent and power of flooding is intensifying and that the 100-year and 500-year Flood Insurance Rate Maps (FIRM) no longer represent what actually happens. The flood zones change before the maps change because, quite inconsiderately, water doesn't bother to read maps.

Local planners work on the level of the individual building lot and can see that residential floodwalls are increasingly topped during tidal events. They see that in many places vegetation requires more water than was planned for them in park maintenance plans as soils dry and the days become warmer. Cities are increasingly telling the public that, due to storms and flooding, parklands are inaccessible more of the year. Urban planners hear about the rising cost of drinking water and know, after talking to local utility providers, that this is due to municipal hunts for potable water that are roving farther and farther out.

Bigger Problems

Climate events must be considered within the totality of human need, however. "The End of the World as We Know It" may be the biggest problem conceivable, but simply does not feel like the most pressing concern to most people. There aren't any immediate solutions, and people just naturally focus on other worries. Urban planners are also busy on other items.

Planners are charged with solving immediate problems like shepherding development proposals through complex processes, solving fights between neighbors over nuisances (real, perceived, and feared), fixing stalls in the development process

Climate Planning Objection 5 ▪ **129**

due to upset applicants and foot-dragging governmental agencies, growing traffic problems, rising local taxes, population stresses on schools, inner-city blight, environmental degradation, and so on.

Local planning departments are increasingly being relabeled *Development Services* as their role shifts from long-range resource protection to short-term economic development. This may be a sign that ideologically the profession has been moved from a protective one to a consumptive one. Planners may find any attempt to protect and conserve at odds with their new name and their new professional commitment. The day may come when "urban planning" and "climate planning" are synonymous or, at least, the one will only be funded when conducted in relation to the other, but that day hasn't arrived yet. Today planners in the U.S. feel they are employed to make development happen. There are no "Climate Planners," just urban planners doing their best with the tools they have.

At the same time, there are planning tools that urban planners have which can be modified to provide climate solutions. Let's discuss those plans.

Emergency Hazard Plans

As of 2013, nine states failed to mention *climate change* in their state hazard plans[4] and so local hazard plans may be the only place a discussion of climate occurs. The key to working on local climate mitigation and adaptation in municipalities which do not prioritize climate efforts is to link climate issues to the local concerns of elected officials, department directors, and the general public. Many urban planners link climate work to the municipality's Emergency Hazards Plans. This is done throughout the southeastern U.S. where flooding is a hazard, in the southwest of the country where heat stroke and exhaustion are growing issues, and in the Rocky Mountain and Great Plains states where wildfires are common.

In Missoula, Montana, for instance, the 2019 Downtown Master Plan, which I co-authored, contained a discussion of climate change even though the plan was primarily an economic development plan for a relatively small, urbanized area. We gave the climate conversation urgency by relating it to the summer of 2019 when Missoula County saw several wildfires approach downtown and the county spent much of the summer in a "state of emergency."[5] The climate section in the plan ends with a discussion of wildfire risk but begins with a discussion about worldwide global temperature increases due to manmade carbon pollution, because a warmer, drier Earth is directly related to wildfires. That section, the section related to the global emergency may prove to be the most relevant part of the plan in the times ahead.

What are the local weather-related emergencies in your community? Hazardous events that should have been mere inconveniences become emergencies when communities aren't prepared. Climate now needs to be part of every planning conversation because catastrophic events are becoming more common and more dangerous.

130 ■ *Why Are We Doing This?*

The Call

There is another aspect to climate change work, which I refer to as "the call." It is a call to action, and at the risk of sounding preachy I recommend that you let yourself "hear the call" and follow it where it takes you. The call disrupts the comfort of ordinary life (including the somewhat straight-forward and safe professional life of urban planners) and leads individuals and communities on a kind of quest. This kind of quest (a kind of quest we see often in movies, literature, religious narratives, and in history) begins with a direct threat to the safety of the community. In the context of this book, the threat is posed by climate-related and weather-related hazards.

Working to avoid calamity can bring communities together in a way few things can. Communities that work together on climate planning develop a connection that makes them more resilient no matter what happens in the future. Why is climate planning so galvanizing? The climate emergency involves a worldwide threat which is playing out on a grand scale; the stakes are high and there is a lot of work that needs to be done. It feels worth people's time. Climate work is also personally fulfilling. One gets to play a small part in a large, important, collective effort. You are no longer a climate bystander. It can feel empowering. As philosopher and author Albert Camus famously suggested, the struggle itself is enough to fulfill the human heart.

Another, less discussed, feature of the climate crisis conversation I have noticed is that it is relatively new in popular culture. People are reading recently published books, or watching newly made documentaries, and sitting down and impressing themselves and others with how much they have learned. There is a kind of climate planning *fandom* afoot in activist circles, or at least, the climate conversation is not the same old "save the trees" conversation. We have to admit that at this point in history the community-character-versus-development dialogue reads from a stale and tired script involving height, noise, privacy, traffic concerns, urban wildlife, and property values. I am not saying that this is not an important conversation to have, just that it is a conversation with familiar talking points and firmly established battle lines. By contrast, the climate conversation is fresh and in my work on climate I have seen new voices, unlikely alliances, interesting ideas, and even surprising friendships arise.

Notes From the Field

Adding Water Conservation and Reuse to Plan El Paso's Sustainability Element

In August 2019 El Paso, Texas mourned the senseless loss of 22 people killed during a mass shooting at a Walmart Store. It was a hate crime committed against Hispanic border residents and it will probably not be the last mass-shooting in El Paso given the political proclivity to demonize immigrants. This kind of event forces us to

Climate Planning Objection 5 ■ 131

Figure 5 Presidio Chapel of San Elizario, Texas

ask: Doesn't El Paso have larger issues to worry about than climate? In a country in which mass killings occur once every two weeks,[6] aren't there much more pressing issues?

To their credit, El Paso residents don't think so. In July 2011, as part of the *Plan El Paso* Comprehensive Plan Process, I co-led a workshop with El Paso's Open Space Advisory Board to review the draft Comprehensive Plan. I met Charlie Wakeem,

132 ■ *Why Are We Doing This?*

the Chairman of the Board, a tall, soft-spoken man who ran a furniture company for 30 years before dedicating his time to Rotary Clubs, neighborhood associations, land trusts, and several city boards and committees. It seemed to me that Charlie found meaning in life by answering many various calls to public service. Despite a quiet voice he had a solid reputation in the community, and city commissioners and citizen activists listened to Charlie.

"You know Jason, this is good," Charlie said of the first draft of the Sustainability Element of the Comprehensive Plan, "but there's a lot of activities that we're working on that we need this plan to support."

Charlie and the Open Space Advisory Board wanted to add more to the plan and make plan language stronger. They wanted a section on dark sky compliant lighting, a section recommending that the city convert its fleet to renewable energy vehicles, clustering requirements for subdivisions to protect farms, a recommendation that stormwater facilities be designed as vegetated, parklike amenities instead of empty pits, and more protections for the arroyos, the dry riverbeds which provide habitat for desert life and provide scenic hiking and biking opportunities.

"The way things are going it is only going to get hotter here in El Paso," Charlie said to me referring to the climate challenge.

On the other end of the political spectrum, our meeting with the Chamber of Commerce the month before had focused on removing items from the plan and making plan language weaker. Their wish list included changing plan language from "shall" to "shall consider" and from "will not" to "should not" when it came to environmental protections. The Chamber of Commerce representatives on our steering committee recommended we add the caveat "wherever feasible" to action items that talked about trail and parkland dedications. They wanted the plan's long-range time horizon to be emphasized, and our illustrative plans of compact, walkable, mixed-use development to be clearly labeled "illustrative" so as not to tie their hands. And when it came to the arroyos, they wanted a distinction made between major arroyos and minor ones because they felt that the preservation of all the dry riverbeds in the city's emerging suburban areas would be too costly in some cases and physically impossible in others.

When drafting city plans, this kind of tug-of-war is to be expected. We encourage it. We draft plans that are consensus documents and palatable to everyone (ideally) and when that's not possible we routinely say, "Everyone gets something they want, and no one gets everything." At that point in the Comprehensive Plan creation process, we had involved over 500 participants at public workshops, over 300 attendees at 50 stakeholder meetings, and more than 18,000 people participating via the project website and Virtual Town Hall. Struggles between various interests were built into the process.

"This is tough," I said to Carlos Gallinar, one of the city's *Plan El Paso* project directors, over lunch at L&J's Café – a small and congenial place where we went to recover after tough meetings. We'd just finished a meeting with the Chamber of

Climate Planning Objection 5 ■ **133**

Commerce in which (and why does this seem so inevitable?) the Chamber's representative to the plan called our work "high-handed interference" and "Mexican-style socialism."

"This is good. We're talking to a lot of people," Carlos said to me with his usual and untiring sangfroid.

However, there was one issue that both the Open Space Advisory Board and Chamber of Commerce agreed on: Water. They both endorsed Goal 10.1 (*Continue developing options to provide sustainable water supply for the City of El Paso for the use and enjoyment of future generations*) and neither had any objections to the policy items which followed – even policies under a climate change banner. The plan's policies supported water resource management and the integration of drought contingency plans into all aspects of city operations, both public and private.

The Open Space Advisory Board, a left-leaning political group when it came to state and local politics, didn't object at all to energy-consumptive desalinization technology, restricting the use of water for agricultural purposes during droughts (even when restrictions meant some farms could become financially infeasible and ultimately disappear), or the conversion of neighborhood parks to xeriscaping, even at the cost of community character.

The Chamber of Commerce, a right-leaning group representing real estate developers, home builders, and ranchers, agreed with policies that protected surface water and groundwater from contamination by hazardous materials by limiting land uses near water reserves, agreed to new requirements for development near aquifer recharge zones and wetlands including a multitude of water harvesting strategies for new development, and even agreed with policies to stop fracking and natural resource extraction that would affect water quality. The Chamber of Commerce's bulldoggish representative also had no problem with climate change language. This surprised me because Rick Perry, the Republican Governor of Texas at the time, called climate science a "contrived phony mess" in his book *Fed UP!* and I saw three copies of that book on the coffee table of the waiting room in the Chamber's office.

This all makes sense. El Paso is dry. Both sides of the political spectrum could see it. Whether plan participants were on the political right or left in El Paso – with all the dogmatic ideology and perceptual blinders that comes with politics – they could still recognize that Homo sapiens have serious water requirements which could not be ignored. Both sides knew that they had to work together when it came to protecting a limited resource.

In some ways the plan divided the city among the two interests. The Comprehensive Plan created a Future Land Use Map which consigned nearly half the city's land to preservation sectors and the other half to intense development. The plan was endorsed by the El Paso Water Utilities Public Service Board as a way to keep water delivery infrastructure costs low and prices low. Endorsement from the Water Board was highly influential.

134 ■ *Why Are We Doing This?*

Plan El Paso was unanimously adopted by the City Council with the support of the Open Space Board and Chamber of Commerce and was the only city initiative to have the support of both except for other plans related to water conservation. This isn't to say they agreed on every detail of the plan. Water supply and water quality is significantly affected by the amount of development a city allows and it goes without saying that the Open Space Board and Chamber of Commerce didn't see eye-to-eye on that issue.

The *Plan El Paso* Comprehensive Plan was about more than water. *Plan El Paso* was about economic resilience as much as climate resilience, because from a certain perspective, these are the same thing. After the plan was adopted, the City approved a US$450 million quality-of-life bond for parks and open spaces, redesigned San Jacinto Plaza following our designs, installed a fleet of restored historic streetcars on two loops, added a downtown baseball stadium, installed 8 miles of two-way protected bike lanes, updated their land development regulations to encourage compact development, and streamlined development approvals. Today, a new children's museum and the first new residential high-rise tower in 80 years are under construction in El Paso's downtown.

Most downtown resurgence is simply a consequence of supply and demand. The supply of land goes down and the demand for passed-over places (like downtown) goes up. What amazes me is how El Paso continues to improve its downtown despite plenty of supply. There are many places at the edge to build new and plenty of places near the downtown to fix up. Even still, the downtown gets better and better without any of the demand-side advantages of places we see in San Antonio, Austin, Atlanta, or Boston. El Paso's downtown continues to improve by force of will and great leadership. Without that force of will and leadership, El Paso would be like so many other places where I work where it feels either nothing is happening, or things are happening so very slowly.

El Paso's downtown is alive again with residences, restaurants, shopping, music venues, and workplaces. Of the many awards that *Plan El Paso* won, I think the most gratifying was the 2011 National Award for Smart Growth Achievement from the Environmental Protection Agency (EPA) because that award said: Yes, the work planners do is essential to the environment and that includes planning for water and planning for a changing climate.

Notes From the Field

Failing (Almost) to Discuss Climate with a Vulnerable Population in the Mission Valley of El Paso

We must continually renew our commitment to climate change work. We're playing a long game. Maybe we're strong for a day, a month, or a year, but new priorities arise, and we lose focus. In the summer of 2019, two major planning projects that

Climate Planning Objection 5 ■ **135**

I headed were concluding and the plans had no mention of climate change. Imagine that! Here were two community plans for the next 25 years that lacked any discussion of climate. How was that possible?

El Paso County's Mission Valley was one meeting away from approving a Comprehensive Plan and despite the claim to be *comprehensive* there was no mention of a warming, drying planet. The Mission Valley is a largely agricultural community in Texas, on the northern banks of the Rio Grande, in eastern El Paso County, and is home to 37,000 people as well as the Tigua Indian Reservation, the Ysleta del Sur Pueblo. Located in the northern part of the Chihuahuan Desert, the Mission Valley only saw 8 inches of rain a year and summer temperatures in the 90s and 100s (°F). By any estimate, the climate crisis would affect Mission Valley dramatically.

El Paso County is a different municipality from the City of El Paso, yet they both face the same challenges. We'd scored a major victory for climate planning with the City's Comprehensive Plan, *Plan El Paso*. It featured a detailed discussion of climate and a variety of goals, strategies, and action items, and yet just a few years later the Mission Valley Plan draft had zero discussion. Why? Because I felt Mission Valley had bigger problems.

Mission Valley is the poorest part of El Paso County and it struggles with low incomes, high poverty, low graduation rates, low homeownership and business ownership, dirt roads, and crumbling adobe structures. Our client was the El Paso County Economic Development Department and our job was to work with the multiple municipalities in the Valley to create a plan for improvement. Our job was also to work to have the historic areas in the valley added to the UNESCO (United Nations Educational, Scientific, and Cultural Organization) World Heritage Site List. Three seventeenth-century Spanish missions remain standing in the Valley and still function as churches: Ysleta Mission (1682), Socorro Mission (1759), and the San Elizario Chapel (1789). The quiet but amazing missions were unaccountably overlooked even though they should have been world famous. The climate emergency seemed the smallest of the place's problems and climate planning felt unhelpful to the job of economic development.

During my presentation of the draft plan to the Commissioners Court, County Judge Ricardo Samaniego sat forward in his seat behind the elevated dais and asked, "What will it take to make things happen in Mission Valley?" He had a long grey mustache, squinty grey eyes, and the kind of tall, angular head shape that looked perfect for a cowboy hat.

"The plan," was my response. "That's what it will take. The whole plan. There is no silver bullet. It will take investments in education, infrastructure, and quality of life." I described how the plan's goals, policies, and projects would work to improve life for locals as well as the experience for visitors. Once implemented, plan strategies would attract investment, and ultimately help secure a UNESCO World Heritage Site designation for the area.

136 ■ *Why Are We Doing This?*

I talked about how it was a long road to a UNESCO designation and how designation was far from guaranteed. However, the Mission Valley was on the old Camino Real, the 1,400-mile trail of cities, towns, missions, presidios, and monuments, that formed the backbone of Spain's Colonial Empire. The Camino Real De Tierra Adentro, the remains of the Camino Real through Mexico, had been recognized by UNESCO in 2010 and so El Paso County simply needed to push for that recognition to be extended across the international border to its three missions. Every place we had studied in our research that had become recognized by UNESCO saw a steady stream of tourists. Tourism and tourism-based economies have their downsides, but overall tourism would help the Valley.

"The plan? That's what will turn things around?" the County Judge asked, sitting back in his seat. "Well, I read it and it is an excellent plan," he said to the commissioners to his right and left. "Thank you for your work," he said to me. I could picture him on a white horse, gently touching the brim of his hat at this point and saying something like, "Much obliged." I could tell that the plan adoption process would go smoothly.

How would a discussion of climate change and the Valley's long-term problems help the people of the Mission Valley? My client was an economic development office, not a long-range planning or sustainability office. The plan's goals came out of the discussions we had locally, and no one had mentioned climate change. Does climate change need to be part of every local plan? Would that conversation jeopardize plan adoption in a place that sorely needed an economic development plan?

The people in the Valley we'd talked to had, however, described how 2019 had been the hottest year they could remember. At one of the charrette tables that I facilitated they talked about the massive floods they had seen years earlier. That flood was caused by fast-moving water down dry slopes that no longer held living vegetation.

We heard a lot about rising water bills. The vast size of El Paso County, its rapid growth, and the drain on the Hueco Bolson aquifer had ended the days of inexpensive drinking water. They talked about decreasing levels of water from the Rio Grande for farming and increased water rationing. They talked about dry soil under their fields. We'd met with hundreds of people and while no one said the words *climate change* they were already dealing with its symptoms. And things would get worse.

Climate change should be part of all local planning, but it isn't a given. It isn't automatic yet. I woke up feeling guilt one morning over my dereliction. I can't say what started it, but it may have been a conversation I had with my kids the night before. I told them stories from when I lived in Cairo. I described the fun parts: Riding a camel past the pyramids and commuting by ferry on the Nile. I told them about the hard parts: I was sick a lot; the water supplies weren't very clean and sometimes a single cube of ice in my fruit juice could make me very unwell. Travelling the Middle East before 9/11, I used to sleep on the floor of mosques to save money and in many of my pictures were men in traditional *galabiyas*. Many

Climate Planning Objection 5 ■ 137

were beggars. My son remarked that the sandy, squalid city in the background of a picture of me having breakfast outside a mosque looked like "a wreck."

"Yeah," I said.

"Why?"

"They are poor and it's a desert."

Was Cairo a glimpse into the future? The capital of Egypt is a city with massive numbers of people huddled on a river that is shrinking. Egyptian developers, including developers I would later work for as an urban planner, wanted to move the city's wealthy out of the crowded, dusty, smog-filled city and into a new area. In the late 1990s when I lived in Cairo, the place felt like it was on the verge of environmental and social collapse. That's what climate change will probably look like across the world. Maybe even in El Paso's Mission Valley.

It's impossible to say what makes us change our mind and it is probably never just one thing, but nevertheless, after talking with my kids about Cairo I sent an email to my client at the County Economic Development Department in which I made the case that UNESCO would want to see long-term thinking in the Comprehensive Plan. I told her I would add a climate change discussion along with goals and strategies even though the County Court had already been presented the plan and the additions might set back the adoption process.

To my surprise, my client, Valerie Venecia, Heritage Tourism Coordinator of the El Paso County Economic Development Department, encouraged the climate discussion even though it meant delays. She saw the need. She saw beyond the narrow parameters of "economic development." I think we were both proud of the plan that El Paso County ultimately adopted.

Just a month later it happened again. I was in Missoula, Montana, working through the adoption meetings on a Downtown Master Plan and climate change wasn't mentioned in the plan. The Missoula Downtown Partnership, Downtown Association, and Business Improvement District had all endorsed the plan, and approval from the City Commission was imminent. I was in Missoula for the adoption meetings and saw a roughly sketched image of what looked like a reticent young girl in a rain jacket on a flyer.

"Who is that?" I asked my team, but no one knew. The flyer had been pasted to a brick building on Higgins Avenue and advertised an upcoming school strike. We should have recognized the young woman's image because months before, in May 2019, Greta Thunberg had been featured on the cover of *Time* magazine.

The Swedish teenager was known for raising global awareness of climate change and holding politicians accountable. Some people attribute Thunberg's success to her autism, her hypervigilant inability to look away from the topic of climate change as the rest of the world averts its eyes. She inspired school strikes across the planet and on September 20, 2019, while I was in Missoula, millions of people took to the streets around the world in one of the largest youth-led demonstrations in history. They delivered a stern message to world leaders everywhere: Do more to combat climate change and do it faster.

138 ■ *Why Are We Doing This?*

How would we include climate in an economic development plan in a relatively climate-resistant place? The city had an aquifer that recharged steadily and had enormous future capacity to accommodate growth. And while smoke from wildfires in the mountains could be a problem, fire had yet to approach even the city's outskirt hillside developments. What would my client say? Just like in El Paso, my client was someone charged with economic development, not resilience.

My client, Linda McCarthy, the Executive Director of the Downtown Business Partnership, said *yes* to a climate discussion immediately. Missoula's Downtown Master Plan now has a section on future climate challenges. It discusses the challenges reduced snowpack will pose to the city's drinking water one day, the increased threat of wildfires over time, the inevitable loss of agriculture, and the fossil fuel sources the city is powered from. The pushback against climate change planning in these two cases came from me, and not from the public or any special interests.

It's a credit to my clients that they both recognized that cities that look these challenges in the eye will be stronger, ultimately, for it. Maybe one day climate adaptation will be part of the scope of work for every project, public or private. At this time in history, though, it is a question of politics, budget, and conviction – conviction to keep climate at the front of everything. This is "the call."

Notes From the Field

Conversations with Skeptics

You can't help but feel like a hypocrite when you fly to a climate change conference – I mean, isn't it kind of like adding jet fuel to a fire you're trying to put out? Isn't it *exactly* like that? Couldn't those presentations be been done via WebEx? Zoom? A conference call? According to my American Airlines app I flew 45,502 miles on 51 flights in 11 months over the 2018 to 2019 period. When I plugged that number into my carbon footprint app I saw that my flights added 2.4 million pounds of carbon dioxide to the atmosphere. I was a super emitter and part of the 1% of fliers causing 50% of global aviation emissions.[8] The feeling of guilt was visceral. I could picture my carbon footprint app strangling my American Airlines app in the middle of the night while I slept.

Nevertheless, I fly to climate conferences quite often. I hope that the good I do with my presentations are worth the environmental cost. So much of our environmental footprint is just baked right into everyday professional expectations. They feel unavoidable. I take comfort in the fact that the personal contact with conference hosts and attendees is probably the most valuable part of the experience – and that can't be done via video communications.

In 2019, Frederic Dalbin of Wright and Dalbin Architects, one of hosts of the 12th Annual Eco El Paso Sustainability Conference, drove me and another speaker up El Paso's Rim Road on the night before we were to present. Some say that Rim

Climate Planning Objection 5 ■ **139**

Road was built as a Works Progress Administration (WPA) project in the 1930s to give visitors to El Paso a scenic view. Others say the WPA simply rebuilt a road that was built much earlier with the purpose of aiming cannons at Ciudad Juárez in Mexico because the U.S. wanted to keep the Mexican Revolution from spilling over. Whatever the case, I gazed southwest across the border from El Paso into Juárez, between the Sierra de Juárez and Franklin Mountains, and at the twinkling lights of a million people huddled together within the pass.

What would climate change be like for these people? A disaster, probably. Both sides. For the American El Pasoans, though, it would probably be an obstacle they could meet. For the people of Juárez who led impossibly tough lives already, it might be the crisis that ended everything. I didn't say any of that to my host. We stayed positive and simply wondered aloud about what made the lights twinkle.

The next day I attended the conference with a ready PowerPoint.

"They banned plastic straws even though all the plastic straw trash in the world comes out of three rivers and none of them are the Rio Grande," a conference attendee, a local architect, said to me between speakers.

"I miss plastic straws," I said. "They gave me one the other day at a fair and I wanted to keep it in my pocket and carry it around."

"McDonald's won't even give you a plastic straw."

"Awful."

The architect laughed and leaned in, building up to his point. I hadn't presented yet but assumed he had read my speaker's bio and knew that I was the "Climate Guy" at the environmental conference.

"My mouth sticks to the wood," he said as he pointed to the wooden utensils they used at the conference held in the Shriner's Auditorium in El Paso. The room outside the Shriner's auditorium had all the mythological paintings and sculpture of a mystery cult: Egyptian snake staves, Arabian scimitars, half-moons and big paintings depicting the weird, less-discussed stories of the Bible. Windowless (of course), it felt like Imhotep's tomb.

"Wooden utensils … imagine *that* splinter," I said. I'm the Climate Guy, sure, but I'm a normal person, too. And every normal person hates wooden utensils.

"So, I checked the weather on Mars yesterday," the architect said. "It's getting warmer. And Saturn is getting warmer," he whispered. I felt that I was being tested for admission into a secret society. It felt like we should have been wearing funny hats with gold tassels.

"Huh."

"No SUVs on Saturn."

"Right."

This is a common climate argument. If warming is happening throughout the solar system then clearly it must be the Sun causing the rise in temperatures, including the temperatures here on Earth. Of course, one can't actually "check" the weather on Mars. Only Earth has weather stations. And even if we could get a weather report from the outer planets, they have vastly longer orbital periods than Earth,

140 ■ *Why Are We Doing This?*

so any changes in their climate would be seasonal. Saturn and its moons take 30 Earth years to orbit the Sun and so three decades of observations equates to only one Saturnian year.[9] The other problem with his assertion that the Sun is getting stronger was the fact that the Sun is, in fact, experiencing a cycle of weaker heat.[10] Should I have told him all this? I didn't want to get the look that said *Don't talk down to me, Climate Guy.* I just wanted to engage in some small talk before my presentation. I was nervous. Small talk helps.

"Don't you think this is all just part of some big cycle?" the architect asked. "I mean, what do you really think about this whole carbon dioxide theory?"

"Well, I think there's a lot of factors when it comes to climate."

"That's right." He leaned in even closer. "What do you think about biking to work?"

Was he going to hate on cyclists? Was he going to blame El Paso's morning traffic on the newly created two-way protected bike lane I helped plan on Mesa Drive?

"Bike lanes, don't get me started. What next? A vegan-only lane?" I could say in order to complete my initiation into the secret club. "I don't know," I said instead. "What do you think?"

"I bike to work. I bike whenever I can. I have solar panels on my home. But you know, I just don't think people are causing this warming thing."

"Okay." That was all I said. It was interesting, though, that this architect biked whenever possible, had installed solar panels on his home, attended an environmental conference, and was still a "climate denier." The problem with "climate denier" (or any other moniker) is that we immediately define the person we're talking about too narrowly. People come in all kinds.

Maybe he was only *green* because architects are expected to be green professionally or maybe he could only be green up to a point. We all have that point. I mean, I fly to climate conferences. It was time for me to present *El Paso: 2050*, a model I'd built of the region described later in this book. I took the stage and after introducing myself and thanking our hosts began to present.

"The world is warming. Whether or not you believe the warming is caused by people is up to you." I hadn't planned to say that. I said it because of the conversation I'd had with the architect. I've noticed that when I'm presenting to a crowd, even a large crowd of a thousand or more, I'm mostly just presenting to three or four people, continuing whatever conversation we'd already had.

My presentation included projections for El Paso in 2050 and 2100, and I concluded by saying, "Climate change is a big problem but we can't be paralyzed by it. We need to do what we can right now." I showed a slide that included recommendations such as:

■ Vote for *solar* candidates, *transit* candidates, and *downtown* candidates in local elections

■ Tell El Paso to apply pressure on El Paso Electric to diversify and encourage decentralized power generation

Climate Planning Objection 5 ■ **141**

- Install solar power in your home and workplace
- Plant one tree on your street and one in your backyard this weekend; if the City says there's a rule against this, then pay the fine and politely ask them to change the rule
- Follow the water discussion and keep in mind that El Paso faces a Day Zero, a day when the water won't turn on

When my presentation was over, I went back to the room with the pyramids, orbs, and oil paintings stained by many years of candle smoke. I went back to the comfortable retreat of small talk.

"Do you know the first item that got a tariff under Trump?" I was asked after my presentation by a different attendee as we all sipped wine and ate cold cuts and cheese.

"I don't."

"Solar panels," the long-haired professor from a local university said to me. "He placed a tariff on solar panels and then the sale of solar panels dropped. The only way Trump's presidency makes sense is if you view it as the installation of a petro-chemical shill."

"Think so?" I asked. I picture myself giving the professor a single arched eyebrow.

"Don't you think?"

I could feel him scanning me for an in-group reaction that would mark me as one of the tribe. Do I think that there's a covert conspiracy, an invisible hand, protecting oil interests? Not quite. I think there is a conspiracy, but I don't think it's covert or invisible. Like any other well-connected, well-funded industry they don't need secret handshakes. Actually, it isn't really a conspiracy, it's just an overrepresented constituency. One of many.

"Don't you think?" he asked again pointing a finger at me. He wasn't going to just let me smile and nod. Did I think that President Trump was "installed" by anyone other than, say, a million or so people who voted for Trump because he spoke to them in a way Democrats didn't? No. "Do you really think that the most powerful industry in the world's history doesn't pick U.S. presidents?" the professor asked.

"I never thought about it that way," I said nodding thoughtfully but moving slowly away from the man. "If you'll excuse me. It's a lot drier here than in Florida." I lifted my empty wine glass. Nevertheless, he followed me to the marble altar table with the crystal wine carafe and the plastic jewel candelabras.

"The last five presidents were petro-chemical shills," he said. "Does it surprise you that I included Obama?"

It surprised me that the wine had gone so fast. With no wine left it looked like I'd be drinking water. I half-listened as I looked around the room at the cruciform swords and paintings of Outer Worlds. I learned from the professor (and when I use the word *learned* in this story imagine me making bunny ears with my fingers in the air each time) about right-wing secret petro-chemical cabals. I learned that every war in history was ultimately fought over fuel of some kind. I learned that the horror that

142 ■ *Why Are We Doing This?*

would be unleashed on the world due to willful climate ignorance was so bad that the political right would one day rank among the world's most genocidal political movements.

As I inched away, the professor closed the gap every time. Now, I am a patient person, as anyone who doesn't know me exceedingly well will tell you, and I nodded and smiled politely, but I don't like sermons. When I am on my soapbox, I hope I don't ever come across as pushy as the petro-conspiracy guy.

"Well, I must be going," I said. I shook his hand. He shook mine. I think he expected that I'd be leaving for the airport that moment, but instead I simply crossed the room and attacked a recently arrived carafe of wine and charcuterie board.

Did I mention the two sphinxes (with noses still intact) outside the Mason Hall and how the shape of the hall was a cross between a pyramid and a spaceship? Weird. In retelling this story to friends, I like to dwell on the secret society iconography and zanier snippets of conversation – even though the conference was really about sensible experts making highly useful local recommendations. Overemphasizing the weird makes a point. I think that climate is a big and interesting topic, some people will be consumed by it, there will not be enough fresh material within the parameters of normality to satisfy them, secrets and things done secretly are interesting, and all variety of theories will abound. Get ready.

Flying Back From the Climate Conference

I flew home the next morning. Flights east from El Paso to Atlanta involve smaller model planes which stay low and let you scan the desert. I passed Dell City, the farm town El Paso would one day raid for water. I passed the Brokeoff Mountain Wilderness Area where no one ever goes because it's as harsh as the planet Mercury. I began to see the tiny beige squares of oil extraction pumps amid the great, fissured landscape. As I flew, I watched how the perfect squares of the pumpjack pads were all connected by roads that turned at right angles. It all looked reminiscent of a circuit board. The pumpjack pads intruded on big circular farms, once green, but now sand and lifeless. Above the craggy landscape, orange plumes of fire, 100 feet in the air, flickered.

I had taken that flight many times and I have started to notice, in the last five years, among the tiny squares of oil rigs that spread like measles as far as one can see, wind farms and even the occasional solar array. East of Midland, a town that has become an almost lunar labor colony of resource extraction, I saw lines of tall, slow-turning turbines. They often outnumbered the pumpjacks. Travelling even farther east, as the sun set pink and purple, at least 600 miles from El Paso, the beige unpaved streets and oil pads disappeared completely and wind turbines took over the landscape, marching up and down the hills in lines.

Windmills look lazy to me. They only seem to be turning half the time. Don't they realize what's at stake? Pumpjacks never take a break. But I must have seen at least 10,000 more windmills on the flight home from that conference than I'd seen the last time I'd taken that flight. I never would have seen any of that had I attended the conference via WebEx or Zoom. It was so incredibly encouraging.

Notes

1 World Meteorological Organization (2020). United in Science 2020. Science Advisory Group of the UN Climate Action Summit 2019. Retrieved from: https://public.wmo.int/en/resources/united_in_science

2 Frazin, R. (2019). Guardian updates style: Climate change now "climate emergency, crisis or breakdown." *The Hill*, May 17. Retrieved from: https://thehill.com/policy/energy-environment/444327-guardian-updates-style-climate-change-now-climate-emergency-crisis

3 *Financial Times* (n.d.). Europe's migration crisis. Retrieved from: www.ft.com/stream/e3dc7191-4121-460a-ab08-89c73d3895e9

4 Babcock, M. (2013). State hazard mitigation plans & climate change: Rating the states. Center for Climate Change Law. Columbia Law School. Retrieved from: https://web.law.columbia.edu

5 Kidston, M. (2019). Missoula County declares "state of emergency" as fire danger grows and weather looms. *Missoula Current*, July 31. Retrieved from: https://missoulacurrent.com/outdoors/2019/07/missoula-fire-emergency/

6 Hoyer, M. and Heath, B. (2012). Mass killings occur in USA once every two weeks. *USA Today*, December 19. Retrieved from: www.usatoday.com/story/news/nation/2012/12/18/mass-killings-common/1778303/

7 Perry, R. and Gingrich, N. (2010). *Fed Up! Our Fight to Save America from Washington*. New York: Little, Brown and Company, p. 98.

8 Carrington, D. (2020). 1% of people cause half of global aviation emissions – study. *The Guardian*, November 17. Retrieved from: www.theguardian.com/business/2020/nov/17/people-cause-global-aviation-emissions-study-covid-19

9 Cook, J. (2010). Pluto warms while the sun coold. *Skeptical Science*. Retrieved from: https://skepticalscience.com/pluto-global-warming.htm

10 NOAA Headquarters (2019). Scientists predict sun's activity will be weak during next solar cycle. Phys.org, April 8. Retrieved from: https://phys.org/news/2019-04-scientists-sun-weak-solar.html

Chapter 6

Climate Planning Objection 6

"Retreat is not an option. Everywhere in the world is prone to some kind of natural disaster. We need to take a stand."

Every part of the U.S. is periodically impacted by some kind of natural disaster: Volcanos in Hawaii, earthquakes on the West Coast, wildfires in the mountains, record-heat in the Southwest, tornadoes across the Great Plains, floods across the Mississippi states, and hurricanes on the East Coast. However, there are some natural disasters that are more predictable, dangerous, and costly than others. Homes on hurricane-prone coastlines, within flood zones, or on fire-prone hillsides, for example, see repeat losses. Urban planning works to restrict development in those areas and in the future we will need to plan for their retreat.

In general, the public can see the logic in this. "You should zone dangerous places for nothing but farms or natural space," people often tell urban planners, but that's rarely possible.

Zoning is the urban planner's main tool. Zoning laws seem inconsequential at times because their primary purpose is merely to designate land uses, and land uses like residential, commercial, office, and industry have natural locations determined by the market and so zoning designations usually just follow the market. However, when the average person talks about *zoning* and the power of zoning, they don't just

DOI: 10.4324/9781003181514-8

145

146 ■ *Why Are We Doing This?*

mean the separation of uses, they are using the word more generically and they are referring to all the tools in the land use and development code toolkit including floodplain management requirements, overlay zoning for fire hazard severity zones, urban development boundaries, rate of growth ordinances, steep slope ordinances, large-lot zoning, the transfer of development rights, and other land preservation tools. Thought of that way, *zoning* can be powerful. Urban planners truly can forbid development and limit density in places where density can be dangerous. We need to do this more.

The fire in Paradise, California, in 2018, known as the *Camp Fire* (and named after Camp Creek Road, its place of origin), was the deadliest and most destructive fire in California history[1] and lax zoning laws were in large part to blame. The densely populated foothill town of Paradise shouldn't have been allowed to grow and it certainly shouldn't have been allowed to reduce the size of its travel lanes on its emergency evacuation route. Urban planners had been warned by one fire hazard study after another, including a Grand Jury report which recommended a moratorium on new home construction in fire-prone areas[2] that was ultimately overturned by the local Board of Supervisors who called the Grand Jury report "not reasonable" and cited improved building codes and fire prevention requirements as reasons a moratorium wasn't necessary.[3] A discussion on whether or not to rebuild followed the fire, which destroyed over 11,500 homes in Paradise (90% of the town's total homes) and killed dozens. Let's focus on that discussion and talk about what went wrong.

"They didn't abandon New Orleans after *Katrina*, they're not abandoning Hawaii although there's a volcano going off, and they're not abandoning San Francisco despite the earthquake dangers," Mayor Jody Jones of Paradise said. "Anywhere you go, there's some risk of a natural disaster."[4]

Natural disasters do happen everywhere, but some areas have a record of repeat emergencies like floods and fires, and because of climate breakdown those areas will see more floods and fires in the future. Urban planners must use everything they have to stop development and keep people safe. There will be opposition. In Paradise, elected representatives stated that their constituents might be homeless if they weren't allowed to rebuild. It's a persuasive argument. California is one of the most expensive places in the world to live. After a devastating event wipes out the entire wealth of a family, how is that family supposed to move? Fire insurance policies and the federal flood insurance program require policy owners to rebuild in the same location in order to pay the claim. And although FEMA has begun to make steps toward changing this rule and has begun to implement pilot projects to encourage retreat, at this time FEMA won't help you if you want to move.

People do retreat after catastrophic weather events, but for how long? New Orleans, for example, lost roughly half of its population after Hurricane *Katrina* in 2005, and the city's population in 2019 was still only 85% of what it was before the storm. Similarly, the population of Miami dropped after the hurricane of 1926.[5] Planning for retreat, however, has been historically confounded by the inevitable return of people. Over time, the population of New Orleans is expected to rise above

Climate Planning Objection 6 ■ 147

pre-*Katrina* levels. Despite many catastrophic storms, the population of Southeast Florida increases by 750 people every day.

They are rebuilding Paradise, California. "Paradise will not be defeated by the Camp Fire," states the draft Long-Term Recovery Plan adopted by the Town Council on June 25, 2019.[6] I can't help but admire the zeal of urban planners working to create a plan based so firmly on the will of local people to rebuild. I, myself, argue that we can save parts of Miami and Louisiana to a world that is unconvinced. But so many people died in Paradise. Fires move much faster than hurricanes and are impossible to hide from. A forest fire can move 50 miles an hour across a landscape.

One planning consultant working in Paradise conducted a listening meeting in April 2019 and asked meeting attendees, "Will you return your kids to school in Paradise?" Some 36% responded YES, 31% responded NO, and 33% were UNDECIDED. I can't help but wonder if a community plan which encourages rebuilding will help convince the people who are undecided. Is that conscionable?

The Long-Term Recovery Plan for Paradise discusses making Paradise more resilient by adding emergency notification systems, placing utilities underground (including power lines which are a frequent cause of wildfires), rewidening evacuation routes that were previously narrowed, and adding missing road segments to improve evacuations. The plan talks about improving construction standards and maintaining 100 feet of clear defensible spaces around homes. Nowhere in the plan can it prove (or even suggest), however, that these additions would make living in Paradise safe again.

What if the people of Paradise rebuild their homes and then sell them to someone else? The current residents of Paradise will foist dangers on to new residents who don't understand the threat – new residents who never had the educational experience of staring into the gaping maw of hell. People forget tragic events. Remembering is the job of government.

I don't agree that Paradise should be rebuilt, and I am glad I wasn't hired to draft that plan. I imagine that there was tremendous influence to simply say "build back." Urban planners aren't hired to tell people what they can't do, or shouldn't do. They are hired to tell people how to do what they want to do. And I understand simply wanting to "get back to normal" after a disaster. It's a dangerous, but not impossible-to-understand, decision.

Local elected officials are highly dependent on outside information from professional planning consultants. Even the elected officials in wealthy communities only employ one or two staff people, and those staff tend to be younger and inexperienced. Too often, by the time these staff people have figured things out they move on to lobbying for vested interests. Local officials can easily be swayed to take no action, marginal action, or even the wrong action for fear of upsetting the public. Local officials reflect community values more than they shape them. When municipalities call in outside professionals to help decide an issue, we owe them more than our work, we owe them our judgment.

148 ■ *Why Are We Doing This?*

Plan for Retreat

In the future, there will be places that do not rebound after major disasters, and retreat will be a necessity. We must plan for this. The retreat from New Orleans after Hurricane *Katrina* was improvised; it was not planned or managed, disaster followed, and the results were often sad. In the aftermath of the storm, Americans everywhere read stories reported by the *Times-Picayune* and learned that there are many cultural, social, political, and economic reasons why people are attached to their neighborhoods and homes. Families were separated, displaced persons found it difficult to find work, and while New Orleans culture took root in several cities around the country, New Orleans refugees experienced economic, social, and cultural impoverishment away from NOLA. Planning for retreat before the storm could have alleviated some of these challenges.

Stories of the *Katrina* refugees were reminiscent of the journey of the Joad family, a fictional farm family in John Steinbeck's 1939 novel *The Grapes of Wrath* who escape the drought of the Dust Bowl during the Great Depression. In the novel, some of the family members make it to California. Others do not. And the ones who do make it find themselves living in inhumane, desperate circumstances. In *The Grapes of Wrath*, there was never government assistance, a state plan, or anything else to assist the Joads. Retreat planning helps prevent the suffering of makeshift resettlement.

When Discussing Retreat, Keep It Simple

In our work locally, we must simplify. Elected officials and the public are often unable to follow detailed explanations and scenarios with a thousand caveats. Paradoxically, urban planners are experts and every detail feels important to unlocking and understanding the big picture when you're an expert. We need to be more conservative when it comes to detail. The big question for shoreline communities like Miami Beach is how much will the seas rise? And when should a retreat begin? These are tough questions because the models can't tell us exactly what will happen in the distant future in large part because human actions are a major variable. Still, we must advise.

Southeast Florida's Climate Compact tells us to expect between 9 inches and 4 feet of sea-level rise by 2060.[7] As I have mentioned before, my *go-to* line (at the risk of over-simplifying) is, "Nine inches is manageable. Four feet is not." You will need a go-to line for your own local retreat planning conversations. "Areas with densities above 30 units per acre can be defended; areas below that cannot," I say. It took a long time and quite a bit of study to come to this conclusion. You'll need a rule of thumb to identify which places can pay for the infrastructure needed to keep a place habitable and which cannot.

"The world is warming, the ice is melting, and the sea is rising, and those are the facts," I say. I know, I know, every half degree of temperature increase or half-inch of sea-level rise is detrimental to someone on the globe, but as a practical matter we must keep it simple. The low-density, low-lying, single-family neighborhoods (which are usually only three to seven units per acre) will not be able to pay to lift their streets, pump their properties, and wall themselves off. Those are the communities that must plan retreat.

On the other side of the nation, the central question for dry places like Las Cruces, New Mexico, is how much hotter will it get and how much more heat can the population handle? The IPCC says to expect a roughly 4–7°F (2–5°C) rise by 2050. "Four degrees Fahrenheit seems manageable. Seven doesn't," I say. I know, I know, temperature increases won't be consistent across the globe, a worldwide rise in temperature tells us little about what will happen locally, but I have yet to find a study that states the exact change in temperature Las Cruces can expect.

What I have learned talking to water managers in Las Cruces, however, is that water levels on the Rio Grande fluctuate based on temperatures. Rising Rio Grande Basin temperatures, already increasing faster than at any other time in more than 10,000 years, are projected to sap the basin of one-third of its surface water supply by the end of the century.[8] It feels like a safe bet that 7°F warmer means that it is likely there simply won't be enough water.[9]

Given the projections for Southeast Florida and Las Cruces area, we should begin discussing retreat planning in the long term. Other places like the areas of Houston, which suffered catastrophic flooding after Hurricane *Harvey* (2017) dumped massive amounts of water, should have detailed plans for the short- and mid-term at this point because they very recently saw death and destruction and must expect to again. Areas of coastal Louisiana are no longer safe and will become increasingly unsafe. Retreat must already be underway. But where will people retreat to? How do we plan areas to receive climate refugees?

Notes From the Field

Planning for Climate Change In-migration in Hammond, Louisiana

"No one is going to move to a safer place until their home is obliterated." I hear this a lot in low-lying coastal communities threatened by sea-level rise and in deserts where long-term water supplies can't be guaranteed. I hear this a lot from, well, myself. "The residents of Miami Beach are here to stay," I said in a video interview for *Seven50* our plan for Southeast Florida. "Miami Beach is an island that we are going to reinforce."[10]

Here to stay. I think about that comment often. At this point in the book, you can already tell that the viability of Miami Beach is something I think about a lot. I spoke in that film as a Miami Beach resident, in, perhaps, a moment of exuberance and optimism.

In 2017, three years after I made that comment, Hurricane *Irma* sent me and my family running and we didn't know if we'd ever return to Miami Beach. Hurricane *Irma* was one of the Atlantic's strongest hurricanes measured by sustained winds (180mph) and central pressure (914hPa). On the morning of September 6, 2017, *Irma* made landfall in Barbuda as a Category 5 hurricane and began its devastating path across Saint Maarten, the British Virgin Islands, and Puerto Rico. On that

Figure 6 A Main Street building in Hammond, LA

morning, CNN had drawn a red line indicating the storm's projected path directly over Miami Beach.

We took our children's little hands (our two kids were pre-school age at that time) and crossed Jefferson Avenue to our packed car. All the parking spaces on our street that we always had to fight for were empty. All week, I had heard power saws cutting boards to protect windows, but the saws had stopped. I had weathered six hurricanes in the Keys during the 2004–2005 hurricane season and my wife had weathered some big ones including the epic Hurricane *Andrew*, but we didn't want to take any chances with our kids. We lived so close to the sea that from the roof of our Miami Beach condominium you could see the Atlantic Ocean. We drove all day and retreated to my in-law's home in Orlando.

As we fed ducks with the kids on a tranquil pond in Orlando my wife and I discussed what we would do if Miami was hit hard. We didn't want to return to a broken, unhealthy city. Not with kids. And we didn't want to return to another coastal Florida community and live in fear of another disaster. We discussed Ohio. We discussed the Northeast where I still have family. California? Where would we go? We could afford to ask that question. We were lucky. We had some savings, the option to work remotely, and skills we could use to get another job elsewhere if needed. We could move far away and start over. Hurricane *Irma* missed Miami and the question of where to relocate was postponed to another day.

One of our options for relocating was Hammond, Louisiana, in part because we had both worked to prepare that town to accept climate refugees. More planning of this kind will be needed in the future. After Hurricane *Katrina*, the town of Hammond, Louisiana saw a population spike as people fled north.[11] Flood victims had been driven from their homes with only the clothes on their backs, unsure if they would ever be able to return, and forced to build a new life in a new place. As the number of storms increased and the seas rose, the urban planners at the non-profit Center for Planning Excellence (CPEX) could see the need to retreat from New Orleans and other low-lying coastal areas. Our firm was hired in 2009 to lead a community involvement process in Hammond working with CPEX, to draft a Comprehensive Plan and a new Future Land Use Map for the town, and to help draft a Form-Based Code to facilitate urban infill.

To reach Hammond from New Orleans you travel across a spit of land between Lake Maurepas and Lake Pontchartrain. Hammond is located north of Interstate 12 and, once there, you feel like you've reached Louisiana's mainland. Hammond has an average elevation of 43 feet[12] compared to New Orleans, which is between 1 and 2 feet below sea level.[13] The small town had a population of around 20,000 people at the time and wanted a plan that would handle newcomers while at the same time maintaining the place's high quality of life.

When we began our work, it was clear that Interstate 12 was already perceived as the safe line for development, and companies and governmental agencies had already started to move their services north of the interstate. The town was over 90-minute drive from New Orleans at rush hour, and so it was unlikely that the development

152 ■ *Why Are We Doing This?*

the area was experiencing was simply suburban expansion for people who planned to work in New Orleans. We were watching relocation.

Hammond had seen millions of dollars' worth of new residential construction since *Katrina* and *For Sale* signs on the lawns of new homes were everywhere. New growth primarily took the form of single-family homes and not the less expensive multi-family homes that would be necessary to house a less affluent, and displaced urban population.

Where should multi-family housing be built? That was the question posed to us. This is a dilemma for urban planners everywhere. The residents of established single-family neighborhoods generally don't want to see apartment buildings appear on the unbuilt lots next door. People living in single-family houses dread the extra height, parking lots, dumpsters, and bright security lighting. New multi-family developments can bring down property values. Homeowners are also afraid that renters will be louder, less respectful, and less accountable to the neighborhood than owners.

Working with the town we realized that the real opportunity to build affordable housing was along Hammond's commercial corridors. In most U.S. municipalities, major corridors are zoned for commercial development and are only allowed to have stores and restaurants. By placing stores and restaurants on the major streets the merchants get the visibility they need to attract customers, and noise and traffic are kept away from quieter neighborhoods. However, most places in the U.S. need a lot less commercial than they have zoned for. Today, urban planners must seek to mix uses more than in the past and reduce the negative externalities like noise, pollution, and blight caused by parking lots. We do this through design. Mixing residential units with stores and restaurants allows people the freedom to walk or bike from home to shopping, dining, and workplaces.

On Hammond's east side, along Roberts' Street, gorgeous Queen Anne Revival homes dated from 1880 and those residents communicated to our team that they would not be against new development as long as it fit in respectfully and didn't lower their property values. In the established neighborhoods around Robert's Street, the plan sought to strengthen the power of local historic districts to require development that fit the historic context. We gave presentations about how local developers once built duplexes and triplexes with just as much concern for design and aesthetics as we see in the town's mansion homes. Our plan required quality construction once again.

The plan encouraged accessory dwelling units, second homes on single-family house properties often referred to as *granny flats* or *tiny homes*, either above garages or in backyards. *Accessory dwelling units* is a building industry term for small units which are self-contained living areas usually located on the grounds of a single-family home.

The plan also encouraged the adaptive reuse of large estate homes into multi-family units by allowing the structures (some old and derelict) to be divided internally into apartments. All the plan's recommendations were voluntary, no one was required to subdivide their single-family lots. The plan simply expanded

Climate Planning Objection 6 ■ 153

the options property owners had. The plan identified specific intersections that were zoned for retail and restaurants that could become new centers with a mix of residential, commercial, open space, and businesses. Instead of single-story commercial and office structures, residential uses would be encouraged on upper floors as well. Townhomes and apartment buildings were encouraged throughout the long linear zones of exclusively commercial development. The Future Land Use Map, a map consulted when applicants seek to change zoning, was upgraded with a *mixed-use commercial* designation in order to unlock development potential.

The Hammond Comprehensive Plan showed hypothetical build-out plans depicting how new development would occur at the intersections. Mixed use buildings, with commercial on the bottom floor, office or residential above, and parking hidden behind, would fill the typically empty parking lots of greying, declining, large retailers. Large expanses of parking would be broken into smaller blocks of roughly the same size as the town's historic blocks. Next, portions of the four-lane major arterial roadways would be redesigned into multi-way boulevards, big streets that could accommodate a lot of cars but use side access roads lined with street trees to make residential living on the major streets more palatable. The multi-way boulevards would help build walkable new pedestrian environments.

When the townhomes and apartments of private investment began to appear, public investments would become feasible with the use of tax capture strategies which spent the increased property tax revenue on amenities like street trees, playgrounds, trails, and even large public parks. Hammond could accommodate far more people while at the same time improving the quality of life of residents. Older residents would have the option of one day selling their larger homes to retire to condominiums with less upkeep and younger residents would have inexpensive places to purchase. And, importantly, as people began to leave the coasts to escape rising seas and storms there would be less expensive housing options for them to rent or purchase.

Hammond's Plan Ten Years Later

It's been nearly a decade since the Hammond Comprehensive Plan was adopted and it is still the City's official plan. The Form-Based Code which followed the plan codified plan principles. The region hasn't seen another direct hit from a major storm like *Katrina* of a Category 3 or higher. Although there have been several serious storms, including Hurricane *Laura* in 2020, Hammond has returned to growing slowly.

The City of New Orleans continues to grow quickly. The city saw its population cut in half after the storm and it has largely rebounded. Specifically, New Orleans' population was roughly 495,000 in 1990, 210,000 in 2006, and 390,000 in 2020.[14] In Hammond, transformations of the drive-only, single-use commercial areas into

154 ■ *Why Are We Doing This?*

areas of walkable mixed-use urbanism like we drew in our renderings have not been seen. However, the Downtown's transformation has, nevertheless, been remarkable.

Thanks in large part to historic tax credits and façade grants recommended by the plan, 90% of historic buildings in Hammond are now occupied. The city's vacancy rate is the lowest in its history. In addition to rehabilitation, several new mixed-use buildings have been constructed in the Downtown and new apartment buildings with affordable units were constructed throughout the town.

One mixed-use building on Morris Street, *200 Downtown*, designed by Holly and Smith Architects, particularly exemplifies the principles of the plan. The building has bank offices on the bottom floor, and 12 affordable rental apartments on the second floor and within its side wings. It's an elegant building with long, linear storefronts and awnings that shade a new tree-lined sidewalk. Parking is located away from the street and accessed by a rear alley.

Another successful infill project, *Square 71*, is a mixed-use block at the intersection of Railroad Avenue and Morris Avenue with restaurants on the ground floors and apartments above. Wrought iron steel balconies and a brick veneer are in keeping with the vernacular of Hammond's historic district. The block is expanding, and multi-family, mixed-use buildings are replacing small shotgun homes. The urban block will be home to many more people and businesses without sacrificing the quality of the place.

Under the town's former development codes, these sites would only have been allowed to become box-like buildings surrounded by parking. The new plan, future land use map, and land development regulations allowed a mix of uses. As a trade-off for the higher quality design and street-oriented architecture required by the code, each site has more area that may to be built on and fewer parking spaces required.

Along Hammond's major streets, new apartment complexes were built in areas that were previously designated for commercial uses. The new apartments address the street better than before; the buildings are located on streets with sidewalks instead of in the center of parking lots and behind gates.

New accessory dwelling units have now begun to appear behind single-family homes. As multi-generational housing becomes more accepted, granny flats are likely to become more prevalent. The City of Hammond allows these granny flats to be rented. This is an important point. Accessory dwelling units are too often prevented by zoning laws from becoming rental units. Every granny flat Hammond adds doubles the housing capacity on a single-family lot.

The Hammond Comprehensive Plan had many transportation, recreation, public facilities, quality of life and resilience goals which, despite the slow growth of the community, are in the process of being implemented. Ten years after plan adoption, the list of plan achievements is long and the plan's primary goal has been advanced. The town is now more ready to accommodate people when the next emergency comes. Retreat from the coast can begin without the panic, rush, and political pushback of a forced retreat.

Notes From the Field

Stormwater and Flooding Management in Miami Beach

I think it is accurate to say that every major coastal municipality in the U.S. is committed to the place they were first settled despite the rising seas and worsening storms of climate change because retreat is not discussed. The plan – at least in the short- and mid-term – is to fortify. In the most vulnerable cities, the plan for the long term is probably best described as "wait and see."

Generally, a wait-and-see attitude is prudent, although building whole new cities and moving populations isn't unknown to the field of urban planning. We study St. Petersburg, ordered by Peter the Great, which is now the second largest city in Russia; Shenzhen in China, a city for 20 million that rose from nothing in 40 years; Brasilia and the many new cities of Brazil; and Saudi Arabia's Red Sea mega-cities. However, those new cities were all built under exceptional circumstances. Every practical cost assessment sides with reinforcing urban centers over retreating. Whatever happens in Miami Beach will provide a blueprint — for better or worse – for the whole world.

On cloudless days, days that haven't seen a drop of rain, the streets of Miami Beach are sometimes flooded as sea water flows up into the streets through the drainage pipes, sewer grates, and manholes. This happens during high tides and every October during King Tide. King Tides are caused by a particular alignment of Sun, Moon, and Earth which makes the Earth's gravity field slightly stronger in certain places.

I lived in Miami Beach from 2008 to 2018 and during King Tides my wife and I had to commute through a vast puddle of seawater in her low-to-the-ground MINI Cooper to reach the causeway that connects Miami Beach to the mainland. No matter what the height of the water my wife shrieked a little as we splashed onward. She pictured the car stalling in the puddle and having to escape through the sunroof. She looked me up and down as I breakfasted on my Cuban junk food and wondered if I'd fit through.

One occasion the water rose higher and higher as we drove –above the front bumper, then to the highest point on the tire, and then mid-way up the car door. The wave action from all the cars ahead of us caused the water to rise to the door window. Would the engine flood?

We drove through an acre-long puddle at the intersection of 5th Street and Alton Road, Miami Beach's front door, for years. When we took my wife's car to a mainland garage to have the tires replaced the mechanic looked at all the salt corrosion on the underside of the car and asked if we had recently moved to Florida from the north where they salted the roads in the winter.

In 2013, the sunny day flooding, flooding not caused by rain, started to make national news and we occasionally drove past news cameras set up on the high dry points of the sidewalk. This sight may have precipitated the startling Rolling Stone article "Goodbye Miami"[15] which concluded that "the unavoidable truth is that sea

156 ■ *Why Are We Doing This?*

levels are rising, and Miami is on its way to becoming an American Atlantis." After that article, every news organization in the world that wanted to feature climate change booked a room on Ocean Drive and reported from America's Atlantis.

Under Mayor Philip Levine in 2013 the city began to install backflow preventer valves, electric pumps, and enormous drainage pipes. The puddle at the intersection of 5th Street and Alton Road, which my wife and I drove through, disappeared. Then the city began to lift the streets. The city's plan was to lift every street to a minimum height of 3.7 feet. For most residential streets that meant a lift of over 2 feet.[16] King Tide in Miami Beach generally reaches about 2.2 feet.[17] My wife and I participated in local meetings and became supporters of adapting Miami Beach.

One of the installations was just a couple blocks from our house on 19th Street and Collins Avenue across from the coffee shop where we often spent Sunday mornings. Flat Miami Beach had its first hills, though they were so slight that only the locals noticed them. The plan was to raise streets and require real estate developers to lift new buildings to the new street level when it came time to build a new building or substantially remodel older ones.

Specifically, every building's lowest floor needed to be raised to a height above the minimum Base Flood Elevation. The Base Flood Elevation (BFE) is a computed elevation to which flood water is anticipated to rise during a flood. In general, buildings would be required to be lifted to a minimum of 8 feet above sea level NGVD (National Geodetic Vertical Datum). For most buildings this only meant 3 or 4 feet given that the average ground elevation of Miami Beach was around 4 feet.

The raised streets and pumps cost US$400 million citywide[18] and many areas that used to flood were suddenly completely dry, even during intense rain. But the move away from a gravity-fed stormwater system to an electric system had to be paid for entirely with local funding. Mayor Levine raised stormwater fees to pay upgrade costs, and this made sense. As a ratepayer I had no problem with the new costs. Later on, however, Mayor Levine realized that this was a politically fatal thing to do.

Federal and state funds were not available for the adaptation projects and that may have to do with the fact that the state's governor, Rick Scott, and the state legislature, especially Senator Marco Rubio, Miami's state representative and a presidential candidate in 2016, stated that they didn't believe in climate change.[19] Governor Scott had banned use of the term "climate change" in state government. Department of Environmental Protection officials were ordered not to use the terms "climate change" or "global warming" in any official communications, emails, or reports.[20] Watching local news at the time, we'd regularly see Mayor Levine "debating" with the governor and senator through the use of clips of recorded speeches.

Watching Mayor Levine, I saw how important local elected leaders can be in times when real leadership is needed. Though they don't receive the same publicity as national leaders they are much closer to people's lives. They determine how much development happens and where, they determine how municipalities spend their

Climate Planning Objection 6 ■ 157

budgets locally, and they rely quite a bit on their local urban planner who is often the only non-political advisor they have.

Just a few years after the debates between Levine, Rubio, and Scott, in 2019, many upper-level Republicans like Scott[21] and Rubio[22] admitted that climate change was a threat and even congratulated themselves on their own efforts to fight it. For many Floridians, the fact that it took until 2019 for state leadership to admit something as demonstrable as a rise in water levels was a dispiriting reminder of how far Florida *hadn't* come. Critics called it shameless. Personally, I find these political inconsistencies easy to forgive. I must assume that these leaders were lied to by people they trusted.[23] Again, those of us who work with elected officials know how easily they are swayed. Maybe the Republican Party is slowly escaping the shackles of the climate deniers.

We see a shift away from climate denial on the local level. The Southeast Florida Regional Climate Change Compact was signed by counties, cities, and other municipalities with Republican majorities at the local level, the level of the city commission or town council. In May 2015, Florida governor Rick Scott signed into law Senate Bill 1094, amending provisions of the state comprehensive planning laws to include the mandatory integration of sea-level rise into local government comprehensive planning. There was no resistance at the local level because Republicans routinely vote for climate adaptation in Florida. Working on mitigation efforts in a city requires patience, but with adaptation you can begin tomorrow because adaptation is absolutely local. It's empowering.

In 2016, Mayor Levine appeared in Leonardo DiCaprio's documentary *Before the Flood* and he walked the actor and part-time activist around Miami Beach to see the lifted streets and new pumps.[24] It was a hopeful point in an otherwise bleak film. In a 2017 documentary, *An Inconvenient Sequel: Truth to Power*, Levine toured Miami Beach with former Vice President Al Gore, and Gore was less than optimistic.

"Kinda hard to pump the ocean," Gore said. "This is a stop-gap measure at best."[25] That moment, by contrast, was a bleak point in an otherwise hopeful film. Watching Levine, it looked to me like he was surprised by the new tone. Was Gore applauding Levine's efforts or mocking him. Was Miami Beach leading the world or giving false hope?

By 2017, several blocks in the city had been lifted to the higher level. Flamingo Park at the end of my street was lifted in places, giving our neighborhood park pleasant, rolling hills. Public buildings in the park were raised on earthen mounds 10 feet higher and upgraded ballfields were made to store water in spaces under the ground to give stormwater time to filter naturally into the earth. At best, the new system only bought select areas of Miami Beach 40 to 50 more years without sunny day flooding, but, locally, it felt like a step in the right direction. In the summer of 2017, Mayor Levine and the City of Miami Beach were also signatories to the defiant open letter to President Trump signed by more than 1,200 mayors, governors, and education and business leaders pledging to abide by the terms of the 2006 Paris Accord even if the U.S. federal government abandoned it. That felt great.

158 ▪ *Why Are We Doing This?*

Levine left the office of mayor to run for the Democratic nomination for governor of Florida in the 2018 election. Levine was labeled "a tax-and-spend liberal" in television attack advertisements for his work to lift Miami Beach's streets. He lost the election. The state voted in Republican governor Ron DeSantis. Governor DeSantis would become nationally known as one of the governors who botched the COVID-19 pandemic relief effort with what could be described as COVID-denial. At least Levine didn't lose to another climate denier like Governor Rick Scott. To his credit, Governor Ron DeSantis hired the state's first Chief Resilience Officer to prepare Florida for the environmental, physical, and economic impacts of climate change, especially sea-level rise.[26]

I've worked on several projects in Miami Beach as a resident and as a city planning consultant, and our firm's main contribution to the city was *Plan NOBE*, the plan for North Beach. The plan was created with public input centering around a charrette – an intensive, open planning process that combines hands-on community brainstorming with "designing in public." The Miami Beach community didn't shy away from hard decisions required by the climate and the *Build to Last* chapter of *Plan NOBE* recommended building sea walls, protective mangroves, and beaches, adding large pipes and pump stations, and raising buildings, public spaces, and streets. Just about every street in North Beach was to be raised to at least 4 feet of elevation. Miami Beach is a built-out city. Raising everything is not easy. However, the community was united. The plan was adopted unanimously in 2016.

Then, suddenly, the City stopped lifting streets and adding pump stations in 2017. Three City commissioners were elected who supported the residents that complained about the nuisance of construction, shared the concern of business owners worried lifted roads would shed water onto private properties, and were sympathetic to the fear that pumped storm water could hurt offshore water quality. Each of the commissioners also said that the cost of tax and fee increases was too much for their constituents. With a new fiscally conservative majority voting bloc, the City stopped pumping the streets during the October King Tides.[27] The City's new policy was only to pump when a storm was approaching. This caused public outrage as the enormous puddle that gave my wife and I so much stress reappeared even though the City had the ability to pump it away.

"New water and sewer mains, critical stormwater pumps and generators, and elevated roads in the works for the last two years may not be realized for another six years," wrote Jon Elizabeth Alemán, Miami Beach Commissioner, in a letter to the *Miami Herald* in May 2018. She wrote the letter to protest a City vote to delay a street-lift project to make the La Gorce area of Miami Beach more resilient to sea-level rise.

> Apparently, it's every homeowner for himself. Community be damned. The Miami Beach commission has apparently lost the nerve to tell people what they need to know over what they want to hear. Individual interests are triumphing over the greater good.[28]

Soon the City replaced its maverick public works director, Bruce Mowry – the man who had worked with Mayor Levine. This was a terrible loss in the opinion of local planners, as Mowry, a Mississippi native, had spent 35 years working on sustainability projects from China to New Orleans.[29] The City then commissioned a study by the Urban Land Institute (ULI) as a rethink of Mayor Levine's approach to resilience. Although ULI recommended to continue to lift streets and add pump stations, it also suggested exploring softer, less expensive recommendations which it referred to as "blue and green infrastructure," referencing the color of water and plants, and referring to solutions for capturing and distributing water in a more environmentally friendly and less expensive way.[30] That sounds good but ultimately this new direction meant a reduced resilience effort.

Blue and green infrastructure includes *water squares*, public plazas for recreation that can also be used for water retention and natural filtration during rainfall events. While our team was working on a park plan for the West Lots of North Beach, we included a water square like the one in the Benthemplein neighborhood of Rotterdam or the Historic Fourth Ward Park in Atlanta. Water squares are only useful as resilience infrastructure in landlocked cities or neighborhoods which flood with rain and have no way to release waters into rivers or seas. I explained to the commissioners that the new "blue and green" strategy was a largely symbolic approach and shouldn't replace actual adaptation measures.

The City Commission called the full stop in resilience progress "a pause," but three years later, in 2020, they were still paused. Talk about resilience continued through that period, but no real action followed. Elected officials described road lifting as "an answer to tomorrow's problems; not today's." New condominium buildings like *Urbin Retreat* on the 1200 block of Washington Avenue, were built 5 feet higher than freeboard, the level water is expected to rise, in anticipation of the street in front of it being raised. What would happen if the street was never raised? Every developer asked that same question and this stalled upgrades.

During "the pause," the City created a program to use state funding to lift sea walls by setting up a 50/50 resilience improvement matching grant of up to US$20,000 per property and Miami Beach's land development regulations continued to require new buildings to be elevated. But without lifting the streets and parks the island remained vulnerable to tidal flooding, storm surge, and the slow rise of water up from underneath Southeast Florida's oolite limestone subsurface. That slow rise exasperated the City's stormwater issues because during flooding events the water below the surface keeps stormwater levels from dropping and flood waters linger for longer.

The problem for the Miami Beach Commission, a governmental body whose members change but which, I believe, nowadays, only attracts people who really do want to build a stronger, safer community, is this: The future has no constituency. Elected officials feel they can't ask people to do difficult things for the sake of future residents. Commission meetings were routinely filled with voters afraid of change and afraid of cost. Behind-the-scenes lobbying efforts continued as property owners with expensive properties with high taxable values worked to convince the commissioners to keep property taxes and stormwater fees low. It may be a while before municipalities automatically plan ahead for climate the same way we do for electricity, drinking water, schools, and roads. It may be even longer before we automatically assess and tax land to pay for resilience the way we do for other public services.

There's an economic benefit to change. A study commissioned by the City in 2019 by ICF, a climate adaptation planning consultant, showed a solid return on investment when it came to resilience spending. Its study showed an increase in values for properties located on raised roadways. In the Sunset Harbour neighborhood, the lowest-lying area of the City where streets were raised, condo units increased approximately US$41 million in total value, or 12% from the time period before the stormwater resilience project began to after its completion. The increase was "specifically due to the road raising project," according to a letter to commissioners from City Manager Jimmy Morales. Overall, the economic model indicates that home prices in Sunset Harbour increased from 8.6% to 11.5% for each 1-foot increase in average parcel elevation, Morales wrote.[31] The higher the elevation of the properties, the more they were worth.

"The neighborhood has also avoided potential damage from tidal flooding due to road elevation," Morales wrote. "Since 2017, the tide levels would have resulted in flooding 44 times." The City does not claim the program prevents all flooding, but it says the results show that areas are flooding less due to the program.[32]

Financial benefit is important to property owners, but it is also important to the City which, in the absence of any significant regional, state, or federal response to sea-level rise, must continue to pay for adaptation with increases to local utility fees and property taxes. If resilience infrastructure must be paid for with taxes levied on taxable property, then rises in property value attributable to resilience spending can be thought of as a system which pays for itself.

And then "the pause" ended. The City adopted a plan by Jacobs Engineering to begin elevating roads again along with other sea-level rise and tidal flood adaptation projects in February 2020.[33] The Jacobs Plan also included a Neighborhood Prioritization Plan to begin lifting the roads in the neighborhoods where there was the most resident comfort with adaptation. In 2021, I co-lead a team which created a Community Redevelopment Agency (CRA) and CRA Master Plan that would use Tax Increment Financing (TIF) to pay for adaptation projects.

"I'd rather do something about sea-level rise now rather than hear from my kids in twenty years that we didn't do anything," said Miami Beach Mayor Dan Gelbert during a City Commission meeting in November 2020.[34]

Questions remain, however. How long will it be before the next "pause"? Will the City continue to lift fast enough? And, ultimately, is any American city even wealthy enough to lift every road, street, and building?

We'll Need to Work a Lot Harder

"Miami, in terms of assets at risk, is the number one city in the entire world for sea-level rise," Vice President Al Gore said in *An Inconvenient Sequel: Truth to Power*. "This is a major crisis."[35] It was a relief to hear that. From the perspective of a local, it too often feels like the *climate people* want Miami to be swallowed live to make the rest of the developed world pay attention. You can practically hear the message on whatever the cartoon equivalent of Captain Planet is nowadays: "So, remember, kids: if we're not nice to Mother Nature she'll kick our butts, just like Miami."

Locally, we believe Miami must be saved because it is home to millions of people, it is the economic engine of Southeast Florida, the infrastructure investments made in the city total trillions of dollars, the total real estate value of Miami Beach alone is US$40 billion,[36] and Miami and Miami Beach should benefit from the enormous amount they generate and pay in state and federal taxes. There is also a tremendous net benefit in maintaining Miami Beach versus the cost of building a new city further inland (though this may not be the case for all the world's coastal communities). Beyond the humanitarian or economic arguments, though, Miami and Miami Beach must be saved for symbolic reasons. If Miami becomes Atlantis, imagine the demoralizing effect worldwide. Saving the City does more for the world's morale than a new, cautionary, Aesop-style fable.

Can the City be saved in the case of a worldwide 10-foot rise in seas? Probably not. But no one is sure when that might happen. If the world's ice melts slowly, we may see a rise of only a few feet by 2100. If the ice melts quickly and the Greenland Ice Sheet collapses, we may see seas 20 to 30 feet higher. Ice sheets are already melting more quickly than models predicted and rapid unpredictable rises in sea levels has happened in the past. Scientists are fairly certain we are locked into at least 3 feet of sea-level rise, and probably more, but we don't know whether it will happen within a century or a somewhat longer timeframe. Generally, planners assume 2 feet by 2060 and 6 feet by 2100. Miami Beach can weather a 2-foot rise.

And so, we return to the question: Is Miami Beach leading the world or just buying time? As a local urban planner, I would answer that Miami Beach is doing both – and it as much as the City can do. It is the job of urban planning to buy time, and it is okay, more than okay; it is important work.

Urban planners I know across the country often complain that the conversation about climate change in their community has not changed fast enough or that it hasn't changed at all. They say climate change discussions continue to fall along party lines. Southeast Florida is different. Decision makers and most residents have gone from ignorance, to denial, to acceptance, to mortal humility, quickly, I think, in my 15 years as an urban planner working in the region. We have gone from mere talk, to plans, to investing tax dollars, and finally to raising new taxes to combat climate change. I believe that the pauses in infrastructure investment, like the one in Miami Beach, are only temporary because our region really can't look away. Unfortunately, it may take an existential threat to make communities focus.

162 ■ *Why Are We Doing This?*

Why is Southeast Florida Still Growing?

Doesn't the fact that Southeast Florida is still allowing the construction of new waterfront development prove that the region isn't taking the climate threat seriously? If Southeast Florida, and Miami Beach in particular, understand the risks, then why are they still allowing development? I am asked these questions often.

The simple answer is to say that the United States is a country whose constitution, specifically, the fifth and 14th amendments to the U.S. Constitution, allow the private development of land as a right. Let me suggest, though, that beyond that right, Southeast Florida is still developing, to some degree, because we have no other choice but to build our way out of our problems. There is no state income tax in Florida. State and local governments are largely funded by property taxes. Property taxes are hugely important to keeping schools open, highways functioning, parks open, and adapting the region for climate change. The communities in Southeast Florida can either raise taxes or build new real estate and add new ratepayers. Politically, elected officials can't always raise taxes and they must choose growth in order to survive.

Another reason Miami is continuing to develop is less deliberate and has to do with the short-term, quick turn-around nature of real estate in America (and in Florida especially). When developers exercise their constitutional rights to develop land and build a condominium tower, they sell the units to investors and then move on to their next projects. Every owner then holds on to those units for four or five years, on average, before selling. As long as each individual owner can make a return on their investment, the cycle continues.

What happens in the case of a devastating storm? Flood and hurricane insurance cover losses and development resumes. Storms like Hurricane *Andrew* in 1992 caused US$27 billion in damage and bankrupted several insurance companies.[37] However, the National Flood Insurance Program (NFIP) rebuilt Southeast Florida after Hurricane Andrew and continues to provide affordable, subsidized, insurance to property owners, renters, and businesses. As long as the National Flood Insurance Program exists, Floridians can expect to secure mortgages.

Without the National Flood Insurance Program, insurance would be unaffordable to most. The program is increasingly criticized for encouraging building, and rebuilding, in vulnerable coastal areas and floodplains. However, the program remains widely supported in Congress. Eliminating the NFIP to save taxpayer dollars would be like eliminating the U.S. Navy to save money. I mean, it could happen, but it isn't likely. Neither Republicans nor Democrats can lose all the voters in Florida along with most voters in other coastal states.

At the same time, the National Flood Insurance Program requires communities to adopt and enforce floodplain management regulations to mitigate losses and Floridians can count on insurance to get increasingly expensive as the seas rise and more properties find themselves in newly designated flood zones. When multiple areas around the globe have simultaneous disasters, insurance prices and rates (especially windstorm premiums) have gone up as insurers demand increases because they need to make up for their losses. We see this in Florida periodically and increasingly often.[38]

Other costs will probably go up as well. The cost of dry streets will be felt because stormwater utilities will need to build pumping systems. User fees will go up at coastal parks as beaches must be replenished and the shoreline must be reinforced. The cost of drinking water is likely to rise because the state will have to desalinate water as underwater aquifers become contaminated with rising salt water. There's a cost to rebuild and lift public buildings and infrastructure, to buy land which can no longer be serviced by public utilities and is therefore ruled *condemned* by government. There's a cost to continually update plans and codes. It's a long list of new costs.

How Long Can Southeast Florida Continue to Grow?

As an attendee at climate conferences I have heard the Florida land development system called a *Ponzi scheme*, a form of fraud in which the belief in the success of a non-existent enterprise is fostered by the payment of quick returns to the first investors from money invested by later investors. The problem with this accusation is that Florida is not a non-existent enterprise, like, say, the non-existent investments of Bernie Madoff's hedge fund which went bust in 2008. Florida is still delivering exactly as promised: Year-round sunny, warm days and relatively cheap living.

Any investment that continues to pay dividends for over 100 years is a good investment. The 1919 swindle organized by Charles Ponzi, whose name became an eponym, only lasted eight months. Ponzi took money from one group of investors and gave it to another, and eventually ended up in a federal prison. Of course, it doesn't help my assertion that we can't label Florida real estate a *Ponzi scheme* to note that after federal prison Charles Ponzi moved to Florida to sell real estate. While the state was in the midst of a property boom, Ponzi worked to set up a bogus real estate scheme to sell land that was still under water to unwitting northerners. He soon landed back in prison, however, before making his fortune, or doing any real damage, in 1927.

I was born in the Northeast, in Rhode Island, and I remember seeing Miami for the first time in 2004. I was living in a chilly apartment in a wooden house in South Kingstown and watching PBS on a bulky Zenith television with click dials which I had placed on top of the stove so that my girlfriend and I could be warmed by our open oven. The camera drove us down Ocean Drive to the tune of a salsa soundtrack, and I saw gorgeous 1930s Art Deco hotels in whimsical pastel shades, coconut palms, pink sidewalks with people strolling here and there in shorts and dresses, teal waters, and the brilliant light of a city made of summer. I had never seen anywhere like it and, sitting at my table 1,500 miles away, I wanted go and see it. In a few

164 ■ *Why Are We Doing This?*

years I'd live just a few blocks from the lavishly restored, architectural jewel box of Miami Beach's Deco District, and its 24/7 open-air carnival. I don't party on poolside terraces as much anymore, but I am glad I invested my life in Florida; it is still a place of sunny beaches and tropical gardens. My vacation has yet to end.

The question is: How much longer can the state deliver as promised?

In a best-case scenario, Southeast Florida continues to be an investment whose assets and liabilities (like sea-level rise, killer hurricanes, and rising insurance rates) will continue to be fully and fairly discussed. This will require urban planners and local media to keep up the conversation about the future and not shy away from discussing the dire straits the state is headed toward.

In a best-case scenario, we can imagine civic leaders at the local and state level continuing to address the risk of sea-level rise in a proactive way. We can imagine leaders continuing to follow Mayor Levine's example, demonstrating the kind of political courage it takes to raise taxes, invest in better stormwater systems, bulwark the shoreline, and lift streets and causeways. We would assume higher and higher standards of construction and the construction of ever-safer structures.

In such a scenario, the water may continue to rise but people would continue to arrive. Construction may slow as Southeast Florida becomes a shakier investment; however, it isn't unreasonable to imagine that the supply of houses and condos would never outmatch the demand. Even with higher temperatures, more severe storms, and routine flooding, Southeast Florida could still provide a nice life. Some locations will likely see a slow, stable, retreat as property values drop due to flooding but, on the whole, city centers would remain defendable, dry, safe, and prosperous.

Difficult decisions would need to be made. Southeast Florida's cities would need to densify around transit stops that could one day contain enough people to pay for an above-ground transit service that connects tall Corbusier-style towers on fortified new islands. This means rapid redevelopment and gentrification as the "old-timer" population of one-story areas clashes with new arrivals in sky-high towers. We'll discuss the ongoing effort to densify around transit momentarily.

In another scenario, the seas rise fast, political leaders dither, the community fails to unite, the problems quickly become insurmountable, and retreat becomes required. In that case, the many urban centers along the Florida coast may be abandoned the way the center of Detroit, Michigan, lost its population and jobs after the collapse of the automotive industry between 1950 and 2010. Southeast Florida has higher ground in its interior for people to retreat to. Much of that land is still farmlands. The state's population could retreat there. Or, maybe, the entire state of Florida would see declining populations as people move out to more temperate climate zones to escape dangerous heat the way people historically left cold climates for Florida. Terrible storms made more intense and slow-moving by climate change could erode the stability of the region as families cash in insurance claims under a modified federal insurance system and use those funds to relocate.

Climate Planning Objection 6 ■ **165**

If the seas rise fast and high, the tourism industry could sink right along with the recreational and hospitality infrastructure built along the shore. We can imagine high unemployment compounded by middle-class flight to other states to find work. The region would be left with a higher proportion of poor in its population, a reduced tax base, depressed property values, abandoned buildings, abandoned neighborhoods, clouds of mosquitos thriving with less spraying, waterlogged parks, and high crime rates. The continuing rise of water would slowly inundate the metropolitan regions as the municipalities would have less money to build sea walls, buy pumps, fix roads, and pay emergency response personnel.

Under this worst-case scenario, by 2100 or 2200, we can imagine Southeast Florida's protracted decline resulting in severe urban decay with thousands of empty buildings in every coastal city. Some parts of the region could be so sparsely populated that cities would have difficulty providing municipal services. Cities might demolish abandoned homes and buildings and remove septic and sewer lines in order to encourage people to move to more populated locations.

Whichever future we face, local plans must talk clearly about the climate crisis, addressing short-term problems and solutions like new seawalls, mechanized stormwater systems, and backflow preventers. The conversation should also include the mid-term future and the bigger, pricier adaption systems that would be required. Every discussion should include the need to mitigate carbon pollution. Any long-term discussion must keep in mind that catastrophic impacts, like the kind that hit Detroit, are possible.

Building Transit

Every day, 11 million people board public transportation in the New York–Newark area. Over two million people in Los Angeles and over two million in Chicago use public transportation each day. More than one million in Washington D.C., San Francisco, Boston, and Philadelphia board transit every day in each. Even in cities that lack historic subway systems, cities known for car-only lifestyles and traffic like Miami, Phoenix, Houston, and Atlanta, over 200,000 people a day use transit in each.[39]

"Americans won't ride transit," urban planners hear all the time, but that's just not true. In the last 25 years public transit ridership is up 20%.[40] Public transportation use saves the equivalent of 900,000 automobile fill-ups every day and conserves 4.16 billion gallons of gas per year. Public transportation saves 37 million metric tons of carbon dioxide annually and that's equivalent to the emissions resulting from the electricity generated by every household in Washington, D.C., New York City, Atlanta, Denver, and Los Angeles combined.[41]

"Are you on board?" asks the American Public Transportation Association.

166 ■ *Why Are We Doing This?*

"No, I'm not," you would say if you are like most Americans, because 76% of Americans drive alone to work according to the U.S. census.[42]

Unfortunately, it seems unlikely that a sufficiently dramatic shift in mode choice from car to transit will occur to lower carbon emissions to a workable point. Cars will, simply, have to become electric in the future. One can imagine a massive subsidy program to build electric cars, like the programs used to build M4 Sherman tanks during World War II, only scaled up roughly 1,000 times because automobile ownership worldwide is growing so fast. In the meantime, we need to work locally to improve ridership on our municipal transit systems.

We are working to triple transit infrastructure in Southeast Florida – a place no one would associate with public transit – and we're making progress. Our progress can provide a roadmap for others. *Roadmap* is probably not the right word; let's say *transit map*.

The Miami-Dade 2045 Long Range Transportation Plan (LRTP)

The Miami-Dade 2045 Long Range Transportation Plan (2045 LRTP) is the long-term blueprint for the region's transportation system and I and my team helped author it. Every region in the U.S. has an LRTP. Your work to build transit in your region should begin with the LRTP. The LRTP analyzes the transportation needs of the region and creates a framework for project priorities. The 2045 LRTP recommends that the Miami-Dade Transportation Planning Organization dedicate US$34 million a year towards the SMART Plan, a plan for transit. Specifically, the Strategic Miami Area Rapid Transit (SMART) Plan involves adding six Rapid Transit Corridors (Bus Rapid Transit and commuter rail) to Miami-Dade County's Metrorail system. The Rapid Transit Corridors would consist of either new rail or Bus Rapid Transit (BRT). The plan also involves land use changes to build walkable places, and a network of new local bus services, trolleys, bike trails, walking trails, and sidewalks to support the transit system. That's an enormous change from the previous spending priorities which almost exclusively focused on automobile infrastructure.

The 2045 LRTP states that by implementing phase one of the SMART Plan with its mix of new trains and bus rapid transit the region would see, by 2045, a reduction of 193,000 vehicle trips and an increase in 272,000 transit boardings. This would double transit ridership in Miami-Dade County. Full implementation of the SMART Plan would result in a reduction of 130,000 vehicle trips and an increase in 182,000 transit boardings. These are conservative estimates based on the assumption that we can connect the 1.7 million residents who live within 2 miles of the SMART Plan Corridors to the 855,000 jobs located within 2 miles. As the numbers of people and numbers of jobs increase so would the numbers of cars taken off the road in favor of cost-efficient, clean transit.[43]

When Does Planning Result in New Transit?

The job of urban planners is to work with the public to draft plans and the ultimate execution of the plans rests with elected officials. This can be a problem. However, if we keep implementation in mind when we draft plans and tie our recommendations to funding opportunities, then the plans have a better chance of success. The LRTP and SMART Plan were officially adopted by the Transportation Planning Organization (TPO) in the fall of 2019. Our team also worked to coordinate our plans with federal and state plans like the Metropolitan Transportation Plans (MTPs) and the Statewide Transportation Improvement Plans (STIPs), and that's important because our region, like most, counts on roughly 50% of its funding for transportation projects from the federal government and another 25% from the state.

The next step in implementation in our region occurs when the transit, bicycle, and pedestrian facility recommendations in the LRTP and SMART Plan make their way onto the Transportation Improvement Program (TIP) – a list of upcoming transportation projects – covering a period of four to six years. The TIP must be financially constrained, and this means that funding sources must be identified. In Southeast Florida we have the People's Transportation Plan half-penny surtax to help fund out transit systems.

In 2002, voters in Miami-Dade County approved a half-penny sales surtax to be added to all purchases subject to a state sales tax in order to fund expansion of transportation and transit service and infrastructure. The problem with the half-penny surtax is that, starting with the 2008 recession, most of the money went to funding the operations of existing transit and a great deal of the money went to highway and road projects. This has been a source of local outrage for transit, bicycle, and pedestrian advocates; however, transit advocates will need to check that outrage because the region will need to unify once again and allocate an additional half-penny sales surtax to fully fund the SMART Plan.

I feel like I've done everything I can both as a resident (my family and I use Miami's MetroRail frequently) and as an urban planner, to support transit. It felt great when in 2020 the Miami-Dade County Board of County Commissioners officially accepted US$1 billion in federal funds for the creation of the Southern Corridor – the first SMART Plan route. The project will provide a mobility connection from Downtown Miami all the way to Florida City. But that's just the first of six transit lines. We still have a long way to go.

Notes From the Field

Local Food and Energy Production at Sandywoods Farm, An Agri-art Community in Rhode Island

America's northern regions have natural advantages when it comes to a changing climate and the north may become a place to retreat to, reversing population shifts

168 ■ *Why Are We Doing This?*

to sunbelt states. Northern communities tend to have colder, moister climates, more dependable water supplies, coasts that rise steeply from the sea, and less hurricane activity. They are still vulnerable, however, and there are low-lying portions of cities that were built on fill like the southern end of Manhattan in New York and Cambridge in Boston. Outside the cities, there are also sandy and marshy areas below 5-foot elevation along the northern coasts. Despite these vulnerabilities, settlements in the American north face fewer challenges compared to U.S. states along the Gulf of Mexico which face heat and flooding, or western states facing heat and drought. How those northern areas develop, how they grow, matters.

In states like Rhode Island with slow growth rates, low risk of wildfires, high coasts, and strong local land use policies that discourage development along the coast and in floodplains, the climate change discussion focuses more on mitigation than on adaptation. However, the conversation hardly ever discusses in-migration from areas that may become too climatologically unstable, or perhaps, just too hot for humans.

Urban planners in Rhode Island work on preservation. Preservation is a form of climate change mitigation. When we preserve land, we prevent costly sprawl which depletes energy and water resources and we protect carbon-absorbing natural environments. When we preserve buildings, we recycle materials and this reduces the amount of energy needed to provide people with homes or workplaces. The pushback to preservation in urban, highly educated, politically *blue* states comes from real estate developers and the elected officials who represent them who see preserving working farms or disallowing development in coastal areas as at odds with job-creation, real estate profits, and municipal budgetary responsibility. In places like Rhode Island, climate change mitigation is simply the latest point of debate in the perennial environmentalist-versus-developer contest.

Preservation was my job as an urban planner in Rhode Island and I worked for years to preserve historic structures, forested landscapes, and working farms. As a student working toward my master's degree in Urban Planning, I worked with Grow Smart Rhode Island to document the cost of urban decay and suburban sprawl and the spread of deforestation and loss of farmland despite the state's relatively static population numbers. I worked for Historic New England at Casey Farm, an organic farm that offered Community Supported Agriculture (CSA) and managed a 400-acre forest for the simple sake of preserving that forest for its scenic value and beneficial environmental processes. I worked for the Town of Richmond's Rural Preservation Land Trust, where I helped create mapping used to buy development rights to keep the rural countryside rural. I was a *green* in local planning parlance, a protector of farms and wild landscapes.

Then I was offered an entirely different job by Ken Paine, an adjunct professor at the University of Rhode Island who headed the State Senate Policy Office. I conducted research for legislation that would build affordable housing. Our policies built affordable housing the hard way, with a state-override of local zoning. The extremely controversial and court-contested Rhode Island Comprehensive

Climate Planning Objection 6 ■ **169**

Housing Production and Rehabilitation Act of 2004 was passed to build homes for people with low- to moderate incomes. To former colleagues, I had become a *grey*, a concrete-bringer, and an agent of the development community. Of course, I didn't see it that way. Urban planners seek to balance competing public goals; we don't wave flags of any color.

I was also young at that time and when I thought about my financial future I couldn't imagine buying a home in Rhode Island on an urban planner's salary. And that was unfortunate because I wanted to own a home, and I didn't want to leave the beautiful little state where I grew up. Sometimes my work to preserve the rural landscape felt like a betrayal of my own generation, a generation that wouldn't be able to afford the American Dream of homeownership. As I tested different roles in the field of urban planning, I found that working to build affordable housing – not luxury homes, not vacation homes, and not investment homes, but places for the average person to live – felt right. It still does.

Today, more than 15 years after I worked on the Comprehensive Housing Act of 2004, thousands of affordable units have been built using Comprehensive Permits that wouldn't have been constructed otherwise, and many of those units are in prosperous places with little poverty and excellent schools. I must believe that these homes have given at least some low-income families an opportunity for advancement.

Looking back on my work through the lens of climate mitigation and adaptation, I see that a few projects even achieved an optimal mix of rural preservation and affordability. Some Comprehensive Permit sites are low carbon polluters or even carbon sinks. They are walkable, mixed-use, and mixed income. A few places embody smart growth that are talked about so often but rarely achieved. One of these places is Sandywoods Farm in Tiverton, Rhode Island.

Sandywoods Farm didn't use one of the zone-busting Comprehensive Permits from the state I helped create, but the threat of a Comprehensive Permit was key to the development of Sandywoods Farm. The town of Tiverton didn't fight Sandywoods Farm in court the way it had fought so many other developments because of the Fair Share Law which was part of the Comprehensive Housing Act of 2004. When communities like Tiverton worked to satisfy the state's requirement of 10% permanently affordable housing and showed real progress to hosting their fair share of affordable homes, they were exempt from the state's zoning-exempt Comprehensive Permits.

Sandywoods Farm is a unique arts and agricultural community which includes 50 affordable units for rent, 25 market-rate lots for sale, and roughly 150 acres of land reserved for a working farm and open space. The farm and open space were dedicated to the Nature Conservancy, a national conservation non-profit, to keep the woods preserved in perpetuity. Power is provided to residents by a 250kW wind turbine on site.

I went back to Rhode Island and toured Sandywoods Farm in the fall of 2016, on a bright and sunny early fall day. I parked by the Grange, the barnlike community center with its wrap-around porch, steep red-tile gables, and weathervane topped

170 ■ *Why Are We Doing This?*

with an iron Rhode Island Red Rooster. The architecture for the entire community was designed by Rhode Island local Donald Powers and his firm Union Studio. The village featured traditional New England vernacular architecture with peaked roofs, vertical windows, deep porches facing the street, balance, rhythm, variety, unity, and timelessness.

Within the Grange, the Sandywoods Center for the Arts provided a venue for community activity and music. Looking at its Facebook page I could see that community activities around the time of my visit included a potluck for a Native American tribe, cooking classes, yoga, Zumba, and a fundraiser for a local Alzheimer's Awareness group. Monthly concerts featured zydeco, mandolin, a strong quartet, a Jerry Garcia tribute, and bluegrass. Down the street with its wide sidewalk, newly planted street trees, and street lamps, were two small stores and an art gallery. The retail spaces had residential units on their second floors and no visible parking lots because the parking was located behind the buildings.

"Well, this is nice," I said aloud, though alone.

The community opened in 2010 near the crossroads of Bulgarmarsh Road and Crandall Road in bucolic Tiverton. The village was a collaboration by local property owners and two non-profit housing developers: Church Community Housing Corporation and RI Housing.

I wandered the simple, narrow residential streets and took in the long views across lawns and meadows. One-, two-, and three-bedroom rental units were located within the homes that were designed to resemble large farmhouses. Behind the dignified two- and three- story homes the backyards were a lived-in clutter of grills, kids' bicycles, toys, kayaks, trash barrels, and recycling receptacles. It was the middle of the day and no one was around. The wind turbine moved slowly in a field behind the board-and-batten homes.

Along Persimmon Drive building fronts were aligned across the narrow street, as if forming the walls of a room. The architecture and landscape design of the best-designed places physically define public spaces. The proper height-to-width ratio of building heights to the width of space between the buildings create a sense of spatial enclosure outdoors. When the eye perceives more street wall than open sky people get a sense of an outdoor room even on a street where the houses are well-spaced.

The farmhouse townhomes looked like they had been built over time with new structures added to the primary mass of the main homes as families had grown or space was added for older generations to move into. Every façade possessed a pleasant symmetry of windows and doors and the specific shades of blue, brown, yellow, and crimson of historic New England.

I had worked for the Rhode Island Senate Policy Council on design guidelines for Comprehensive Permit projects in order to encourage a high degree of design quality for the projects, but the guidelines initiative was scrapped. It was argued by members of the State Housing Appeals Board (SHAB) that people didn't care what their homes looked like from the outside – they just wanted a place to live. But, of course, the ironically named SHAB (as in *shabby*) had it wrong. People identify with the homes they live in, even the homes they rent, and take pride in them. I remember showing friends and family around the big farmhouses I had lived in as a student near the University of Rhode Island. I took pride in those. They were internally subdivided into tiny rooms with creaky floors, thin walls, comically small bathrooms, and they all lacked closets, but they had architectural character and offered a sense of place. The residents of Sandywoods Farm had stately traditional architecture, but also new floors, solid walls, bathrooms that were large enough even for people with disabilities, and deep closets with interior lights.

As a practical matter, urban planners know that handsome, context-sensitive affordable housing is more likely to be approved by their host communities. Design matters and good design doesn't always add to cost; it's often just a matter of hiring an architect that knows what they are doing. Architects who study traditional architecture, especially, know how to produce self-respecting homes with simple, classic designs that are cheaper to build because those architects know to skip the numerous gables, dormers, double-story high entries, and multiple clashing materials of flashy contemporary residential architecture. In the world of residential architecture, expense and taste are too often inversely correlated.

I walked Sandywoods' Meadow View Lane, reached the edge of the settlement, and stood in the street between empty housing lots where utility boxes poked out of the long grass on the lots waiting to be developed. At the time of my visit, Sandywoods was still under construction. The distant windmill slowly spun its long arcs on the breeze. Homes behind me. Forest ahead. By clustering the units, the total development footprint was lessened, yet green lawns and meadows still weaved through the community, lengthening views, creating an awareness of nature, and cleansing rainwater. The oaks, hickory, and native pines of the surrounding forest preserve hid the marshy wetland systems of the interior, though the reds and orange hues of the swamp trees like red maples and cottonwoods showed through the branches.

"Well this is nice," I said again into the cool autumn air.

Trees and the Environment

Forests absorb more carbon that they release, taking carbon out of the atmosphere. U.S. forests alone store 14% of all annual CO_2 emitted in the U.S.[44] New England was once a far more deforested place. The land had been cleared of trees and used for grazing and farming. Ralph Waldo Emerson, perhaps the most quintessential of New Englanders, deplored the loss of trees for spiritual reasons, but now we know that in addition to their transcendent value, trees are a life support system. Trees absorb carbon, water, and sunlight, and release glucose and oxygen. The carbon becomes part of the plant as wood, *sequestering* it. When the tree dies the carbon the tree stored is released into the atmosphere. Forest fires create mass releases. In most cases, however, forests absorb more than they release. They are *carbon sinks*. Carbon

172 ■ *Why Are We Doing This?*

sequestration, the long-term storage of carbon is essential to decreasing our carbon output. Every tree is a net win for the environment.

I walked tractor trails across the co-op's farmland and took the dirt road to a gravel parking area with newly planted oaks in the center. Since learning about the carbon cycle, I occasionally see trees as frozen carbon. My imagination goes further, and I picture oil, coal, and gas stored underground in a kind of pitch-black hell escaping as billowing smoke like vaporous monsters released into the atmosphere. The smoke goes around and around the world forever unless trees pluck it from the air. In recent years the black vapors are thickening and speeding up. I suppose this isn't too far off given our planet's increasingly lop-sided carbon cycle.

Which trees store carbon best? I'd have to guess it was the slow-growing, long-living, oaks. They planted oaks just about wherever they could at Sandywoods Farm. One day the tree and shrub planting guides used by backyard gardeners that list hardiness zones, care requirements, fruits, nuts, color, shape, height, and spread will list the sequestration levels of individual species.

The communal garden was located on a plot of land near the Grange and appeared to have about half an acre under cultivation, boarded by forest. Simple pine boards marked squares and rectangles for beds and shrubby sage and lavender had overtaken a few boxes. Other boxes had been cleared in preparation for winter. Unpicked perennial flowers drooped in the western boxes but some still had beautiful yellow and orange blooms. Flower bulbs had been recently planted under patches of newly added dirt to root before the frost and four plastic chairs in a semi-circle suggested that whomever planted the bulbs made it a family activity. Even when there are no people in these Traditional Neighborhood Developments (TND)s you see places designed for people and you don't feel alone.

I read on the Sandywoods Farm website that the farm and communal garden grew a range of vegetables for co-op consumption, for sale to Sandywoods residents and the greater community, and for donation to a soup kitchen in the nearby city of Fall River. I read that a café and bed and breakfast were planned. I also read that the farm was certified organic. Organic farms take far more carbon out of the atmosphere than the conventional farms that use synthetic fertilizers.

The number of organic farms in Rhode Island is growing and local agriculture plays a key role in the state's economic, environmental, and nutritional health. Local agriculture improves the environment by lowering the amount of fossil fuels that must be devoted to processing and shipping fruits and vegetables long distances. Organic, small-scale agriculture can improve the environment by protecting watersheds from the chemical run-off that is typical of large-scale, conventional industrial farming. Producing food close to home keeps food dollars local. It also ensures that the produce will be fresh and retain more of its nutrients, improving the health of the local community.

I couldn't help but wish that Sandywoods Farms did more with the farm and communal gardens. There was room for twice the cultivation, a farmhouse and full-time farmer, a roadside farm stand at the edge of the property, and mobile chicken coops. But then, I am a farm snob having worked at Casey Farm in Saunderstown,

Rhode Island, one of the state's most successful Community Supported Agriculture (CSA) programs. And as an urban planner I tend to think big, but half of urban planning is knowing when to stop.

Community Supported Agriculture (CSA)

CSAs are jointly owned by the members of a community who receive a fresh mix of locally grown fruits, herbs, and vegetables. Most items are made available to CSA members the day they are harvested to insure peak flavor, ripeness, and nutrition. CSA farms often involve a small full-time staff with CSA members volunteering their time. This keeps the full-time staff small and gives participants a shared community activity and an understanding of the food they eat. CSA members assist with the routine tasks of planting, harvesting, and preparing the crops for distribution. Farm staff supervises the work and assumes the specialized tasks involving farm machinery and livestock.

At its smallest scale, a CSA could consist of a single tenant-farmer raising free-range livestock on pastureland that productively maintains the community's long-views. Larger CSAs in Rhode Island provide fresh produce to hundreds of members and have summer camps and educational experiences for local schoolchildren. I remember gathering eggs from the mobile chicken coup with kids on Casey Farm and the abject horror inner city kids expressed when I pulled up a carrot, brushed the dirt off, and ate it.

"It's organic," I'd say. "No pesticides, so as long as you ..."

"You can't eat that! You can't!" the little kids said. "Well, I won't. You can't make me. You're going to die, crazy farm teacher."

I remember shucking oysters I plucked from the Rhode Island Bay at the foot of the farm and eating them in front of the kids. I explained to my students that thanks to the hundreds of acres of forested buffer provided by the farm, the pollutants from runoff was largely ...

"O my God, you're going to die!" the inner-city kids said. "Like, any minute!"

CSAs aren't just a New England thing. Forerunners to CSAs began in the early 1960s in Germany and Japan, and there are now over 2,000 cooperative farming partnerships in the United States alone. The Serenbe community, outside Atlanta, includes a 25-acre CSA which features an acclaimed restaurant serving CSA produce. The farmhouse restaurant shares the traditional architectural vernacular of the entire community, with front-porch homes and hidden parking. Serenbe hosts festivals, wine-tastings and culinary competitions, and has become a weekend destination for Atlanteans.

New Urbanism

Complete, walkable, garden-like new communities such as Sandywoods Farm and Serenbe aren't a new idea. In 1898, the prominent British urban planner and social

174 ■ *Why Are We Doing This?*

thinker Ebenezer Howard published *To-Morrow: A Peaceful Path to Real Reform*, which offered a new vision for the cities of the twentieth century. Written in reaction to the poor living conditions born out of the Industrial Revolution, Howard's seminal work proposed the first *suburbs* – new garden cities that combined the best qualities of both towns (with their opportunity, high wages, and recreational possibilities) and country (with its beauty, fresh air, and low rents). He imagined carefully designed and balanced new villages with homes, industry, and agriculture, that were limited in size, self-contained, and surrounded by *greenbelts*, the undeveloped spaces we call *agricultural preserves*, today. The *Garden City*, Howard's vision, widely influenced the planning of many of America's most beautiful early twentieth-century towns.

Since then, attorneys, developers, and builders have proposed alternative visions for our towns and cities. Zoning laws segregate uses thought to be incompatible, spreading uses so far that even a cup of coffee requires a long drive. Roads are widened to better accommodate ever-increasing traffic congestion. Roadways are a clutter of large signs and parking lots. Though well-intentioned, these efforts have resulted in the placeless suburban sprawl of today.

The New Urbanism, the philosophy of firms like Donald Powers, the designer of Sandywoods Farm, and my own firm, Dover, Kohl & Partners, is rooted in the planning tradition of Howard's garden city suburb and seeks to rebuild connected, pedestrian-friendly, self-sustaining neighborhoods. New Urbanism is a rejection against low-density anonymous subdivisions, ugly suburban shopping complexes, and the modernist-inspired large-scale high-rise housing blocks which produce lightless concrete canyons of development.

New Urbanists advocate for the densities that gave European and American cities and towns their distinctive character. The New Urbanists haven't had much luck changing the development world at a large scale, however, as land in cities is valuable and built to the maximum allowed every time. Land outside cities is also still plentiful, relatively inexpensive and home buyers like big houses on big lots. That said, some remarkable examples of New Urbanism have been built. In new communities like Glenwood Park in Atlanta, Wheeler District in Oklahoma City, and South Main in Colorado – projects my firm has had a chance to contribute to – a high percentage of energy is drawn from renewable sources, homes have fewer cars (some homes have none), and many trips are made on foot or bike. Sandywoods Farm is one of those communities.

New urban communities located in busier places than sleepy Tiverton, Rhode Island, can support a wider range of employment and commercial uses. Larger new urban communities can contain just as large a percentage of open space, but with a wider variety of green spaces, from playground lots to vast gardens which connect the neighborhood physically and socially. Sandywoods Farm was small, but a considerable improvement from neighboring conventional subdivisions to the west and south.

The neighborhoods around Sandywoods Farm were better described as *subdivisions* than *neighborhoods*, and they were more *zoned* than *planned*. The strongest tool the urban planner has is zoning. However, zoning works to separate uses to avoid conflict, and it violates an essential characteristic of neighborhood planning when it separates every use. There is an overhaul process happening in the world of zoning in favor of more balanced communities. Progressive urban planners today work to build entire neighborhood units, each with a place for recreational, industrial, educational, retail, and residential uses. The main streets of those centers offer the opportunity for social encounters and exchanges we typically only experience in historic centers.

Snakes in the Garden

I walked to my car to leave Sandywoods Farm, heading down the center of the carless street, disappointed that so few people lived and worked in the community that I never had a chance to talk to anyone about the place. But maybe that was okay; I might have heard stories of discord and hostility. I might have gotten an earful. *O solitude, my sweetest choice*, goes the line. Sandywood Farm isn't perfect.

According to articles I'd read, Sandywoods Farm had disappointed its founders. They had envisioned a community of artists, but later learned that the community's subsidized, affordable units couldn't be rented exclusively to artists because of fair housing laws.[45] Residents fought over the wind turbine which some complained was too noisy. They fought over how open to the general public they wanted their settlement to be, and some residents even wanted to build a gate and gatehouse. Music festivals and farmers' markets had been scheduled and cancelled due to spats between housing board members. The community had seen foreclosures, lawsuits, and arguments the size of compost piles after sunflower season.

People are people, and, to be frank, I have observed the same problems in other new communities my team and I have designed. I have seen the same tensions in the hill towns of Northern Thailand I visited, in the ashrams of India where I studied, in the storybook island towns of Martha's Vineyard, Nantucket, and Block Island where I'd lived for short periods, and in every neighborhood association or homeowner's association I have ever been part of. I have heard it put this way: The smaller the village, the more people want to kill each other.

From what I have seen, though, turmoil waxes and wanes, and the people who live in Traditional Neighborhood Developments like Sandywoods Farm prefer it to the alternative. When the disillusioned people move on, upset, outcast, and sometimes with a court date for a civil trial on their calendar, I have observed that they tend to move to other traditional neighborhoods.

The low carbon footprint and high carbon sequestration of traditional neighborhoods surrounded by preserved forest or farms could help bring people together, though. They can rightfully feel that they are playing a part in the climate crisis. Better designed communities chip away at the problem, and while threats to

176 ■ *Why Are We Doing This?*

the planet should inspire more than a slow *chipping away*, it's the best we can do at times.

It is possible that one day the U.S. will adopt land development laws similar to the UK and Europe and agricultural preserves, carbon sequestration, walking trails, architectural quality, renewable energy, an optimal mix of uses, and financial mechanisms that combine public and private funding to make affordable housing profitable will all become part of the real estate development process. But short of a holistic national housing policy we must cobble together the financing for complete, compact, and connected communities where we can and look to non-profit agencies and developer-philanthropists to build better, greener, more sustainable places.

Notes

1 Baldassari, E. (2018). Camp fire death toll grows to 29, matching 1933 blaze as state's deadliest. *East Bay Times*, November 11. Retrieved from: www.mercurynews.com/2018/11/11/crews-continue-to-battle-strong-winds-in-deadly-camp-fire/

2 Butte County (2009). Butte County Grand Jury report 2008/2009 (PDF). Retrieved from: www.buttecounty.net/Portals/1/GrandJury/08-09/Grand_Jury_Report_FY08-09-Pages_56-110.pdf

3 Gafni, M. (2018). Rebuild Paradise? Since 1999, 13 large wildfires burned in the footprint of the Camp Fire. *The Mercury News*, December 2. Retrieved from: www.mercurynews.com/2018/12/02/rebuild-paradise-since-1999-13-large-wildfires-burned-in-the-footprint-of-the-camp-fire/

4 Ibid.

5 Gannon, M. (2012). *The New History of Florida*. Gainesville: University Press of Florida.

6 Make it Paradise (2019). Long-term community recovery plan: Paradise, California. Urban Design Associates. Retrieved from: https://makeitparadise.org/community-vision

7 Southeast Florida Regional Compact Climate Change (2016). Integrating the unified sea level rise projection into local plans. RCAP Implementation Guidance Series, supported by the Institute for Sustainable Communities. Retrieved from: https://southeastfloridaclimatecompact.org/wp-content/uploads/2017/01/SLRGuidance-Doc.pdf

8 Fleck, J. (2013). Climate change affecting Rio Grande water supply. *Albuquerque Journal*, December 12. Retrieved from: www.abqjournal.com/318542/rising-temps-affecting-our-water-supply.html

9 Llewellyn, D. (2013). West-wide climate risk assessment: Upper Rio Grande Impact Assessment. U.S. Department of the Interior Bureau of Reclamation Upper Colorado Region Albuquerque Area Office. Retrieved from: www.usbr.gov/watersmart/baseline/docs/urgia/URGIAMainReport.pdf

10 Elisara, C. (producer), Padget, J. (director) (2014). *Seven50 | Seven Counties 50 Years | Southeast Florida Prosperity Plan*. United States: First + Main Media. Retrieved from: http://seven50report.org/

11 City of Hammond (2011). Hammond Comprehensive Plan, Page 5.5, Table 5.3: Building Permit Activity and Value. Retrieved from: www.hammond.org/wp-content/uploads/2013/01/masterplan.pdf

12 Ibid.
13 City of New Orleans website. Retrieved from: www.nola.gov/
14 U.S. census. Retrieved from: www.census.gov/glossary/#term_Populationestimates
15 Goodell, J. (2013). Goodbye Miami (also appears as Miami: How rising sea levels endanger South Florida), *Rolling Stone*, June 20. Retrieved from: www.rollingstone.com/feature/miami-how-rising-sea-levels-endanger-south-florida-200956/
16 Dover, Kohl & Partners (2016). Plan NOBE: North Beach Master Plan. Retrieved from: www.miamibeachfl.gov/wp-content/uploads/2018/07/PlanNoBe_Adopted 101916_sm.pdf
17 Weiss, J. (2019). Miami Beach's $400 Million sea-level rise plan is unprecedented, but not everyone is sold. *Miami New Times*, April 19. Retrieved from: www.miaminewtimes.com/news/miami-beachs-400-million-sea-level-rise-plan-is-unprecedented-but-not-everyone-is-sold-8398989
18 Ibid.
19 Korten, T. (2015). In Florida, officials ban term "climate change." Florida Center for Investigative Reporting, March 8. Retrieved from: www.miamiherald.com/news/state/florida/article12983720.html
20 Ibid.
21 Iannelli, J. (2019). Rick Scott brags about his nightmarish climate change record in letter to environmentalist. *Miami New Times*, September 10. Retrieved from: www.miaminewtimes.com/news/florida-sen-rick-scott-brags-about-his-climate-change-record-11263292
22 Rubio, M. (2019). Rubio on climate change: "We should choose adaptive solutions." *USA Today*, August 19. https://eu.usatoday.com/story/opinion/2019/08/19/rubio-on-climate-change-we-should-choose-adaptive-solutions-column/2019310001/
23 Adragna, A. (2019). Luntz: "I was wrong" on climate change. *Politico*, August 21. Retrieved from: www.politico.com/story/2019/08/21/frank-luntz-wrong-climate-change-1470653
24 Stevens, F. (Dir.) (2016). *Before the Flood*. RatPac Documentary Films, U.S.A.
25 Cohen, B. and Shenk, J. (Dir.) (2017). *An Inconvenient Sequel: Truth to Power*. Actual Films, U.S.A.
26 *Sun Sentinel* Editorial Board (2019). Gov. DeSantis goes bold on climate change. Even Rick Scott says it's real. Now what? Editorial. *Sun Sentinel*, May 29. Retrieved from: www.sun-sentinel.com/opinion/editorials/os-op-desantis-climate-change-2019 0528-zxfc3aq4qbc5xnre27i4bbhp6u-story.html
27 Askew, S. (2018). Mayor says Miami Beach is "reorienting" its Resiliency Plan. *RE Miami Beach*, May 24. Retrieved from: www.remiamibeach.com/citywide/mayor-says-miami-beach-is-reorienting-its-resiliency-plan/
28 Aleman, J. (2018). Letters to the Editor: Wake up Miami Beach commission! Resiliency matters. *Miami Herald*, May 22. Retrieved from: www.miamiherald.com/opinion/letters-to-the-editor/article211640179.html.
29 Weiss, J., op. cit.
30 Askew, S. (2018), op. cit.
31 Askew, S. (2019). The business case for Miami Beach's resiliency efforts. *RE Miami Beach*, September 28. Retrieved from: www.remiamibeach.com/citywide/the-business-case-for-miami-beachs-resiliency-efforts/
32 Ibid.
33 Jacob Engineering (2020). Miami Beach Integrated Water Management. Miami Beach Rising Above, February 28. Retrieved from: www.mbrisingabove.com/climate-science/innovative-studies/

178 ■ *Why Are We Doing This?*

34 Miami Beach Commission Meeting (2020). A video of the meeting which took place November 18. Retrieved from: https://miamibeachfl.new.swagit.com/videos/107364

35 Cohen, B. and Shenk, J. (Dir.), op. cit.

36 Askew, S. (2019). Miami Beach FY 2020 budget approved. *RE Miami Beach*, September 26. Retrieved from: www.remiamibeach.com/citywide/miami-beach-fy-2020-budget-approved/

37 Rappaport, E. (1993). Hurricane Andrew. National Hurricane Center (Preliminary Report). Miami, Florida: National Oceanic and Atmospheric Administration National Weather Service, December 10. Retrieved from: www.nhc.noaa.gov/1992andrew.html

38 Harris, A. (2020). Brace for insurance shock: Windstorm premiums are soaring in Florida again. *Miami Herald*, June 26. Retrieved from: www.miamiherald.com/news/weather/hurricane/article243766772.html

39 American Public Transportation Association (APTA) (2018). *2018 Public Transit Fact Book*. Table 3: The 50 Metros with the Most Transit Travel (Ranked by Unlinked Passenger Trips). Retrieved from: www.apta.com/wp-content/uploads/Resources/resources/statistics/Documents/FactBook/2018-APTA-Fact-Book.pdf

40 American Public Transportation Association (APTA). (2019). *2019 Public Transit Fact Book*. Retrieved from: www.apta.com/wp-content/uploads/APTA_Fact-Book-2019_FINAL.pdf

41 Ibid.

42 U.S. Census Bureau (2013). American community survey, Table S0801. Retrieved from: www.census.gov/history/pdf/sdcommute2013.pdf

43 Miami-Dade 2045 (2019). Long Range Transportation Plan: Transportation planning organization for the Miami urbanized area. Prepared by Gannett Fleming, Inc. Retrieved from: https://miamidade2045lrtp.com/the-plan

44 Friedel, M. (2017). Forests as carbon sinks. *Loose Leaf*, July 18. Retrieved from: www.americanforests.org/blog/forests-carbon-sinks/

45 Dunn, C. (2015). Owner's dream of turning Tiverton farmland into thriving artists colony unrealized. *The Providence Journal*, May 14. Retrieved from: www.providencejournal.com/article/20150514/NEWS/150519511

Chapter 7

Climate Planning Objection 7

"It's a lost fight. It's too late."

The bad news is that the IPCC reports it will be "very difficult" to keep the global temperature rise below the internationally agreed danger limit of 2°C.[1] The two degrees Celsius goal was considered a long shot at the time of the Paris Agreement in 2015. We can't help but ask: Why are we failing? Is it a lost fight? Is it too late?

The good news is that while it will be "very difficult" to keep the global temperature rise below the internationally agreed danger limit of 2°C, the worst-case scenario for CO_2 emissions and the warming of up to 6°C by 2100 also no longer looks likely. It is not a lost fight. It is not too late to make a difference.

In 2014, the IPCC contained within its 5th Assessment Report (AR5) four climate futures, all of which were considered possible depending on how much greenhouse gases are emitted in the years to come.[2] The four scenarios were called Representative Concentration Pathways (RCPs) and the RCPs contained projections regarding worldwide global warming, sea level rise, and other effects. RCP Scenario 8.5, the so called "business as usual" scenario, assumed a 500% increase in the use of coal. The price of clean technology has fallen, and global coal use peaked in 2013 and has been flat since. Researchers say that given current trends, a rise in temperature of around 3°C is far more likely.[3]

At 3°C of rise the world is still in peril with coral reefs largely wiped out, Arctic sea-ice mostly gone in the summer, large-scale melting of permafrost, and decreasing crop yields. Still, the limited attempts to cut carbon that the world has

DOI: 10.4324/9781003181514-9

179

180 ■ *Why Are We Doing This?*

adopted to date are having an impact and the worst emissions scenarios are no longer realistic.

There is time to improve future outcomes. It isn't too late. Fifty years from now also won't be too late, something can still be salvaged, but let's start now. One of the advantages of local government planning versus the micro-level of household planning or macro-level planning of world policy is that we can more easily break the problem of local mitigation and adaptation into smaller pieces, each with a milestone, and have everyone take a piece and work on it.

The ultimate success in mitigation would be to move a community from being a carbon source to being a carbon sink, absorbing carbon. The ultimate success in adaption might be confidence that a community will be inhabitable in 2100. There are many steps that we can take toward those goals.

Notes From the Field

Returning to the Florida Keys to Plan for a Changing Climate

In 2004, I was an urban planner for Monroe County in the Florida Keys and I lived in a tiny shack by the ocean in Tavernier, on the island of Key Largo. Our office was working to complete *The Liveable CommuniKeys Plan*, a Comprehensive Plan for the county. That spring, our office's principal planner had returned from a conference on climate change and I remember his report back to our team at our Monday morning meeting.

"It's something we need to be aware of, but we shouldn't worry," he said. He probably said more but that's all I remember because I stopped thinking about it that moment. There was nothing I needed to do. There was nothing I needed to add to the Comprehensive Plan draft.

Pause with me a moment as we put this into perspective: In 2004, 16 years after the creation of the Intergovernmental Panel on Climate Change (IPCC) was established, the plan for the Florida Keys, a chain of islands none higher than 10 feet above sea level, one of the most vulnerable places on Earth, didn't contain a mention of climate change or rising seas. It was a place that was periodically annihilated by hurricanes; in fact, on my way to the Upper Keys Planning Office every morning I passed a monument, set atop a mass grave, dedicated to hurricane victims. And thanks to climate change, Huracána, the mad goddess I learned about from the Haitians in the Keys, would have 2–4 feet more water to work with the next time she decided to scour the islands of people. Nothing to worry about? Looking back now, I believe fear and panic were in order.

To be fair, I was probably the one the most at fault in our office for not incorporating climate into the plan because five years earlier I had been working in the Tarutao Islands in Thailand researching fish stocks, coral bleaching, and sea level rise. I knew the world was warming and the seas were rising, but I was new to my

Climate Planning Objection 7 ■ 181

job in the Keys and new to my profession. I wasn't clear on how much the sea would rise, I wasn't sure how much more intense storms would become, and there were no local reports for me to reference on topics such as increased flooding from rain events, higher storm surge, or even the effect of salination on our drinking water. In my office no one was talking about sea level rise, and I didn't want to sound alarmist.

Figure 7 Tavernier Hotel, Key Largo, Florida

182 ■ *Why Are We Doing This?*

Our draft Comprehensive Plan was dedicated to preserving historic wooden conch houses, protecting white-crowned pigeons and Key deer, and defending Ironwood, Gumbo Limbo, and Sea Grape trees. These were important goals, but to say our local planning office *missed the forest for the trees* is precisely right.

Then things changed for our island community. In 2004 four destructive hurricanes hit the Keys: *Charley, Frances, Jeanne,* and *Ivan.* In 2005 three more hit: *Dennis, Katrina,* and *Wilma.* The year 2005 was the first time in the historic record that two storms in the Gulf had reached Category 5 in the same season. Yan Egalond, the emergency relief coordinator for the United Nations, called it "a wake-up call for the world" but the call was still not heeded in our county planning office.

Despite mandatory evacuations I didn't leave the islands. Once, during *Katrina,* while the sea lapped my mailbox and the water pounded my wooden door so hard that the inside of the door was as wet as the outside, I thought I might die. Worse, I remember looking over at my girlfriend as she slept in our one-bedroom shack. She had relocated with me from Rhode Island when I got the job, and I worried for her. I felt responsible. No one I knew in the Keys understood what was happening because no one had seen anything like that season, but I felt responsible.

Four hurricanes hit us in six weeks. In between, the gusts always seemed to be blowing through the tops of the coconut palms and the shallow bay waters were always white capped like the deep oceans back in Rhode Island. During the day I worked without sunlight in offices barricaded with metal shutters as tempests raged. The power was out so often that when we wanted to watch the US tv Weather Channel to know when we would be hit next, we needed go to a bayside bar with a generator. I remember frequenting Hog Heaven and Snappers. I remember that part fondly, though hazily. I remember being scared a lot, too.

And then one day a hurricane changed my life. It isn't your usual story of disaster. I know so many people who suffered true disasters that I hate to make a comparison, but nevertheless, a hurricane changed my life. On the drive down to the Keys to take the job, a job in a place I had never even visited before, my girlfriend talked about how back in Rhode Island we were already married by common law. We'd been together for over ten years. Did Florida have the same law she asked. We were close. We grew up together. I had known her since I was eight – she was my cousin's best friend.

She evacuated when Hurricane *Ivan* was tearing its way across the Bahamas and threatened to devastate the Keys. She didn't want to go through another storm like *Katrina.* She evacuated like so many others. She never returned to our little shack. Or to my life. Can I blame the hurricane? Can I blame a hurricane season that went through the entire alphabet and six letters into the Greek alphabet? Or had our relationship simply run its course like the mad downpours of rain bands or the brief double rainbows over the Florida Bay? I'll always wonder. Every natural disaster changes lives.

Returning to the Keys

In 2014, eight years after leaving the Keys, I returned to sound the alarm. I was working for the regional government on the *Seven50 Plan* which I described earlier in the book. I began my self-appointed mission in the Keys by turning two Kiwanis Club lunchtime speaking invitations (presentations which could have been on any aspect of the plan – from economic development to transportation) into a presentation strictly on the effects of sea level rise. I showed a series of maps and compelling watercolor aerial renderings drafted by James Dougherty, an illustrator at our firm, which showed the Keys wiped out. I had failed to mention climate change in the County Comprehensive Plan a decade before. Those plans had not been updated, the world's climate problem had increased exponentially, and I felt I needed to make up for lost time.

In 2014, some 26 years after the creation of the IPCC, climate was finally on the minds of most urban planners, but the crisis still wasn't part of the dialogue in Florida. Those *Seven50* presentations to the Kiwanis Club were, astoundingly, the first time that many in the audience had ever heard of climate change.

At one of the Kiwanis Club meetings in Islamorada, I discussed a *retreat to the heart of town* strategy which showed densifying, bulwarking, and pumping various locations on the island. The rest of the island would probably need to be abandoned, regrettably, I reported. How would they react I wondered as I made my way through my presentation, and they made their way through their chicken parmigiana lunches? They nodded gravely. One woman took a seat nearer the front for a closer look at my maps. Several people exhaled loudly. I heard a *wow* now and then.

When I finished, they clapped, and I was warmly thanked by the organizer. It was time for questions and answers, but several people left the room immediately. That's never a good sign. The crème brûlée and coffee hadn't even been served yet. One attendee pointed to the big glowing rendering on the screen behind me, which showed a four-story, mixed-use center protected by a levee, and his finger wagged in angry accusation. "I wouldn't want to live there," he said. He explained that he liked the one-story, single-family design of the Keys. "If the place starts to look like your drawing then I'll leave."

"Me too," another man said. "I'll just sail away." People laughed. I laughed with them. I was as nervous as you'd expect; the *end of the world* wasn't the usual Kiwanis Club guest presentation. Its list of speakers for the year included the author of a book about World War II romances, a birder, a local historian talking about bat towers, and an update on local Boy Scout Eagle Badge projects. By contrast, I had shown more than half the Keys underwater by 2100.

"That was interesting," one man said after the question-and-answer session had concluded. He shook my hand. I recognized him: He had been the county's building inspector and one of my co-workers ten years earlier, but I could tell that he didn't recognize me. "They can be a tough crowd," he said.

184 ■ *Why Are We Doing This?*

He told me that he had been privy to conversations in the back of the room and while everyone had been polite to me up front, in the back it was outright hostility. I told him that we had worked together for two years. He smiled non-committally, pretending to remember. He probably would have remembered me if I had introduced the Keys to sea level rise eight years earlier. I had simply failed to stand out back then.

Why was there such apathy and hostility? Kiwanis are people who give scholarships to kids, donate to charities abroad, and organize politically to find candidates in their ranks for local government. They are do-gooders who care about the future. Their apathy may have had something to do with the fact that the Kiwanis Club members I talked to went to the Keys to retire. They hadn't been born in the Keys, or Florida, and hadn't grown up or raised families in the state. Maybe it would have rattled them more if I had shown Cleveland, Trenton, or Brooklyn disappearing – the places they were from, where they still had family, children, and grandchildren. They had a lifetime of memories attached to those places.

Why the hostility? Maybe it had to do with national politics. Or maybe the problem was simply too great and seemingly impossible problems put people in a bad mood. Just where do you begin as a charitable organization when it comes to the climate crisis? When I left the Kiwanis, I must assume they got back to their normal agenda, back into their comfort zone, and didn't discuss climate again. I believe the main reason the average person doesn't hear more about climate change is because they don't want to know. The implications to our lives are enormous and life is hard enough.

Today in the Keys

I continue to work in the Keys every chance I get and the conversation on climate has gotten far more sophisticated in the last few years. At the last Rotary Club meeting I was invited to present at in 2019, I was asked, "There is so much heat trapped in the ocean that the seas will rise anyway. What if the heat in the system has already become self-sustaining? What does it matter what we do?" Good question.

"I don't know what will happen in the long term, but there's a lot we can do to improve things in the short- and mid-term," I said. "Saltwater upwelling has yet to reach the roots of trees. They aren't brown and dead yet." I pointed to the Silver Buttonwood bushes just outside the window which lined the parking lot and had grown large enough in the warm, wet tropical environment to be called trees. "When the trees die, it will be a powerful sign, but it hasn't happened yet. Let's do all we can first."

I am currently working in Key West, the last in the 125-mile string of islands. It is the southernmost point of the continental United States and is surrounded by some of the world's warmest coastal waters. When you stand on the south side of the island on a clear day, Key West feels like it is within waving distance to Cuba. The

Climate Planning Objection 7 ■ **185**

town is known for its historic center with its traditional wooden homes that date from 1880 to 1920, sunset happy hours, snorkeling, and scuba diving. It doesn't feel like the proverbial canary in the coal mine, but it is.

Key West has an average elevation of 4.7 feet but the famed center of the community, along Duval Street, can be quite high by South Florida standards, between 7 and 18 feet. Residents have learned to live with destructive storms and frequent flooding, but the storms haven't resulted in widespread devastation in recent memory. Even given the island's extra elevation the challenges ahead are dire, though. An NOAA tidal measure in Key West has tallied an increase of 9 inches in sea level over the past century. The total population of Key West was 26,039 in 2016, the total number of homes at risk is estimated at 6,921, and the total value of threatened property is around US$3.3 billion.

To combat flooding, Key West has invested in one-way valves on storm drains to block seawaters from surging on to city streets and prevent sunny day flooding like in Miami Beach.[4] The city also has many resilience measures contained within its local plans which they have yet to implement. One of my roles in Key West is to keep the conversation on climate going. In my presentations I talk about how, by 2045, the sea level in the Florida Keys will rise another 15 inches according to projections made by the U.S. Army Corps of Engineers. As a result, the city of Key West – the economic powerhouse of Monroe County, Florida – would see more than 300 tidal flooding events per year within the lifetime of today's 30-year mortgages. By 2100, Key West could expect 6 feet of rise and at that point things would be much worse.

The people I talk to point out that as vulnerable as Key West may be it is far less vulnerable than most of the Florida Keys. Unlike areas like Cudjoe Key, Big Pine Key, and parts of Key Largo, Key West has better prospects for survival because it has some of the highest ground in the Keys. "Don't worry, we will survive," I hear.

"The responsibility on you is even greater, then," I say. "Over long enough a timeline, Key West may become the last refuge of Key's culture and history."

Even if Key West loses all of its 7 square miles except for its core 300 acres in the next 200 years (a core with elevations, again, up to 18 feet) we can call our effort to sound the alarm a success, in my opinion. Even if the entirety of the Florida Keys and the state road that connects the island keys disappears, then, I believe, the salvaging of that tiny island core can be considered an achievement. It may be a Pyrrhic victory given the ultimate cost, but the locals I work with are the judge of ultimate success and they seem to agree.

I believe that even with a much smaller footprint, the place can maintain a high level of diversity and versality. Key West is a beautiful tropical oasis of natural, manmade, and cultural assets. Anyone who has visited Key West never forgets the classical Caribbean homes and exquisite historic conch houses, Bird of Paradise trees and block-large banyans, and picket fences covered in jasmine and hibiscus. The place hosts literary festivals, art walks, fetish parades, historic tours, bar crawls, breathtaking sunsets, Easter Sundays, and family reunions. No matter where one's interests lie, that experience awaits them in Key West.

186 ■ *Why Are We Doing This?*

On my desk at the moment are plans to update, lift, and bulwark Key West's Duval Street. I have learned that Duval Street is really several different main streets through several unique places: The nightly celebration at Mallory Square, the raucous afternoon partying in front of Sloppy Joes', the quiet solemnity of St. Paul's Church, the locals' night off in Bahama Village, and the charm of shopping and galleries near Virginia Street. In the distant future everything closer to each other.

The plan includes a range of approaches from permeable materials, bioswales and raingardens, to lifting the street in select areas, and adding sea walls and new pump systems. The plan proposes a wonderful new streetscape with more shade, places to sit, plazas to visit, and things to see. Every climate plan must benefit current residents as well as future generations. Despite the best effort of my team, too many of the locals we talk to feel that the ultimate survival of Key West and Keys culture is still the responsibility of another generation. Still, we persevere.

Touring the Keys

During my return trips to the Keys after having worked there, I had a chance to evaluate the results of my work to protect coral and animal habitat eight years earlier. Just about all the water around the Florida Keys is part of the Florida Keys National Marine Sanctuary but the centerpiece is Pennekamp State Park in Key Largo. I snorkeled Pennekamp to examine the coral and was disheartened. Far more of the coral was rumble and dust than I remembered. If I had tapped transect squares and counted fish I'd count less fish than eight years before.

There is only so much anyone can do at the local level to protect coral. We required sewer systems to replace leaky septic tanks and that helped, though the cost to both the homeowner and to the municipality was high and the upgrades had to be slowly phased in. Our rate of growth ordinance was made to slow development long enough to help the sewer projects keep up. That ordinance helped too.

New development in the Keys had to be set far from the water and buffered by the mangroves wetlands. Mangroves are essentially forests that grow along the coastlines and they protect coastal regions from waves, erosion, and rising sea levels. Mangroves are a haven for biodiversity and sequester carbon which can help address both global heating and ocean acidification. In the Florida Keys new construction wasn't allowed on offshore islands at all. That helped keep vegetative barriers in place and reduce indefensible development.

In the Keys, I helped map and draft the Tier system in 2005 and 2006, Monroe County's land conservation system, and it remains the most effective regulatory land preservation tool that I know. We designated Big Pine Key *Tier 1, Environmentally Sensitive Land*, and shaded it in green on county maps to protect the endangered Key deer located on the island. This meant that getting a building permit was nearly impossible. There were 24 endangered species in the Keys and we had the ability to control development to a degree that is rare in America. A property owner's best financial option was often to sell their land to the county.

We designated land on Key Largo *Tier 2, Sprawl Reduction*, in subdivisions that were only partially developed in order to begin a conversation about county acquisition. Many of the thousands of lots we designated for protection were mapped for multiple reasons including reducing the stressors on coral created by development. Another goal was to reduce construction in areas of repeat flooding. Though we didn't discuss it at the time, I could see that these areas would be inundated as seas rose.

The public meetings got heated. People didn't like having their land colored green or any other color except yellow for residential and red for commercial on the Zoning Map (which our Tier map superseded). We were an Area of Critical State Concern monitored by the state, but some of our county commissioners felt that it was their role to stand up to the state and to the urban planners applying state law. The commissioners disagreed with staff reports and granted exceptions, basically granting building permits in places of high environmental quality or in places likely to flood in the future.

The champion of the pushback effort was Monroe county mayor Murray Nelson. Granting exemptions one at a time (as was a commissioner's prerogative) wasn't enough for him. He met with county staff to redraw the maps and grant more properties Tier 3 status, allowing the owners of the environmentally important lots to build. Mayors are not supposed to give direction directly to staff. Nelson didn't care.

Commissioner Nelson was a large man, bald, with thick bi-focal glasses, a fondness for florid fishing shirts and a CEO's way of giving speeches, subtly hinting at what he wanted, and expecting his requests to be carried out without him ever having to be overt. The first two times we met I listened politely and nodded quite a bit.

"We don't need the state telling us what to do down here do we?" he asked. "Tallahassee is a different world. What do you think?"

"Tallahassee is practically Georgia," I said.

"That's right." He liked that. His rakish, pirate smile broadened.

The next time he met with me he asked my supervisor to attend the meeting because I didn't seem to take any of the mayor's hints. I, in turn, asked our staff biologist to attend the meeting to contribute their expert advice on the habitat value of the lots which Mayor Nelson wanted me to re-map. Maybe it was the presence of the biologist, but on our final meeting I gave him a speech which almost got me fired. I talked of the barn swallows back where I grew up in Rhode Island, of all things: "They came in the spring and darted in and out of haylofts squeaking and fluttering. Their feathers fell to the ground. We could tell that the numbers of swallows were decreasing every year. It is down here that the swallows live most their lives and we're paving their habitat. We're paving paradise."

This time it was Commissioner Nelson's turn to smile and nod. He wore a banana yellow shirt with a wild-orchids-in-Hawaii motif that day. I still remember it. Whatever his plan for me was he didn't give it away. He just smiled.

188 ■ *Why Are We Doing This?*

"I'm not going to tell you what to do," my supervisor, David Daquisto, the director of the Upper Keys, said to me. "But you might want to be a little more careful. The commissioner is complaining about you."

I didn't want to be more careful. The mayor was costing the Keys animal habitat and coral. People were building in places where they shouldn't have been.

On my return trips to the Keys eight years after wrestling with Commissioner Nelson, I felt slight vindication over the fact that he granted building permits in places that saw continual flooding. The low-lying neighborhoods along the Backwater Sound like Stillwright Point and Twin Lakes, places where Nelson owned lots or had friends, are inundated for weeks at a time today. The ubiquitous manatee mailboxes of the Keys sit in still, black water that pools in the center of the road during King Tides.[5] Those homes experience mold, subsidence, and cracks in their support foundations. Commissioner Nelson didn't do those owners any favor by granting building permits. At the same time, thanks to our work on the Tier system, many of the flooding lots don't have homes on them. Newspaper articles which describe flooding in the Keys don't mention the Tier system. When risk reduction works you never hear about it. No one cares about the bomb that didn't go off.

Commissioner Nelson only slowed the inevitable. In 2020, the U.S. Army Corps of Engineers released a US$5.5 billion plan that involved strengthening the U.S.1 Highway in six places, elevating 7,300 houses, floodproofing 3,800 buildings and, importantly, buying and demolishing about 300 homes. State-run buyouts which began with the Tier system and focused on undeveloped land have begun to focus increasingly on removing homes.[6]

Commissioner Murray Nelson died of cancer just months after our last meeting. He died with two years left on his term and was replaced by Sylvia Murphy, a local Emergency Medical Services medic and environmental activist. The county's Government and Cultural Arts Center was named after Commissioner Nelson. I helped design the waterfront facility on Tier 3 land suitable for development. Commissioner Sylvia Murphy fought off attacks on the Tier system for 14 years as a commissioner and only recently retired.

Notes

1 IPCC (2013). Summary for Policymakers. D. Understanding the climate system and its recent changes. In: Stocker, T.F., D. Qin, G.-K. Plattner, M. Tignor, S.K. Allen, J. Boschung, A. Nauels, Y. Xia, V. Bex and P.M. Midgley (eds), *Climate Change 2013: The Physical Science Basis. Contribution of Working Group I to the Fifth Assessment Report of the Intergovernmental Panel on Climate Change.* Cambridge and New York: Cambridge University Press. Retrieved from: www.ipcc.ch/site/assets/uploads/2018/02/WG1AR5_SPM_FINAL.pdf

2 Ibid.

3 McGrath, M. (2020). Climate change: Worst emissions scenario "exceedingly unlikely." *BBC News Online*, January 29. Retrieved from: www.bbc.com/news/science-environment-51281986

4 Harrington, J. (2019). From Atlantic City to Key West: 21 beach towns that will soon be under water. *USA Today*, July 18. Retrieved from: www.usatoday.com/story/money/2019/07/18/atlantic-city-key-west-beach-towns-will-be-under-water-climate-change/39697819/
5 Mazzei, P. (2019). 82 days underwater: The tide is high, but they're holding on. *New York Times*, November 24. Retrieved from www.nytimes.com/2019/11/24/us/florida-keys-flooding-king-tide.html
6 Harris, A. (2020). In Florida Keys, $5.5 billion hurricane protection plan would buy 300 homes, raise thousands. *Miami Herald*, July 3. Retrieved from: www.miamiherald.com/news/local/environment/article243931482.html#storylink=cpy

Chapter 8

Climate Planning Objection 8

"Someone will fix this. Some new technological invention will save us."

"We need to save the planet," we often hear, and we do, and we will, but a qualification might be in order when it comes to the climate variable of the planetary equation. This isn't a problem we can *fix* any longer. Given the amount of additional carbon dioxide already present in our climatic system it may be too late to save, or *prevent*, damage to the world's most vital systems. *Salvage* may be a more accurate word, though how bad a situation we face is still a question. And there is also no one technological invention – not solar panels or carbon capture technology, for instance – that can fix the problem because the problem is multifarious.

Our coastal cities, for instance, are already locked into higher sea levels because of the heat which has already been trapped in the oceans. We're likely to see several feet of sea level rise regardless of any preventive action we take now. The only question is how long it will take. Southeast Florida planners often talk about "2 feet by 2060" based on Army Corps projections. Even if we can halt rise at 2 feet, 2 feet will have an overwhelming effect. Local shipwreck stories, the stories we read on panels at local museums in Florida dedicated to piracy or storms, teach us that when you're in a fight with the ocean your best hope for survival is salvaging what you can. The ocean really is just too big to fight.

The IPCC 2007 Summary for Policymakers states that "carbon dioxide emissions will continue to contribute to warming and sea-level rise for more than a

DOI: 10.4324/9781003181514-10

191

192 ◾ *Why Are We Doing This?*

millennium due to the time scales required for removal of this gas from the atmosphere."[1] However, more recent studies using more elaborate computer models report that the situation is perhaps less dire and that if we stop emitting carbon right now the oceans will absorb carbon more rapidly. The lag between halting CO_2 emissions and halting temperature rise might not be 50 to 100 years and might be closer to three to five years.[2] If true, then that's empowering.

If nothing is done to stop carbon pollution, then we will find ourselves in impossible positions. Additional warming of 3.6°F (2°C) could translate to 15.4 feet (4.7 meters) of global sea level rise one day. That would necessitate the displacement of over a hundred million people by some estimates.[3] Whatever the case, it is safe to say that if we do everything we can to restore equilibrium in the world's carbon cycle and are successful, then we will still have several years of sea level rise to contend with.

Many of the planners I know in the Great Plains and Rocky Mountain states have resigned themselves to the idea that their communities will simply run out of water one day and my colleagues have become, I hate to say, graceful losers, reiterating the phrase: "Enjoy it now, because it is not going to last." I hear this phrase in relation to the water shortage predictions in Colorado, the Texas Panhandle, and South Texas, especially. Maybe this is a sound, rational assessment of the situation. The American West is strewn with ghost towns and dead main streets. We do not know. But I hate to hear people give up.

Even if we avoid all discussion of the calamitous results of climate change – like the retreat from coastal regions and abandonment of desert cities – we must assume that even the smallest effects will be calamitous for vulnerable populations in our country. In Laredo, Texas, on the plains of the Lower Rio Grande, the water bill is getting harder and harder to afford. This is the case in many towns across the country and this problem will only get worse. This isn't a problem that can simply be solved, or one that Laredo can be saved from. Still, we must salvage what we can.

In 2019, while I was working on a Land Development Code update in Laredo and co-leading a meeting on affordable housing, water became the main discussion topic. At our table of housing experts, Carol Sherwood of Habitat for Humanity described the plight of a homeowner in a Habitat house who she said paid US$110 a month on his home payment and US$119 a month on his water bill. She said that the tenant had already given up trying to keep the grass and front yard trees watered, and his wilted grass and browning trees were a source of shame for the man.

"This is a struggling city," Sherwood said. According to Laredo's Community Development Department's Five Year Plan, 37% of Laradoans pay more than 50% of their income on housing.[4] "After they pay for housing, the people I work with sometimes don't have the money for water," she said. And then, making things worse, just weeks after our conversation, the City instituted higher rates to pay for US$70 million in water infrastructure. Included in the City's plan was a search for an additional source of water to supplement the Rio Grande. The city of Laredo can't be blamed; as the world gets warmer and drier, drinking water will simply get more and more expensive.

Climate Planning Objection 8 ■ 193

I often hear that a technological solution is on the way, but it isn't here yet. I hear that changes to our lifestyles and systems aren't necessary now because we simply just need to wait until the solution is invented. "Technology not taxes." This all may have to do with the fact that in America today the Democratic Party owns the renewable energy conversation and there's a hope held by the Republican Party that some wonderchild company philosophically aligned with their views will top the Democrat's puny efforts with some genius new invention.

Scientific studies have determined that today's renewable technologies are sufficient to reduce greenhouse gas emissions and avoid some of the worst aspects of climate change. There will be improvements to technology including the efficiencies of batteries, the practicality of carbon capture mechanisms, and the efficiencies of nuclear technologies, but we have what we need. This is a fact we need to make clear in our work: The challenge may be made easier but will not be solved by some a new invention. We must employ the tools we have now.

I often hear the persistent myth that renewable energy sources can't meet baseload (24 hour per day) demand. *The wind doesn't blow all the time, and there's no sunlight at night*[5] is a continually stated justification for not switching to wind and solar power even though, batteries, of course, store energy when there is no wind or sunlight. With lithium-ion battery prices falling 76% since 2012, energy storage is becoming an increasingly cost-competitive option to pair with large-scale solar generation.[6] Hawaiian Electric Industries announced it was building the world's biggest battery. Then, the next day, Florida Power and Light announced it was building a larger battery, a battery (technically, an energy *storage center*) that would cover 40 acres of land. The Florida battery would be enough to power 100 million cell phone batteries as people slept. The "world's biggest battery" is an ongoing contest, and Texas will soon have its entry.[7]

Across the world, plans to move to 100% renewable energy at the local, state, and national level all may assume technologies that are available today. The shift will involve both increases in energy efficiency and a switch to renewable power generation paired with batteries. The European Renewable Energy Council (EREC), for instance, prepared a plan, entitled *Re-Thinking 2050*, for the European Union (EU) to meet 100% of its energy needs with renewable sources by 2050.[8] Local municipalities should all be working on similar plans despite the pushback they will inevitably receive from fossil fuel energy providers who will label the initiatives costly vanity projects that put an undue cost burden on ratepayers.

There is no calvary coming over the hill at the sound of the bugle, no line of horses about to crash the battlefield and save us like in the classic Westerns. No gunship rescue, medevac, or SOS Tomahawk missile bombardment like in contemporary war movies. No metaphoric D-Day. No silver bullets in the form of carbon-capture technologies or clean nuclear fusion, I am sorry to report. The villains are many, and the heroes are few and in it alone. But it isn't time for last words either; the heroes have taken a stand. Though somewhat untheatrically, the heroes have taken the form of photovoltaic panels, wind turbines, energy storage centers, purple

194 ■ *Why Are We Doing This?*

pipes, desalinization facilities, international climate accords, Green candidates, and, I like to think, urban planners.

The Problem of Droughts

Out West, "whiskey is for drinking; water is for fighting over," Mark Twain once reputedly wrote. In the world of urban planning, however, water adequacy should come before development, not the other way around. Land use and drinking water quantity, quality, dependability, and availability are connected. Most arid states have rules that tie development to water availability like the Co-Water Adequacy Rule in Colorado, and new building permits are not issued until applicants can first establish that water is available. However, when our plan projections look beyond today's water availability and to the future, we tend to find a water gap. Colorado, for instance, will have a municipal and industrial water gap of between 25,000 and 750,000 acre-feet per year by 2050 according to the Colorado Water Plan Analysis and Technical Update.[9]

The water problem can go relatively unnoticed until a community hits a drought, but as the world warms and dries we can expect more droughts. In 2018, 23 U.S. states had no state-level plans of any kind regarding water supply resiliency and climate adaptation.[10] While many states like Colorado, California, and Oregon have statewide water efficiency requirements, no U.S. state has yet to adopt statewide drought mitigation requirements. What this means is that in 2020, when Colorado was in the middle of one of the worst mega-droughts in its history and suffering the largest wildfire it had ever faced due to dry conditions, all Coloradoans really could do was pray for rain.[11]

Droughts are something we expect to ride out. The water will come eventually. But what if it doesn't? Or, at least, what if doesn't come soon enough to avoid damage? What if it doesn't arrive with enough volume to restore stability? The relationship between climate and water is a complicated one but it is a safe bet that warmer futures mean drier futures for most places. The *2018 IPCC Special Report* confirms the escalation of global warming and how this will aggravate drought risks.[12] As the number of droughts and water shortages continues to increase nationally, laws that advance water efficiency and conservation at the state and local level are becoming more critical.

There are tools to help urban planners. The U.S. Drought Monitor is a way to tell when your community is in drought, though the monitor doesn't offer local solutions. The best guidebook for local planning solutions may be the American Planning Association report, *Falling Dominoes: A Planner's Guide to Drought and Cascading Impacts* (2019).[13] The guidebook teaches planners to ask these questions:

- ■ Where does our water come from?
- ■ How much water do we have?

Climate Planning Objection 8 ■ 195

- How much water do various land use sectors use?
- How do we pay for water system repairs and improvements?
- How is water conserved?
- Is our water system sufficient, safe, and reliable?

The report describes drought mitigation assessment tools (such as water resource inventories, drought risk assessments, and Hazard Mitigation Plans), legislation and public policy tools (like water bans), ways to increase or augment water supplies (this list includes water recycling projects and watershed protection), and public education.

Drought is a complex topic and is caused by a variety of factors from meteorological drought caused by a lack of precipitation to socio-economic drought caused by supply and demand gaps. When it comes to long-range climate planning, drought due to aridification is our biggest concern. Aridification is the process of a region becoming increasingly arid, or dry. It refers to long-term change, rather than seasonal variation. Aridification transforms ecosystems, economies, and communities permanently.

Aridification is often measured as the reduction of average soil moisture content. Hotter temperatures create more evaporation and less evapotranspiration. Evapotranspiration is the process by which water is transferred from the land to the atmosphere by evaporation from the soil and other surfaces and by transpiration from plants. Aridification results in less precipitation in the form of snow and less water storage in the soil. Lower soil moisture means less drinking water, crop failures, and greater potential for wildfires. As global temperatures warm the rate of evaporation increases worldwide and while some areas may experience heavier than normal precipitation in the future due to climate change, they may also see higher evaporation rates and may become more prone to droughts.

Climate planners working around the world are often asked: Are the droughts we're seeing today the new normal? And that's a hard question to answer. When it comes to your community's long-term water and drought prognosis, the largest source of uncertainty is, as with all climate questions, human actions. However, our long-term plans need to be tailored for a more drought-prone and fire-prone world.

As urban planners write long-range plans they typically ask:

- What is our population, housing, and employment growth?
- What are our development expectations?

Going forward, they will also need to also ask:

- How much water will we need?
- Do current water supplies line up with projected demand?
- What water challenges does a changing climate pose?

196 ■ *Why Are We Doing This?*

After a thorough exploration of these questions new policy can follow. These policies might include water supply diversification initiatives, requirements for proof of adequate water for all new development, water conservation programs, and land use changes.

Notes From the Field

Fighting Heat Island Effects in Laredo, Texas

The term *heat island* describes built areas that are hotter than nearby rural ones. The annual mean air temperature of a city with a million people or more can be roughly 2°F to 5°F (1.1°C to 8.3°C) warmer than its surroundings. In the evening, the difference can be as high as 22°F (12°C). Heat islands can affect communities by increasing summertime peak energy demand, raising air conditioning costs, adding to air pollution and greenhouse gas emissions, triggering heat-related illness and mortality, adding to water costs, contributing to water pollution, and adding to regional aridification.[14]

We can design cities, neighborhoods, and individual development projects using techniques that reduce heat absorption and the heat island effect while at the same time sequestering the carbon which is the root of global warming. Planning controls already in place in most areas work to add heat-absorbing greenery to the cityscape. Zoning codes and land development codes usually contain requirements for at least one street tree on the lot of every new subdivision, parking lot landscaping for new businesses, vegetative buffers between properties, and open space preservation (usually around 20% of a newly developed greenfield site).

Our first job as urban planners is to protect these requirements even as land becomes more valuable and our cities and towns densify. In the state of Montana, I was notified by city planners that the 20% open space requirement which we were recommending for a new neighborhood site we were planning and coding was too high, even though the 20% open space rule of thumb has been employed by urban planners in America for over a century. We were informed that the maximum open space we could require had been whittled down to 11% by the state courts. We weren't allowed to require more than 11% open space from development no matter what the environmental context of the project. From a climatological point of view, that's appalling, and we must fight efforts like this.

Developers frequently try to avoid providing 20% open space with the use of Planned Urban Developments (PUDs) which allow them to draft their own codes for large projects. Developers also use form-based codes, a tool I am usually quite in favor of as a proponent of quality design, to reduce their open space. As climate planners we can't let private or public developers out of their responsibilities to provide parks and trees no matter what the argument.

Urban planners need to go further than conventional setback, buffer, and open space requirements. Planners should update their municipality's code requirements

Figure 8 La Postada Hotel, Laredo, Texas

and local and state road design standards to require street trees on all new streets and require a plan to water the trees for their first year. Locally, tree protection ordinances can require a tree removal permit before valued trees (as defined by the ordinance) are cut down. Additionally, we want to encourage native species and xeriscaping practices, and the integration of landscaping with stormwater management

198 ■ *Why Are We Doing This?*

techniques such as bioswales and raingardens. As we will discuss later, all of these goals are far harder to implement in practice than in theory.

The U.S. is losing its urban tree canopy at a rate of 175,000 acres per year. This is approximately 36 million trees per year. A study in 2018 by the National Forest Service found that 23 states had a statistically significant decrease in tree cover, with a total of 45 states showing a net decline.[15] This is happening at a time when the country needs street trees to save energy by providing shade, to cool air as leaves evaporate water, reduce storm water runoff, reduce flooding, clean water prior to its return to aquifers, improve air quality by absorbing carbon dioxide and other pollutants, and, in general, make life on Earth more pleasant.

The loss of street trees is happening for many reasons, including lowered code requirements, inadequate maintenance, and a well-meaning desire to give street trees more space to grow than the urban or even suburban realm allows. Our existing urban canopy is also a kind of infrastructure which is being allowed to age and decay along with many other categories of infrastructure. Trees are a particularly fragile form of infrastructure and prone to rot, diseases, pests, and damage from cars. Replacement campaigns need to be part of a city's budget.

We see a whittling down of street tree requirements in communities across the country because street trees add expense to development and so they are targeted by developers seeking to reduce capital costs. Often urban planners obligingly remove tree and planting requirements to reduce the cost of development in the hope their actions will translate into greater affordability. I must say that in my experience, reducing requirements almost never lowers sales prices because those prices are set by the market. And even in those cases in which decreasing the cost of development might just decrease home prices we need to remember that neighborhoods need trees too.

City engineers, public works departments, parks departments, and even tree wardens are often anti-tree because they do not feel that they have the budget to maintain trees. Often these departments inherit trees from the subdivision process and as the number of subdivisions increase the green areas these departments are responsible for increases even though their budgets remain static. Developers are loath to create the homeowners' associations that will take care of the trees and parks they build because the existence of a homeowners' association can hurt home sales.

Sometimes new requirements even make it impossible to replant areas that once had trees. Narrow planting strips, playgrounds, and areas under power lines which once had trees are being deemed unsatisfactory, unsafe, or inadvisable for new canopy trees. Tree wardens across the country ban trees near sidewalks in order to allow the trees all the impermeable space they need for feeder roots. Again, this is well intentioned, but impractical.

The highly successful *Right Tree Right Place* campaign from the United States Department of Agriculture (USDA) Forest Service Urban and Community Forestry Program produces beautiful posters with illustrations of local trees and then forbids those same trees in just about every area other than the centers of backyards in fear

Climate Planning Objection 8 ■ 199

that those trees might interfere with telephone lines and power lines. Thanks to this campaign, the city of Coral Gables in Florida, a planned city with a 100-year history of careful tree stewardship and some of the greatest oak and banyan lined trees in the country, was reduced to planting several hundred dinky Foxtail Palms along its otherwise grand and centrally located SW 57th Street because of a telephone line that happened to sporadically line parts of the roadway. Palm trees add little to no shade to an urban canopy and have a low overall ecological value.

Let me describe one effort to preserve the street trees in an arid city and let me break the narrative into rounds, like a boxing match, because boxing is an apt metaphor for a day that seemed to involve one hard hit after another to those of us who care about trees.

Round 1

In the summer of 2019, from the conference room of Laredo's Transit Center, I looked down on Jarvis Plaza with its Live Oaks, Rio Grande Ash, and the violet summer flowers of the Queen Crepe Myrtle. Under that canopy of trees where people sat and waited for buses, the humid summer heat was tamed: It was between 5 and 15°F cooler than just about anywhere else in the city. The shade was helping to retain soil moisture and fighting the heat island effect. At that same moment I was admiring the trees from that conference room, I learned that Laredo had made street trees illegal. Worse still, many of the trees in Jarvis Plaza were no longer compliant with the city's Code of Ordinances and could be removed, or, at least, would never be replaced.

I was invited to Laredo as part of a team working to update the city's code. The project was called *ReCode Laredo*, and our job was to align the code with the Comprehensive Plan that our same team co-wrote, which was called, quite unimprovably, *Plan Viva Laredo*. The code meetings were headed by Able City, a Laredo-based planning firm which had led the *Plan Viva Laredo* project. According to the plan's Sustainability Chapter, improving the city's urban tree canopy was part of our job.

I read the tree-ban ordinance handed to me by one of the city's engineers which effectively made street trees illegal.

"Did you know about this?" I asked one of the city's urban planners. He didn't. "This is pretty bad, right?" I asked. He shrugged indifferently.

Apparently when the city had amended the Plumbing chapter of its Land Development Code it included language that stated, "no vegetation shall be installed within forty-eight inches [four feet] of a public street."[16] Of course, in Laredo, like in most of the United States, street trees are typically placed within 4 feet of the street because there's no more than 4 feet available in the adjacent side planting strips. Because of the ordinance, the city's tree canopy could not be replaced as trees died, and new streets, except those with uncommonly wide planting strips, would not host street trees. Over a long enough timeline Laredo would lose its entire urban forest.

200 ■ *Why Are We Doing This?*

Without trees, the heat island effect would raise temperatures, soil moisture would be lost, and fewer people would choose to walk or bike the city's unshaded streets – and this would, foreseeably, increase automobile usage. The city would also lose the exquisite charm of its Live Oaks, Ebony, Honey Mesquite, Cypresses, Ash, and Cedars.

"We need to fix this," I said to my team. They agreed. The city's urban planner said nothing. We had only just begun to talk about trees and we were already on the ropes – leaning against the ropes of the proverbial boxing ring for support, on the verge of collapse and defeat.

Round 2

In our first meeting of the day, I talked to an engineer on the city's Technical Review Board Ad-Hoc Committee, which recommended the changes which the City Council adopted, and he explained to me that the intent of the ordinance wasn't to eliminate street trees but instead to prevent public and private irrigation systems from leaving puddles on the streets. The engineer attributed cracks in the streets along a new subdivision called Concord Hills to the watering of its line of oak trees. I didn't know that water could cause cracks in asphalt. I'm from Florida where it rains all the time and we still have streets, but I accepted his explanation.

I showed the engineer an image from an online map of a home on Victoria Street in the historic part of the city which had gotten permission to install five new oak trees in the planting strip parallel the street.

"Would that be allowed in the future?" I asked.

"Well, no," he said. He then went on to reiterate that eliminating street trees wasn't the intention of the ordinance; the intention was to preserve the city infrastructure.

"You must have seen this coming," I said.

He narrowed his eyes defensively. Was this truly a foreseeable though unintended consequence or was it the case that the development community was simply pushing an ordinance that would eliminate street trees in order to reduce their development costs?

"We're going to fix this," I told the city's urban planner again. Code updates are precisely the right time to fix specific problems.

He shrugged again. "I don't see the big deal," he said.

"It's a big deal."

The street trees were not winning.

Round 3

The next input meeting on the code update project was with service providers. AEP Energy, a local provider responsible for erecting and maintain power lines, came to the meeting with a list of changes to the code that it wanted to see. The changes involved eliminating every portion of the code which required street trees and trees on people's property. When questioned about this, AEP's representative said that her company wanted to lower the number of power outages caused by tree limbs which knocked out wires during windstorms. She made a good point. Outages in a hot, arid place could mean lives lost when the air conditioning was out, especially among the older population.

I looked up AEP's website a found a graphic depicting how small trees such as redbud, dogwood, and crabapple which were under 25 feet high could be located under power lines. The graphic was reproduced from the *Right Tree, Right Place* campaign.

"Can we do this?" I asked, showing the AEP representative the image. "This is from your company's website. It says that we can have small trees."

"Any tree could cause a problem," she said.

"Why can't you put the lines underground?" a planner from Able City asked.

"It costs too much," she said.

"We'll do this," I said tapping again on the image of small trees under the power lines. "It's better than nothing."

Again, I am no fan of the *Right Tree, Right Place* campaign. No tree-lover is. In my experience, the amiably named *Right Tree, Right Place* campaign has done more harm than good to the tree canopy of the country. At its least destructive, the *Right Tree, Right Place* campaign is causing tall, shade-producing, canopy trees like oaks to be replaced with non-canopy, bushy trees like Crab Apple, Holly, and dwarf Crape Myrtles, and cities and towns are losing shade and losing the large trees that act as carbon sinks. However, the campaign was endorsed by power companies across the country and while the gist of the policy is anti-tree, it does allow small trees to be located under overhead lines – like the foxtail palms that were planted in Coral Gables, Florida. We would add the graphic to our code and talk about low canopy trees like Guajillo and Mesquite, small flowering trees like Texas Mountain Laurel or Retama, and even trees that produced edible fruit like Texas Persimmon, Kumquat, or citrus.

"We're going to allow small trees," I said.

"I love trees," the AEP representative agreed. "Fine, plant small trees."

Maybe the trees won that round. Maybe.

Round 4

The next meeting involved representatives from the development community, and a planner from Able City asked about trees. A member of the Laredo Builders Association stated flat out that the new code needed to decrease the cost of development and that trees were too costly.

"It's less than US$500 for a decent oak here," I said. I had checked the websites of local nurseries. The price was three times higher in other places I'd worked. Nurseries were abundant because the land needed to grow trees at plant farms was still plentiful in Laredo.

202 ■ *Why Are We Doing This?*

"We want to keep houses affordable," the builder said. "People think that when you give us a requirement we simply learn to accept that much less profit but what really happens is that we pass that cost to the homebuyer."

"I don't think a homebuyer will disagree with paying US$500 more if it means they get an oak in their front yard."

"Big subdivisions mean a lot of trees. That's a high up-front cost for us."

"You'll make your money back."

"We're not going to accept a new code that raises the cost of development," the builder said flatly. The Laredo Builders Association is a non-profit organization made up of member builders, developers, and sub-contractors. Most growing cities have a builder's association and they usually have enough influence to stop updates to municipal codes.

"Was it a builders' representative on the city's Technical Review Board Ad-Hoc Committee that pushed to eliminate street trees?" I asked the builder. "You know, to prevent cracks in the road."

The builder didn't answer.

After the meeting, a planner at Able City told me that when the technical committee was created it was intended to offer a purely technical review of proposed city policy, but that one by one the City Council appointed developers and builders to the committee instead of technical experts, like engineers and landscape architects, so that the committee had begun to push developer-friendly policies exclusively. It seemed plausible. I had seen that kind of thing occur on many local Planning Commissions, Development Review Boards, and Technical Review Boards across the country.

I had even seen developer representatives on appointed boards make street trees illegal, sometimes under the guise of water conservation, in order to make sure that no one, not even developers that wanted to, were planting trees. Anti-tree laws are sometimes pushed by builders and developers afraid that trees planted in any subdivision anywhere raised the community's standards for new subdivisions.

A short digression is in order here: When we use the commonly heard expression *development community* we can't help picture a happy village of real estate developers, not unlike, to use a Dr. Seuss reference, Whoville, with all the happy Whos standing hand in hand. In reality, my experience is that developers are in cutthroat competition with each other and will do whatever they can to quash competition and keep standards low.

I felt it better to give the city's Technical Review Board Ad-Hoc Committee the benefit of the doubt, however, and assume that eliminating street trees was an inadvertent mistake. If it was really the case that puddling due to irrigation caused cracks and not, say, the underlying soils or the city's inadequate road specifications (specifications that might have been watered down by representatives from the development community), then I was confident we could find a way to accomplish the goal of avoiding cracks without costing the city its trees. Perhaps a high-efficiency, drip irrigation system could be required in the city's Plumbing Code. However, if

Climate Planning Objection 8 ■ **203**

the Builders Association put absolutely no value on trees and if the City Council deferred to the Builders Association then no clever solution would help.

I felt dazed, disoriented and punch drunk. It was time to find my corner, spit out the mouthguard, look around the ring for that guy who treats a boxer's cuts between rounds, and take some encouragement from the crowd.

"What do you think about requiring a drip irrigation system to avoid puddling?" I asked the city's urban planner.

"Sounds expensive."

Rounds 5 Through 12

Street trees have a lot of enemies in Laredo and as our meetings continued, I met more. One resident said that he didn't like leaf litter and bird droppings on his car, and he admitted to cutting down a tree in the right-of-way in front of his house even though it was on city-owned land. Another resident said he'd had all his trees taken down for fear that they would become a hazard during a tornado. The engineers in the city's Streets Department agreed with outlawing street trees because their roots could lift sidewalks and the sidewalks would need to be repaired. The Assistant Fire Marshal spoke of forbidding trees because low limbs could be an obstacle to his fire engine. State traffic engineers were against trees because cars sometimes crashed into trees. Keep in mind, each of these anti-tree policies has a corresponding pro-tree mitigation and compromise.

"We can solve for all of these problems in the code and keep the trees," I said to the city's urban planner as the day wore on and we were all getting tired.

He shrugged again.

I stood, leaned across the conference room table slowly, and slapped him hard in the back of the head. Actually, I didn't do this, but imagining it made me feel a lot better. Now, I am not suggesting that these incidents typify the Laredo Planning Department, City Hall, or Laredo in general. Far from it, I have met many outstanding people working hard to revive Laredo's Downtown, like Viviana Frank-Franco and her husband Frank Rotnofsky of Able City, especially. They are urban planners but also property owners in Downtown Laredo and every one of their projects, from the restaurants and shops they co-own to their company's downtown office in a renovated gas station, are remarkably eco-conscious. I met many inspiring, capable people working on *Viva Laredo* during a public process that was phenomenally well attended. Every city should be so lucky as to have Mario and Diana Peña of Able City in residence because somehow after a work-week spent improving their city they became tireless boosters and advocates for the city on weekends by saying "yes" to every charity event and social occasion that might help them to organize, advocate, or educate. Laredo has great people. I am simply saying that despite those people, I worry that Laredo will no longer have an urban canopy in 50 years, even though every cut tree is a step toward suicide for the city's local micro-climate.

204 ■ *Why Are We Doing This?*

Even if our team managed to change the code to allow (and maybe require) trees, after our work was done Laredo's trees would undoubtedly have to go another 12 rounds again, sometime in the future. After the day's meetings the team and I waited until it was a respectable enough hour to go have a beer and we drank a few for purely medicinal purposes.

"That's just how it is here," one of my team members at Able City said.

"Don't blame Laredo," I said, "That's how it is everywhere."

Speak For the Trees the Lorax Told Us

Think global and act local (if only because it is all you can do). Immediately after returning home from Laredo I bought a Royal Poinciana tree and planted it in the planting strip in front of our house. Just 50 years ago everyone in our part of Florida would have planted a tree (or two) before moving into their home because trees were their air conditioning. That's changed. The trees on my street were planted over 50 years ago, are getting old, and are not being replaced.

I involved my kids. I dug the hole with a long-handle digging shovel and they removed the dirt and repacked it around the tree with gardening trowels. That felt good.

Just a few weeks later we bought a Jacaranda and squeezed it into our SUV – the feathery green leaves sitting atop my kids' heads as we drove home. We planted the Jacaranda in the planting strip just 15 feet from the Royal Poinciana. Ideally, I would have given the trees more space from each other and more from the pavement, but it will be decades before that becomes an issue.

Puerto Rico is planting 750,000 trees.[17] The Scottish Highlands are being rewilded.[18] India has pledged to plant 40,000 square miles of forest.[19]

I filled out the Right-of-Way Tree Planting Request Form with the city of South Miami, the town where we live, and asked for two trees: One for the last portion of the planting strip (I requested a Live Oak); and another for our yard (it would shade the sidewalk and so it had a public benefit, I argued in the note section of the form). I was proud of my town because as a Tree City USA it had a policy to provide two free trees to every lot and even install them. However, after multiple communications with the city planner and assistant city manager those trees never arrived. Months and months passed. I gave up waiting for them and went back to the nursery. The Royal Poinciana and Jacaranda in my yard were looking great and so I purchased a Hong Kong Orchid.

China is reforesting 16 million acres of land, an area roughly the size of Ireland.[20] Pakistan is committed to planting 10 billion trees.[21] A coalition of Latin American countries has planned 77 square miles of forest restoration.[22]

As my wife watered the street trees one night a car pulled up alongside her and the older woman in the driver's seat looked at her and said, "One day those roots will rip up the sidewalk."

"That's a long way away," my wife said. "And we can always fix the sidewalk."

The busybody neighbor drove on.

One night, as I watered the Hong Kong Orchid, and the peacocks that live in South Miami gave their whooping call announcing sunset, I decided that it wouldn't be much more work to water a fourth tree, even though, unfortunately, I had run out of room in the planting strip in front of my house. The next weekend I bought another Royal Poinciana and placed it in the planting strip in front of a neighboring house. The bank had foreclosed on the family that lived there, the house had sat empty for over a year, and I didn't think anyone would mind.

Australia will plant a billion trees in the next 11 years.[23] Ireland will plant 440 million trees by 2040.[24]

I planted a native Slash Pine in my backyard and a second Hong Kong Orchid next to it. Technically, they were in the wrong place according to the *Right Tree, Right Place* poster I have hanging on our solarium because they were under power lines at the edge of our backyard and side yard. Big deal. Maybe in ten years those trees would have to be cut back a little.

My community, South Miami, has a goal of planting a million trees. We were six trees closer to that goal. Worldwide 100 gigatons of carbon will be pulled from the air. Tree planting seems to be the only climate policy that both political parties can agree to. I am not so sure Laredo will keep its trees, but my side of the street in South Miami will. My trees seem to be the only newly planted ones in our neighborhood, and I have resolved to move on to other streets and other blocks with my guerilla tree planting.

The 1952 movie *Ikiru*, by Akira Kurosawa, is about a city planning director who spends his career accomplishing nothing (except a weekly paycheck) until he realizes he has terminal cancer, and then he upends the entire city fighting to install one small children's playground in a poor slum before he dies. By the end of the movie, he succeeds, and we see him on a kid's swing just before, presumably, he passes away. It's one of my favorite films. Kurosawa made more than samurai movies. When the uphill battle of working as an urban planner gives me the Sisyphean blues, I can always just go plant a tree.

Seoul is planting 30 million trees.[25] Milan plans to plant 3 million trees. Niger and Senegal in Africa are planting 10 million trees.[26]

Notes From the Field

Discussing Drought in Lubbock, Texas

There are social norms in every society, community, office, and family. Social norms are the rules that prescribe what people should and should not do given their social surroundings. Often those norms are at odds with finding solutions to the climate crisis – even in a progressive urban planning office.

206 ■ *Why Are We Doing This?*

"We need to talk about climate change," I told my team in a briefing before we were to travel to Lubbock, Texas, for an on-site public workshop in 2019. We had already covered the basics regarding trip logistics, our workshop schedule, and the work products we were to generate. Everyone was briefed and it was time to talk strategy.

"We're not experts in climate change," I heard from one of the team members, an illustrator who was a little older than myself. "We would be safer if we stick to what we know. It's Lubbock." He had worked in Lubbock, an oil town, before. I had not.

We know enough, I wanted to say but I didn't because I suspected that the illustrator wasn't the only one with these kinds of thoughts.

"Our plan will make the city more walkable and bikeable," another team member said. "Do we really need to take the climate issue head on?" This was a surprise. He was ten years younger than me and I generally assume that younger people are more inclined to talk about climate than I am.

If we don't talk about these issues then who will? I wanted to say. "Good point," I said instead, discovering an unspoken office rule I didn't know we had, namely: *Don't talk about climate directly*. To be fair, our office is more environmentally aware than most. Several people bike to work, a couple walk, and several take transit even though parking is plentiful and cheap in our local parking garages. Victor Dover, our firm's co-founder, had an office shower installed for bike commuters and he proudly touts our *executive parking lot*, the hallway at the top of the stairs where the cyclists keep their bikes, when he gives office tours. That's where he parks too.

I began to discuss Lubbock's climate challenges with the team. I'd made a model of the future using a program called Urban Footprint. The future looked bleak.

"Are you really going to talk about climate change in Lubbock?" I was asked twice more. I didn't reply.

We went to Lubbock in September 2019 to help update the city's Downtown Plan and Development Code and to begin to implement the city's recently adopted city-wide Comprehensive Plan: *Plan Lubbock 2040*. The Comprehensive Plan's goals were to support downtown, manage growth, create an identity for the different areas of the city, improve connections with the universities, add a greater range of housing choices, add more parks, and support local businesses.

Nowhere in *Plan Lubbock 2040*, a 288-page document, were the words *climate change* mentioned. My first thought was that this omission was a kind of professional negligence on the part of plan authors. How could a plan for an arid Great Plains city that included a timeframe that extended to 2040 (in the title no less) not include a discussion of the world's changing climate? But I knew what it was like to write a plan for a community who hadn't adopted *fighting climate change* as a cultural value. The planners who wrote the Comprehensive Plan may have been specifically told not to include the entirely accurate, but still politically polarizing term, *climate change*. Texas is a red state and our firm had faced a similar dilemma just months earlier.

When our firm was commissioned to co-write a recovery plan for the downtown and waterfront of Panama City, Florida, after Hurricane *Michael* in 2018, our draft plan didn't include the words *climate change* or *sea level rise*. The words simply didn't appear in the first draft of the report, called *A Strategic Vision for Panama City's Historic Downtown and its Waterfront* (2019). There was a chapter called *Resilient Infrastructure* and one called *Sustainable Buildings*, but the plan never mentioned the root cause of the city's growing resilience and sustainability problems. Like the character Harry Potter, the plan fought a challenge which could not be named.

Imagine that: Hurricane *Michael's* eyewall passed directly over Panama City, and numerous shopping centers, hotels, and office buildings sustained major structural damage or were destroyed. Homes lost roofs. Yet there was no mention in the report that these problems would worsen in the future. While it is true that hurricanes had a history of hitting Florida well before human activity had begun to warm the planet, the rising seas and increasing damage caused by storms due to climate change are now major factors going forward. Why say nothing?

I was told that our planning team was asked by the prime consultant, the local firm leading the project, to say silent on the topic of climate change. I was told that our team, feeling that they needed to work within the boundaries the prime consultant set in order to stay at the decision-making table, conceded.

"You can get more done if you are on the inside than on the outside," I was told to me by one of our planners.

But that wasn't the whole story. I talked to key members of the Panama City team and they each communicated a reticence to address the controversial issue of climate. Each told me something to the effect that they didn't want to make the difficult job of drafting a consensus plan even harder. It was easier just to go along with what the prime consultant was asking. It was better to stick to neutral topics. That's the thing: Being on the inside changes us.

Climate change and sea level rise aren't the only items covered by informal gag orders set by social norms. There's a lot we don't talk about or don't attempt to address, including racial and economic inequity, unequal representation in local government, environmental justice, and gentrification – the displacement of local residents and businesses in the form of evictions and extreme rent increases caused by urban planning policies. But those are all topics for another book. There's a lot we don't talk about in America when it comes to local planning. Climate has simply been added to that list.

After some professional soul-searching our firm did include the words *sea level rise* and *climate change* in the final draft of the plan for Panama City and we did add to the report a frank discussion about rising seas.[27] After a discussion on the topic, Victor Dover insisted on it. *A Strategic Vision for Panama City's Historic Downtown and its Waterfront* (2019) eventually won a Charter Award from the Congress of the New Urbanism for addressing climate change head on.

Back to Lubbock.

208 ■ *Why Are We Doing This?*

Instead of saying *climate change*, Lubbock's Comprehensive Plan talks about the symptoms of climate change without mentioning the ultimate cause. The plan has sections on water conservation, air pollution, and making it safe to exercise outside despite worsening heat. This was the same approach our firm initially took in Panama City.

Would we just play along in Lubbock?

The city of Lubbock, Texas, has a population of roughly 254,000[28] and its main industry is farming. The city is highly dependent on the Ogallala Aquifer for both drinking water and irrigation, and the Ogallala is running dry.[29] The Ogallala Aquifer is a shallow water table aquifer beneath the Great Plains states and is one of the world's largest aquifers, stretching from South Dakota to Texas and covering an area of over 174,000 square miles.[30] Producers are extracting water faster than it is being replenished, which means that parts of the Ogallala Aquifer are considered a non-renewable resource.

Picture a windmill on a tower with a slatted fan wheel rotating in the wind on a grassy Midwestern prairie. Chances are that the windmill you are picturing, whether from memory or from a movie, was pulling water from the Ogallala. That windmill either stopped being able to fill its water tank long ago or will soon stop.

Agricultural communities like Lubbock are highly threatened by increases in temperatures and drought because farmers are dependent on water. Yields of major U.S. crops such as corn, soybeans, wheat, rice, sorghum, and cotton are expected to decline over this century because of increases in temperatures and changes in water availability.[31]

Even Lubbock's *2018 Strategic Water Supply Plan* had no mention of climate change, though it did describe "variable climatic conditions"[32] and water "diminishment" in multiple aquifers over time. The plan described how Lubbock, since 1911, relied solely on groundwater until 1968 when surface water from Lake Meredith was made available. It discussed how Lubbock utilized water from the Bailey County Well Field and the Roberts County Well Field, two groundwater sources which ultimately drew from the Ogallala Aquifer, which, again, were drying, and how the city would rely more on surface water sources Lake Meredith and Lake Alan Henry. The water supply from Lake Meredith was temporary, the plan stated. Lake Alan Henry, roughly 60 miles from Lubbock, would then supply the city with water for the next 100 years provided "its yield does not change due to dramatic changes in the lake's environments."

But dramatic changes are coming. Dramatic changes are already here. We live on a warmer and drier planet than we used to. You see the problem with using code words like *variable climatic conditions* instead of *climate change*: Variables can be helpful or hurtful and they presumably alternate. Some years you are up and others you are down. However, the changes that are expected in the Great Plains are headed in one direction: Desertification.

Given just how vulnerable Lubbock was, I couldn't help wondering if urban planners, certified by the American Planning Association, should be compelled to

Climate Planning Objection 8 ■ 209

talk about climate or risk their American Institute of Certified Planner (AICP) certification. The American Planning Association described climate as "one of the most important planning challenges of the 21st century" and stated that planners have an "obligation" to address it.[33] What if the AICP Rules of Conduct had a new rule that stated planners cannot allow political considerations to interfere with a frank discussion of climate? Perhaps a charge of ethical misconduct could be made against an urban planner who saw the symptoms of climate change but failed to discuss it, and failed to link it back to human activities, in the way a medical malpractice charge could be made against a doctor who saw the symptoms of diabetes or cancer in a patient and refused to diagnose the disease and prescribe treatments and lifestyle changes for fear of upsetting their patient and losing a client.

What if the urban planners who wrote Lubbock's Comprehensive Plan and water supply plan were required to talk about climate change? We can presume they would have addressed the issue if required to. I looked up the plan authors. They were fully educated experts from prestigious firms. The question of whether planners should be required to talk about climate change and the impact of human activities had never occurred to me until Lubbock. I am not sure I have ever seen so vulnerable a place – and I am from Miami.

Lubbock has plenty of reasons not to talk about climate change. As oil and gas exports from the United States surge West Texas has boomed.[34] Companies in Lubbock and others in the Permian Basin – an ancient, oil rich seabed that spans West Texas and southeastern New Mexico – are exporting millions of barrels of oil thanks to the U.S. Congress. Congress lifted a 40-year-old restriction on the export of crude oil in 2015. Oil from the Permian Basin will account for 80% of the growth in global supply for the next several years.[35]

At a stakeholder meeting with the topic *Environment*, I showed scenarios I had made from my computer model. The most compelling calculation, I think, demonstrated how, by focusing on rebuilding Lubbock's leveled downtown, the city could save 11 billion gallons of water per year and avoid 6 million metric tons of CO_2 carbon pollution per year. The downtown had been levelled in part by a tornado in 1970 and then finished off by bulldozers to make parking lots for a few office towers in the years that followed.

"According to the Comprehensive Plan, Lubbock will grow by 70,000 people between 2018 and 2029 and the way those people live will affect the planet," I said. People nodded. They waited for my next point. "We need to plan in a way that reduces water and energy use per person for a lot of reasons, but also to do our part as the world gets warmer and drier." They listened politely. When the presentation was over and we began to talk about their environmental concerns, no one objected to what I had said about climate change.

My next meeting was focused on transportation and, just like in the environment meeting, we invited attendees to give input on the code update. I talked about how the downtown would struggle to grow economically as long as the city continued to build highway loops that bypassed the downtown. Loop 289 went out 10 miles from

210 ■ *Why Are We Doing This?*

the downtown and circled the city. Another loop highway, Loop 88, the Lubbock Outer Loop, was planned and it would open up land to suburban development up to 20 miles out. The local transportation representatives from the Metropolitan Planning Organization, Department of Transportation, and local Streets and Public Works Department agreed that, yes, the downtown would face some fierce competition. However, they said that the people of Lubbock wanted to live in single-family houses and the city's land use policies and transportation investments were simply responding to that desire.

I showed images from a visual preference survey we had done with over 50 people which suggested that the participants we had talked to preferred downtown living and new, walkable, mixed-use communities to suburban ranchettes. The transportation providers responded that the preferences of people who come to public meetings about the downtown weren't representative of the average person from Lubbock. That was a valid point.

"Maybe the average person wants a big house in suburbia, but you have to concede that there a lot of people who would like something different. People want to live downtown again," I said. "We're just trying to create options."

They agreed. I talked about how El Paso, Texas, had funded bike infrastructure and downtown transit and saw a downtown regeneration.

At first, my audience had no problem with the idea of creating more options. One of the city's engineers said that he'd like to move to a condominium downtown one day. But as the conversation progressed, the transportation officials began to say that they had no way to fund the sidewalks, street trees, bike lanes, and transit which people had asked for. They said that their budgets were predominately dedicated to loop roads and their accompanying car-only infrastructure.

We discussed a shift in the way that federal and state monies could be spent in favor of multi-modalism. Just a fractional shift would make a difference. I talked about how the upcoming Long Range Transportation Plan (LRTP) process would provide an opportunity to have that conversation. My audience wasn't defensive about that, and a few were positive. Then I talked about climate change and the effects our transportation choices had on the planet. None of them disputed a thing I said.

"The city needs to begin calculating greenhouse emissions when it makes transportation decisions," I said. Everyone at the table agreed. Where was the resistance to climate conversations that we all expected?

For the next couple of days our meetings ranged from Historic Preservation to Education and whenever I talked about climate change no one disagreed that the climate was changing, that people were to blame, and that the city and country needed to make changes. Climate change was never at the front of anyone's minds; they always wanted to discuss other, more local, goals. They talked about flooding, parking shortages, the heat island effect, the lack of people downtown, and the deficit of downtown amenities. But they didn't object when I made the connection between the issues that they wanted to discuss and climate issues.

Climate Planning Objection 8 ■ 211

I began to wonder: Who was it that we were worried about upsetting? We'd had climate conversations with more 200 people in four days. We discussed future challenges, both local and global, and no one raised an objection. Was it possible that the authors of the city's Comprehensive Plan, consultants from out of town like myself, had censored themselves for no good reason?

"Can I talk about climate change?" I asked Steve O'Neal, Director of Development Services, before our final presentation. "Will it upset the City Commission?" I wondered if maybe it was the City Commission that had vetoed the climate discussion in *Plan Lubbock 2040*. We hadn't talked to the City Commission yet.

I sensed that Steve was the right person to ask. He had been in the city for a long time, and he had a thick Lubbock accent. It's a distinct brand of Texan accent and I believe that when we adopt or retain an accent it's a sub-conscious way of showing belonging. When I asked Steve if it was okay to talk about climate change, I felt like I was asking the entire city.

"Well," he began, "as long as it's not all you talk about, sure, because I don't think it's the most important thing to people," he said. "Got it?" he said like *Git it?*

"I do."

"We're talking about all kinds of things this week," he said, "and the conversations we're having are going well. I can't believe that we are talking about impact fees." Steve believed that new development had to do more to pay for itself when it came to water, stormwater, transportation, and parks. With more people came a need to upgrade city utilities and new revenue sources were needed. "If you told me 15 years ago that the developers would be okay with impact fees – and even want them – I wouldn't have believed it."

"I can talk about climate?" I asked again.

"Yessir."

As the project continued, we continued to talk about climate. From the big public events with over 200 people, to the City Council, to meetings with selected participants on specialized topics, I talked about how 2015 to 2019 was the warmest five-year period on record, how the world's temperatures had risen 1.1°C above pre-industrial levels, and how climate change impacts were hitting harder and sooner than predicted a decade ago. I didn't bang my audience over the head with this topic; I stayed brief and concise and stuck to my scope of work (broadly defined). My audience listened. Maybe they simply waited me out, politely, but it seemed to me like they were listening. Perhaps the public had become more comfortable talking about climate since the drafting of *Plan Lubbock 2040*. The national conversation has changed a lot in just a few years.

Donald Trump, perhaps the most influential climate denier in an elected position in the world, had received 66% of the votes in Lubbock County during the 2016 national election, according to the Lubbock County Elections Office. I would have welcomed a conversation with people with different opinions. It's not that I like confrontation – I dislike it as much as anyone – but I worry that the people who voted Trump were staying home and not participating because they didn't feel

212 ■ *Why Are We Doing This?*

welcome. I worry about the retreat from community life. I see fewer and fewer pNeople at public meetings.

"You work in oil extraction?" I asked a man who had come to one of our open houses. I had heard him talking to his daughter. We stood in front of a board our team had made that discussed climate change risks.

"Yeah. And I want to continue to," he said with a wry smile. The man's daughter, a college-age young woman, raised her eyebrows in alarm and quietly shuffled away.

"I hope you can, too," I said.

"This isn't about stopping oil?" he asked.

"No. It's about a better downtown." I talked about the plan for the downtown and the new code, and the man was absolutely in favor of re-building the downtown. He owned a scrap yard and metalworking shop in the Depot district on the edge of downtown. Though he spent most of his time driving a truck for an oil company, the yard provided a weekend hobby for him.

"Would you like to turn that hobby into a business?" I asked.

"Never mind about that. Just don't stop oil."

"I got it," I said like *git it*. And I do. I believe we must help places like Lubbock plan their shift with a kind of measured, slow, sensible, transition.

Lubbock's Green New Code

The land development code we co-drafted with the planning firm Kendig Keast has incentives for greener development. The code allows energy efficient development and light impact development to build on more lot area than conventional development, adding tangible value. Specifically, development which has a LEED Platinum or LEED Gold certification, or equivalent, may increase the maximum impervious lot coverage by 20%. Development that incorporates a blue roof (water retaining roof) or a green roof (vegetated), or other building or site features that reduces the first 1 inch of rainfall by at least 50% may reduce any required building setback by 20%. Buildings that include photovoltaic panels sufficient to power the entire building may also reduce setbacks by 20%. Homes that include Level 2 EVSE (electrical vehicle supply equipment) – charging stations for electric vehicles – may reduce setbacks 10%. Having a Level 2 EVSE at home is ideal because most electric vehicle owners find they do the majority of their charging at home.

The new code allows an entire range of light imprint storm drainage methods that will keep more water on the landscape, nurturing plant and animal life in a warmer world. The previous code required all new neighborhoods to convey water along curbed streets and into pipes and retention ponds. The new code includes methods for allowing water to sit or be absorbed where it falls and includes formerly disallowed elements like pervious asphalts, trenches, French drains, landscaped tree wells, filtration ponds, and rain gardens. The world is becoming warmer and drier, and so we need places that are cooler and wetter.

Other incentives for green development include the ability to build urbanism. Urbanism means dense, walkable, mixed-use places that provide more shade for walking and biking. These places use resources more efficiently. The code highly incentivized traditional neighborhoods with walkable block sizes, a mix of units, and a range of open spaces (including the smaller, easily shaded neighborhood parks which are becoming more and more rare). Front setbacks are reduced so that buildings may shade the street. Bicycle parking is required of all new development and parking for cars is greatly reduced below the usual land development code norms.

Shade structures over sidewalks like galleries, arcades, colonnades, awnings and even free-standing covered walkways are allowed as heat-mitigation strategies. Prior to the new code, shade structures could not span into the right-of-way of the street. The code conversation overcame objections related to potential legal liability, the "canyon effect" created when buildings or structures are too close to the street, or lost revenue from renting out the public realm. Heavy-duty, privately built shade was allowed.

Admittedly, our work in Lubbock merely allows for and incentivizes energy and water efficiency, multi-modal urbanism, and green infrastructure. Green infrastructure involves rain gardens, bioswales, green roofs, small municipal greens, regional parks, and conservation lands. In other places, usually in bigger cities or places farther along in the climate conversation, our codes require these things. But communities can start with incentivized regulations that they ratchet up in time.

Plan and Code Adoption

The Lubbock Downtown Plan and Code were adopted in 2021. I believe that Downtown Lubbock will begin to re-build its downtown and that the downtown will provide jobs and economic empowerment to the people of declining rural areas. I believe that the city will hire the people it needs, like a Downtown Management District and Parking Authority, and that it will even bond to create the funding necessary to build downtown parks, green their streets, and add big amenities dedicated to the arts. I believe that a sizeable portion of the 70,000 people Lubbock will see in the future will locate downtown, younger generations will live differently than their parents by choice, and that over time the "return to the city" we've seen across the country will happen in Lubbock. Despite more than a century of downtown neglect it seems to me that in less than 25 years Downtown Lubbock might just be on the map of great places within the Great Plains states to live, work, and play.

I also have every reason to believe that in the future the city's per capita water use and carbon footprint will lower significantly. As part of our work on the Downtown Plan and city-wide code we recommended the drafting of a Climate Adaptation Plan. I will watch for that.

In the long term, I don't know if Lubbock will solve its water problem, or if it will diversify its economy away from farming and fossil fuel extraction fast enough

214 ■ *Why Are We Doing This?*

to avoid an economic bust. I do, however, believe that these topics can be discussed as openly as I discussed them, at least among the people who matter most to the city's future.

I recommend that even if a population votes for a notorious climate change denier like Trump it may not be because he was a climate change denier. There may have been other reasons. And one is politically true red or true blue, everyone is a blend, everyone has a different shade. I recommend treating your audience like responsible adults despite preconceptions you may have about them created by watching the national news. I've worked everywhere and, believe me, people are no less intelligent in one area of the country than in any other. Assume the best of the people you are talking to. Be diplomatic but be honest when talking about the future.

Notes

1 IPCC (2007). Summary for Policymakers. In: Solomon, S., D. Qin, M. Manning, Z. Chen, M. Marquis, K.B. Averyt, M.Tignor and H.L. Miller (eds), *Climate Change 2007: The Physical Science Basis. Contribution of Working Group I to the Fourth Assessment Report of the Intergovernmental Panel on Climate Change.* Cambridge and New York: Cambridge University Press, p. 17. Retrieved from: www.ipcc.ch/site/assets/uploads/2018/02/ar4-wg1-spm-1.pdf

2 Hertsgaard, M. (2020). A second Trump term would be a "game over" for the climate, says top scientist. *The Guardian*, October 2. Retrieved from: www.theguardian.com/us-news/2020/oct/02/donald-trump-climate-change-michael-mann-interview

3 Strauss, B.H., Kulp, S. and Levermann, A. (2015). Mapping choices: Carbon, climate, and rising seas, our global legacy. Climate Central Research Report, pp. 1–38. Retrieved from: https://sealevel.climatecentral.org/uploads/research/Global-Mapping-Choices-Report.pdf

4 City of Laredo, Community Development Department (2015). 2015–2019 Five Year Consolidated Plan. 2015–2016 Annual Action Plan. Retrieved from: www.cityoflaredo.com/CommDev/Admin/Consolidated_Plan/5_and_1_Yr_Consolidated_Plan-FINAL.pdf

5 Skeptical Science (n.d.). Can renewables provide baseload power? Retrieved from: https://skepticalscience.com/print.php?r=374

6 Roselund, C. (2019). Florida Power and Light enters the race for the world's largest battery. *PV Magazine*, March 28. Retrieved from: https://pv-magazine-usa.com/2019/03/28/florida-power-and-light-enters-the-race-for-the-worlds-largest-battery/

7 Ibid.

8 Zervos, A., Lins, C. and Muth, J. (2010). Re-Thinking 2050: A 100% renewable energy vision for the European Union. European Renewable Energy Council. Retrieved from: http://citeseerx.ist.psu.edu/viewdoc/download?doi=10.1.1.638.5765&rep=rep1&type=pdf

9 Colorado.gov/State of Colorado (2019). Analysis and technical update to the Colorado Water Plan. Retrieved from: www.colorado.gov/pacific/cowaterplan/analysis-and-technical-update

Climate Planning Objection 8 ■ 215

10 Schempp, A. (2018). Water efficiency and conservation: The state of the states. Environmental Law Institute, April 18. Retrieved from: www.eli.org/vibrant-environment-blog/water-efficiency-and-conservation-state-states

11 Brennan, C. and Rojas, R. (2020). Colorado wildfire grows into largest in state history. *The New York Times*, October 18. Retrieved from: www.nytimes.com/2020/10/18/us/colorado-wildfires-cameron-peak.html

12 IPCC (2018). Global Warming of 1.5°C. An IPCC special report on the impacts of global warming of 1.5°C above pre-industrial levels and related global greenhouse gas emission pathways, in the context of strengthening the global response to the threat of climate change, sustainable development, and efforts to eradicate poverty. Masson-Delmotte, V., P. Zhai, H.O. Pörtner, D. Roberts, J. Skea, P.R. Shukla, A. Pirani, W. Moufouma-Okia, C. Péan, R. Pidcock, S. Connors, J.B.R. Matthews, Y. Chen, X. Zhou, M. I. Gomis, E. Lonnoy, T. Maycock, M. Tignor and T. Waterfield (eds). Retrieved from: www.ipcc.ch/sr15/

13 American Planning Association (2019). *Falling Dominoes: A Planner's Guide to Drought and Cascading Impacts.* Chicago: American Planning Association. Retrieved from: www.planning.org/publications/document/9188906/

14 U.S. Environmental Protection Agency (EPA) (n.d.). Heat Island Effect. Retrieved from: www.epa.gov/heat-islands

15 Nowak, D.J. and Greenfield, E.J. (2018). Declining urban and community tree cover in the United States. *Urban Forestry & Urban Greening*, Volume 32, pp. 32–55.

16 City of Laredo (2019). City of Laredo Ordinance No. 2019-O-073. City of Laredo, May 6. Retrieved from: www.cityoflaredo.com/Building/images/ordinances/2019-O-073_irrigation_ordinance.pdf

17 Simmons, J. (2018). Puerto Rico planting 750,000 trees to defend land from natural disasters. *Eco Watch*, September 28. Retrieved from: www.ecowatch.com/puerto-rico-news-trees-2608395449.html

18 Editorial Board (2019). The Guardian view on rewilding Scotland: An immodest proposal. *The Guardian*, March 21. Retrieved from: www.theguardian.com/commentisfree/2019/mar/21/the-guardian-view-on-rewilding-scotland-an-immodest-proposal

19 Aggarwal, M. (2018). India has brought 9.8 million hectares of degraded land under restoration since 2011. *MongaBay*, September 4. Retrieved from: https://india.mongabay.com/2018/09/india-restored-9-8-million-hectares-of-degraded-land-since-2011/

20 Pharr, C. and Liu, L. (2018). The WorldPost Opinion: China is reforesting land the size of Ireland. Here's what that looks like. *The World Post*, June 1. Retrieved from: www.washingtonpost.com/news/theworldpost/wp/2018/06/01/china-forest/

21 Constable, P. (2018). In Pakistan, an ambitious effort to plant 10 billion trees takes root. *Washington Post*, October 14. Retrieved from: www.washingtonpost.com/world/asia_pacific/in-pakistan-an-ambitious-effort-to-plant-10-billion-trees-takes-root/2018/10/12/18f14474-c015-11e8-9f4f-a1b7af255aa5_story.html

22 Vidal, J. (2014). Lima climate talks: Pledge to plant 20m hectares of trees. *The Guardian*, December 8. Retrieved from: www.theguardian.com/environment/2014/dec/08/lima-climate-talks-pledge-to-plant-20m-hectares-of-trees

23 Hirsh, S. (2019). Australia will plant 1 billion trees in the next 11 years. World Economic Forum, February 21. Retrieved from: www.weforum.org/agenda/2019/02/australia-to-plant-1-billion-trees-in-the-next-11-years-bringing-the-country-closer-to-paris-agreements-goals/

24 Brent, H. (2019). Ireland will plant 440 million trees over the next twenty years in a bid to tackle the growing issue of climate change. *The Irish Post*, September 3.

216 ■ *Why Are We Doing This?*

Retrieved from: www.irishpost.com/news/irish-government-plant-440-million-trees-2040-tackle-climate-change-170870

25 Hyun-ju, O. (2019). Seoul to plant 30 million trees by 2022 to fight fine dust. *The Korea Herald*, March 26. Retrieved from: www.koreaherald.com/view.php?ud=20190326000754

26 Whiting, A. (2018). Cities are planting more trees to fight climate change and improve healthy living. World Economic Forum in collaboration with Thomson Reuters Foundation, December 4. Retrieved from: www.weforum.org/agenda/2018/12/cities-are-planting-more-trees-to-curb-wild-weather-and-boost-healthy-living-ec92b137-4610-4871-a341-0c10ea1b3954

27 City of Panama City, Florida (2019). *A Strategic Vision for Panama City's Historic Downtown and its Waterfront*. Final draft, October 2. Retrieved from: www.rebuildpc.org/wp-content/uploads/2019/10/Strategic-Vision-for-Downtown_Final-Draft-100219_web-version.pdf

28 United States Census Bureau (n.d.). QuickFacts: Lubbok city, Texas; Lubbock County, Texas. Retrieved from: www.census.gov/quickfacts/fact/table/lubbockcitytexas,lubbockcountytexas/PST045218

29 USGCRP (2018). Fourth National Climate Assessment: Volume II: Impacts, risks, and adaptation in the United States. Washington, D.C.: U.S. Global Change Research Program. Retrieved from: https://nca2018.globalchange.gov/downloads/NCA4_2018_FullReport.pdf

30 Mcguire, V.L. (2007). Changes in water levels and storage in the High Plains aquifer, Predevelopment to 2005. USGS Fact Sheet 2007–3029. Retrieved from: https://pubs.usgs.gov/fs/2007/3029/

31 USGCRP, op. cit.

32 City of Lubbock, Texas (2018). 2018 strategic water supply plan. City of Lubbock, August. Retrieved from: https://ci.lubbock.tx.us/storage/images/4G1pIUEKJzRJftCGkkPQyFewa9PVdySLl4ekNLWV.pdf

33 APA (2011). Policy guide on planning & climate change (adopted April 27, 2008; updated April 11, 2011). American Planning Association. Retrieved from: https://planning-org-uploaded-media.s3.amazonaws.com/legacy_resources/policy/guides/pdf/climatechange.pdf

34 Collier, K., Smith Hopkins, J. and Leven, R. (2018). As oil and gas exports surge. West Texas becomes the world's "extraction colony." The Center for Public Integrity. Retrieved from: https://apps.publicintegrity.org/blowout/

35 International Energy Agency (n.d.). World Energy Outlook 2017: A world in transformation. IEA. Retrieved from: www.iea.org/reports/world-energy-outlook-2017

Chapter 9

Climate Planning Objection 9

"The future can't be predicted. Climate models are unreliable."

In coastal states, when we hear that a tropical storm with 65 mile-per-hour winds is expected to strengthen and hit our area as a Category 4 hurricane, we react. That information comes from the National Hurricane Center at the National Oceanic and Atmospheric Administration (NOAA). So, if we take NOAA so seriously when a storm approaches why don't we do the same when NOAA warns us about a changing climate? The National Climate Assessment released by the United States Global Change Research program (and endorsed by NOAA) tells us the earth is warming, and to react. Why are we so skeptical?

It may be because in coastal states we know the limits of forecasts. We pay attention when we see our homes within the forecast cone of NOAA's full five-day forecast, but it isn't until we see our homes in the three-day forecast that we begin to make plans. Coastal residents have seen so many day-to-day changes in the trajectory of hurricane cones. One can't help but ask: If we can't predict the weather next week, how can we predict the weather in 50 years?

The reality is that the movement of hurricanes is based on several chaotic factors like the strength of global winds, the presence of high- or low-pressure systems, and variations in wind shear, while the Earth's temperature and sea level rise are based on long-term averages. This means that while meteorologists succeed or fail based on their ability to predict the track of storms within 100

DOI: 10.4324/9781003181514-11

217

218 ■ *Why Are We Doing This?*

miles or so, the success of a climatologist's ability to forecast is judged based on the average temperature worldwide or the average sea level rise along the shoreline of an entire continent. The climatologist doesn't need to be specific for their message to prevent disasters and save lives. Climate modelling is both less exact and more reliable than hurricane planning. Climate modelling can be taken more seriously than any weather report. The future can be predicted. The models are reliable.

Notes From the Field

Disaster Planning For My Own Home During Hurricane Dorian

We had four days before Hurricane *Dorian* was forecast to hit and it was time to make the decision to stay or go.

At 3:35am on August 29, 2019, 14 years to the day after Hurricane *Katrina* had made landfall in Louisiana, I was looking at my glowing NOAA Radar Map app as I lay in bed. It didn't look good. The trajectory of Hurricane *Dorian* had moved south according to NOAA's 11pm update and the eye of the storm was projected to hit closer to Miami than in the last projection. *Dorian* was only a Category 1, but it was rapidly intensifying.

Hurricane *Dorian* was to make landfall on the mainland in Fort Pierce, 120 miles away, but, still, our home was within the forecast cone. Stay or evacuate? *Dorian* was strengthening and a direct hit to Miami would be devastating.

Or would it?

My wife and I had moved our family off of Miami Beach a year and a half earlier and our new home in South Miami was 3 miles away from Biscayne Bay and away from any rivers. Our new home was on 8.5 feet of elevation – not bad by Southeast Florida standards. Climate change and flooding was definitely a factor when we left Miami Beach. We still own there. My plan is still to retire under swaying palms and with my feet in the warm sand. But I have kids and so we left.

I went to FEMA's National Flood Hazard Layer Viewer on my phone and entered in our address. I waited as the FEMA Flood Insurance Rate Map (FIRM) loaded. I waited. I knew that it was the storm surge and flood waters that did the real damage. I continued to wait. Why had I never done this before? When we lived in Miami Beach I had advocated for a sign campaign that read "Do you know your flood zone?" and now, after a year of living in a new home, I didn't know my flood zone.

The map materialized. Our home was Zone X. The screen read: *An area of minimum flood hazard.*

"Everything okay?" my wife asked groggily from beside me.

"Yeah, it's fine." I felt much better. I closed my eyes.

Climate Planning Objection 9 ■ **219**

I opened my eyes. Had I seen that right? Was our house just half a block from a flood zone, Zone AH? I checked. Yes – Zone AH was just 200 feet away. I turned off the phone and laid in the dark, but I couldn't sleep.

What was the margin of error on the FIRM maps? Would a new map that took into consideration the world's changing climate place us into Zone AH? What was Zone AH? I turned my phone back on and looked up Zone AH. Zone AH meant we didn't need flood insurance because homes in AH were in a low risk area that saw less than a 2% chance of annual flood. Okay. Even if an updated FIRM map placed us in Zone AH the chance of a flood was so low that we weren't required to have flood insurance. Good. I closed my eyes.

I opened my eyes. Wait – did we have flood insurance? What if *Dorian* was Miami's doomsday storm? How was it that I didn't not know if we had flood insurance? If we owned a flood policy the paperwork would be in the cabinet next to our bed, but I didn't want to wake my wife. So, instead, I researched doomsday storms as I lay in bed. I was acting paranoid, I knew. This could all wait until morning. Nevertheless …

Mexico Beach on the Florida Panhandle met its doomsday storm on October 10, 2018 when the town was hit by Hurricane *Michael*, a Category 5 hurricane. I panned to Mexico Beach on the FEMA app and I toggled between the FEMA map and Google Earth to see how good a predictor flood zones were of actual damage. Not so good. Dozens of the homes around the Mexico Beach pier were vaporized despite being in Zone X.

I sat up in bed. Anyone living in Mexico Beach who did the research I was doing before Hurricane *Michael* would have been proven justified. Was I even being paranoid at all? Wasn't fear of hurricanes in Florida a rational fear?

I read how Mexico Beach lost its city hall, elementary school, and water tower. Some homes were reduced to bare foundation slabs when the storm surge rose 14 feet. However, from what I could see, many of the homes, especially the new ones, survived. And when I looked at the neighborhoods that were not directly on the coast (neighborhoods like mine) miles from the shore, I saw little to no damage, or at least, no damage that was visible from an aerial. Relief.

Then again, those homes could have flooded. Everything inside may have been destroyed and mold could have formed within the walls which made them unlivable. I promised myself I'd buy flood insurance in the morning.

Still, I couldn't sleep.

I downloaded another app which showed tidal highs and lows. At 4am, I was downloading apps. I learned that when *Dorian* was expected to arrive it would be King Tide, our highest high tide of the season. Not good.

Scientists say that the chance of hurricanes becoming a Category 3 or higher have increased each of the past four decades.[1] Much of the death and destruction from hurricanes comes from major storms of Category 3 strength or higher. Our home was only 3 miles from the coast and a surge of 15 to 20 feet would one day reach our front door, just as they have in the past.

220 ■ *Why Are We Doing This?*

I turned off my phone. I closed my eyes. We'd be okay. My wife and our two kids would be okay, I told myself. We wouldn't lose all we owned. I went to sleep. Eventually.

The next morning as Hurricane *Dorian* intensified, and as sandbags were beginning to be placed along the doors of the main street our office was located on, my wife and I went to buy flood insurance. The policy I wanted was quoted to me at US$500 a year and it seemed like a small price to pay thanks to massive federal subsidies. However, coverage sold through the National Flood Insurance Program required a 30-day waiting period before going into effect. If our house was flooded during *Dorian* there would be no insurance monies, and for our family, like most, that would mean financial ruin.

"I really have to wait?" I asked the insurance salesperson.

"You do," she said.

"Is there someone else I can talk to?" I asked.

"You can talk to me," said a middle-aged man in the desk right next to the insurance salesperson I was talking to. "I own the company."

"There must be a way to get coverage."

"Where do you live?" he asked.

I told him.

"You're fine. It won't flood." As it turned out, the owner of the insurance company lived near our house and he didn't have flood insurance either. "Don't be paranoid."

"The world is changing. Climate change. Sea level rise."

"I mean, maybe," he said. "But climate change is slow." He looked at me, my wife, and his salesperson and then shrugged resignedly. "I'd be a fool if I talked you out of buying something from us." He paused. "What we sell here is piece of mind. That's well worth the cost," he said just like a salesperson. He looked at me again and could see concern in my eyes. "But, don't worry. I mean, not really."

"I want it today."

"That ... we can't do." He turned his swivel screen around and showed me how the word BLOCKED appeared on every line he'd use to take my information and submit for flood insurance. "Come back after the storm."

Dorian slowed down to 8mph as it approached Miami. It strolled. It took days and days. It was like waiting for an enraged, Godzilla-sized, turtle. I looked at my NOAA Radar continually over the next few days, and I watched the great green and yellow swirl of *Dorian* approach. I felt the immensity of nature and smallness of man. It's an awful feeling.

As sea temperatures rise, hurricanes have been increasing in intensity. Over the past 169 years there have been only 35 Category 5 hurricanes on the Atlantic. That's roughly one every five years. Yet in the past four years there had been five Category 5 hurricanes in the Atlantic Ocean: *Matthew* in 2016; *Irma* and *Maria* in 2017; *Michael* in 2018; and *Dorian* in 2019.[2]

Dorian hit.

Climate Planning Objection 9 ■ 221

If my life was a movie then you would know what happened next: A downer ending to the story, my last-minute attempt to get flood insurance was too little, too late. In the original *Godzilla* (1954), after all the heroic sacrifice, it turned out Godzilla wasn't the only one of his species and human civilization was still doomed. At the end of *Dr. Strangelove* (1964), despite the attempts of both sides to save the world, a nuclear warhead still dropped, triggering the doomsday machine. In *Game of Thrones* (2019), despite the fact the city bells were rung to signal the surrender of the Lannister forces, Daenerys refused to accept their surrender and her dragon still barbecued the city.

Luckily, life is more forgiving than movies.

Hurricane *Dorian* was a monster which inflicted terrible damage on the Bahamas, but the winds, stormwater flooding, and tidal surge didn't cause damage in Miami. Our home wasn't flooded. And by the time the next storm arrived we had flood insurance.

While we can't say that this or that drought, hurricane, refugee crisis, or even war was due to climate change, we can say that warming temperatures make it more likely. And that's the same thing. In military terms, global warming is a *threat multiplier*. We need to be as vigilant with climate change as the military is with absolutely everything. You only need to be right once for what we'd call paranoia to be worthwhile.

Notes From the Field

Cost-based Decision-making; South Miami's Septic Tank Problem and the Switch to Solar

In August 2019, my family and I attended an informal get-together for Mark Lago, a candidate running to be the mayor of our town, South Miami, and the inevitable question of climate change came up.

"I think we need to add sewer systems before our septic tanks back up," one of our neighbors, a software designer in his early 50s, recommended to the candidate as we sat with beers and pizza around a dining room table. "The water is rising under us and our septic tanks will fail one day."

"Well, they say that would cost millions," Candidate Lago, a commercial real estate appraiser, said. "There would be special assessments and hook-up fees." He wasn't a fan of the idea.

"Septic-sewer conversions would protect us from the rising water tables and keep harmful nutrients out of Biscayne Bay," my neighbor said.

"I heard that a single conversion would cost US$5,000 a household," Candidate Lago said. I think that American politicians must advocate crippling cheapness in order to get elected, whether they believe in it or not, and so I didn't feel it necessary at that point to finish my beer, make our exit, and find out if the guy's opponent

Figure 9 City Hall, South Miami, Florida

had a fundraiser with better food. "I mean, I personally don't feel like I have any extra money to pay for a sewer system," Candidate Lago said. "Do you?" He was looking at me.

"I think septic tanks are a problem," I said. One-third of all Florida homes, about 1.6 million households, use backyard septic tanks. In Miami-Dade County, the majority of homes and businesses don't use septic tanks. They are connected

Climate Planning Objection 9 ▪ **223**

to a municipal sewer system which collects waste using a network of underground pipes and pumps and sends it to the Central District Wastewater Treatment Plant on Virginia Key where it is treated. Treated waste is either released into Biscayne Bay or sent into deep injection wells.[3] However, roughly 20% of the homes in the county are not connected to that system and must rely on septic tank systems and the aging, leaky systems for disposing of human waste have provided a public health and environmental hazard for bay waters and drinking waters since the 1950s.

South Miami is one of the towns that rely almost entirely on septic. Septic tanks are concrete tanks which collect solid waste and send water into a backyard drain field.[4] As sea levels rise the groundwater rises and the drain fields of septic tanks won't filter like they are supposed to in the soggy soil. By 2040, 64% of the county's septic tanks (more than 67,000) could have issues every year.[5] This would affect homeowners, whose yards could turn into putrid swamps. During major rain events people might be forced to wade through contaminated floodwaters. Septic leeching also could affect the health of our drinking water.[6]

"I think we need to do something," I said to Candidate Lago, though I assumed that most people in town would be against sewer lines. Laying down new pipes to connect homes to the county's sewer system is expensive and while federal and state monies are available in some cases, property owners generally pay most of the costs. Lago had said that the average price was US$5,000 but to my knowledge it was higher. The average price to homeowners in Miami-Dade County is US$15,000 and, in some cases, it could cost far more. Costs also continue after installation as special taxing districts paid for by homeowners are used to maintain the systems.

"Well …," Lago said, "maybe." He had told us earlier in the night that he had run for the city commission a few years before and lost by just 45 votes. He couldn't afford to lose his first crowd. "We need a plan," the candidate said. "We can look at it." I saw, once again, urban planning, my profession, as a way for government officials to put off confronting a difficult issue or making an important decision. *We need a plan* was his way of saying *let's wait awhile before doing anything.*

"Maybe it wouldn't be your administration. Or even the one after it, but it needs to happen," my neighbor said, keeping the evening congenial and light by giving the candidate the opportunity to kick the proverbial can down the road.

"That's right," Candidate Lago said, but he didn't let the issue go. He then began to argue that the septic upgrade problem should be left to the future because, politically, people wouldn't want to pay for upgrades until septic tanks had begun to fail. Once things got bad the cost in taxes and the disruption of having roads torn up would feel necessary. South Miami's septic tanks hadn't begun to fail and because the town was, on average, 8 feet in elevation it could be years before septic failure became a widespread problem he argued.

At this point I was more inclined to leave the party, but my kids were eating their pizza. The event's hostess also promised my kids that they could see her pet bunnies. I was trapped. Maybe for hours.

224 ■ *Why Are We Doing This?*

One person, a local architect, defended Candidate Lago, arguing, "Do we have a moral imperative to pay for a sewer system that will solve the problem created by the last generation and will only really help the next generation?"

"Right," Candidate Lago said. There it was again, the climate dilemma faced by every elected official: The costs would be borne immediately, the public would likely push back, and the greatest benefits of those costs would not materialize until after the deaths of those same elected officials. In other Florida municipalities where I had worked elected officials didn't act until sewer systems were required by law. When I was an urban planner in the Florida Keys the installation of sewer systems was required by court order after it was shown that septic leakage led to coral die-off and poisonous algae blooms.

"In my opinion," I said, "given all the challenges ahead when it comes to climate change, getting started on a foreseeable problem now makes sense." It makes sense to me both as an urban planner and as a property owner, despite the household costs. I stopped there, figuring that I'd save the complete climate sermon for after the candidate was elected. "What's your feeling on street trees?" I asked Lago, bringing the conversation back to more comfortable territory.

"I am all for them," Candidate Lago said.

"Great."

"As long as the town isn't paying for them."

"You should run for mayor," my wife suggested after the pizza and bunnies and we were back home.

I considered this. As a candidate I'd seek sewer systems, solar panels on every home, public building, and business, low-water drought-tolerant landscaping (at least at all municipal sites and parks), and reroofing with high albedo materials like white barrel tile. I would fix the city's tree-planting program to make sure that it gave every resident two free trees. I also liked requiring all new homes and businesses to include high-output charging stations (Level 2 EVSEs) for electric vehicles. And these were the things that came to mind immediately – imagine if I had a two-year term. No, I wouldn't win the election.

In February 2020, Mark Lago lost the election to Sally B. Philips, a retired psychologist, who ran on two issues: Revitalizing South Miami's downtown, and getting homes off of septic tanks.[7] Maybe I didn't know my town as well as I thought. Philips received over 300 more votes than Lago and locally many people attributed the win to her endorsement by scientist environmentalist Mayor Philip Stoddard. Now, I need to tell you about Mayor Stoddard.

A Mayor For Our Time

Mayor Stoddard is a biology professor at Florida International University and has the unusual niche of being a small-town mayor-scientist who built a national profile as a climate leader by appearing in shows like the National Geographic Channel's *Years of Living Dangerously* in which he talks with actor Jack Black in an episode called "Saving Miami." Under Stoddard, the town joined the ICLEI (Local Governments for Sustainability) while the rest of the state was decrying ICLEI's connection to the Agenda 21 conspiracy theory. Stoddard also frequently made Florida news by fighting Florida, Power & Light. He lived in a house entirely powered by the solar array on his roof which he installed in 2014 to FPL's dismay.

Stoddard is a phenomenally outspoken Mayor. He told *The Guardian* in 2014 that Senator Marco Rubio was "an idiot" and called Florida Power & Light "an evil genius."[8] He has a bumper sticker on his car which says "Back off, Man. I'm a scientist." Thanks to people like Mayor Stoddard, our little town of South Miami with its small population of 12,000 leads the state in environmental performance.

Florida ranks 47th and is behind Mississippi on the list of states producing the most renewable energy.[9] A mere 2.6% of electricity in the Sunshine State is from renewables. To be fair, Florida is the second-highest energy generator in the country producing 238.4 million MWh a year and it is easier for the top five states on the list (Vermont, Idaho, Washington, South Dakota, and Maine) to make the transition to renewable because all together they generate just over half of the power that Florida must. And, really, hydroelectric is the largest renewable energy source in those top five states, it always has been, and so for those states there was hardly a transition to make. Flat Florida has very few hydroelectric opportunities. However, looked at another way, California generates nearly as much power as Florida and 47% of its electricity is from renewables. Texas generates nearly twice the power as Florida, and it derives 16% of its electricity from renewable sources. One can't help but feel that Florida, which is a purple state politically, should be somewhere in between blue California and red Texas when it comes to renewable power. Florida should at least be working on the problem. It is the "Sunshine State" after all. However, I think it is fair to say: It isn't.

Florida Power & Light, the state's investor-owned electric utility company, is notorious for fighting the move to rooftop Photo Voltaic panels because there's no financial incentive for FPL to empower its customers to produce their own power. Rooftop solar power would only reduce the utility's revenues by reducing sales. Every kilowatt of solar Florida produced on our roof would be one less kilowatt that the utility could sell us.

FPL has only minimally invested in utility-scale solar and for this reason continually ranks as one of the worst utilities for clean energy.[10] The state is largely powered by natural gas-fired plants, coal-fired plants, and nuclear energy.[11] In the Southeastern U.S., state energy efficiency requirements and renewable portfolio standards are weak compared to other regions and there is no mandate to shift to renewables.

Along with other large utilities, FPL has been criticized for using its influence with state politicians and political organizations to encourage them to reject laws which would make it easier for home and business owners to adopt rooftop solar.[12] According to the Florida Center for Investigative Reporting, several of the top utility

226 ▪ *Why Are We Doing This?*

companies in Florida, including FPL, have contributed over US$12 million towards the election campaigns of state lawmakers since 2010.[13] In 2016, FPL was a sponsor of Amendment 1, a measure that would have protected the electric utility by creating barriers to entry for competitors. The amendment was ultimately defeated by voters after media reports revealed that the measure was presented as pro solar though it was actually an attempt to limit alternatives. The utility industry spent nearly US$22 million promoting the amendment.[14] As a Florida ratepayer, I hate the idea that the money I send to the power company to keep my lights on is being used to thwart climate change mitigation.

My neighbors in South Miami aren't waiting for Florida Power & Light to make the change. When you walk my neighborhood you see solar panels on many houses. The panels face every direction and defy the idea that only one house orientation works for solar. My wife and I were inspired by our neighbors and we made a goal to get rooftop solar. We both want one of those "We went solar" signs we see on other people's front yards. Part of my motivation is simply to "join the club" and provide an example to others.

"People will willingly shoulder a burden," wrote George Marshall in his excellent book *Don't Even Think About It: Why Our Brains Are Wired to Ignore Climate Change*, "even one that requires short-term sacrifice against uncertain long-term threats, provided they share a common purpose and are rewarded with a greater sense of social belonging."[15] That describes my wife and I. However, we purchased our home less than three years ago and it will take some time before we're financially capable of installing solar power.

South Miami isn't the wealthiest or highest educated community, it was the local political leadership and the local culture which that leadership helped create that made the difference when it came to sustainability. Mayor Stoddard deserves a great deal of credit for what he accomplished. For instance, anyone building a new house in South Miami – or in some cases renovating existing ones – will have to install solar panels under a groundbreaking law approved by the City Commission in July 2017.[16] The law was the first of its kind in Florida. South Miami was the first city in the United States outside of California to approve the requirement. The ordinance was based on similar laws in San Francisco and Santa Monica, California. The law applies to single-family residences that are larger than 1,100 square feet, including townhomes and some multi-story residential buildings.

The law was fought by vested interests like local builders' groups and by Florida, Power & Light. During Commission meetings, local builders argued against the mandate in favor of local incentives and a tax break. In a letter to the *Miami Herald*, Eric Montes de Oca, president-elect of the Miami chapter of the Latin Builders Association, described the law as "counter to individual freedoms" and used language suggesting the law was discriminatory, saying that people would feel "not welcome to live in South Miami."[17]

Florida, Power & Light's representatives argued that because the average residential energy bill in Florida is lower than the national average there would be no financial advantage to customers. FPL also pointed out that the City of South Miami received US$1.4 million in fees from FPL which residents paid on their FPL bills and that this accounted for nearly 7% of the city's budget. They argued that if power consumption dropped as a result of the solar requirement then the city would lose out. Robo-calls from several well-funded anti-solar groups popped up to scare residents. In short, FPL tried everything to stop South Miami's solar panel law.

The U.S. Department of Energy estimates that a medium-sized photovoltaic system costs about US$11,000 after factoring in federal credits. To incentivize photovoltaic panels, South Miami waived its permit fees for solar installations. Under the solar power requirement, new residential construction would require 175 square feet of solar panel to be installed per 1,000 square feet of sunlit roof area, or one panel with 2.75 kilowatt capacity per 1,000 square feet of living space, whichever was less.

Your Neighborhood Needs Solar Too

Asking your community to adopt a solar requirement may sound like too much to ask. South Miami is a tiny municipality of only 2.3 square miles and is largely built-out (although homes are being torn down and replaced at a high rate), and so passing a solar requirement wasn't too big a deal. It would be much more difficult in a community in the process of building many new homes. South Miami also didn't require solar on commercial properties and taking that next step will be contentious. However, if you are interested in solar for your U.S. town, Solar United Neighbors helps communities assemble solar co-ops.

Co-op members leverage bulk-purchasing power to get discounted pricing and a quality installation and Solar United Neighbors was essential to South Miami's success. Even though FPL is a sole energy supplier, South Miami residents could get solar on their houses through buying cooperatives. The Solar United Neighbors website lists co-ops people can join and gives information on creating new co-ops. Essentially, as soon as 30 qualified homes with sunny roofs sign-up Solar United Neighbors issues a Request for Proposal to installers. Installers submit competitive bids and participants in the co-op volunteer to be on a selection committee and choose one installer to serve the entire group.

Talking About Climate at Home

Climate change is starting to become a personal issue for a lot of people. Increasingly, my friends have their own climate stories – some talk about close calls, others tell tragedies – involving hurricanes, rising seas, and wildfires. So many people are talking about the increasingly high cost of water. As climate heating affects more

228 ■ *Why Are We Doing This?*

communities people will band together despite the pushback they receive from energy providers and slow-to-act governments.

We should start relating our climate stories to the next generation and preparing them for the task ahead. For my wife and I, with two young kids, that means talking about planting trees, recycling, and solar panels as we walk around our neighborhood. It means discussing the world's various environmental challenges and the endangered status of the animals we see at the zoo. When my son told me that a girl in his class was vegan, we talked about the environmental benefits of veganism.

"She can't eat pretzels," my son gravely informed me.

"I think she can eat pretzels," I said.

Starting early may just reduce the need for behavioral changes when they get older. Schools are doing their part; we see climate discussion in their lessons and homework. We also see a commitment to building an environmental ethic in just about every animated show they watch. I like *Octonauts*, especially; the show is about a submarine filled with stuffed animal characters who work to save polar bears stuck on ice flows and reef fish populations displaced by bleaching coral. Maybe if the next generation's loyalty is to the Earth they can put differences of race, class, nationality, and religion aside. Maybe that's asking too much. Somehow the Octonauts put aside their differences and the pale white teddy bear captain gets along just fine with the green bunny Tweak.

"We need trees," my five-year-old said on the ride from school the other day. "I would rather live in a world with no ice-cream than with no trees because we need trees to live," she said, sagaciously.

Banding together creates a sense of camaraderie. I look forward to the next time we host a backyard birthday for the kids with a bounce house and a cotton candy machine and the neighbors notice our new solar panels. In this respect I want to spend money and time to keep up with the Joneses.

"Why, yes, we're making so much power we give back to the system," I'll tout breezily as I flip hamburgers (ahem, *tofu* burgers). A little bragging doesn't mean you're a shallow person. Getting noticed for pitching in is a strong motivator. Sometimes I wonder if it isn't one of our strongest motivations.

Notes

1 Rice, D. (2020). Global warming is making hurricanes stronger, study says. *USA Today*, May 18. Retrieved from: www.usatoday.com/story/news/nation/2020/05/18/global-warming-making-hurricanes-stronger-study-suggests/5216028002/

2 Berardelli, J. (2019). Intense hurricanes like Dorian produce 1,000 times more damage – And they're becoming more common. Retrieved from: www.cbsnews.com/news/hurricane-dorian-1000-times-more-damage-becoming-more-common/

3 Miami-Dade County (n.d.). Wastewater disposal and treatment. Retrieved from: www8.miamidade.gov/global/water/wastewater-disposal-and-treatment.page

4 Ibid.

Climate Planning Objection 9 ■ 229

5 Miami-Dade Government (2018). Septic systems vulnerable to sea level rise. Retrieved from: www.miamidade.gov/govaction/legistarfiles/Matters/Y2018/182728.pdf (local report, not published). This report was developed collaboratively by the Miami-Dade County Department of Regulatory & Economic Resources Miami-Dade County Water and Sewer Department & Florida Department of Health in Miami-Dade County (Dr. Samir Elmir).

6 Ibid.

7 Ruse, G.A. (2020). Sally B. Philips. *Miami's Community News*, January 14. Retrieved from: https://communitynewspapers.com/featured/sally-b-philips/

8 McKie, R. (2014). Miami, the great world city, is drowning while the powers that be look away. *The Guardian*, July 11. Retrieved from: www.theguardian.com/world/2014/jul/11/miami-drowning-climate-change-deniers-sea-levels-rising

9 Stebbins, S. (2019). States producing the most renewable energy. *247 Wall St*, July 24. Retrieved from: https://247wallst.com/special-report/2019/07/24/states-producing-the-most-renewable-energy-2/

10 Savenije, D. The worst-ranked utilities for clean energy. *Utility Dive*, August 8. Retrieved from: www.utilitydive.com/news/the-worst-ranked-utilities-for-clean-energy/294943/

11 Energy Information Administration (n.d.). *Electric Power Monthly*. Retrieved from: www.eia.gov/state/?sid=FL#tabs-4

12 Pentland, W. (2015). Solar alliance In Sunshine State may be bad news for Jeb Bush. *Forbes*, April 14. Retrieved from: www.forbes.com/sites/williampentland/2015/01/15/solar-alliance-in-sunshine-state-may-be-bad-news-for-jeb-bush/?sh=3b9842a95ee3

13 Barton, E. (2015). In Sunshine State, big energy blocks solar power. Florida Center for Investigative Reporting, April 3. Retrieved from: https://fcir.org/2015/04/03/in-sunshine-state-big-energy-blocks-solar-power/

14 Klas, Mary Ellen (2016). Florida voters say no to misleading solar amendment. *Miami Herald*, November 8. Retrieved from: www.miamiherald.com/news/politics-government/election/article113449438.html

15 Marshall, G. (2014). *Don't Even Think About It: Why Our Brains Are Wired to Ignore Climate Change*. New York: Bloomsbury. Retrieved from audio version on Audible.com, 2015.

16 Dixon, L. and Teproff, C. (2017). South Miami is going solar but not everyone is on board. *Miami Herald*, July 19. Retrieved from: www.miamiherald.com/news/local/community/miami-dade/south-miami/article162582838.html

17 De Oca, E.M. (2008). Latin Builders Association: South Miami should not make solar panels mandatory. *Miami Herald*, May 13. Retrieved from: www.miamiherald.com/opinion/article161881308.html

Chapter 10

Climate Planning Objection 10

"I'll be dead when this happens."

When we present climate change, we reference distant years like 2050 and 2100 because the worst effects of climate change are still ahead, and the most significant changes will take decades or even centuries to manifest. However, urban planners must also emphasize that climate change is happening here and now. "We have to behave like our house is on fire, because it is," Greta Thunberg says.

We tend to present climate change with statements like: "Sea levels could rise by as much as 19 inches by 2050 in Atlantic City." This is a fine and accurate way to present. However, we've all watched our audiences do the math and decide that the problem is for the next generation to solve. "Atlantic City can expect a 75% chance of risk of at least one flood topping over 5 feet to hit between now and 2050," is a good additional point, because it frames the discussion in terms of what could happen tomorrow.

The disastrous seasons in California and Australia in 2017, 2019, and 2020 are evidence of the problem we face today. The hurricanes of the 2004–2005 season and 2018–2019 season on the Atlantic and Gulf Coasts were either triggered or exasperated by the warmer and drier climate. There's always been fires and storms, but in recent years we've all lived through record-breaking infernos and tempests.

If this were a disaster movie, we'd be past the early scenes when the scientist warning the authorities of the potential for disaster is being ignored. We're at the point when the scientist is finally being taken seriously, and we're just about to reach

DOI: 10.4324/9781003181514-12

231

232 ■ *Why Are We Doing This?*

the *fighting to survive* point in the story arc. So why doesn't it feel that way for everyone? It may, in part, be because we keep referencing 2050 and 2100.

Climate change is already occurring, but the average person can't see how it affects their daily lives yet. We can show that today's fires and floods, food costs, energy costs, infrastructure costs, and the hardships and tragedy created by displaced persons are all related to a changing climate, but I have found that most audiences, while interested in these topics, feel them academic. The everyday fears and anxieties people carry around with them are all more immediate than climate.

Sadly, even the people tasked with "the future" are too often uninterested in climate change challenges. In the fall of 2020, I implored a Florida Department of Transportation engineer to consider lifting Highway 44 in the town of Crystal River as part of their scheduled reconstruction of the road because the highway was just a mile from the shore, already in a flood zone, and was the evacuation route for an economically disadvantaged African American community. I talked about how the road could be seasonally submerged during hurricane seasons.

The FDOT engineer literally laughed at my suggestion. She even laughed at the idea of simply studying the problem and told me that there wasn't enough money in the project budget for sea-level rise to be considered in any way.

"This road will flood. And one day it will be permanently under water," I said.

"I'm glad I will be dead when that happens," she said flippantly on a video conference call involving a dozen people. She couldn't have been more than 30 years old. Maybe she'd heard the phrase "I'll be dead when that happens" so often in her department that it felt quite natural to repeat it.

"No, you won't be dead," I wished I'd said. "Speak up for your generation. Stop fighting yesterday's problems and fight today's." The really good retorts only occur to you a week later.

I try to make climate change part of every planning presentation but conservation and preparedness, while responsible, can be boring and though it's the urban planner's job to prepare the public for the future, no one likes to be the bearer of bad news. This is one reason, I think, that urban planners shirk the responsibility. Maybe the engineer I mentioned did not want to report to Crystal River that despite the millions of dollars she and her department were willing to invest in the roadway it would probably never stand the challenges of the future.

"We toured the woods north of the site," I said to a crowd of several dozen in the food court of a dying mall outside Richmond, Virginia, in the early spring of 2020, "and along with the redevelopment of this site can come the creation of a new trail system."

People seemed to like that idea. I thought I saw heads nodding and a person or two pointing up at the areas we'd labeled for trails and whisper enthusiastically to others.

"I saw the tiny white flowers of the Bradford Pear in bloom everywhere I went," I continued. "They are blooming earlier and earlier every year as the world warms, but that's another conversation."

Climate Planning Objection 10 ■ 233

I could hear an older woman in the front row say *whew*, glad to be spared a climate crisis sermon. Her concern wasn't climate change. Her concern was the blight and crime the dying mall was creating. She had attended my presentation for the bright, shining renderings of the future and so I proceeded to show the artist's renderings of the dead mall transformed into a wonderful mixed-use center with happy people sauntering around. She liked that.

People may not want to hear about climate, but we must insist. As climate change is studied further and the problem intensifies, there will be, sadly, more alarming statistics and examples of ruin and loss that are closer to home. However, the older woman in the dying mall helps illustrate a difficult point: If our audience is under a certain age, we can appeal to an enlightened self-interest, but if our audience has advanced beyond a certain age, one must admit that the benefits of climate change mitigation and adaptation will largely be enjoyed by future generations. The way we view things has a lot to do with the time we think we have left to live. How do we get people to care about a world they won't see?

"Think of your children," we can say. "Think of your grandchildren." Kids temper our natural self-centeredness and shortsightedness. The problem, however, is that people are already thinking of their children and grandchildren all the time and the difficulties they are dealing with today are scary and complicated. Drug use, teen pregnancy, school violence, police violence, bigotry, health issues, stagnant workplace pay, and rising living costs are a lot to deal with.

"Think of what your children and grandchildren will say about you when it comes to climate change. If the next generation finds themselves in an even scarier world, will they blame you?" I have yet to say anything like this to an audience because it sounds a bit intense. "Or will they say, 'Dad did everything he could do,' and 'Mom fought this?' *The fiery trials through which we pass will light us down in honor or dishonor to the latest generation*, wrote Abraham Lincoln." I'd never quote Lincoln. Planners aren't politicians – they aren't comfortable with such rhetorical grandiosity. Even still, "Where were you and what were you doing when all this was going on?" is truly a question our kids and grandkids might ask.

For me, this book, and my work in urban planning, is how I show my concern. My kids might read this book and think their dad silly for thinking local action could amount to anything. Or maybe they will think me alarmist because the world fixed the problem before they inherited it. But they will know I cared. As City Councils and Boards of Supervisors across the country passed statutes that made my work illegal – specifically, outlawing any ordinances that were traceable to the UN's Agenda 21 (and by extension, the Paris Accords and climate change) – I kept talking about climate and adding resilience and sustainability to my plans, codes, and ordinances. Even when my audiences, clients, and employers didn't want to hear it, I persisted. I did what I could.

What do I have to show for it? Quite a lot if I view my work this way: We don't need to convince everyone. We only need to convince the small, thoughtful, committed groups who the scientist Margaret Mead said was all that were needed to

234 ■ *Why Are We Doing This?*

Figure 10 Water Tower, Newfield, Martin County, Florida

change the world. There are many young people brimming with energy who want to invest time in the growth of themselves and others. There are many people in the later stages of their lives who feel a pressure to improve the lives of generations to come. Continue to seek out those people. They will do what they can. Advocates are a climate plan's most important asset. They will push quietly for years.

Climate Planning Objection 10 ■ **235**

"I will be dead when it happens," I hear surprisingly often given the self-centered nature of this statement. It sounds so selfish to me. Fortunately, not everyone feels this way and that's why the world is acknowledging the problem and making changes.

There are people who are very much concerned about their legacy. I want to tell you about one person because his work makes him a champion of climate planning (though he would probably never identify himself as one). He has a fitting first name for a hero. His name is *Knight*.

Notes From the Field

Planning Compact Urban Gorm and Knight Kiplinger's Legacy at Newfield in Martin County, Florida

Newfield, outside Stuart, Florida, if constructed faithful to the vision, could become a model for new settlements in Florida's interior, away from the vulnerable shore. Located on Citrus Boulevard, a highway that no longer has any citrus along it, the community could one day host small-scale farming, providing fruits and vegetables locally, as well as the kind of walkable urbanism that people move to historic coastal communities to enjoy.

I traced a finger-shaped wetland onto my base map, drew with my pencil a 50-foot buffer around it as was required by Martin County's wetland protection regulations, and then turned the odd shape into a pleasing parallelogram. At the terminus of the wetland park I'd drawn, I used my rolling ruler to design a civic building with a hipped roof and a portico that would look out across an expanse of tall slash pine trees, and wild grasses with clumps of saw palmetto. The building would be a community center for the southern neighborhoods of the new development in Martin County's interior. The 3,400-acre development was located on a plateau which was on average 26 feet above sea level – *high plains* by Florida standards.

Beginning in 2017 our team started imagining Newfield as a new town for a population of 15,000–20,000 people with a diverse mix of uses and housing types and large swaths of preserved open space at the edges. The original name of the new town was Pineland Prairie, and it was a name that had to be pried away from Knight Kiplinger, the developer and property owner, by his marketing department. Knight believed Florida's natural interior was itself an amenity and he wanted a name that communicated that belief. However, his marketers eventually convinced him that the name needed to sound more like a place where people lived than an open space restoration project. Newfield will be both.

When you imagine development in Florida, you picture golf courses ringed by apartment pods sitting behind gatehouses. You picture drive-thru restaurants announced by enormous backlit signs on long suburban strips where the air boils

236 ■ *Why Are We Doing This?*

above parking lots. You picture condominium towers on the ocean with pools on the tenth floor and a phalanx of security people and valets at ground level. You picture traffic – four lanes in both directions and bumper to bumper. Sadly, walkable neighborhoods where people can live a car-light or car-optional life are hardly ever built in America today and almost never built in Florida. Placeless, conventional, sprawl development is often marketed as places where one can "live, work, and play," but they aren't, and I often wonder if the marketers know the difference. Newfield will be different.

The Newfield property is shaped roughly like the state of Nebraska and bisected by Citrus Boulevard. Today you'd drive past the site without feeling the slightest need to look to either side at the featureless landscape. In the future, as one enters the site travelling west on Citrus, the vistas will remain natur..l for the first two miles, with open fields. Cattle will graze the prairies and alligators will continue to live in the creeks.

Visitors will then reach the center of town and find a buzzing, prosperous place with a country café facing a grocery store. Each structure, though new, will feature *old-time* storefronts with transom windows, kickboards, and wide awnings shading the sidewalks. One could stop for a coffee and then stay to browse the shops. Local vendors will sell paintings, pottery, metalwork, and woodwork in the various one- and two-story shops. A water tower will sit just behind the central square with an ivy-covered trellis and large letters that read "WELCOME."

We designed the town center with a feeling of spatial enclosure like an outdoor room and we hid all the unsightly parking at the interior of blocks. One will be able to walk from the central square along a connected network of tree-lined streets to see homes designed in the local, rustic style and facing the street. Front porches will be within conversation distance of the sidewalk. On even the most searing hot day the sidewalk will be coolly shaded.

Newfield will be a new place but reminiscent of an old mining town out West, the kind of towns that have become destinations for day-trippers and tourists. Newfield will resemble a picturesque hilltop town in Italy or France, except without the hill (because it is still Florida). I picture narrow pedestrian streets that will be home to tapas bars, a microbrewery, a bakery, and a bookstore. I picture a bike shop where one can rent a bike and explore the nearby trails that traverse the landscape.

This isn't suburban development so much as suburban retrofit because if you zoom out a bit on a map you see that Newfield is at the center of an endless bewildering sprawl of single-family houses – and nothing but single-family houses. Our new community will provide a town center. Unlike a bedroom suburb which everyone has to drive out of in the morning and return to at night, this will be a place people drive, walk, and bike to for work.

As one continues further west along Citrus Boulevard, they will leave town and see agriculture along the boulevard. Citrus will return to the street along with tomatoes, potatoes, sweet corn, strawberries and ornamental plants. Community-owned gardens located around a new barn that will look like an old barn will host

Climate Planning Objection 10 ■ 237

community events such as weddings and community farm-to-table meals. For the design of the barn and farmhouse I looked to Casey Farm as a precedent, a seventeenth-century gentleman farm in Rhode Island where I once worked. One of the problems with development today is that there's nothing that distinguishes it. There are no images that fix in the mind. It's all a vast urban nowhere. By contrast, the barn will be a landmark.

Do water towers, barns, and shopfronts with awnings have an old-fashioned air? Yes. But a charming and engaging one. It is okay to build the way people did for centuries before the modernist fashion began to dominate. Our design team drew all the streets, public spaces, and building lots after studying the nicest and most functional communities of Old Florida. We studied the charming, laid-back towns of Stuart, Winter Garden, Apalachicola, Cedar Key, Winter Park, and DeFuniak Springs and applied what we learned.

Farther along Citrus Boulevard there will be, well, nothing. Except for a few hiking and horse trails the area will stay fields, wildflowers, pines, and native sable palms. In total 70% of the site, nearly 2,000 acres, will be kept as open space. The land will be open to everyone and will become one of the largest natural parks in Martin County.

And all this will happen, I think, because it has one thing going for it that so many ideal communities our team has planned before does not – namely, Knight Kiplinger.

Knight is a rare kind of client. The former editor-in-chief of the Kiplinger financial media company in Washington D.C. lives part of the year in Martin County and contributes time and resources to local philanthropy. He's known in Martin County for donating land to build churches, homes for civic organizations, hospitals, and libraries. During the plan unveiling process, he went out of his way to meet with local leaders, community groups, and neighbors to explain what he was trying to do, and to solicit feedback. Large developments are proposed all the time in Martin County and rejected. Local opposition to any kind of new development is fierce. Newfield wasn't rejected, it was approved, and it wouldn't have been approved were it not for Knight.

When it comes to climate change adaptation, new communities like Newfield present an opportunity to shift development that would have occurred on barrier islands and coastal communities away from the shore and reduce Florida's economic reliance on the beach. As the seas rise, beach tourism could transition to a more sustainable kind of ecotourism. Our team designed a system of boardwalk trails and paths that explored the pine forests and cypress swamps. Our team walked the routes where the trails would be located. I walked under the boughs of tall pines and across fields of wild grasses. We skirted the freshwater ponds ringed by cypresses that were covered in Spanish moss that blew in the breeze. It was clear to me on those walks that the state's interior can be quite beautiful in its natural state.

Most of the site can stay natural while still delivering a profit thanks to a dense center with apartments, townhomes, triplexes, duplexes, and single-family homes

238 ■ *Why Are We Doing This?*

with accessory dwelling units in the back. In America today there are roughly 328 million people living on 1.9 billion acres of land. That's about 6 acres per person. What if every person really did live on 6 acres? There would be no room for parks, trails, and wilderness. But that's what we are building when we design large lot gated subdivisions and McMansion mini estates. At Newfield the average household would live on one-tenth an acre. That means there's room for vast open spaces and trail networks that people can share. People aren't so much buying a house as buying into a town that will stay rural by design.

Was climate change adaptation part of Knight's vision? Was he thinking about Florida's migration away from the coasts? I talked about it with him at a party at his home on Sewell's Point in Martin County in 2017 and he shied away from the topic. I suspected that he had stronger views on climate change than he was willing to let on because *Kiplinger's Personal Finance* magazine doesn't shy away from the topic.[1] Maybe he understood that it was dangerous to talk openly about climate in conservative Martin County. Martin County had voted two-to-one in favor of Trump during the 2016 National Election[2] and if you felt climate change was a problem you didn't vote Trump. Martin County was also the second county to leave the *Seven50* Partnership described earlier in the book.

Kiplinger will not build Newfield alone, however. He will have to partner with other investors and real estate developers and sell pieces of the land in phases. While he plans to retain control over Newfield's overall design and town center, it will be a 25-year building process and Knight is not a young man. It is possible that his vision for a perfect community where people of various income groups and ages meet on shared greens and break bread at locally sourced restaurants – with all the turn-of-the-last-century friendliness he talks about – will, in time, become just another Florida real estate project with conventional garage-front homes and strip-style commercial. I hate to admit it, but my agritopian heart has been broken many times before. However, Newfield got one thing right from the beginning: It is in the right place. The rising seas and increased storms will not impact Newfield like places along the coast. The homes are more likely to remain insurable. The people won't have to evacuate except when facing the worst storms.

"I want to build a place where I would want to live and a place my grandkids will want to live," Knight told me. Knight talks so often about his legacy that it makes sense to give him the benefit of the doubt and have faith that he can make the picturesque little hamlet happen. When it comes to climate, real estate developers will need to consider their legacy, the places that they will hand down to future generations because the issue of climate will probably prove more important than questions of a place's architectural character, quality of life, trail networks, or built-in congeniality.

The biggest issue when it comes to the relocation of vulnerable populations in Florida (and everywhere else) is that people love their homes and don't want to leave them. It takes catastrophe or multiple washouts with high replacement costs before people decide to change their lives. That could change. We could realistically imagine a statewide policy one day that doesn't allow large new construction projects along the coast. We could imagine a day when the cost to insure buildings on the coast will simply be too high, or when taxpayers and insurance ratepayers who don't live on the coasts will get tired of paying for continual reconstruction. Until that day, we need to design places on higher ground with a high quality of life and recreational and scenic amenities that are not the beach in order to give all Floridians a choiceworthy place to retreat to.

Let's picture a new Florida with complete, compact, walkable, mixed-use communities amidst the inland pinelands and vast sawgrass prairies, atop upland ridges, and far from the shore. Let's picture continuity (of a kind) in Florida, and new places that combine high quality natural environments with high quality man-made environments, beauty and grace, by design. That would be a worthy legacy for us all.

Notes

1　Smith, A.K. (2016). How to invest for climate change. *Kiplinger*, February 5. Retrieved from: www.kiplinger.com/article/investing/T052-C008-S002-how-to-invest-for-climate-change.html

2　*Politico* (2016). 2016 Florida presidential election results. Retrieved from: www.politico.com/2016-election/results/map/president/florida/

CREATING CLIMATE PLANS

2

Chapter 11

Drafting the Plan

The Main Stages

Climate planning is a *process* more than a *product*. This section discusses the methods we use to educate decisionmakers and the public and create a vision that people will commit to. In the field of urban planning, vision is important, but commitment is of greater importance.

Jane Jacobs, a writer and activist who influenced urban studies, suggested that the great majority of urban planning is ineffectual, if not harmful, and I am afraid I find myself agreeing with this too often. However, some plans do work, in large part because those plans are made *with* and *for* the community. Those plans are structured with goals, strategies, and action items that agencies and individuals can work into their collective and personal missions.

Here, we discuss the elements of climate planning and provide one specific (though modifiable) process to draft a Climate Plan (or any kind of plan). These steps include: drafting the plan, co-authoring the plan with the public, plan adoption, and implementation. Once you have a plan adopted be prepared to deal with setbacks.

There is also advice on staying productive even after the inevitable political pendulum swing.

Different Kinds of Climate Plans

Climate planning involves **mitigation** (reducing greenhouse gas emissions) and **adaptation** (contending with a hotter, drier, and more turbulent world and getting ready for an even worse situation). It comes in many forms including Climate Action Plans (CAPs), Sustainability Plans, Resilience Plans, Comprehensive Plans, the Sustainability or Resilience Elements within Comprehensive Plans, Transportation

DOI: 10.4324/9781003181514-13

243

244 ■ *Creating Climate Plans*

Plans, Neighborhood Plans, and other forms of municipal plans, policies, initiatives, investments, or expenditures. To simplify we will call these various kinds of plans **Climate Plans** and provide an approach to community engagement that could work in any situation.

The **Mitigation Element** of a Climate Plan provides an inventory of Greenhouse Gas (GHG) emissions across all sectors along with recommendations to reduce emissions. The Mitigation Element includes both **indicators** (measurements that provide information about trends to assist community leaders in making decisions that affect future outcomes) and **benchmarks** (quantifiable targets that crystalize community aspirations). Indicators and benchmarks are used to measure progress over time.

The **Adaptation Element** describes upgrades to streets, buildings, and public spaces and proposes adaptation infrastructure. When the goal is to reinforce, we use one set of strategies. When the goal is to retreat, the Adaptation Element identifies places to evacuate from and strategies to return the land back to a use that is less vulnerable.

Writing the text for a Climate Plan is just one part of a larger planning process. To maximize success in implementing the plan, community involvement is integral. For this reason, crafting a Climate Plan can take anywhere from six to 16 months based on staff (or volunteer) capacity, availability of data and information, and the level of public engagement.

The approach described in the following two chapters aims for the maximum possible public involvement and includes a five-day **Public Design Workshop** as the centerpiece of the longer process. This intense, comprehensive method of public involvement allows stakeholders to come together and form consensus.

These events are often called **charrettes** by urban designers. The word *charrette* has its roots in the curriculum of the École des Beaux-Arts, the architecture school in Paris, at around the turn of the twentieth century. Purportedly, the word *charrette* refers to the small cart students would add their work to when it was time for the work to be graded. We can imagine students working frantically on their canvases as the cart proceeded through the streets of the Latin Quarter. Similarly, the Climate Plan team will need to work fast.

Of course, the word *charrette* is … well … French, and in my experience, a French term can be off-putting in some communities because it is foreign. In the United Kingdom, designers use the phrase *Enquiry by Design* and we can reasonably assume they do that to avoid using a French term (the two countries have a long history). You don't have to use the word *charrette*. *Public Design Workshop* works fine.

We like the charrette method because it is focused and quick. If you took all the work our teams could complete in one week while on charrette and put it into the normal business schedule the deliverables would be comparable to one or two months of activity. Charrettes respect the community's time and provides a less expensive option for municipalities. There is also something fun, democratic, and

Drafting the Plan: The Main Stages ■ **245**

maybe heroic about working late nights to complete the plan for a community in that same community with a door open to anyone who wants to contribute.

Charrettes aim to maximize public involvement by being open to absolutely everyone. Get ready; if you conduct charrettes for a living you come to realize that while not all people who come to charrettes are strange, all the strange people in a town will come to the charrette. I could tell a few stories at this point, but you will have your own stories soon enough.

Sometimes during a charrette the biggest foes become the strongest supporters. This is hard to believe, I know, and harder to explain, except to say that the strong impulse which compels people to attend public meetings (usually it is a form of fear and anger) sometimes can be turned into an equally strong impulse to work with the team and help get the plan approved and implemented. If you can, include your opponents in everything. Allow them to share an _esprit de corps_. In a few instances, the leaders of the pushback morph into staunch supporters who continue to hold the elected officials to the promise of plan implementation. I know, I know, you have to see this to believe it, but it happens, though it only happens as part of a well-ordered public process.

Chapter 12

Co-authoring the Plan with the Public

Phase 1: Plan Direction and Team Creation (Month 1)

Task 1.1: Decide on Plan Type

Once there are people within a community who want to see improvement and change, along with a municipality willing to work toward a plan, the first task in creating a Climate Plan is to decide what kind of plan or plan update provides the best framework for climate work.

- **Climate Action Plans (CAPs)** focus primarily on reducing greenhouse gas emissions. This could be limited to the local government's operations or include the entire municipality's net emissions. CAPs are compact documents, rarely more than 30 pages, and common projects include expanding a municipality's electric vehicle fleet and providing more transportation options. A CAP is unlikley to talk about land use considerations as those would need to be placed in the Comprehensive Plan. One guide to creating a CAP is the *Climate Action Planning Guide* from Climate Smart Communities (2014).[1]
- **Sustainability Plans** seek to "meet the needs of the present without compromising the ability of future generations to meet their own needs," (as this common expression in planning goes) The three pillars of sustainable development are usually the environment, social equity, and economic development. Sustainability Plans tie together a community's goals, strategies, implementation plans, and metrics for improving sustainability. These are mid-length

248 ■ *Creating Climate Plans*

documents between 50 and 100 pages. One sustainability guide is the *Sustainability Planning Toolkit* (2009) written by ICLEI–Local Governments for Sustainability USA.[2]

■ **Resilience Plans** seek to improve urban resilience, which has conventionally been defined as the "measurable ability of any urban system, with its inhabitants, to maintain continuity through all shocks and stresses, while positively adapting and transforming towards sustainability."[3] These plans contain elements of Sustainability Plans and are comparable in size but have an additional focus on adaptation to changing conditions.

■ Resilience Plans identify resilience factors which can be labelled as **basic** (dealing with the rudimentary requirements for living after acute shocks) and **beyond basic** (the elements which facilitate healthy living and social and economic empowerment and help to alleviate chronic stresses). A hierarchy of needs might include basic issues such as clean water, affordable energy, safe places to live and gather, clean and safe environmental conditions, access to jobs and education, and access to health care and preventive health services. Beyond the basics, these plans may include healthy food choices, access to open space and active living, community connectivity and empowerment, and opportunities for economic advancement. The organization 100 Resilient Cities, which was funded by the Rockefeller Foundation for several years (ending in 2019), produced numerous resilience plans for cities around the world, which could be studied as templates.[4]

■ **Comprehensive Planning** is a process that determines local goals and aspirations in terms of community development. Most municipalities in the United States have Comprehensive Plans and most update them regularly. These plans describe public policies related to urban design, transportation, utilities, land use, recreation, and housing. Comprehensive Plans typically encompass large geographical areas, a broad range of topics, and cover a long-term time horizon. Comprehensive Plans are made up of elements, and Sustainability Elements and Resilience Elements are increasingly common. *The Practice of Local Government Planning* (2000) is the most common reference for developing Comprehensive Plans.[5]

■ Additional plans that may include sustainability or resilience components include Transportation Plans, Neighborhood Plans, Development Studies, Master Plans, Parks and Open Space Master Plans, Utility Master Plans, Capital Improvement Plans, and other municipal plans.

The charrette that helps everyone understand the plan can be **on-site** or **virtual**. During the COVID-19 pandemic, which began in 2020, we learned how to conduct virtual charrettes, and now we do not need to travel to a municipality in order to engage many people substantively. During a five-day period we use teleconferences, webinars, open Design Studios, on-line polls and questionnaires, and real time, interactive presentations to host a conversation about the future. Virtual events, or _telepresence_, is also an emissions-reduction strategy which helps avoid emissions from both business air travel and local commuting to public meetings.

Task 1.2: Assemble the Plan Team

At the start of the project, a Plan Team must be identified to work both as community organizers for the public process and as authors of the Climate Plan. The creation of Climate Plans doesn't involve specialized knowledge. Although a background in the fields of urban planning, architecture, landscape architecture, sustainability, and resilience are helpful, there are guides to both preforming the necessary analyses and drafting the policies of every kind of Climate Plan. Climate Plans are also public documents and communities that have adopted them make them available for review and download. I recommend you review at least one Climate Plan from another municipality with comparable geographic and socio-economic challenges before you begin.

The Plan Team can be composed of volunteers from the community working with city staff from the Planning or Engineering departments. Elected officials or chief municipal staff members can also direct their staff to draft a Climate Plan. A municipal Planning Department is the most likely candidate to lead the process. However, in some small towns, the Climate Plan process is conducted by the mayor's office or the town engineer. In larger cities, there may be a sustainability officer or resilience officer with offices and staff members. Elected officials can also direct municipal staff to draft the report or hire outside experts, like local universities, nonprofit organizations, or urban planning consultants, to draft the Climate Plan.

Though the Plan Team can come in many forms, there should be a **Project Coordinator** designated by the municipality. That person may be either an existing staff member who is tasked with coordinating the plan, or a new hire specifically designated for this task. The Project Coordinator acts as the primary point of contact within the local government and externally to the public. They will participate in all meetings – including advisory boards, interdepartmental meetings, and outreach meetings – and keep the municipality focused on their desired outcomes. The coordinator needs to be well versed in climate issues to guide and often _push_ the planning process forward.

Task 1.3: Determine Plan Boundaries and Their Adoption

Climate Plans are typically for entire municipalities (towns, cities, and counties in the U.S.) but can involve multiple municipalities or entire regions. The best Climate Plans tend to involve all government and private operations within a municipality. They are typically adopted by a municipality and become an advisory policy document.

250 ■ *Creating Climate Plans*

Some Plan Teams also work to secure the endorsement of influential local groups before the plan begins the adoption process and it is important to consider the geographies that concern those groups. Such organizations could include the local Chamber of Commerce, homebuilders' associations, Sierra Club (an environmental organization that is widespread throughout the U.S.), nature conservancies, and land trusts.

Task 1.4: Assemble a Plan Advisory Committee (Optional)

Advisory Committees are common for public planning projects. They are composed of informal leaders in the community and provide feedback throughout the creation of the plan to the Plan Team. Committee members work as plan ambassadors in the community by inviting people to meetings personally. When the plan is finished, the endorsement of Advisory Committee members helps the municipal adoption process.

Advisory Committee members should come from diverse backgrounds representing many points of view and should be interested in sustainability topics. Committees could include elected officials, business owners, real estate developers, educational institutions, and philanthropic organizations, among others. Forming the Advisory Committee requires striking a balance between being inclusive while ensuring that the committee stays small enough to be manageable and productive.

The term "Advisory Committee" is better than "Steering Committee" and the term "Think Tank" may be even better. We don't want the Advisory Committee to feel they are in-charge of the project because it is difficult for a diverse group to agree on action. *If Christopher Columbus had an advisory committee he would probably still be at the dock*, goes the old adage. The committee act as advisors to the Plan Team. Valued advisors, but advisors.

Advisory Committees usually comprise seven to 11 members who meet regularly, often once a month, and their meetings involve an agenda with presentations from the Plan Team. Each meeting should have a facilitator, agenda, and minutes taken. Limiting meetings to a maximum of once per month can help ensure that participants will not be overloaded with unnecessary meetings. Committee members can be tasked with research to contribute to the plan at meetings and they can even co-write the plan.

Advisory Committee members should attend working group meetings in person (or virtually), but since they tend to be very busy people, they should be allowed to send a representative from their organization with expertise in the issues. The Committee works best when there is one representative who attends all the meetings so they can stay abreast with all of the issues.

Why should someone join the Advisory Committee? I am asked this often by municipal planners afraid that they won't be able to get people to join. Too often our projects don't have an Advisory Committee because the local urban planner just can't see why a person would volunteer their time.

Some people join because they have a vested interest and want to learn more to further the interests of their businesses. Local developers, architects, landscape architects, and land use attorneys are often willing candidates. Others aspire to an elected position locally and want to build their resume. For most people, though, it is the need to do something to help the world that motivates them; it is "the call." It's a complicated motivation. It's a mix of needing to be important in some way, needing to stay busy and engaged in the world in ways other than jobs and family, and needing to feel like they are a *good* person.

After many years of helping assemble Advisory Committees, I believe that working toward a better world gives people meaning, fills them with energy, helps them put aside anxieties regarding health, family, and finances. Don't be afraid: just ask. Chances are you will have more people interested in volunteering than you can make use of.

Phase 2: Kick-off and Previous Plan Review (Months 2 and 3)

Phase 2 involves an official kick-off for the project and the compilation and review of all relevant information, including previous studies – for example, Comprehensive Plans and Sustainability Plans, and Transportation Plans at the local, county, and regional level. These plans provide a foundation to build from. They provide ideas and inspiration. This phase also includes meetings with key stakeholders, on-site analysis, and the first chance to get the word out about the plan and the planning process to the general public.

Task 2.1: Hold Project Kick-off Meeting

The Plan Team should schedule a meeting with municipal staff to review base information needs, identify key stakeholders including the Advisory Committee, strategize on the Public Design Workshop, and develop a detailed schedule for the creation of the Climate Plan.

Task 2.2: Develop Public Outreach and Participation Plan

The Plan Team works with the municipality to develop a public outreach and participation plan that will provide the framework for integrating the public into the planning effort. The Plan Team also works with the municipality to create a list of key individuals, local leaders, community organizations, and stakeholders to include throughout the planning process, and to determine a strategy for distribution of public awareness materials to them. The Public Design Workshop will be the centerpiece of the public outreach and participation strategy; however, the team may employ various techniques for information gathering like focus groups,

252 ■ Creating Climate Plans

individual interviews, meetings with community groups, and informative and interactive websites.

We seek to talk to everyone who could be impacted by our policies but that is likely to be impossible. It is therefore not necessary that planners talk to every person in a community, but it is important that every viewpoint be heard. This means we need the viewpoints of people typically left out of the public process, especially minorities and the poor. Similarly, we must involve climate skeptics and their viewpoints.

During the charrette (or workshop), the Climate Plan is co-created with the community and in full view of anyone who is interested. While maximum of public involvement isn't strictly required of a Climate Plan, I have found that the climate change denial factions within a community will find the time to attend at least part of a five-day Public Design Workshop – and that's good. They have a chance to be heard, they will be more willing to work with you after they feel listened to, and they are more likely to learn.

In five days we can change minds (free coffee and snacks help). Of course, there are hard cases who will never be convinced that the climate is changing, that our actions affect the climate, or that it is worth the time and expense to plan, mitigate, and adapt. At the very least, the mystery that surrounds Climate Planning will be dispelled by a Public Design Workshop. The curtain is pulled back on many conspiracy theories. Attendees see that the team working on the plan are well-meaning, ordinary people, and not extremists sent by a political party or shadowy organization.

Task 2.3: Review Previous Plan and Gather Information

Most municipalities have conducted significant amounts of urban planning and those plans are applicable to the Climate Plan. The team should review existing local planning efforts, including the municipality's Comprehensive Plan, to guide and inform the plan process. Specific information also needs to be gathered for the Mitigation Element and the other elements of the Climate Plan.

- **Mitigation Element:** A Greenhouse Gas Emissions (GHG) inventory will indicate which sectors are the greatest contributors of GHG emissions in a community and establish a baseline from which to set goals and measure progress. The baseline GHG emissions inventory provides the data needed to prioritize actions that will offer the best return on investment when it comes to reducing energy consumption and reducing GHG emissions. The Mitigation Element also involves an Implementation Plan listing actions that will reduce GHG emissions within the relevant sectors.
- There are several online tools for generating an GHG emissions inventory. The U.S. EPA (United States Environmental Protection Agency) provides a

free Local Greenhouse Gas Inventory Tool[6] which I use. The free, interactive spreadsheet calculates GHG emissions for many sectors, including residential, commercial, transportation, waste, and water management.

- GHG tools include User's Guides that explain data collection and how to calculate emissions. Ultimately, the Plan Team uses the tool to develop a base year community GHG inventory, track emission trends, develop mitigation strategies and policies, and regularly assess progress towards meeting their goals.
- **Other Plan Elements:** A Geographic Information System (GIS) is a system designed to gather, analyze, and present spatial or geographic data using maps and graphics. GIS application tools allow users to create interactive queries, analyze spatial information, edit data in maps, and present results. A city's GIS may consist of data layers called *shapefiles* that can be downloaded and used with an ArcGIS software license. At minimum, we usually request the following GIS shapefiles from municipalities to make our base maps and analysis maps: streets, buildings, open spaces, water (lakes, rivers, shoreline), flood zones, and aerials.
- If the Plan Team or municipality does not have GIS there are many online map programs like Google Maps, Surging Seas, local Property Appraiser sites, and online FEMA websites that can be used to compile base information and create informative analysis maps. We also use online applications such as WalkScore and Zillow. Other data includes basic socioeconomic data, education statistics, housing data, employment data, and health statistics, and much of this data is available from sources like the Center for Disease Control (CDC) and the U.S. census at census.gov.

Task 2.4: Communicate Publicly Through Interactive Websites

Although public meetings and workshops play an important role in engaging people, it is challenging to engage people from all sectors of the community in-person. Web-based tools can be a convenient and low-cost method for centralizing information and remotely engaging community stakeholders.

The Plan Team should create a project website and generate content for posters, flyers, and marketing materials like e-mail blasts (using special email addresses created for receiving feedback), and mailers; local newspaper Op-Ed pieces; social media outlets; public radio broadcasts; public access channels or YouTube broadcasts; and local news reports and programs.

Plan websites (or webpages on municipal sites) publicly announce the plan and the opportunities for the public to participate in the planning process. The Plan Team keeps the public and key stakeholders updated on major achievements by routinely updating the website. The Plan website should also build on past successes by identifying past achievements and recognizing the work the municipality has done already.

254 ■ *Creating Climate Plans*

Websites host information and solicit feedback and are often combined with social media platforms such as Facebook, Twitter, Instagram, and LinkedIn. Online participants can learn about the climate planning initiative, learn who is involved in the process, understand their role in climate initiatives, and learn about upcoming educational events and meetings. Innovative methodologies for online engagement and crowd sourcing data are continually being developed.

We use multiple online engagement tools to gather information from the public. Our websites have an *Engage* tab where people answer poll questions, respond to surveys, complete visual preference surveys, place their ideas on maps, and post digital idea cards. We also work with online engagement platforms with their own special purpose tools. This includes companies like Engagement HQ (developed by the company Bang-the-Table), MySidewalk, MapSeed, Social Pinpoint, Konveio, Ethelo, and MetroQuest. These tools all offer different tools or combinations of tools to facilitate a two-way conversation between stakeholders and allow the Plan Team to collect the feedback and analyze it for inclusion in the plan.

A Virtual Charrette Hub is a website page used for Virtual Charrettes or workshops that lists all the meetings the public can engage in when public meetings or events use video communications instead of on-site meetings. The Hub explains how and when people can connect with the Plan Team using webinars, video meetings, or public involvement tools. The Hub should also include the results of each day of the Virtual Charrette or workshop including meeting minutes and draft plan materials.

Short films can help people understand the project. Our plans include a variety of film types from long professional-quality films made by documentarians to short films recorded in PowerPoint by individuals on the team. Make films. They endure after the project ends and will continue to be viewed by people. Nothing explains a project better than a short film featuring a person explaining, as best they can, why the project is important and how people can get involved.

Task 2.5: Conduct a Listening Workshop

The Plan Team should conduct a two-day Listening Workshop in the community engaging local government staff, elected officials, and members of the public before the Public Design Workshop or charrette.

Government staff typically include planners, public works staff, fleet managers, transportation planners, finance and budget staff, emergency management, public safety staff, park staff, human resources, water and wastewater staff, and other municipal agencies and quasi-municipal agencies involved in housing, economic development, public health, and education. Local government officials and staff will be implementing many of the initiatives recommended in the Climate Plan. They are experts in their field and know the surrounding community well, and they will know how to implement the Plan.

Outreach should also involve individuals representing the various interests of the community, including residents, businesses owners (small and large), real estate developers, neighborhood groups, local industry leaders, educational institutions, regional planning agencies, state agencies, local school district partners, religious groups, and non-profit organizations.

My team usually schedules two days of meetings, four meetings per day, and groups the various invitees with general meeting titles like: Mitigation, Adaptation, Environment, Transportation, and Urban Design. After a brief introduction to the project, I invite everyone around the table to introduce themselves and tell us a little about their group's mission and how the Climate Plan can further their goals. I do my best to take their input and attempt to use their ideas to develop new and innovative ways to build community resilience with every plan.

The Listening Workshop can be on-site and in-person or conducted virtually using video communications. Attendees are sent a link they can use to join a meeting with the Plan Team from their office or home. In-person meetings can be supplemented by video meetings in order to reach people who are less likely to have the time or inclination to attend an in-person event.

Phase 3: Visioning (Month 4 or 5)

Plans must be both aspirational and actionable. They must be visionary and galvanizing. It is easier to make large plans a reality than small ones because small ones haven't the power to excite people, *to stir men's blood* as the American architect and urban planner Daniel Burnham once suggested. *Make no little plans*. But plans must also be implementable in order to translate into real change.

Public input should represent diverse interests within the community and involve people from as many different demographics, neighborhoods, and perspectives as possible. To create a fully inclusive and transparent process, the public at large should have the opportunity to provide input into the plan through a variety of outlets. These include public meetings, smaller meetings with key stakeholder groups, a website for public comment, and online forums.

In the format we recommend, the Visioning Phase is centered around a five-day workshop which, again, we call a charrette or Public Design Workshop. When the work is conducted remotely using video conferencing tools, we call these events Virtual Charrettes or Virtual Design Workshops. During the event, the Plan Team leads a series of public meetings, design sessions, interviews, and technical meetings in one room (whenever possible), to quickly engage the community.

Task 3.1: Co-lead a Public Design Workshop

The Public Design Workshop (or charrette) can be any number of days but typically ranges from five to nine. I find that five is optimal. It doesn't ask too much of the community, and it provides enough time for the team to do the work. The workshop can be done live and on-site or virtually and remotely using webinars, video communications, films, and interactive websites.

256 ■ *Creating Climate Plans*

Charrettes provide a spirit of shared undertaking. It's a social occasion. I like talking hopes and fears. I like open questions. I enjoy pointing things out to people and having things pointed out to me. At this point in my career, it is working with people that I take the most satisfaction and enjoyment from.

The Public Design Workshop includes the components listed in Tasks 3.1.1–3.1.6.

Task 3.1.1: Co-lead a Hands-on Event Community Involvement Session

We typically begin the Public Design Workshop with a Monday night Hands-on Event. At the event, the Plan Team gives a short PowerPoint presentation that outlines the overall planning process and emphasizes the role of attendees in shaping the future of their community.

During the presentation we report to the community the findings of the draft Mitigation Element. This involves a presentation on the community's baseline Local Government Operations (LGOP) inventory for a chosen base year. The inventory is related to facilities, vehicles, and infrastructure directly owned and controlled by the municipality and is expressed in terms of metric tons of CO_2. If we are updating a Climate Plan, then we report on decreases or increases from the base year. Ideally, our initial reports also include not just government operations, but a snapshot of the entire municipality's CO_2 pollution.

The next part of the presentation, the *Food for Thought* portion, educates participants on the climate emergency worldwide. We don't shy away from the future challenges of climate change and discuss property loss, food system stress, increased storm intensity, flooded infrastructure, extreme heat, water scarcity, and so forth. We describe national best practices in mitigation and adaptation measures. We discuss livable transportation and sustainability success stories from communities working to adapt municipal systems and infrastructure. We then explain the Hands-On Exercise and help the public begin to think about what they will contribute during the break-out session.

- **Keypad Polling:** Live, interactive polling can be added to the presentation. PowerPoint presentation tools such as Turning Point˚ or Poll Everywhere can collect polling results in real-time and display data on a projected computer screen for everyone to see. Keypads can be passed out to the community members or they can supply answers using text messages on their phones. A series of questions are asked during the presentation, and the participants answer these questions. The results are immediately sent to and processed by the program, and are presented as part of the presentation, allowing the planning team, the municipality, and the community to immediately understand the many viewpoints and goals of the participants.

  Interactive polling can be employed during a Virtual Public Design Workshop as well using the Zoom video communications or Poll Everywhere.

Questions are asked of the public, they reply on their computer or cell phones and the compiled results appear on the presenter's screen.

We ask questions we categorize as "Who's in the room?" about age, background, and where people live or work. Later in the process we pin up our work and ask participants to react to or even score our work. One series of questions I use often goes like this: "Did your parents walk to school as children?", "Did you walk to school as a child?" and "Do your kids of grandkids walk to school?" You can imagine the result. The fact that fewer and fewer kids walk to school every year has significant impacts on both the health of children and the amount of carbon added to the environment. During the Hands-On Exercise community members will discuss solutions.

- **Community Image Survey:** Our Community Image Surveys are like the Visual Preference Surveys perfected by Anton Nelessen in the late 1970s[7] but are more casual and less scientific. As part of our presentation, or using separate boards, we show the public a variety of images that give pairs for comparison (though we present them out of order) to add interest to the exercise. The typical images show two varieties of streets – one tree-lined and multi-modal, and another six-laned and traffic-filled; two kinds of multi-family unit – one on a street and providing visual interest to a pedestrian, and the other poking from a parking lot, and so forth. Generally, people choose the kinds of streets, buildings, and public spaces we find in walkable mixed-use places and we discuss the result with the public in relation to climate mitigation and adaptation goals.
- **Hands-On Exercise:** The Hands-On Exercise follows the presentation. We use a break-out session with meeting participants in small groups and then reconvene the group towards the end of the meeting. This can be done in person or virtually. As a technical matter, our team distributes base maps, typically printed at 24 inches long by 36 inches wide which show the entire community with streets and landmarks marked. We divide the community up – five to ten people per table and per map – and then give them one or two packages of coloured markers to draw their ideas on the map. When conducted virtually, participants find themselves in virtual rooms with a digital map and annotation tools they can use. Each team may have a scribe or note-taker, as long as everyone feels comfortable to grab a marker and write whatever they'd like.

On climate projects we give the community mitigation questions like, "What are some creative suggestions for reducing energy use and associated GHG emissions?" An adaptation question could be: "As the world's climate changes, what are the community's threats? What are potential solutions?" Participants list their ideas for their community and draw potential adaptation projects on the map. Other approaches could include breaking up the larger group by topic or geographic area. I usually give participants 30 to 45 minutes to work together the maps.

Some people may become disruptive. A certain amount of this must be tolerated. Don't lose your temper. Don't lose your self-confidence. Steer them

258 ■ *Creating Climate Plans*

back to the group. When people can't settle down, I usually give them their own table and my personal attention so that they don't interfere with the other participants. Unruly people are surprised to find that I really do enjoy one-on-one conversations with those who hold contrarian or even radical viewpoints. And I do. It's interesting. I appreciate passion. I can agree with everyone up to a point. And I believe that the best way to persuade someone is to listen to them. Try to find a facilitator who feels the same.

The Hands-on Exercise is one of the key times where you will encounter people who will pushback on the plan. Encourage it. Starting to hear objections and listening to people early can help you to frame the plan, solutions, and implementation in ways that address pushback concerns.

The Hands-on Exercise ends with a spokesperson from each table standing at the front of the room (or being given centerstage in a virtual meeting) and relating, in 5 minutes or so, what their table discussed. As each table is done, I ask the entire room to applaud that table's contribution. It isn't easy to get up in front of strangers. I always appreciate when people volunteer to do this.

Once every table is finished, I explain to the audience the next steps for the project. I discuss the project website, other events in the workshop they can participate in, the overall timeline, editing process, and adoption process for the plan.

Task 3.1.2: Set up On-site Design Studio

Following the Community Involvement Session, the Plan Team sets up an On-site Design Studio, preferably in a central location in the community, for the duration of the Workshop. The studio is usually a donated space like a gymnasium, library conference room, or city hall chamber. We also use rented conference facilities at hotels or other venues when necessary. The team works on-site in order to refine the vision and continues to gather input for the development of the Climate Plan. The community is encouraged to stop by the Design Studio whenever it is convenient to them, to share their insight and to check in on the plan's status.

A Virtual On-site Design Studio is also possible. A Charrette Hub, a page on the project website, is created with a schedule of meetings and access information to participate in those meetings. Films are made daily to summarize the day's discussion. A website tab allows participants to engage with surveys, maps, and project exercises. Live events occur which people can participate in virtually through video and telephone communications. Social media is used to create interest and report back findings.

As part of our work in the studio, we introduce a Mitigation Element along with other Plan elements. The team discusses local climate strategies and that discussion is intended to be educational. We discuss topics people aren't familiar with and it is helpful to list a few briefly:

Co-authoring the Plan with the Public ■ 259

- **Cleaner transit** means discussing policies and investments that reduce vehicular speeds to make places safe for walking, add protected cycle-ways, expand public transit, and add dedicated lanes on central streets for transit. We talk about what a street needs to be safe, comfortable, interesting for pedestrians, and encourage walking. This includes a mix of shade, wind protection, street-oriented buildings, street furniture, on-street dining and pedestrian signage.
- **Greener design** involves making brownfield sites a priority for future construction, slowing construction on undeveloped and environmentally sensitive land, planting micro-forests to provide shade and air-cooling, making sure every citizen has a green space within a 10-minute walk, and using public funds to curb energy use, reduce emissions, and better insulate homes.
- **Going local** policy proposals are about locally focused development. During the COVID-19 pandemic this discussion grew. Municipalities and citizens can prioritize goods and services created within or near their community. School meals can be made 100% organic and in certain areas we have seen that up to 50% of all ingredients can be sourced from the surrounding region. Local sourcing reduces the carbon pollution of shipping food from far away.
- **Affordable housing** is a major concern in the world at this time. Building at higher densities near transit can often lessen the need to build in green areas. Communities can commit to facilitating the construction of a certain number of homes per year and working to keep a certain percentage affordable.

Once these ideas have been discussed we will pin up what we hear from the public under headings like Leadership, Transportation, Buildings, Housing, Environmental Stewardship, Food, Consumption of Natural Resources, Mitigation, Adaptation, and Resilience. We then categorize the public's recommendations as short term (0 to 5 years), mid-term (5 to 10 years), and long term (10 years and up).

We often encourage participants to discuss *what* they would like to see and not dwell too much on *how* to achieve those goals. How to pay for an idea is the job of the final plan, elected officials, technical committees, and urban planners. The final plan will make all the usual compromises between utility and cost, and we don't need to burden the brainstorming conversation with those compromises too early in the process.

It's also important that the team pinning up the public's ideas commits beforehand to deal with those ideas honestly. This is to say that if a green idea faces a lot of skepticism or outright protest then the moderators will not include that idea in the final plan. This can be difficult, and can feel like shirking one's responsibility, but, personally, I believe in only listing the consensus ideas, because in my experience governing by consensus is the only way to move forward. Search for the small hard core of common agreement.

I tend to side with the people in the community labeled *moderates*. Sometimes I think that a successful plan cannot afford to be more than 10% brave new ideas.

260 ■ *Creating Climate Plans*

In choosing my multi-disciplinary teams and steering committees, however, I like to work with strident and often extreme pro-green voices. Sometimes, thanks to their help, we score victories that I secretly applaud – while staying aware that just because a progressive policy makes it into the plan doesn't mean it will be implemented. If nothing else, when I work with *greener* people than myself, I learn from them (and so does the public) and when public opinion takes a step forward a bit, I am ready to work those ideas into the next plan because I am familiar with them.

Task 3.1.3: Co-lead Technical and Stakeholder Meetings

While in the Design Studio, the Plan Team works closely with the municipality to ensure the feasibility of the plan. It is in these meetings that we talk about *how* we implement the plan as well as *what* the plan should focus on. This involves leading meetings with government agencies and local experts in order to gain technical feedback on important issues. These meetings usually focus on one element of the plan like Mitigation, Adaptation, Environment, Transportation, or Urban Design. Within any one goal, such as "Promote green building," there can be a number of measures that help to implement the strategy. We invite the attendees to brainstorm all possible strategies for achieving the goals. We include departmental directors in the outreach meetings, so they can hear direct feedback from the public and can incorporate public opinion into their daily work.

Though we are talking more about feasibility and cost in these meetings, I still believe that the most important part of public meetings is simply letting people talk and contribute their ideas. Keep the brainstorming going. Take a lot of notes. The more people see their ideas (and even their own words) in the plan the more likely they are to endorse and promote the plan. Prevent the technical discussions from becoming narrow, politicized discussions, which can provoke defensive thinking. The general public often has good ideas about possible solutions – even on technical topics. During these meetings (which last 30 minutes to an hour) I stay on my feet, giving the group a person they can direct their comments to, moving the conversation along, and helping every voice to be heard.

Task 3.1.4: Create Visualizations for Plans, Renderings, Graphics, and Photographs

Words alone fall short of describing the experience of being in a place. People often need to see what their ideas really mean when pen is put to paper in order to understand the options and opportunities that exist in their community. Visualizations are an integral part of our planning process; we use hand-drawn plans and renderings along with computer technology to create before-and-after and change-over-time images.

The plans and renderings address what we heard from the public and what we heard during the stakeholder meetings. They depict land use, transportation, recreation, public works, and community character strategies. The plans and renderings often show selected sites within the municipality that should receive focused attention and new or improved buildings, streets, and public spaces. Renderings (both bird's-eye and ground-level) are also drawn to explain how the municipality can develop over time.

The renderings often depict walkable urbanism: Mixed-use pedestrian-friendly destinations where people can arrive by transit and then walk or bike. Every American municipality needs more of these places. In 1791, the English poet William Wordsworth coined the term "pedestrian." Before that, there was no special word for someone travelling by foot because walking was such an unremarkable feature of everyday life. Today we must design for walkability and pedestrians.

Participants can see the social, economic, and quality-of-life benefits of a mixed-use centers where people can live, work, and play without using their car. Alternative strategies for city-wide infrastructure, such as stormwater management and multi-modal transportation networks, will often be illustrated with diagrams. The plans, renderings, and diagrams become an integral part of the Climate Plan.

Admittedly, Illustrative Plans and Renderings sometimes do require design professionals. However, photos and graphics can also demonstrate concepts effectively. If you don't have a professional renderer don't worry: Simply refining what you heard from the public by adding to their ideas and reorganizing them by theme and timeframe – short term, mid-term, and long term – does a lot.

Task 3.1.5: Refine the Vision Plan and Policy Plan Framework

The Vision Plan component of the Climate Plan serves as the foundation for the rest of the document. The Plan Team continues to work with municipal staff, elected officials, and the broader community to establish a concise vision. During the Public Design Workshop, the Plan Team also focuses on developing a detailed framework for the Policy Plan. Creating principles for each of the elements of the Policy Plan during the Workshop, in coordination with the establishment of the Vision Plan, allows the team to gain consensus on the fundamentals of the plan. Policy Plan ideas will be further refined and detailed following the Public Design Workshop.

Task 3.1.6: Lead a Work-in-Progress Presentation

At the conclusion of the Public Design Workshop, the Plan Team presents the work generated during the week at an evening Work-in-Progress Presentation. At this presentation, the team presents the ideas gathered from the community and discusses how these ideas were incorporated into the draft plan. We demonstrate to the public that their ideas have been heard; quoting the public's feedback directly has a powerful effect.

262 ■ *Creating Climate Plans*

The team presents the draft illustrative plans, renderings, and visualizations of the mitigation and adaptation strategies. We explain the issues and challenges to ensure the public understands background concepts and the need for action. We use interactive polling devices to test public opinion on measures being considered for the plan. We show policies, plans, and renderings and ask, "Do you like this?" and people can answer *Yes, No,* or *Not Sure.*

We ask people their opinions for several reasons, but one is to keep them engaged and interested. It's a crime to bore an audience, James Howard Kunstler, known for his public speaking, once said to me. You must make what is important interesting and fun.

We see at this point in the process if the plan is being made for the community, with their goals, needs, and limitations in mind, or if the Plan Team is drafting a plan based on its own pre-conceived agenda and with the its reputation and professional peers in mind. These are two different things, and the plans I have seen absolutely fail were designed to be impressive, state-of-the-art, publication-worthy award winners and not practical, implementable, and highly tailored to the community. The community will push back when asked "Do you like this?" and during any question-and-answer sessions. The Plan Team has a decision to make at this point and hopefully all team members realize that their job is to serve the community and not the other way around.

The Work-in-Progress Presentation can reach more people if the team uses online video communication tools. Even when conducting live, on-site, in-person events we use tools like Zoom, Microsoft Teams, GoTo Meeting, WebEx, and Facebook Live. The Work-in-Progress Presentation should also be available for people to watch online. Ideally, the presentation is broken up into topics and short films that are each less than 10 minutes. Short, bite-size films will be watched by many more people than long ones. The Work-in-Progress Presentation is not the end of the process; rather it is an opportunity to solicit feedback on the work that has been produced.

Finally, on the topic of presentations, it is important to practice, practice, practice before presenting. You don't need to practice with a set script and aloud (although that doesn't hurt). You can practice in your head by thinking through the material. The best speeches, the ones people thought were impromptu, always involved days of solitary thought. Also, don't be too worried if you are new to presenting. Every great public speaker was a bad public speaker once. And big, important causes make people eloquent – in time.

Phase 4: Development of the Preliminary Draft (Months 5 to 8)

The compact, high-energy format of the Charrette or Design Workshop is designed to make major advances towards the creation of the Climate Plan. Refinement of the plan continues after the workshop. The team further details the elements of the plan and also produces the Implementation Strategy component of the plan.

Task 4.1: Refine the Vision Plan

The Plan Team takes the preliminary vision established during previous phases and refines it to further match the community's goals and expectations. The preliminary vision and policy planning groundwork are further defined and become the final plan.

Task 4.2: Refine the Illustrative Plans and Renderings

The Plan Team refines the illustrative plans and renderings created during the Workshop for use in the Plan document. These graphics demonstrate and guide the development, redevelopment, and innovation and conservation principles established by the plan.

Task 4.3: Tailor the Policy Plan

The Plan Team takes the draft principles defined during the Workshop and further tailors them to form a detailed policy framework for each element of the Climate Plan. Land use, economic development, natural hazards, housing, mobility, urban design, critical and sensitive areas infrastructure, and neighborhoods are typically some of the topics addressed. The illustrative plans and renderings are integrated into the Policy Plan in order to make the Climate Plan an easy-to-understand document. The Plan Team should strive to make the plan as visual as possible with graphics, infographics, photographs, charts, plans, and renderings. Graphically rich plans have a higher degree of usability and are more likely to be implemented.

Plan Elements

There are several chapters within Climate Action Plans, Sustainability Plans, Resilience Plans, Comprehensive Plans (or the Sustainability or Resilience Elements within Comprehensive Plans), Transportation Plans, and Neighborhood Plans that can be helpful in meeting the community's goals. The following provides examples of what some of the plan chapters could include, and some mitigation and adaptation tools that should be explored. Resilience and the environment cannot be viewed in isolation and should not be approached piecemeal. I recommend including as many elements as you can in your planning.

- **Community Goals:** A Community Goals Statement, developed by the community during the Public Workshop process, can serve as a guideline for future development in the municipality. Sometimes we call this "The Big Five Ideas"

264 ■ *Creating Climate Plans*

of the plan and organize the plan according to action statements. Whatever their format, the Community Goals should be clearly stated. The plan will explain and illustrate the goals in detail and with nuance later. Although certain details of the plan may change over time, the Community Goals will serve as the guiding principles to steer future discussions and development in the municipality.

■ **Mitigation:** This element includes GHG emissions baseline, future projections, and reduction targets, GHG reduction goals, strategies, and supporting actions for a variety of sectors, recommended actions for preparing for climate change with climate adaptation measures, and a monitoring and implementation strategy. Some Climate Action Plans are limited to a Community Goals Element and Mitigation Element.

■ **Growth Framework:** The Growth Framework Element illustrates the past, present, and future land use and urban form within the municipality. A Future Land Use Map is often included, and it could take several forms depending on the expected regulatory tools that will be used to guide future development. A Sector Plan approach delineates areas for intended growth and restricted growth and then ties development in those areas to specific public approvals processes. The existing codes and regulations are examined, and alternative coding methods are explored and discussed with the municipality.

■ **Economic Development:** The purpose of this element is smart economic development in education, infrastructure, and quality of life that creates jobs, increases the tax base, encourages development, and increases the jurisdiction's competitiveness. Workforce training, youth skills, employment, wages, and youth skills are all discussed. Green jobs in solar panel installation, tree planting and maintenance, insulating, and water system conversion are discussed.

■ **Community Design:** The Community Design Element reflects the community's vision and is based on Smart Growth principles. The illustrative plan and small area plans created during the Public Design Workshop are used as a guide for shaping future development.

Green Building principles are increasingly discussed in the Community Design Element of municipal plans. A Net-Zero Building is one that has zero net energy consumption, producing as much energy as it uses in a year. These buildings use natural lighting. Their walls, windows and ceilings have maximum insulation to retain heat in winter and coolness in summer. Heating and air-conditioning systems are placed to maximize efficiency. Many communities have a plan to reach Net-Zero by a specific time horizon, like 2050. These buildings and communities often use Leadership in Energy and Environmental Design (LEED) as a standard.

Community Design also aims to build walkable cities, which prioritize walking, biking, and transit over the automobile in their design. Pedestrian-oriented urban environments dramatically reduce GHG emissions from driving. They are inclusive and equitable in that they enable people of every socioeconomic demographic to get around. Homes, workplaces, parks, shops, and restaurants are intermingled at higher densities than car-oriented, suburban sprawl. Costs for public infrastructure and services are reduced.

As urban populations continue to grow, designing walkable streetscapes becomes increasingly important. Streets must be tree-lined and shaded during the day. Tools like Walk Score and metrics like mode share (the percent of trips made without an automobile) are used to evaluate the walkability of places. Tools like form-based codes are used to build walkable places.

- **Infrastructure:** The Infrastructure Element should also look at water resources, stormwater and wastewater capacity, and other items critical to the work of a municipality's civil engineers. This element is concerned with what's below the surface of the manmade world, especially in a Climate Plan.
- **Housing:** Recommendations are made for developing policies and changing existing regulations that allow the development of new housing types in a way that respects and enhances existing buildings and provides quality affordable housing for all sectors of the population, especially low/moderate income households. The housing analysis explores policies from inclusionary zoning to community land trusts and recommends strategies, policies, and regulations that will best meet the need to provide quality housing for all residents of the municipality.
- **Natural and Cultural Resources:** The Plan Team expands on the efforts begun during the Public Design Workshop to address the environmental issues within the plan. Conservation of agricultural and natural lands and watershed protection strategies are explored. Sustainable development practices are identified, including building design, and sustainable infrastructure. Access to arts and cultural amenities is also discussed along with mechanisms to fund public art and local artists.

    Specifically, carbon sinks are identified especially for protection and restoration. Coastal wetlands where the land and ocean meet provide a first line of defense against storm surges and flood waters and sequester huge amounts of carbon in plants, roots, and soils. These areas enhance biodiversity and improve water quality. Once viewed as mere "swamps" in need of draining the environmental services, coastal wetlands are now better understood.
- **Sustainability:** The plan discusses using resources more efficiently by identifying opportunities to conserve energy and save money through smart investments. This element seeks to improve the environment by monitoring and improving local air quality, reducing GHG emissions, cleaning up waterways, reducing auto dependency by increasing transportation options, and decreasing waste.

    Half the waste generated in the world comes from households, and managing it tends to be the responsibility of local government. Recycling reduces emissions created by the production and landfilling of wastes. A community's recycling program should be investigated. Cities and towns can offer curbside

266 ■ *Creating Climate Plans*

recycling with specific dumpsters for collecting recyclables. At the least, a plan should identify local recycling centers where households, offices, and factories can drop off metals, plastic, glass, and other materials. Paper products and organic wastes can be recycled using separate waste management solutions. Pay-as-you-throw programs bill households for trash sent to the landfill but carry away recycling and compost for free.

A municipality's potential for green roofs and cool roofs are investigated. Green roofs are vegetated to sequester carbon in their biomass, filter air pollutants, reduce rainwater runoff, mitigate the urban heat island effect, and add pleasant and attractive greenery to people's lives. Cool roofs reflect solar energy back into space in order to reduce cooling costs and use light-colored materials. Tropical places have used "white roofs" all through time and it is only recently that this commitment was lost.

■ **Health:** The Health Element discusses community health and wellness, access to health care, and public safety. Transportation and mobility, parks, open space, and recreation all factor into community health. Increasingly, the Center for Disease Control (CDC) has focused its work on the built environment and how it affects lifestyles. Focus on improving the health of children and older people, especially, to help those who need the most assistance and also to build plan support.

■ **Mobility:** The Mobility Element examines how residents, employees, and visitors transport themselves. Key strategies promote non-auto travel including public transit services, parking strategies, bicycle facilities, car-sharing programs and pedestrian components that are well coordinated and connected with a larger regional transportation system.

Transportation is the single greatest source of carbon emissions and it is growing due to the growing availability of cars. In the U.S. less than 5% of commuters use mass transit and the plan works to increase the number of transit options including buses, Bus Rapid Transit, streetcars, and commuter rail. Beyond the benefit of emission reductions, transit also helps slow the growth of traffic congestion because transit moves greater numbers of people using less space than cars. In this way, transit can benefit all people, not just those who use it. High-speed rail systems, electrified rail, electric vehicle charging points, ride-sharing programs, and even telecommuting programs are discussed and recommended by the plan as strategies to reduce carbon pollution.

■ **Energy:** Wind power, especially in the form of offshore wind turbines, is underused in the United States, and local plans should identify candidate communities. Geothermal taps underground heating and cooling and new subdivisions in many areas could access geothermal. Utility-scale solar PV must be allowed "as of right" wherever possible.

The "macro" grid is the massive electrical network of energy sources owned by energy providers and typically connected to fossil fuel plants that we all plug into. Microgrids are localized groupings of renewable energy sources such as rooftop solar, micro-wind, in-stream and tidal hydro, and biomass. Locally, energy monopoly, not technology, is usually the key hurdle for microgrids. Municipalities must plan for, but also advocate for, microgrids in local plans.

- **Community Facilities:** The location, placement, and design of public facilities is of great importance in a community. Civic buildings serve an important role by standing as the centerpiece of a neighborhood or community, creating a sense of place and identity. Public facilities can serve to foster community recovery and revitalization, corridor redevelopment, and environmental sustainability.

  Community buildings should be the first to adopt efficient heating and cooling systems, smart glass which responds to admit visible light while blocking heat, smart thermostats which take independent action to maximize energy, and district heating and cooling which use renewables, better insulation, green roofs, cool roofs, and LED (light emitting diode) bulbs.

  The Plan Team works to make LED the standard lighting fixture in all community buildings and streetlight systems. Though LED bulbs are double the cost of incandescent or fluorescent fixtures they use far less energy. Plans must encourage not only local government but all households and commercial spaces to replace less efficient lighting with LEDs.

- **Capital Improvements Program:** The Capital Improvements Program is closely coordinated with the plan in order to link prioritized planning efforts with the capital necessary to complete each project. Included with the plan will be a series of implementation strategies and prioritized implementation projects.

- **Implementation Strategy:** The plan must have a clear implementation strategy, including designation of a responsible department or party, funding source, timeline, next steps, short- and long-term milestones, and indicators for measuring progress. The Plan Team prioritizes the components of the plan working with the stakeholders and technical experts and establishes a schedule by which items should be completed.

  This Implementation Strategy helps the municipality make short- and long-term decisions about future planning. The Implementation Strategy also includes measures for residents to monitor the implementation of the plan.

Climate Change Impacts

Climate impacts will vary by region. Urban planners must understand the regional effects of climate change in their communities in order to tailor effective mitigation strategies. The 2009 U.S. Global Change Research Program produced a publication called *Global Climate Impacts in the United States*[8] which includes a list of climate challenges by region – summarized below.

268 ■ *Creating Climate Plans*

The U.S. Global Change Research Program's list of *direct* impacts works well for local planners though it does not identify large-scale *indirect* impacts including inundation of coastal areas, diminished drinking water due to drought and saltwater intrusion, mass migration (people will seek to escape sea-level rise, hot weather, political instability and violence), food production shortfalls, and so forth.

Get ready: The list reads like a rather dismal weather report.

■ **U.S. Northeast region**
- Shorter winters with fewer cold days and more precipitation; significant reductions in the winter snow season
- Under the higher emissions scenarios, 20 to 30 days in which the high temperature in cities exceeds 100°F; more frequent heat waves; and, on average, six weeks longer of summer conditions
- More frequent flooding as a result of sea-level rise and heavy precipitation events
- Economic effects including negative impacts on agricultural production, including dairy, fruit, and maple syrup, reduced snow cover adversely affecting winter recreation, and a northward shift of lobster fisheries and diminution of Georges Bank cod fisheries

■ **U.S. Southeast region**
- All variety of heat-related stresses for people, plants, and animals
- Decreased water availability due to increased temperature and longer periods between rainfall events
- Sea-level rise and the potential for increased hurricane intensity, significantly affecting coastal areas and ecosystems

■ **U.S. Midwest region**
- In the summertime, the region will see increased heat waves and reduced air quality
- A longer growing season, potentially generating increased crop yields, provided challenges such as heat waves, floods, and greater numbers and varieties of pests can be managed
- Increased volatility in precipitation, resulting in more frequent flood and drought conditions
- Significant reduction in Great Lakes water levels as a result of higher temperatures that promote greater evaporation, affecting shipping, infrastructure, water-based tourism/recreation, and ecosystems

■ **U.S. Great Plains**
- Negative impacts on the region's water resources resulting from increased temperature and evaporation and frequency of drought
- Stresses on agriculture, ranching, and natural lands management resulting from changes in precipitation and higher temperatures

- Negative effects on key habitats and ecosystems, especially wetland systems

- **U.S. Southwest region**
  - Increasing scarcity of water supply, requiring policy decisions to prioritize allocation among competing uses such as urban populations and agriculture
  - Increased temperature, drought, and wildfire, significantly affecting ecosystems
  - Negative effects on tourism/recreation industries, including reduced snowpack in ski-resort areas and unique ecosystem degradation

- **U.S. Northwest region**
  - Declining snowpack negatively affecting regional water supplies
  - Higher temperatures increasing risks to forestry from wildfires and insect pests
  - Negative impacts on coastal areas resulting from sea-level rise
  - Decreasing habitat for cold-water fish, such as salmon

- **Alaska**
  - Higher temperatures increasing risks to forestry from wildfires and insect pests
  - Longer growing season and longer periods for outdoor tourism due to increasing temperatures
  - Damages to infrastructure due to thawing permafrost
  - Negative effects on coastal areas from loss of sea-ice buffers, increasing frequency of strong storms, and thawing permafrost

- **U.S. Pacific and Caribbean Islands**
  - Reduction in availability of freshwater supplies due to changing rainfall patterns, including reduced precipitation in the Caribbean region and contaminated groundwater from flooding in the Pacific islands; sea-level rise will threaten underground freshwater supplies
  - Negative effects on marine ecosystems, creating problems for tourism and fisheries industries
  - Greater frequency of coastal inundation resulting from sea-level rise and increased intensity of storms

Phase 5: Preparation of Final Draft and Adoption (Months 9 to 12)

In Phase 5 of the project, the Plan Team works with the municipality to review, revise, and present the Final Plan.

270 ■ *Creating Climate Plans*

Task 5.1: Prepare for Plan and Report Review

The team submits the Draft Plan to the municipality for review. The municipality is given adequate time to review and submit comments to the Plan Team. The Plan Team strategizes with the municipality on how to solicit public comment. This will depend on local laws, the breadth of the outreach process, and historic precedence in the community for engaging the public. Often, the Plan Team uses the project website and social media to enable the public to review the plan, post comments, and review other comments.

Task 5.2: Prepare for Plan Presentations and Adoption

Once reviewed and revised, the team presents the plan to the municipality in either informal meetings or official public hearings. Outreach and communications focus on getting people to the presentations. Presentations can be in person or virtual and include an overview of the creation of the plan as well as a detailed explanation of each plan component. If a plan is to be adopted by a municipality then the Plan Team should expect several Planning Commission and City Council meetings. All meetings should be recorded and each draft of the plan posted on the project website.

Regardless of how well the city publicized its Climate Plan initiative and no matter how many public meetings were held, it is inevitable that someone (often someone influential) will claim never to have heard about the effort. Elected officials will wonder if this person is representative of a much larger group and they may begin to think seriously about starting the entire process over. Don't begin again. Make sure, however, that you can assure that elected official of three things:

1. **The plan did everything it could to involve everyone.** The municipality did an excellent job (a better job than any previous effort, hopefully) of creating the plan in an open way, advertised the plan in print and on the internet, gathered extensive public and stakeholder comment, and documented the effort. Your Climate Plan presentations should begin by listing every event you held, the number or people who attended, photographs of people actively engaging with the Plan Team, and a reporting of what you heard. It should appear impossible that a concerned citizen did not hear about the project and couldn't find a venue for giving input. The numbers of people who participated should be so high that the elected official worries that if they don't adopt the plan they will have wasted too many people's time.
2. **The plan team created an atmosphere of compromise.** Most local policy discussion is dominated by small groups of citizens who are highly vocal about specific issues. We refer to them as *single-issue extremists* and I use this term affectionately because I should hope that when it comes to our own communities we all have an issue we're too passionate about to see past or compromise on. However, it should be clear that the public process involved more than the

Co-authoring the Plan with the Public ▪ 271

loudest people in the room and the usual suspects at City Council night, and that the plan reflects multiple perspectives. The plan's facilitators and authors must have demonstrated a willingness to hear all sides and to compromise – right up until the last minute.

3. **The plan has something for everyone.** Elected officials will look for *the deal* – one or more items that all key stakeholders can agree on. There may be vocal opposition to this or that portion of the plan but there should be enough consensus issues to make many people happy. Elected officials routinely admit they can't make everyone happy, but they will not approve a plan that doesn't make most people happy. Most climate planning has the long-term interests of the municipality in mind. Elected officials like that aspect of the plan but they can only approve a plan that advances the causes of the people they see, hear from, and answer to, at election time.

If you find you have reached the adoption period and the plan doesn't satisfy these three criteria, don't worry; a plan is ultimately words on a page and you can, quickly, add what you need to make sure the plan works for the elected officials. The last edits that plan authors make are usually the most critical to adoption.

Phase 6: Implementation and Evaluating Progress

After the plan is released and adopted, it is time to start implementation. Implementation can take a variety of different forms such as passing new regulations, forming taskforces, initiating pilot projects, educating the public, or developing specific plans for specific issues identified in the plan.

Task 6.1: Assist in Implementation

Once a plan has been adopted several things have been accomplished thanks to the planning process alone. The plan has raised awareness within the local community on key challenges and opportunities affecting long-term development and quality of life. Common goals have been identified regarding the desired future development of the jurisdiction. Interdepartmental cooperation has increased by bringing staff, elected officials, and appointed officials together, asking tough questions and discussing complex issues. Local government transparency has been increased thanks to the interactive dialogue. The fact-driven plan educates the public in a way that allows them to participate better in future planning processes and to monitor and evaluate plan progress.

After the local government adopts the plan, implementation should begin immediately. The various local government departments should be responsible for implementing the plan, and staff should coordinate and monitor implementation progress. It is difficult to work on all measures at once, so the Plan Team needs to give strategic advice on how to utilize staff resources and volunteer time to

272 ■ *Creating Climate Plans*

implement the plan. Implementing the quick wins first will serve to maintain the momentum generated through the planning process and will lay the groundwork for implementing the longer-term measures.

Task 6.2: Transition the Advisory Board to Become an Implementation Team

After the plan is released, the role of the Advisory Board can shift to advising on the implementation of the plan and/or monitoring implementation of the plan. Some local governments may choose to "sunset" their boards after the plan is developed, whereas others may continue to keep the board involved in the plan implementation. Regular interdepartmental team meetings should be scheduled to keep the planning process moving forward and to make sure the municipality stays committed and engaged. The Plan Team works with the coalition to develop a public education and outreach campaign.

Task 6.3: Track Implementation

The Plan Team should submit an editable spreadsheet or database to keep track of the key milestones, deliverables, and achievements. Local governments should publish an annual progress report on the implementation status of the measures in the plan. The progress report should include a description of the actions taken and the next steps in the upcoming year and beyond. In addition to the progress report, local governments should track their performance using a set of sustainability indicators identified with the plan.

Task 6.4: Codify Implementation

We recommend that local governments define a periodic timeframe for updating the plan (once every five years is common), to ensure that the plan meets the changing needs and conditions of the jurisdiction, and is an active part of government's agenda. A *living plan* is far preferable to one that sits on the upper shelf silently collecting dust. The Plan Team can remain available to answer any questions and refine parts of the plan as needed. Sometimes we help codify the process and timeframe for updating the plan and define a process for monitoring implementation progress through a resolution or local law. Monitoring is essential because it allows the municipality to set specific measurable goals and work toward those goals.

Notes

1 Climate Action Planning Guide, March 2014, produced for Climate Smart Communities by VHB, Vanasse Hangen Brustlin.

Co-authoring the Plan with the Public ■ **273**

2 ICLEI–Local Governments for Sustainability USA (2009). *Sustainability planning toolkit*. Written in association with the City of New York's Office of Long-Term Planning and Sustainability, December. Retrieved from: www.hud.gov/sites/documents/20399_ ICLEI_SUSTAINABIL.PDF

3 UN-Habitat (2018). Urban Resilience Hub. Retrieved from: www.hud.gov/sites/ documents/20399_ICLEI_SUSTAINABIL.PDF

4 The Rockerfeller Foundation ceased this funding in 2019. The 100resilientcities.org website no longer exists, although it was active at the time of writing.

5 Hoch, C., Dalton, L.C. and So, F.S. (2020). *The Practice of Local Government Planning*. Washington, D.C.: International City/County Management Association.

6 The tool can be found at: www.epa.gov/statelocalenergy/local-greenhouse-gas-inventory-tool

7 DePalma, A. (1989). Architecture rejuvenates main streets. *New York Times*, March 28. Retrieved from: www.nytimes.com/1989/03/28/nyregion/architecture-rejuvenates-main-streets.html

8 U.S. Global Change Research Program (USGCRP) (2009). *Global Climate Change Impacts on the United States*. New York: Cambridge University Press. Retrieved from: http://downloads.globalchange.gov/usimpacts/pdfs/climate-impacts-report.pdf

Chapter 13

Dealing With Setbacks

Let's imagine that your public process was successful, the Climate Plan was adopted, and implementation is underway. At some point – let's say mid-way through the short-term action items and with only a few mid-term items begun – plan implementation will probably stall. This may happen because elections require people seeing public office to campaign against the policies of the incumbent, and even good ideas, like climate mitigation and adaptation, inevitably become political hot topics. Or maybe after a few years of successful policy implementation the new city council simply adopts other priorities. Whatever the case, there are multiple approaches to keeping your Climate Plan alive as you wait for the political pendulum to swing back to responsible action. Climate Plans have been in place in the U.S. for over 25 years and that's long enough for them to have been challenged, abandoned, and reactivated. You know the phrase: It's a marathon, not a sprint.

In 1993, Portland, Oregon, was the first U.S. city to create a local action plan for cutting carbon. The plan dealt with every aspect of municipal operations and city life. In 1997, Miami Beach, Florida, adopted its first Stormwater Master Plan and a Capital Improvement Plan, and millions of dollars were spent to eliminate flooding and build a system that could survive sea-level rise. Nevertheless, 1993 and 1997 were a long time ago, and in both Portland and Miami Beach, urban planners eventually had to wait out long periods of political pushback and deliberate inaction. It is inevitable. Behind every successful plan there's a lot of unsuccessful years.

Here's six steps for helping climate planners deal with setbacks.

Step 1: Settle Down

It's a long emergency. Climate change is happening fast, but it is happening fast in geological time. Understand the perspective of the opposition and learn to *play the*

DOI: 10.4324/9781003181514-15

275

276 ■ *Creating Climate Plans*

long game. This means having a long-term plan and long-term goals. Even though it can feel like preparing for climate change is the most pressing issue in the field of urban planning, that's not how it feels to others. As best you can, continue to deal with the obstacles placed in front of the plan with the same civility, humility, and tolerance that was used to draft the plan.

Remember that urban planning as we would like to imagine it probably doesn't exist in America. We don't look ahead often enough to make decisions. We solve problems today at great expense on the brink of calamity (or after the calamity has passed) that could have been solved far more easily in the past with … let's call it … planning. The tension between the way urban planning should be conducted and the way it actually pans out places most planners into a state of low-level depression. When you meet with your local urban planner you encounter *a countenance more in sorrow than in anger,* to quote Shakespeare's *Hamlet.* They are people who aren't listened to enough, and this fact haunts them. That's all fine as long as they don't quit. The community can't afford to lose their urban planner at this time in history.

Step 2: Work With the Opposition

Remember that in the American political system the challenger must oppose the policies of the incumbent. There's a lot of people who are against everything all the time and tapping those voters can be the key to political victories on the local level. What does the challenger actually believe? It can take time before they even know. Keep the conversation going with them. Wait them out, without losing your job or losing influence in the community. Once elected, it is often possible to convince those who publicly derided the Climate Plan to become advocates of it.

There's a common misconception about political leadership. The leader doesn't decide what the group will do as much as they figure out which way people are heading and then get out in front. *I've got to follow them, I am their leader* was the tactic of Alexander Ledru-Rollin, the French revolutionary. Leaders may be at the front of the parade, so to speak, but only as a conduit of public will. Government is organized public opinion. And here's the thing: If public will and public opinion are the important parts, one doesn't need to be an elected official to influence them.

When the climate planner's ideas represent public sentiment, elected officials listen. Again, this is something you have to see to believe, but it happens all the time at the local level because contrary to popular belief, we aren't dealing with professional politicians hardened by party philosophy and bought by special interests, we're dealing with normal people open to persuasion and truly interested in staying popular with their constituents. Work to educate the public and elected officials will follow the public's lead.

If you can't make progress with a city's leadership then learn to wait. There's a French proverb: Everything passes. Everything wears out. Everything breaks (*Tout passe. Tout lasse. Tout casse*). Look for trade-offs and compromises where possible, absolutely, but learn to wait. To make a difference we must last.

Step 3: Rebrand the Effort and Stay PC

Urban planners working under administrations that are ideologically or politically against climate change mitigation and adaptation learn to avoid using words like *climate change* and *sea-level rise* and to talk in terms of incidents, like *wildfires*, *hurricanes*, and *flooding*. Climate change will just exasperate problems you are already working on, and the only upside to this fact is that it provides cover for working on climate planning under a different name.

Elected officials and higher-level municipal staff know that when something goes wrong during their administration (and weather-related catastrophe is high on the list of things that could go wrong), the public will search for signs of pre-catastrophe lack of preparedness or dereliction as they hunt for a scapegoat. Help the elected officials and their staff understand that their day in the post-disaster spotlight will come and that they had better be able to say they did everything, absolutely everything, to mitigate the damage and stave off calamity (i.e., blame). Appeal to your elected officials' sense of self-preservation. It isn't manipulative, they are used to people doing this. Without discussing climate, discuss calamity and the steps municipalities can take. Without discussing climate, talk about how a day will come when advanced planning and precautions are vindicated and even celebrated publicly.

Step 4: Seek Outside Validation

Update your climate plan's carbon assessment portion. Has your community reduced carbon emissions? If it has, then work to win an award for plan implementation. Award-winning plans recognized by non-profit organizations like the local chapter of the American Planning Association gain new attention, new traction, and renewed influence, locally. When plans I have written won awards from the Environmental Protection Agency, Department of Environmental Management, or the Congress for the New Urbanism, I made sure to have a representative from that organization present the award live to the elected bodies. This can reinvigorate plan implementation.

Outside validation can be sought at conferences and through online correspondence as you wait out periods of local plan stagnation or hostility. Keep learning facts and skills which, if they can't be applied to your current position as an urban planner or implemented in your town, can help you on the next job. If your climate planning work has been thwarted at the local level, get involved at the state level. Only 22 U.S. states have state resilience plans at the time of writing.[1] A state resilience plan helps fund (and sometimes compel) resilience efforts locally. State resilience plans are sometimes drafted by volunteers from the local American Planning Association chapters.

Get involved at the neighborhood level. Help homeowner associations, park and open space non-profits, and even local political candidates with their climate

278 ■ *Creating Climate Plans*

planning. I have found tremendous satisfaction simply helping the park down the street from my house switch to drought-tolerant, native plants (which are still beautiful) and educating my neighbors on climate simply by talking about the resilience of shrubs like Firebush and wild coffee. I have helped local candidates for office draft their statements and policies on climate and they appreciate my time. When I volunteer locally, I feel that I am still heading "the call" even when climate planning shrinks to a small part of my job.

Step 5: Keep Conversations Going

If plans are shelved, realize that keeping the conversation going is the most important part.

There is a cynical view of local planning that asserts government policy is not contained within the reports and plans it commissions; government policy IS the reports and plans it commissions. This is to say that government finds it enough just to let the public make plans or commission plans because the planning process creates the impression that something is being done and then, after that, no real action is necessary. Elected officials just want to be seen as doing something. Having a plan becomes a substitute for taking action.

There is truth to this. We've all observed local plans that sit on the proverbial shelf. To some degree this is due to human nature. *Status quo bias* is a built-in preference which psychologists tell us affects our decision-making, and leads us to choose, more often than not, the current state of affairs over other possible futures, even when we know better. Habit is stronger than reason. There is also *psychological inertia*, a natural predisposition to always avoid breaks with tradition, especially among elected officials who tend to be, in democratically elected governments, firmly *of the people*, and no more or less aware or enlightened than the average person. There is also the *bystander effect*: Our tendency to wait for others to act rather than act ourselves. Few people want to rock the boat.[2]

However, for concerned community members interested in positive change the local plan is just about all they have. The plan's legal weight varies state to state and community to community, but it is the only tool the average person has to hold elected officials accountable besides the ability to vote, and the perfunctory three minutes or so that local government allows for public comment at official meetings. Even when the plan is shelved, remember that it did educate many people. Judge the plan by what it achieves in five years and not month to month. In my experience, in certain places, at the right time, and in the hands of convinced people, the local plan can be extremely powerful when the effect of the plan is considered over time.

Remember to be realistic about the efficacy of city plans. In our field we talk about architect and urban designer Daniel Burnham's *Plan for Chicago of 1909* – the plan that turned a mid-western cow town into an international metropolis (as the story goes). Yet, I'd estimate that only 30% of that plan was implemented. Burnham

Dealing With Setbacks ■ **279**

may have considered his plan a failure, but history does not. Burnham's plan taught a generation of urban planners what an urban plan could be with its grand imagery and recommendations at every level. The educational value of the plan considered nationally was tremendous.

Work to learn the varying opinions on the topic of climate change and understand where they are coming from. There is an outlook, an emotion (often fear) at the heart of every strong opinion. Sympathize with *that* at least. Try to understand, just for a second, what it is like to be that person (we all know how unpleasant it is to be afraid) and why that person might hold such an opinion. The criticism we receive helps us recognize our own assumptions and biases. Study the illusions of others, and your own, for their causes. Reply to your detractors only after you see the opposition's point and any potential flaws in your own. Again, all this can happen in a second in your head if you're open to it.

Listening wins friends. Courtesy and understanding wins friends. But keep the climate change conversation going. The only way to avoid pushback is to say nothing, do nothing, and be nothing. That's not you. You probably wouldn't have purchased this book if it were.

Step 6: Keep At It (In Different Ways)

Sometimes your municipality just won't adopt a climate plan. Even when that happens, you can still work on policies that could reduce emissions and build a community that will be safer and stronger in the future. And if you have adopted a plan but the current administration just doesn't consider implementation a priority, keep at it, in different ways, quietly adding teeth to your community's climate policies through revisions to the Land Development Regulations (LDRs) and zoning. Periodic updates to the zoning and LDRs are expected in municipalities. Updates provide a chance to make communities more sustainable, green, and resilient. Big LDR overhauls provide cover for smart climate policies that, by themselves, would receive undue scrutiny and ultimately fail to be approved.

Climate planning backlash is one reason why we shouldn't be looking for one big climate policy – like carbon taxing on an international level or the requirement of solar panels on every new home on the local level – to save us. We need a variety of climate planning options on every level. A variety of climate policies and a long list of potential investments help build multiple coalitions of people who are really going to fight for the climate plan. There's climate action steps that can help everyone from housing advocates to environmentalists, from historic preservationists to exercise enthusiasts, advance their cause. There are many climate solutions which even the local chamber of commerce can endorse because they create jobs or attract investment. Well-written climate plans are completely actionable at every scale, so even when there is a stall in government at the federal, state, or local level, everyone can take a piece locally, at the level of the block, street, and lot, and continue to make a difference.

"Every town wants a city planner but no one really wants you to do anything," was something I heard as a young urban planner at my first internship in Hopkinton, Rhode Island. I have since found that this statement is only true of certain municipalities at certain times – but still, it's true too often. If you don't see an end to your local political lethargy when it comes to climate planning then consider moving on to another municipality. As the world warms, dries, burns, and floods, climate-planning skills will be increasingly in demand.

Notes

1 Climate Action Tracker. Retrieved from: https://climateactiontracker.org/countries/usa/
2 Marshall, G. (2014). *Don't Even Think About It: Why Our Brains Are Wired to Ignore Climate Change*. New York: Bloomsbury USA.

TWO AMERICAN CITIES IN 2050

3

282 ■ *Two American Cities in 2050*

Introduction to Part 3
Two American Cities in 2050

Let's imagine the future. Writing about your community's future is a way to understand the challenges ahead and create a compelling narrative that encourages discussion. Let's avoid describing the future with dystopian imagery. We're beyond the point of needing an ear-splitting wake-up call. We need to look ahead the same way a person with life-threatening heart disease or cancer might: With self-respect, a resolve to change, and hope.

There are reports that can help you interpret the future. In 2014, the IPCC contained within its Fifth Assessment Report (AR5) four climate futures, all of which are considered possible, though each assumes a different level of greenhouse gases emissions in the future.[1] The four scenarios are called Representative Concentration Pathways (RCPs) and are named RCP2.6, RCP4.5, RCP6, and RCP8.5. The RCPs contain projections regarding worldwide global warming, sea-level rise, and other effects. Urban planners can start with an RCP and then use other online or municipal GIS (Geographic Information Systems) programs, the long-range plans of energy and water providers, and transportation and land use plans, to create multiple scenarios of their own municipality's future.

Planners have been doing this for a long time. The Futurama Exhibit of the 1939 World's Fair, which took place in New York, predicted quite accurately the world of glass towers, superhighways, and easy motoring we live in today. Going back even further, Edward Bellamy's 1888 bestselling book *Looking Backward: 2000 to 1887* imagined a future with debit cards, e-commerce like Amazon, and radio music. Of course, he imagined music arriving through underground pipes; Bellamy's versions were all a bit nineteenth-century when it comes to specifics. He also more or less imagined gender liberation, social security, retirement, and socialist democracy. More important than his actual predictions, his work inspired his contemporaries to write thoughtful papers with support or rebuttal for decades. The conversation is the important part. We learn a lot by studying the future.

While no one has a crystal ball, future modelling is something urban planners do very well when it comes to planning for new schools, transportation infrastructure, and water infrastructure. Today we need to add climate adaptation infrastructure to the list. As an example of a plan that puts all these things together, I recommend the *Seven50: Prosperity Plan for Southeast Florida,*[2] but there are many examples. The description of Southeast Florida's future in this chapter draws from that plan.

I have chosen to describe Miami (Southeast Florida, specifically) and El Paso (and its region) because they are two cities with acute, but different, climate challenges and they are both working hard to become sustainable. Before we imagine the future, I will describe their current sustainability efforts. Those efforts lead me to believe that neither city is a lost cause.

Instead of the far-off year of 2100 that is often described by futurists, let's imagine 2050, a year that many readers of this book will live to see. Instead of assuming an

DOI: 10.4324/9781003181514-16

unlivable, apocalyptic future in the hopes of encouraging action, and then hoping for the best (as many futurists maddeningly do), let's stay optimistic that humans, the great variable in the climate story, continue to work toward resilience.

Modelling Assumptions

Let's imagine a global median temperature rise of 2°C (3.6°F) by 2050. Why? Because without any new policies to mitigate climate change, our projections suggest an increase in global mean temperature in 2100 of 3.7°C to 4.8°C, relative to pre-industrial levels.[3] However, if significant action is taken, warming in 2100 could stay below 3°C.[4] Let's err on the side of optimism.

Let's assume 2 feet of rise for our Southeast Florida study area by 2060.[5] Why? Because while sea level rise is projected to reach anywhere between 11.5 inches and 20 inches by 2060 (above the 1992 mean sea level)[6] the U.S. Army Corps of Engineers (USACE) and the National Oceanographic and Atmospheric Agency (NOAA) tend to revise upward with every new reporting. Keep in mind, however, that in the year 2100, we might have to assume 6 feet rise on average globally, and 10 feet of rise in Southeast Florida.[7]

These assumptions are in line with RCP8.5, the so-called "business-as-usual" emissions scenario that assumes the Earth will continue to rely heavily on fossil fuels as the global economy grows. I don't think the Earth will continue *business-as-usual*. I think the world will change dramatically socially and economically to combat the climate threat. However, in terms of fossil fuel use, it appears that the growing world population will demand the same standard of living that developed nations enjoy. This is significant, because it offsets, in a negative way, much of the positive action that will be achieved elsewhere in the world.

Developed nations use resources at hundreds of times the rate as the planet's other citizens and those of us who live in developed nations are a privileged fraction of humanity. The developing world also wants to reach the point advanced nations are at as easily as advanced nations. Will this require more carbon emissions than our planet can handle? Impossible to say. However, it does appear that developing nations are more likely to use renewable energy more to supplement fossil fuels than to replace them. For this reason, we are using the RCP8.5 emissions scenario.

Caveats are called for at this point. It should be noted that some scientists would consider a 2-foot rise optimistic because there is no scientific consensus that warming of 2°C (3.6°F) will correspond to only 0.6m (1.9 feet to 2 feet) of rise. Scientists also describe a 1.5°C (2.7°F) rise as a situation which means 3.5m (11.5 feet) of inevitable rise, in time. This is referred to as "committed sea level rise." Commitment levels are achieved when the ocean equilibrates to the combined effects of an expanding warming ocean, melting of land ice primarily at the poles, and other factors. So,

284 ■ *Two American Cities in 2050*

while we stop our forecasting at 2050, much higher seas may come inevitably – and way too quickly – if we do not act.[8]

Notes

1 IPCC (2013). Summary for Policymakers: D. Understanding the climate system and its recent changes. In: Stocker, T.F., D. Qin, G.-K. Plattner, M. Tignor, S.K. Allen, J. Boschung, A. Nauels, Y. Xia, V. Bex and P.M. Midgley (eds), *Climate Change 2013: The Physical Science Basis. Contribution of Working Group I to the Fifth Assessment Report of the Intergovernmental Panel on Climate Change.* Cambridge and New York: Cambridge University Press, p. 15. Retrieved from: www.ipcc.ch/site/assets/uploads/2018/02/WG1AR5_SPM_FINAL.pdf

2 South Florida Regional Planning Council and Treasure Coast Regional Planning Council (2013). *Seven50, Seven Counties, 50 Years: The Southeast Florida Prosperity Plan.* See also http://seven50report.org/

3 IPCC (2014). Summary for Policymakers: SPM. 3 Trends in stocks and flows of greenhouse gases and their drivers. In: Edenhofer, O., R. Pichs-Madruga, Y. Sokona, E. Farahani, S. Kadner, K. Seyboth, A. Adler, I. Baum, S. Brunner, P. Eickemeier, B. Kriemann, J. Savolainen, S. Schlömer, C. von Stechow, T. Zwickel and J.C. Minx (eds), *Climate Change 2014: Mitigation of Climate Change. Contribution of Working Group III to the Fifth Assessment Report of the Intergovernmental Panel on Climate Change.* Cambridge and New York: Cambridge University Press, p. 8. Retrieved from: www.ipcc.ch/site/assets/uploads/2018/02/ipcc_wg3_ar5_summary-for-policymakers.pdf

4 Ibid., SPM.4.1, p. 10.

5 South Florida Regional Compact Climate Change (2015). Unified sea level rise projection for Southeast Florida: Relative sea level rise near Key West, FL (inches relative to mean sea level). Retrieved from: https://southeastfloridaclimatecompact.org/wp-content/uploads/2015/10/2015-Compact-Unified-Sea-Level-Rise-Projection.pdf, pp. 4–5.

6 Ibid.

7 Kopp, R.E., Horton, R.M. and Little, C.M. (2014). Probablistic 21st and 22nd century sea-level projections at a global network of tide-gauge sites. *Earth's Future*, Volume 2, pp. 383–406.

8 Levermann, A., Clark, P.U., Marzeion, B., Milne, G.A., Pollard, D. Radić, V. and Robinson, A. (2013). The multimillennial sea-level commitment of global warming. *PNAS*, Volume 110 (34), pp. 13745–13750.

Chapter 14

Miami and Southeast Florida

Today, Florida is the third largest U.S. state with roughly 22 million people.[1] If Florida were an independent nation it would have one of the world's largest economies, ranking above Saudi Arabia, Turkey, Argentina, the Netherlands, and Switzerland.[2] Southeast Florida is the state's primary population and employment center and includes Miami-Dade County, Broward County, Monroe County, and Palm Beach County. Often referred to as "Greater Miami," or just "Miami," Southeast Florida is the sixth most populous metropolitan region in the nation. When writers of popular climate change articles blithely report that Miami will be lost before the end of the century, they are referring to a region that includes more than the City of Miami, they mean Southeast Florida, and they are giving up on a region whose population outranks Boston, Massachusetts, and all its surrounding communities. They are writing off an area larger than Philadelphia and its entire region.

At the same time, it's easier for Americans to imagine losing Miami than Boston or Philadelphia because Miami has had a comparatively short history. Miami was born just 120 years ago, when Standard Oil founder Henry Flagler's train reached the sandy peninsula. Boston and Philadelphia were well established around that time – the start of the twentieth century – and had already made significant contributions to the history of our country. It was also only very recently, perhaps in the early 1970s, that Miami had become entirely livable with the proliferation of air-conditioning. However, since about the year 2000, Miami has become the center of the Latin American and South American economy and the significance of that fact has yet to enter into American's understanding of the place.

The region grew by 4.8 million people from 1970 to 2010 and today is referred to as the "Gold Coast" – not because of the large gold resources found in the area (like

DOI: 10.4324/9781003181514-17

285

286 ■ *Two American Cities in 2050*

Figure 11 Boardwalk in Fort Lauderdale, Florida

the Gold Coast of Africa) but because of the value attributed to real estate investment. That brings us to another point about Miami's image: It has the reputation of being a vacation place for people from elsewhere. The world seems more ready to part with Miami than with Boston, Philadelphia, New York City, or even Norfolk, Virginia, because Miami is largely known as a playground for the idle, rich, and famous.

If you're looking for a modern city to play the role of Atlantis in your allegory on hubris, well, Miami will do nicely. One day, tourists will scuba dive the mansions of Star Island and the former homes of Elizabeth Taylor, Madonna, Jennifer Lopez, and Pitbull. Miamians hear this all the time. There's a passage in the Book of Job which talks about rich people with fat waistlines dwelling in houses that will become the rubble of desolate, ruined cities when the breath of God blows them away. Yeah, we've heard it. Several times. Thanks.

To be fair, Miami is actually a poor city with low median household incomes and high living costs.[3] Miami is an Ellis Island providing opportunity to millions of refugees and immigrants just getting their start.[4] Spanish is the first language of half the people in the region.[5] For those of us who live in Southeast Florida and understand it, Southeast Florida feels too important to lose. It is no more than a cheap shot to label this home for millions, this economic powerhouse, this rising place in a country where so many other regions are in decline, as Sodom and Gomorrah, and kiss it goodbye.

Miami faces challenges that Boston and Philadelphia do not, however. Southeast Florida is low-lying and the average elevation in the City of Miami is 6.6 feet (though heights range from sea level to 30 feet).[6] The average elevation of the City of Boston is 141 feet[7] and in Philadelphia it is 39 feet.[8] Southeast Florida also has an oolite limestone subsurface, and saltwater from the ocean moves upward, underground, and can appear underfoot regardless of whether there are sea walls.

Many years before climate change was widely discussed, Miami Beach had begun to fight the rise of the oceans. The 10-mile-long shoreline fronting Miami Beach was replenished between 1976 and 1981. The project cost US$64 million and it revitalized the area's economy. Prior to nourishment, many parts of the beach were too narrow to walk, especially during high tide. Now, the sandy beach has become home to festivals and concerts year-round. The initial investment cost has been paid back many times over. The beach system also provided a critical barrier against storm surge and sea-level rise.

Floridians could leave the coasts. The state has a relatively high and undeveloped center, and we could retreat from areas below 16 feet to areas that will survive all but the most cataclysmic effects of climate change. But the coast is essential. The coast *is* Florida. In 2010 Florida's coastal counties contributed 80% of the state's economy, nearly US$600 billion in regional gross product. More than 75% of the state's population lived in the coastal counties, and the counties represented a built-environment and infrastructure worth US$2 trillion, estimated to be worth US$3 trillion by 2030.[9] Unlike Jakarta in Indonesia, Dhaka in Bangladesh, or even New Orleans in Louisiana, Southeast Florida feels wealthy enough to save itself. But can it?

The Effect of Sea-level Rise

Just 1 foot of sea-level rise has serious implications for Miami and Southeast Florida and, at 3 feet, the very existence of many areas would be threatened.[10] Urban

288 ■ *Two American Cities in 2050*

planning in Southeast Florida assumes 2 feet of rise by 2060[11] though the seas could rise locally anywhere from 14 to 26 inches by 2060 (above the 1992 mean sea level). Increasing greenhouse gas concentrations, accelerating melting of the ice sheets on Greenland and Antarctica, and accelerated thaw of permafrost, are among the many factors affecting the rate of rise.

What Could Happen After 1 Foot of Rise

Regionally, nearly 80% of the lands potentially affected in the 1-foot scenario are conservation lands, especially coastal wetlands. These low-lying natural systems of buttonwood, mangrove, scrub mangrove, and herbaceous saltwater and freshwater wetlands slow wave action, keep the sea at a distance, and provide nursery habitat for aquatic life. Those environments would be significantly affected, and this includes the Everglades National Park. Losing these protective systems would further increase the region's vulnerabilities to extreme weather and devastate the local fishing industry.

Beaches would begin to wash away and expensive replenishment efforts would be necessary. Miami and Southeast Florida's 80 miles of beaches are the iconic images of the state. Unlike much of the west coast of Florida, the east coast is highly urbanized and the interface between city and ocean give Southeast Florida some of the most accessible and best maintained beaches in the world.

Southeast Florida depends on canals to drain stormwater into the ocean. A 1-foot of rise could severely affect almost half the regions' existing flood control capacity. The region's gravity-drained systems would need to be mechanized and the costs to taxpayers would be enormous.

There are also many low-lying, high-investment areas that become vulnerable after just a 1-foot rise. The upper estimate of current taxable property values in Monroe, Broward, and Palm Beach Counties vulnerable in the 1-foot scenario is US$4 billion.[12] Three of Monroe County's four hospitals, 65% of schools, and 70% of emergency shelters are located on property at elevations below sea level after 1 foot of rise. The cooling canals of power plants in Miami-Dade and Broward and the high voltage power lines in Monroe County may find themselves in water with just 1 foot of rise.

By 2050, an analysis by the First Street Foundation shows Monroe County alone could see 35% of its properties flooded 50 or more times a year. That's more than 12,000 homes flooded nearly every week. At that point, the study assumes, those properties could lose all their value.[13]

What Could Happen After 3 Feet of Rise

In Broward, Palm Beach, and Monroe Counties more than US$31 billion in real estate and public investments become vulnerable in the 3-foot rise scenario. Many barrier islands would require significant bulwarking to stay intact; others face the threat that they may disappear. Communities near the Everglades would have to increase pumping dramatically to stay dry. Water rise in many canals would make neighborhoods expensive to insure. The cost to repair storm damage due to flooding would rise with the water. The entire region, even upland areas in the north, would be affected by the loss of coastal drinking water well fields due to saltwater intrusion. Expensive, and energy-consumptive new desalination efforts would be necessary.

The Future

We've described the present situation well enough, so now let's discuss the future. Imagine that you are listening to a hypothetical news program broadcast. Picture a voice like Walter Cronkite or, I suppose, Trevor Noah, depending on your generation, presenting a *dispatch*, a communication, from the future.

Miami and Southeast Florida in 2050: A Dispatch From the Future

In 2050, Hurricane *Xu* took an unexpected turn and that meant several lives were lost in the Miami and Southeast Florida region. Still, locals felt it wasn't too bad a storm, especially for anyone who had experienced Hurricane *Zeta* 15 years earlier. Southeast Florida prided itself on the fact that the long-term uphill battle against the sea was well underway when Hurricane *Xu* hit and so *Xu* hardly left a scratch.

Hurricanes in 2050

When Miami residents went to bed, *Xu*'s swirling yellow and green eye on the radar screen was just west of Santa Clara in Cuba, and the storm track showed the hurricane crossing the Florida Keys and moving up the west coast of Florida as a Category 2 with 100-miles-per-hour winds. Miamians knew they'd feel it. Thousands evacuated to Orlando just in case of coastal flooding. But most locals considered the storm nothing to worry about. The eye of the storm was projected to pass more than 150 miles from the center of Miami.

However, anyone awake at 1.30am, when the storm hit, heard a continuous howling fury that made them reconsider the wisdom of staying. The eye of Hurricane *Xu* passed directly over Miami's downtown as a Category 3 hurricane. Sustained winds of 120 miles per hour were recorded at Miami International Airport. The hurricane's storm surge swept into Downtown Miami and Brickell, flooding the streets with knee-deep water. Luckily, it was a fast-moving storm at 15 miles per hour; it dumped less than 8 inches of rain, and the tides were low when the winds peaked.

Even still, the storm damaged hundreds of structures in its path and the total cost of storm damage was estimated at US$50 billion. Ten people drowned in the

290 ■ *Two American Cities in 2050*

South Beach area of Miami Beach when the storm surge breached low levees made of mangrove and muck on the island's west side. The victims were later identified as squatters living on the abandoned portions of the barrier islands. People continued to be drawn to the unsafe, unpoliced, but still often picturesque Evacuation Zones of Florida's barrier islands for unfortunate reasons related to poverty, drug use, legal issues, and mental health issues.

Hurricane *Zeta*, in 2035, was far more catastrophic than Hurricane *Xu* and after *Zeta*, lessons were learned. Following *Zeta*'s devastation, a debate was held on whether to hold the line at all, and it became a national conversation involving Congress, the Federal Emergency Management Agency (FEMA), the Environmental Protection Agency (EPA), presidential candidates, and taxpayers across the country. The State of Florida and the municipalities that composed Miami and Southeast Florida said *yes* to staying and bulwarking, and effectively decided to double-down despite the risks.

Hurricanes were not more frequent than in the past, the time before manmade climate breakdown, but warmer ocean waters from climate change were making hurricanes lose power more slowly because the water acted as fuel tanks for moisture. The storms were getting bigger, living longer, growing wetter, becoming slower, and doing far more damage. They also intensified faster, and the threat of overnight intensification gave everyone in the region nightmares. The kind of multi-day monsoon rainstorms that used to hit only once every five years hit every year.

Rising Seas in 2050

The world's temperature had risen 2 degrees Celsius and expectations were that it would reach 4 degrees by 2100. The most dire sea-level predictions had yet to occur, however. The sea level had risen in Southeast Florida to only 2 feet and was on course to rise to 6 feet by 2100. This was far less than the doomsday scenario projected by some.

The region rose to the challenge of climate change by accelerating efforts already underway to update building codes and reinvent capital projects. Local efforts were boosted by Federal relief when after Hurricane *Zelda* Congress approved US$2 billion for the Central and South Florida Flood Control Project. Southeast Florida continued elevating more than 5,000 miles of roads, installing 800 new pump stations, upgrading stormwater drainage utilities, and raising sea walls in the most vulnerable areas by up to 7.5 feet. All new structures were higher, often on block-sized pedestals, and streets and infrastructure were lifted in every community that had urban densities. Despite the outrage of top-tier taxpayers and political oscillations between fiscal conservatives and people of a more forward-looking nature, Miami and the rest of urbanized Southeast Florida had successfully worked to build its way out of its problems. To a point.

As the region was building stronger and safer, a retreat from low-density coastal areas and the lower parts of all but a few barrier islands had begun. High insurance rates, the significant down-payment requirements needed in order to secure mortgages, and dropping home sale prices resulted in sluggish sales and high vacancy rates in areas that had been hot markets before Hurricane *Zeta*. Repeated calls to evacuate low-lying neighborhoods during the hurricane season were felt to be too disruptive to normal life for many people and they wanted out.

Miami-Dade County established sea-level rise thresholds at which county services and infrastructure maintenance would be terminated to low-lying neighborhoods. Concurrent with that policy – a policy some described as draconian but most agreed was necessary – a retreat-to-the-heart-of-town strategy was implemented in every municipality to give people a place they could go to while staying relatively local. The result was increasingly complete, compact, and connected new centers and new local main streets away from the shore.

Commentators continued to call Miami and Southeast Florida an "Atlantis in the making," as the region suffered vicious cycles of run-for-your-life storms. Category 3 and 4 storms, far scarier than the 1926 and 1935 storms that once broke the city, began to hit once per season. The warmer ocean water made hurricanes move more slowly and drop more water. Southeast Florida saw more severe rainfall than ever before and Downtown Miami was often inundated around the iconic Freedom Tower. Pictures of the tower surrounded by lakes of water made national news and demoralized locals.

As it became more and more clear that the sprint to build stronger, safer municipalities would need to become a marathon, Southeast Florida converted its regional government into a regional public works department called the Rising Above Commission. The Rising Above Commission began to fund sea walls and pumping systems through the sale of general obligation bonds paid for by property taxes. Other tax capture funding mechanisms (like Tax Increment Financing provided by local Community Redevelopment Agencies) helped build local levees and these projects succeeded in bolstering confidence in Southeast Florida's will to survive – if not its ultimate ability.

Migration in 2050

Southeast Florida's multinational and multicultural diversity proved to be its strength. The number of foreign buyers in Miami from Latin America and South America escaping civil war, unrest, security issues, and food and water supply problems caused by climate change, kept the real estate market going. Simply put, other places had it worse, and the population of Southeast Florida had reached nine million people by 2050. Miami remained the U.S. city with the largest immigrant population despite prognoses that climate refugees would skip Miami altogether.

The increase in world temperatures caused a precipitous decline in crop yields in South America. Extreme and recurrent droughts in South America made corn, soybeans, and cotton largely ungrowable south of the 37th parallel. This problem was exasperated by increased weed and pest invasion. The Southern hemisphere was becoming dependent on the Northern for food.

292 ▪ *Two American Cities in 2050*

Tens of millions of people worldwide were displaced due to climate change by 2050 and this spurred a mid-twenty-first-century building boom in places like Miami. People arrived there by boat and plane – even though its international airport flooded regularly, making air travel in and out of the city more difficult. Residents talked about the *flood of people* more often than the *flood of water*. Florida adopted a tax on residents' incomes, including those earned from dividends, and applied those monies to the infrastructure needed to accommodate all the new residential towers that seemed to hover in the air above cresting flood waters.

Mass migration had positive and negative effects on the region and one negative was that unemployment tripled from 3% to 9% during the 2020–2050 period. Southeast Florida saw an increase in poverty from 25% of the total population in 2020 to 35% in 2050, due, in large part, to migrants from the Caribbean Islands, Latin America, and South America.

While some of the municipalities that composed Southeast Florida planned to work toward a slow and graceful depopulation, rather than a sudden and catastrophic one, no serious government-initiated abandonment efforts of urban areas could be observed in 2050. No urbanized area had yet to see the value of homes spiral down in the way prognosticators assumed would occur. Economic and social conditions were, simply, more dire elsewhere in the world.

Temperatures in 2050

Miami heated up by more than 3 degrees Fahrenheit on average. However, other places in the country saw far greater increases and suffered a greater jolt. Southeast Florida was already comfortably acquainted with living with heat. Cities depended on the cool shade of trees for outdoor life and urban tree canopies became well-funded municipal infrastructure. Cities that took their urban tree canopies seriously enjoyed Mediterranean pleasantness in their city centers. At the same time, it was no longer safe to cool homes exclusively with shade, open windows, and fans, and air-conditioning became necessary for public health. Some people reportedly left the region simply because they were tired of the murderously hot summer temperatures and living like cave dwellers in air-conditioned spaces. Out-of-doors construction was prohibited when temperatures reached 100 degrees and, for much of the spring and summer, the cranes and earthmovers on construction sites sat unmoving.

Drinking Water in 2050

By 2050 the State of Florida operated 30 solar-powered desalinization plants managed by the Rising Above Commission. Desalinated water made up 50% of water consumed in the state because, as underground salinity levels rose, only 50% of potable municipal water could be pulled from groundwater. Desalinization came with a high energy cost, paid in large part by a new nuclear reactor located in the state's interior, at Belle Glade.

The Economy in 2050

The region embarked on a new, massive beach replenishment and bulwarking program to save its beach tourism. Sand costs rose as sand was imported from farther and farther away: The Caribbean, Mexico, and even Africa. Sand from offshore was pumped back to shore, essentially resetting the sands for the erosion cycle to start again. Beach renourishment cost millions and was paid for using both state monies and a large portion of the "bed taxes" collected from overnight visitors staying in hotels.

Flooding from each successive year's King Tides reached farther inland and affected more and more homes and businesses with some areas effectively shut down for weeks every year. Large, rural parts of Miami-Dade and Broward counties saw water sloshing around for months in places where the South Florida Flood Control Project's pumping stations, canals, and levees simply had nowhere to send the water. Declines in marine fisheries due to flooding seriously affected the seafood cuisine of Southeast Florida with locally harvested oysters, shrimp, and fish like snapper and grouper, reaching the price of delicacies.

After years of consternation over environmental impacts, Miami and Southeast Florida began a serious effort to build new barrier islands and extensions to existing islands. The islands added 10 to 20 feet of elevation to the land. Just as Miami had been largely built by dredging in the 1920s, the dredge again became the symbol of Southeast Florida's climate adaptation effort. Environmentalists howled as the first real coastal walls rose, and for good reason: Soft shorelines of mangroves and natural beaches became hardened shorelines of walls and levees within new, artificial dunes. Local flora and fauna was displaced in favor of lifeless coasts made of cement and sand.

In Greater Miami, the islands of Virginia Key, Fisher Island, and Miami Beach were linked with storm surge barriers which closed during storms and protected the downtown from surges of up to 15 feet. *The Barbican Wall* (as it was referred to locally) was less a wall and more an archipelago of manmade islands, super-levees, barriers, and gates topped with mini-cities with front doors sometimes 30 feet above sea level. New lagoons sheltered thousands living in houseboats. The population of Miami continued to grow and, in true Miami fashion, the effort to build vital infrastructure became a real estate project. Selling real estate to people from the cold North or turbulent South remained Southeast Florida's main economy.

Energy in 2050

The Turkey Point Nuclear Generating Station, a twin reactor nuclear power station located 25 miles south of Miami near the southernmost edge of Miami-Dade County, sat in the middle of a walled island with pumps running around the clock. All the state's nuclear generators had originally been placed on coastal edges and their long-term survival hinged on the world's ability to cut carbon emissions and halt the rise of the seas. A new nuclear generation plant had been constructed in Florida's inland at Belle Glade and several other inland generating stations were in the planning stages.

294 ■ *Two American Cities in 2050*

Protesting nuclear power became a pastime for environmental advocates who felt that Southeast Florida simply hadn't done enough to harness renewable energy. Objectively, however, the region was on track to maximizing its harvest of solar energy and nuclear power was still needed. All new construction in Southeast Florida was required to be equipped with photovoltaic panels and vast solar arrays located just outside the urban edge generated millions of gigawatt-hours. The state had no potential for conventional wind power, and little potential for hydro power other than large-scale tidal facilities that were under development. Without nuclear power the state's renewable energy sources were not forecasted to be sufficient to meet the region's need for energy.

Environment in 2050

In Southeast Florida 20% of local plant and animal species had experienced extinction by 2050. Coral reefs in Southeast Florida had died a decade earlier along with most other coral systems worldwide. Every year during record heatwaves, fires would light in the Everglades and people wondered if it was possible for temperatures to get so high, and remain so steady, that the Everglades, despite all the water in the system from rising seas, would simply burn down.

Looking Forward: From 2050 to 2100

What would the next 50 years bring? Wider abandonment, most likely. Astronomical adaptation costs, undoubtedly. While Miami had bought itself another several decades of existence, even the city's most dedicated boosters looked ahead and saw that the challenges posed by the warming Earth and rising seas would one day prove insurmountable.

People continued to live in Southeast Florida despite the sultry heat and violent weather, however. There was nothing wrong with Florida that wasn't wrong with the rest of the world, people said. Florida's upland northern interior was still delightfully inhabitable, and people continued to leave cold northern cities and retire to tranquil suburban neighborhoods. People who used to wake to the sight of the ocean now spent their mornings gazing across the wooded glades of the state's interior and taking walks on sun-dappled paths far from the salty air and tempestuous seas. At the same time, on the coasts with their walled, pumped, tower cities, people continued to live and work and tourists continued to swim the emptying oceans.

Notes

1 This information is from the U.S. Census Bureau. In 2018 the population was 21.3 million. Retrieved from: www.census.gov

2 South Florida Regional Planning Council and Treasure Coast Regional Planning Council (2013). Seven50, *Seven50, Seven Counties, 50 Years: The Southeast Florida Prosperity Plan.* See also http://seven50report.org/
3 Wile, R. and Wooldridge, J. (2019). South Florida workers are among the poorest-paid. The "Miami Discount" may be to blame. *Miami Herald*, June 5. Retrieved from: www.miamiherald.com/news/business/real-estate-news/article229904864.html
4 Deibert, M. (2015). Making sense of Miami: What America's refuge city says about the US's future. *The Guardian*, July 2. Retrieved from: www.theguardian.com/cities/2015/jul/02/miami-florida-cuba-multicultural-metropolis-diversity-hispanic-haiti
5 Ibid.
6 For further information see www.miamigov.com/Home
7 For further information see www.boston.gov/
8 For further information see www.phila.gov
9 Bolter, K. P. (2016). SFRPC South Florida Regional Planning Council Coastal flood resiliency South Florida Initiatives. Retrieved from: www.fgcu.edu/cas/communityimpact/celatega/archives/files/2016archive/SouthFL_initiatives_Bolter.pdf
10 South Florida Regional Planning Council and Treasure Coast Regional Planning Council (2013), op. cit.
11 Southeast Florida Regional Compact Climate Change (2015). Unified sea level rise projection: Southeast Florida. Retrieved from: http://southeastfloridaclimatecompact.org/wp-content/uploads/2015/10/2015-Compact-Unified-Sea-Level-Rise-Projection.pdf
12 South Florida Regional Planning Council and Treasure Coast Regional Planning Council (2013), op. cit.
13 Harris, A. (2020). Sea rise won't sink all of Florida's real estate market, experts say. Just parts of it. *Miami Herald*, April 28. Retrieved from: www.miamiherald.com/news/local/environment/article242305881.html#storylink=cpy

Chapter 15

El Paso, Texas

El Paso is hot. The first time I saw El Paso, driving on the highway from the airport in 2010, it looked harsh enough to make me gasp: Dry, cracked soil and blown litter riding the wind up and over the tacky billboards and between the homes that sat on parched, treeless hills. I remember wavy heat rising off asphalt roads that had long ago been bleached white by the sun.

I got out of my rental car at San Jacinto Plaza. It was a summer day. Airless heat. Baking desert. Even in the shade I had perspired through my shirt. I thought about how climate heating had yet to even really kick in. I walked San Jacinto Plaza, the city's *plaza mayor*, the main square of the city, and found that a walk in the park in El Paso was no *walk in the park*. There were few trees except for low Acacia, bent Eucalyptus, and palms that were all jutting jackboots and no fronds. The dominant visual image was brown concrete. I was the only person in the park. I was the only person outside at all.

At that time, there wasn't a single restaurant I could find open in the downtown and so, after a big sigh, I left the downtown and went to L&J Cafe by the Concordia Cemetery. I quickly found that in El Paso life happens indoors in the air-conditioned cool of restaurants, living rooms, and workplaces with the blinds closed. I found that once indoors, El Paso is as welcoming as the outside is intimidating. Under a chandelier made from a wagon wheel (as I remember it), I enjoyed spicy food and cold beer and conversations with three customers who were waiting for a table and just decided to strike up a conversation with me.

I know that you can't really describe an entire city's population with a few adjectives, but after working in El Paso for many years my experience of El Pasoans is that they are family-oriented, easy-going, quick-to-laugh, artistic, community-minded, and spiritual. I take the same comfort from the food – the heaps of rice, cheesy burritos, and cheap beer like they serve at L&J's – as I do in the warm *abrazo* the people express. Everyone I know that knows El Paso loves El Paso, and it is the warmth of the people that makes the difference.

DOI: 10.4324/9781003181514-18

Figure 12 Union Depot, El Paso, Texas

In my first days in El Paso, I was alone for sometimes a week at a time and I was invited to watch boxing and soccer on TV at people's homes, concerts in the park, book readings, birthday parties, and backyard barbecues. I was even invited to a *quinceañera* celebration. Some of these events were arranged just for my benefit (not the *quinceañera*, obviously) because the people I met felt it heartbreaking that I was eating at the hotel alone in the deserted downtown. It felt like I saw the homes of all the city's staff and elected officials – including Beto O'Rourke who would go on to the U.S. House of Representatives and run for U.S. president. I tell you sincerely: It's a wonderful city.

Once you get to know the city's pocket parks with their Palo Verde trees and dappled sunlight, nighttime restaurant patios lit with chic Edison bulb lights, and cool arroyo canyons (the dry stream beds that ran down the mountains), you realize that, if you're smart about it, the city and surrounding river valley can be experienced out of doors comfortably, even in summer. Part of my team's work in El Paso included the redesign of San Jacinto Plaza and today, thanks to the work of SWA Group and Kale Flato Architects, it is a state-of-the-art urban space with axial paths and informal ambles shaded by a complete canopy of trees. The park includes a children's splashpad, gaming areas for chess, checkers, and washoes (a game similar to horseshoes but with water), public bikes and electric scooters for rent, and the Coffee Box restaurant which is housed inside two brightly painted metal freight containers stacked on top of one another. They sell fantastic, sugary ice coffees. Today, the downtown is back, people abound, and El Paso has become one of the best places in the country for outdoor nighttime concerts. The local music scene is a fantastic mix of genres and culture.

I've worked in El Paso on various projects involving every aspect of urban planning from transit, to parks, to development codes, economic development, arts and culture development, and climate (by one name or another). In 2018, El Paso was being recognized for its "cool" – not least by the Lonely Planet travel guides. After working so long with so many to improve the place, that felt terrific. Still, despite the fact I got to know the city fairly well and became very fond of it, that first impression off the plane has never left me entirely: *I can't believe people live here.*

A lot of people live in El Paso or within the pass which gives the region its name. There are 650,000 people in the City of El Paso.[1] El Paso County, which includes the city, has a population of 840,000.[2] Within a short drive from the city center live more than 2.7 million people in the bi-national Borderplex (as it is known), which includes Las Cruces in New Mexico and Ciudad Juárez in Mexico.

The cities on the plain (as they are referred to in Cormac McCarthy's modern cowboy novels) are in the center of the sizzling Chihuahuan Desert, but because of the high altitude of the desert plain, the region is cooler than many desert areas. In El Paso, the average high is 31°C (88°F) with lows of 17°C (63°F). However, rainfall is still scarce. El Paso, Texas, gets 10 inches of rain, on average, per year, with the U.S. average being 38 inches.

The region will face severe climatological challenges. El Paso experienced 31 days of triple-digit heat per year on average between 2008 and 2018.[3] Heatwaves, storms, and high winds knock out power for thousands of homes and businesses several times a year and this can result in life-threatening conditions in the desert heat. Rain is scarce and lessening, and droughts are common. The last major drought lasted five years, 2010 to 2015.[4] The dangerously dry, hot, and harsh days will become repeat occurrences in the near future as extreme weather events increase.

300 ■ *Two American Cities in 2050*

However, the people of El Paso are resilient. Living in the middle of the harsh Chihuahuan Desert they have no other choice. In terms of climate change adaptation, El Paso is on the cutting edge of water conservation and reclamation. Immigration to El Paso has caused the city to sprawl and this creates additional carbon pollution, yet El Paso mitigates its rising carbon levels by providing more mass transit options than cities five times its size. El Paso strives to improve energy efficiency, energy conservation, alternative fuels, recycling, waste reduction, and climate protection. Even though it is precariously situated in one of the driest inhabited places on Earth, its focus on climate protection puts it far ahead of cities with twice its natural advantages. Nevertheless, despite El Paso's proactive efforts, one day – and that day will come all too soon – the city will be surely challenged like never before.

Desalinization in El Paso Today

Desert settlements were the first to be confronted with water shortages and they were the first communities in the U.S. forced to rethink water use priorities. El Paso is a forerunner in developing and testing innovative, efficient, and, it must be said, globally relevant, water-use technologies and policies. El Paso draws water from surface water plants on the Rio Grande, wells on the Hueco Aquifer east of the Franklin Mountains, wells on the Mesilla Aquifer west of the mountains, and the world's largest inland desalinization plant.

The desalinization plant might be of the most interest to the rest of the world, as this is a technology that we must assume will need to be deployed everywhere. El Paso has vast brackish (salty) groundwater resources – imagine underground rivers wider and deeper than the Rio Grande – and until the city began filtering salts these waters were undrinkable. The Kay Bailey Hutchison (KBH) Desalination Plant opened in 2007 and can produce up to 27.5 million gallons of fresh water daily. At the time of writing, it operates at a small percentage of its potential, currently producing just 3.5 million gallons per day.[5] The plant was opened primarily to accommodate growth at Fort Bliss.

Fort Bliss is a U.S. Army post in New Mexico and Texas, with its headquarters in El Paso. The name isn't ironic; it wasn't picked out of sheer sadism to toy with the minds of new arrivals to boot camp. It was named after an army officer, Lt. Col. William Wallace Smith Bliss, who had the good fortune to marry Zachary Taylor's (the 12th U.S. president) daughter. Fort Bliss contains over 1,700 square miles of area and, when combined with the adjacent White Sands Missile Range, it is one of the world's largest Army bases.[6] Fort Bliss is home to the 1st Armored Division, "American's Tank Division," which returned to the U.S in 2011 after 40 years in Germany, as well as many other commands and brigades. Fort Bliss has gained its importance in the military because it has the unique ability to train troops for desert warfare while still on U.S. soil.

The base received tens of millions in federal dollars for the Kay Bailey Hutchison (KBH) Desalination Plant project. Desalinization is reliable and drought-proof. It uses reverse osmosis which forces the salty water through a thin membrane that removes the salt and other impurities. It is tremendously expensive, however, and costs US$540,000 a year to produce roughly 3.5 million gallons.[7] The high price of desalinization makes it prohibitive. Desalination technology will get cheaper over time, but it will always introduce a technological dependency that comes with risk. We have to imagine a future in which the Federal government will need to build desalinization plants for cities across the country, even cities without such military importance, and then pay the enormous cost of their operation.

Water Recycling in El Paso Today

As important as desalinization may be, it is El Paso's commitment to water recycling that keeps the city hydrated. El Paso has decreased its water consumption from 220 gallons per capita per day (gpcd) in 1977 to just 125gpcd today, by passing water conservation ordinances, operating rebate programs, and periodically increasing the cost of water. El Paso Water Utilities treats and reclaims over 100 million gallons of water a day.[8]

This isn't to say that the water problem is solved. The population continues to grow in the region and El Paso is still dependent on the Rio Grande surface water for 45% of its water production. That's a precarious position to be in. The Rio Grande provides water for six million people in Colorado, New Mexico, Texas, and Mexico, and two million acres of cropland. Water levels in the Rio Grande are expected to decline by 10–30% between 2020 and 2050. A water supply shortage of almost 600,000 acre-feet is expected by 2060 in El Paso without ever factoring in climate change.[9] To give some perspective: Finding 600,000 acre-feet of additional water will be the equivalent of finding a surface water source about two-thirds as big as the State of Rhode Island.

Renewable Energy in El Paso Today

Continuously high solar radiation makes deserts ideal locations for solar cell installations, but El Paso has not yet tapped the potential of solar energy as an alternative to fossil fuels in any major way. Possible incentives to encourage the shift towards renewable energy sources could include taxes on pollution-generating burning of fossil fuels, and loans and grants for the use of solar and other renewable energy resources.

Fort Bliss is working on the U.S. military's largest solar power station, however, and that's exciting.[10] The Army will work with El Paso Electric to create a 20-megawatt solar farm that will power the division's headquarters and most of the

302 ■ *Two American Cities in 2050*

eastern sector of the sprawling military installation. The partnership would be the first between the military and a major local utility on a renewable energy project of such scale. Despite anti-renewable political rhetoric from various commanders-in-chief through the years, the military understands the importance of energy self-sufficiency and the value of cheap, solar energy. Elected officials in Washington D.C. who want to cut defense spending do not realize that the military does more than fight wars; it innovates when it comes to climate adaptation.

Mass Transit in El Paso Today

Transportation has surpassed power generation as the sector with the highest greenhouse gas emissions in the U.S. today.[11] In 2017, light-duty vehicles in the United States (including cars, SUVs, pickups and most of the vehicles used for everyday life) produced 1,098 million metric tons of CO_2 equivalents. That's about one-fifth of the country's total emissions footprint.[12]

In 2010, the El Paso City Council pledged to make El Paso the most walkable city in the Southwest. The city's Comprehensive Plan, *Plan El Paso* (2012), a planning project that I co-led, gave detailed strategies to accomplish that goal. The *Climate Change* section of the Sustainability Element in El Paso's Comprehensive Plan also tied that effort to climate resilience. The plan set a mitigation goal of reducing greenhouse gas (GHG) emissions by working to decrease the vehicle miles travelled (VMT) by car and increasing transit usage, cycling, and walking. The plan also seeks to use LEED (Leadership in Energy and Environmental Design) standards in new construction and encourage non-polluting energy generation.

Since the adoption of *Plan El Paso*, Sun Metro, the public transportation provider that serves El Paso, has completed a number of major initiatives and helped the city make quick progress toward the goal of becoming a more walkable city. Sun Metro began operating its express bus service, named *Brio*, in 2014, serving the west part of the city and travelling between Downtown El Paso and the Westside Transfer Center in Northwest El Paso. The frequency of Brio buses ranges from just 10 minutes during weekday rush hours to about 20 minutes on Saturdays. The line uses 22 purpose-built curbside stations with shelters, ticket vending machines for pre-boarding payment, and real-time arrival information. The system had an annual ridership of 12 million people in 2019.[13]

The Brio fleet consists of 60-foot-long buses powered by compressed natural gas, able to carry a total of 72 passengers at a time. The project cost US$27.1 million to implement, using local funds and a grant from the Federal Transit Administration. Sun Metro plans to open its second Brio route, extending the system east to Mission Valley via Alameda Avenue at a cost of US$35.5 million. Further routes north on Dyer Street and Montana Avenue are also planned.[14]

If I may be allowed a personal favorite when it comes to El Paso's growing transit alternatives, it would be the new electric streetcars. Sun Metro installed the El Paso Streetcar in 2018, a clean energy system which uses a fleet of restored historic streetcars that had once served both El Paso and Juarez, Mexico until the system's dismantlement in 1974. The revived system covers roughly five miles in two loops from Downtown El Paso to the University of Texas at El Paso.

The streetcar was the idea of Peter Svarzbein, an El Paso native and local artist, who has since become a city councilperson. Svarzbein began generating excitement for a streetcar by painting murals on the sides of buildings and hanging posters around the city which flatly stated that a bi-national streetcar would soon be arriving to pick up passengers. "Let us take you home ... on either side of the border," read one poster as part of a fictional ad campaign that included promotional videos. Svarzbein was hanging posters and making films advertising the streetcar before any transit agency had even begun discussing the idea. His fictional mascot, "The Conductor," smiled affably from the wheel of a fictional streetcar on murals all around the city.

People looked up at the murals and asked. "Why don't we have a streetcar?" The streetcar concept gained public support, and now El Paso is home to one of the country's most effective, and stylish (thanks to Svarzbein's artistic flair), new streetcar systems. In 2014, a US$97 million grant from the Texas Department of Transportation was used to retore six iconic streetcars which had been abandoned for 40 years in the desert near the El Paso International Airport.[15]

The *Plan El Paso* Comprehensive Plan project, headed on the city's side by Carlos Gallinar, now of Gallinar Planning & Development, was critical to securing TIGER grants (Transportation Investment Generating Economic Recovery) from the U.S. Department of Transportation for the buses and streetcars. Public transit and VMT reduction are two pillars of local greenhouse gas reduction strategies and El Paso is working to make multiple modes of mobility just as convenient as automobile usage. The move towards lower carbon vehicles and mass transit has been complemented by the development of walkable, compact urban fabric, especially around transit nodes. This theme was first discussed in the 2011 document *Connecting El Paso*, a project I also co-led working with Gallinar. The sprawling, car-dependent city of El Paso is urbanizing once again, and slowly kicking the car habit.

Has all this commitment to transit and walkable urbanism helped El Paso decrease the amount of GHGs it puts into the air? We don't know. This metric usually appears in a Climate Action Plan (CAP) and El Paso has yet to develop one. They need one. Gallinar ran for Mayor in 2020 and, had he won his bid, there is no doubt in my mind that El Paso would have a CAP today. While it is unlikely that carbon pollution is down given the rise in population, it is likely that the amount of vehicle miles travelled (VMT) per person has been significantly reduced. That's a start. I look forward to the day we can prove this.

Access to Parks in El Paso Today

In 2015, 46% of people living in El Paso County lived within a half mile of a park compared to 36% of people living in Texas.[16] Having access to places for physical

304 ■ *Two American Cities in 2050*

activity, like shady parks or indoor community facilities, encourages people to get active and do so more often. The closer you live to a park, community center, or community pool, the more likely you are to walk or bike there.

El Paso County had 92 days with maximum temperatures above 90°F from May to September 2016. Extreme summer heat is increasing in the United States, and climate projections indicate that extreme heat events will be more frequent and intense in coming decades. Extremely hot weather can cause illness or even death. That said, in the mornings and evenings, when people are more likely to go outdoors for exercise, the weather on El Paso's high desert plain is usually quite pleasant. El Paso has approved multiple quality of life bonds in order to build open spaces and recreational spaces, and we may reasonably assume that this kind of commitment will be needed in the future in order to keep parks accessible and the city livable as the world gets warmer and drier.

The Future

Let's study El Paso's future. Let's imagine a report, like you'd hear on National Public Radio or you'd read in *National Geographic*, from the year 2050.

El Paso, Texas in 2050: A Dispatch From the Future

Day Zero passed and the water stayed on. Day Zero, the name given to the day it was projected that half the city would turn on the faucet and not see a drop, was September 1, 2050. However, the crisis was averted – for a time, at least. The world's temperature had risen 2°C (3.6°F). Expectations were that it would reach 4°C (7.2°F) by 2100. Drinking water for the growing city was getting harder and harder to find in the Chihuahuan Desert.

Population in 2050

El Paso County's population had reached 1.7 million residents in 2050, sooner than anyone had expected.[17] The nearly 60% increase in population from 2010 was due in large part to migration from the failing farms of Latin America and South America and refugees fleeing other forms of climate-related instability. Mercifully, the U.S. had adopted a new conciliatory refugee category for those fleeing the effects of climate change, especially famine. Even Americans of a more conservative nature were not inclined to let the U.S. hide behind a wall while its neighbors to the south starved.

Just south of the border, within sight of El Paso, the Mexican city of Ciudad Juárez had topped 2.2 million residents. That city had also become a gathering place for people fleeing climate crisis instability. Water from the Rio Grande and

El Paso, Texas ■ 305

underground aquifers was shared across the border with Ciudad Juárez and dividing water resources required a delicate balance requiring new international treaties. Occasionally lawsuits erupted and political rhetoric over water rights flared.

Drinking Water in 2050

Six months before Day Zero in March 2050, El Paso had prudently begun drawing water from the Victorio Peak-Bone Springs aquifer in Dell City, roughly 100 miles east. The Dell City aquifer was a source of water El Paso did not have to share. While everyone was relieved that the water was online in time to avoid Day Zero, it was the first time in 150 years El Paso had to leave its county to secure water supplies. All of Texas was going farther for water, the number of legal fights over water at the State Supreme Court was rising, and El Paso felt lucky it had no other large American metropolis it had to share with. El Paso had, effectively, no eastern neighbor. The vast desert around El Paso and the relatively low per capita population densities of the region proved to be a saving grace. The harsh desert had saved the city.

In September 2050, the Victorio Peak-Bone Springs aquifer at Dell City was contributing 40 million gallons of water per day to the approximately 100 million gallons El Paso was using. The Dell City oasis would be drained and farming would cease there in time. Dell City got its name from the nursery rhyme, "The Farmer in the Dell," but it would be farmed no more. The cost to buy out the farmers and move water roughly 100 miles was enormous, and that cost was felt in local water bills.

In 2050, El Paso County drew 50% of its water from the aquifer wells of the Mesilla Bolson, Hueco Bolson, and Victorio Peak-Bone Springs; 40% from the surface water of the Rio Grande; and 10% from the Kay Bailey Hutchinson Desalinization Plant. The KBH Plant remained the largest non-seawater desalinization plant in the world and became a frequently toured facility by water managers from around the planet seeking to learn about desalinization in the desert. But desalinization was tremendously expensive and, worldwide, relatively few desalinization plants were planned.

El Paso continued to treat and reclaim 100 million gallons of water a day using a "pipe-to-pipe" system (specifically, wastewater pipe to kitchen faucet) and this was far more essential to the city's water portfolio than desalinization. Wastewater was no longer sent into the aquifer to be shared with Mexico; instead it went right back into the tap people drank from after advanced purification involving many steps – reverse osmosis, UV light, advanced oxidization, the application of activated carbon to absorb the remaining organic matter, and, finally, chlorination.

El Paso had perfected a kind of city-wide *Dune Suit*. The novel *Dune* (1965) by Frank Herbert described a desert planet where people survive because they have learned to conserve and recycle every possible trace of moisture. The *Dune Suit* (the *stillsuit* was its proper name in the book) was a full body suit that consisted of various layers that would absorb body moisture otherwise lost through breathing, sweating, or urination and then filter the impurities so that drinkable water would

306 ■ *Two American Cities in 2050*

be circulated to *catchpockets*. The suit's wearer could then drink the reclaimed water from the pockets using a tube attached to their neck. El Paso had put the "icky-ness" factor aside relatively quickly and received publicity and prestige for its commitment to never wasting a single drop.

Technological advancement aside, the primary water source remained the aquifers, and the Hueco and Mesilla groundwater bolsons were draining as the aquifers were being used faster than they could replenish. Leaders in El Paso, Juarez, and Las Cruces talked about giving the Hueco and Mesilla bolsons "a rest" to regenerate. They talked of reducing water draws to less than the natural recharge capability of the water sources. However, population pressures proved too great and El Paso had to admit that the bolsons were unsustainable water supplies. Still, the city had no other options.

The Rio Grande was also drying as the Colorado snowpack that melted into the Rio Grande began to decline. Rio Grande water levels declined 30% between 2020 and 2050, yet the Rio Grande continued to provide water for ten million people in Colorado, New Mexico, Texas, and Mexico, and three million acres of cropland.

El Paso Water, the regional water utility, was quietly progressing with land and water rights acquisitions even farther away than Dell City in order to enable El Paso to continue to survive. As it carried on its search for a drought-proof, sustainable supply of water, the water-provider was named a *Water Hero* by the Environmental Protection Agency every year the honor was given. The city's water consumption had gone from 250gpcd (gallons per capita per day) in 1997 to 125gpcd in 2050, thanks to some of the country's most progressive water conservation ordinances, advanced water reclamation and reuse technologies, expanded desalinization, and, ultimately, high water rates. The cost of water made people conscious of water use. When adjusted for inflation, the cost of water and sewer utilities for households in El Paso had more than doubled. Local programs helped lower income households pay their water bill but could only shield the most vulnerable.

El Paso looked drier in 2050 than ever before, and this was a major quality of life issue. The population had doubled, and the city grew in size west and north, but outdoor water use could not be allowed to increase correspondingly. Smaller home lots with less vegetation were the norm. Swimming pools were an increasingly rare luxury. The days of beautiful, but water-consumptive exotic shrubs, groundcover, and trees in the planting strips along the streets and in backyards had passed. Neighborhoods like Sunset Heights and Kern no longer hosted Date Palms, tulips, hydrangeas, or turf grass. Local households used cacti, ocotillo, sage, agave, yucca, and rock xeriscaping to create beauty, and, thus, make a virtue of necessity. Tree cover was used strategically to add shade to pedestrian areas. Mesquite, Palo Verde, and other desert trees were drip-fed with highly economical, but still expensive, systems.

Dust storms became a common phenomenon in El Paso and the surrounding Chihuahuan Desert lowland areas, especially in the spring season. Every day brought an encounter with blowing dust. On some days, consequences ranged from simple irritations and increased particulate matter concentrations to serious disruptive

El Paso, Texas ■ 307

events aggravating respiratory health problems. Deadly fatal collisions in near-zero visibility on city roadways and highways in the surrounding desert were tragically common.

Flooding in 2050

Although El Paso received only approximately 8 inches of total rainfall a year in 2050, flooding still occurred under light rainfall conditions and unexpectedly. Even 2–4 inches of rain could become dangerous when focused on a small geographic area with steep slopes, slick soils, a lack of supportive plant material, degraded arroyo systems, and inadequate stormwater infrastructure. Fatal flash floods rocketing down from the Franklin Mountains cost lives. The city and county gave greater protections to the arroyos so that the stream channels could help direct and absorb water. New neighborhoods were built around the arroyos instead of paving over them, and the chaotic and dangerous effects of flash floods were largely mitigated.

CO_2 Pollution in 2050

When global carbon pollution peaked in 2040 so did El Paso's. But the world had decoupled economic growth with rises in CO_2 emissions and so did El Paso. The widespread use of the electric engine in trucking and freight services helped El Paso, one of the world's largest inland ports, to reduce local particulate pollution from vehicle exhaust and to reduce the carbon emissions previously emitted by all the fossil fuel engines that travelled the pass. In 2050 El Paso measured its greenhouse gas emissions at 60% below 2020 levels despite the city's tremendous population growth. Total GHG Emissions were estimated at 3.1m metric tons CO_2 per year by the City of El Paso's Climate Adaptation Plan. LEED building requirements had reduced building emissions to 4.1m metric tons CO_2 per year – a decrease of 30%. Transportation systems emitted 1.1m metric tons CO_2 per year – a decrease of 65%.

At the same time, El Paso, like many desert cities, became an energy power-house, capturing solar energy with a 10-square mile solar farm located in the desert east of the city in an area that was previously slated for suburban expansion. The city made use of cheap, easily accessible, treeless, and flat land. The La Ciudad Solar installation consisted of 4 million solar panels. The plant's sheer size and 850 megawatts capacity made it the largest solar farm in Texas. The solar park generated around 220-gigwatt hours of electricity per year, which is the equivalent of powering 200,000 households.

Following the 2015 Paris Agreement, there was a surge in the number of solar farms being built as governments all over the world worked to reach their national clean energy targets and contribute to reducing global carbon emissions. For a long period, the U.S. had led the world in mega solar farms but, in time, India and China dominated the space with multiple large-scale projects. When it was completed, El Paso's La Ciudad Solar was not even in the top 25 list of world's largest solar farms.

308 ■ *Two American Cities in 2050*

Even still, El Paso's proximity to Ciudad Juarez in Mexico and Las Cruces in New Mexico meant lengthy power connections were not necessary to capitalize on the manufacturing of energy. Many remote desert locations in the world were unable to benefit from the world's shift to solar because of their remoteness. Not El Paso. Thanks to cheap, locally available solar, El Pasoans saw no rise in energy costs per household after the region made the shift to 55% solar power (8.7b kilowatt hours per year), and solar became a major industry in the city and paid significant local property taxes which funded city services.

Far more El Pasoans were employed by what was termed *the Green Economy* than the fossil fuel economy in administration, construction, deployment, and maintenance of solar technologies. El Paso saw an increase of 30,000 additional professional and technical services and most were related to the Green Economy. Juarez, Mexico, was home to two electric car factories and electric cars produced nearby made up 32% of the El Paso-Las Cruces combined statistical area's automotive fleet. This was less the 55% national average due to the fact that El Paso had lower median incomes and residents had a low rate of car replacement. Subsequently, the City of El Paso and El Paso County offered property tax credits to encourage the proliferation of electric vehicles.

Formerly "wasted space" had been retooled for the Green Economy. Most surface parking lots in the city were shaded by solar arrays and long shaded walkways topped with photovoltaic panels allowed residents to walk along a central downtown path. Outside the city, carbon sinks and storage in the form of wild grasslands and alfalfa cover crops over fields watered by the Rio Grande were estimated to pull 2.1m metric tons of carbon from the atmosphere. Re-wilding and re-foresting efforts involved the planting of millions of trees and bunchgrass shrubs wherever the soil could support vegetative life without additional watering. Wild land protection and reforesting were supported by State and Federal grants.

Land Use and Transportation in 2050

El Paso did its best to follow its Climate Adaptation Plans and Sustainability Plans. The Future Land Use Map in the City's Comprehensive Plan set the groundwork for growth management controls which created a kind of greenbelt around the city and slowed outward expansion. The rate of city expansion to the east of downtown had decreased significantly from previous periods. On the whole, El Paso was a city that was infilling, building up and not out, *re-filling* its formerly emptied downtown with buildings and parks, and densifying the surrounding neighborhoods around transit investments. Rising skyward, 20-story towers were constructed once again in the downtown in a way the city hadn't seen done since the 1930s.

A massive expansion of public transport reduced transportation emissions as the city (like the rest of the world) worked to phase out fossil fuel burning engines. Over 40% of the population lived within a 5-minute of walk quality transit, and high-speed rail connected El Paso to Denver in seven hours. Increased transit in the core of the city led to the construction of affordable housing around transit centers. Historically, the lack of density and affordable housing in downtown had pushed people farther and farther out, but by 2050 this outward migration had largely turned inward. El Paso remained an affordable city despite the population increases thanks to policies requiring urban infill, suburban retrofit, and higher density living.

Between 2020 and 2050 the city had continued to sprawl, however, as an additional 75 square miles of arid desert had been converted to water-consumptive suburbs. To the west of downtown, 14,000 acres of farmland had been converted despite transfer of development rights and clustering requirements that worked to contain new development to previously developed lands.

"City Apologizes as Traffic Jams Worsen," was a repeated news headline. El Pasoans spent more time in traffic in 2050, though they traveled less far on average. Multiple major roadways dropped below a Level of Service F, a failing level of performance by Department of Transportation standards. As the city became practically immobilized at peak times by traffic, El Paso moved from 92% of trips by car to 86% of trips by car. In 2020, households traveled 24,100 miles a year per household, or 66 miles a day. In 2050, households traveled 22,900 miles a year per household, or 62 miles a day.

Household transportation costs were less. Automobile ownership and maintenance per household went down as El Pasoans more and more tended to own one car per household. In 2020, households spent US$18,000 per year on car ownership, maintenance, fuel, and transit, and that number went down to US$10,100 per year by 2050.

Economy in 2050

El Paso's economy saw an increase from 326,000 total jobs in 2020 to 660,000 total jobs in 2050. At the same time, El Paso saw an increase in poverty. The percentage of households in poverty went from 20% of the county population in 2020, to 35% in 2060, due, in large part, to migrants from Mexico, Latin America, and South America. Unemployment doubled from 4% to 8% during the same period. Poverty and unemployment was clustered in two areas: City neighborhoods near the border, and in new settlements out east.

With the increase in displaced persons, El Paso saw a renaissance of arts and culture including music (from traditional Mariachi to world dance club), public art installed in newly revamped public spaces (from local hobbyists working with pottery to international celebrities painting three-story high concrete canvases), new museums, a variety of holiday celebrations, inexpensive cantinas that exhibited art on every wall, and galleries of all kinds. The artistic resurgence was centered in the downtown and El Paso was compared to Juarez, Mexico, during its artistic heyday in the 1970s, and to Mexico City with its perennially exuberant and colorful culture.

310 ■ *Two American Cities in 2050*

Fort Bliss, headquartered in El Paso, retained the 1st Armored Division with its 21,000 soldiers. However, the base did not see increases in soldiers or in military investment. Military engagements around the world occurred less in Middle Eastern desert regions because of the United States' decreased reliance on foreign oil and increased use of renewable energy sources. The world's Oil Wars were winding down.

Some increases in the base population occurred as Fort Bliss remained home to missile, artillery, and drone training and testing. In general, conflicts occurred around the world in more varied environments and this meant more training areas in mountainous states, plain states, and sub-tropical states were needed. Fort Bliss continued to contribute US$1.7 billion to the economy of El Paso. One notable contribution the base made was on the "green front," as it was described nationally. By 2050, El Paso had succeeded in becoming a net zero energy installation and the Fort was home to the largest solar farm within the U.S. military. Military expenditure remained popular in America and that spending was refocused on a threat greater than war or terrorism: The Climate Emergency.

Severe heat meant low crop yields for row crops such as corn, leafy greens, peanuts, and onions in the Mission Valley and Mesilla Valley. Lower yields ruined many livelihoods in farming. However, farm yields on row crops remained high enough to still employ large numbers and to continue to export farm products. In the city's river valleys, pecan farms, ornamental plant farms, palm tree farms, and vineyards could still be found, but their numbers were decreasing as the cost to supply growers with water increased.

Heat in 2050

The 2°C (3.6°F) increase in worldwide temperatures by 2050 was a global average, and in El Paso and other desert regions it was hotter. El Paso heated up by more than 2.7°C (5°F) on average. Every year the city experienced more than three months of temperatures over 100 degrees. Local weather forecasters talked routinely of "triple-digit days," and "off-the-charts" heat conditions.

Heat exposure continued to be the biggest killer of El Paso residents in terms of natural hazards. Outdoor construction during the middle of the day had become prohibited by state workplace safety standards. The prohibitions on construction during unhealthy weather hampered the construction economy. The difference between daytime and nighttime temperatures decreased and for the first time El Paso experienced nighttime deaths involving heat and dehydration. These deaths were due in large part to preexisting health conditions but, nevertheless, new restrictions were issued regarding outdoor work during nighttime heat.

As a heat mitigation response, El Paso planted thousands of low-water trees and brought down temperatures in urban areas under the new desert tree canopy. Trees weren't enough, however, and El Paso erected outdoor walkways topped with solar panels between all the major downtown walking destinations. Downtown buildings once again had galleries, arcades, and colonnades to shade pedestrians. Thanks to the commitment to building outdoor shade, walking and cycling remained a safe and even comfortable experience during commutes in the mornings and evenings.

Prior to 2020, El Paso averaged 3 inches of snow per year. The white powder that once lightly dusted the wide expanses and blew in the wind hadn't been seen in a long time by 2050. No one could say when the last snowfall had been – it seemed too common an event to be recorded by local meteorologists/ However, by 2050 snow was a distant memory.

Worldwide, global warming did not continue unchecked and absolute disaster was avoided. Greenhouse gas emissions were curtailed, and the average annual temperatures did not rise beyond the climate niche in which humans had thrived for the 6,000 years. This shift prevented conditions warmer than suitable for human life and the world stayed livable. However, in desert places like El Paso, the effects of climate change were felt the hardest.

Energy in 2050

By 2050, El Paso was on track to use 100% renewable energy in the form of solar and wind power, thus synching it with the State of Texas' commitment to total renewable energy by 2100. The effort began in earnest when the City of El Paso and El Paso County, with the help of state and federal funding, spent millions of dollars to retrofit public buildings for energy efficiency, and coated the rooftops of public buildings in solar panels to decrease their reliance on fossil fuel sources. The next step involved powering all of the city's public schools with solar arrays. After 2050, all of El Paso's new buildings were required to include solar panels by city ordinance.

Like most large, private utility monopolies across the U.S., El Paso Electric initially resisted the switch to solar power and spent ratepayer dollars to lobby intensely against public mandates to upgrade facilities and against the individual's right to choose home energy generation. However, a ballot measure approved by voters and upheld by the Texas Supreme Court allowed customers to pick their electricity providers from a competitive market and gave residents the option to produce solar energy themselves. Eventually, El Paso Electric transitioned to large scale solar facilities in response to microgrids of autonomously operating energy providers capable of disconnecting from the traditional El Paso power grid. Similarly, the nation's electric utility industry was reinvented one state at a time. By 2050, large-scale photovoltaic solar farms covered 2.6 million acres of land in the U.S., more than three times the size of Rhode Island.

Many El Paso homes used geothermal heat pumps to decrease energy costs. Geothermal pumps took advantage of the fact that the ground beneath homes tended to stay about 50°F in summer or winter. Pipes placed 6 to 8 feet below single-family houses and apartment buildings cooled the liquids they carried to around 50°F. That liquid was then piped up to the buildings and used to cool indoor temperatures. During hot summer days in excess of 100 degrees, El Pasoans could cool their homes with almost no expenditure of energy.

Looking Forward: From 2050 to 2100

Despite the political vacillation, the rhetorical pendulum-swings, and the endorsement and rejection of world climate accords, the U.S. government continued to deal with climate change seriously. The American public viewed climate heating as a major threat to national security and citizen wellbeing. Moratoriums on oil and gas leases on public lands quietly went unchallenged, fracking and offshore drilling were limited to only a few states, and carbon was taxed like any other pollutant in order to discourage its use. While the U.S. economy had not achieved carbon neutrality by 2050, the promise of net-zero carbon emissions remained a perennial campaign promise of every major political party.

Human settlement continued in the Chihuahuan Desert, against the backdrop of the indigo Sierra de Juarez Mountains and the tall black Franklin Mountains. The cities and towns continued to provide oases. The vast urban nowhere of the suburban sprawl era were slowly becoming dense with clustered people wherever there was still water. On most days, it was 102°F at El Paso's Downtown Farmer's Market, but El Pasoans continued to go. The sky was flower orange, more Martian than earthly, but the vendor's trucks still arrived, pulling dust behind them. People continued to stand shoulder to shoulder to listen to music in the plazas most evenings, and the shining Milky Way still continued to humble everyone at night.

Notes

1 2018 population according to U.S. census for city of El Paso. Retrieved from: www. elpasotexas.gov
2 2018 population according to U.S. census for El Paso County. Retrieved from: www. epcounty.com
3 National Weather Service. Retrieved from: www.weather.gov/epz/elpaso_100_degree_page
4 Texas Water Development Board. Retrieved from www.waterdatafortexas.org/drought
5 El Paso Water in collaboration with Alan Plummer Associates (2019). El Paso water utilities 2019 water conservation plan. Retrieved from: www.texaswater.org/all-resources/el-paso-water-conservation-plan-2019
6 GlobalSecurity.org (2006). Fort Bliss. Retrieved from: www.globalsecurity.org/military/facility/fort-bliss.htm
7 El Paso Water in collaboration with Alan Plummer Associates, op. cit.
8 Ibid.
9 Rio Grande Regional Water Authority (2013). Lower Rio Grande Basin Study, 2013. Retrieved from: www.usbr.gov/watersmart/bsp/docs/finalreport/LowerRioGrande/LowerRioGrandeBasinStudy.pdf
10 Amusa, Malena (2013). The military's Fort Bliss solar farm will be its biggest. Retrieved from: https://tinyurl.com/3snexf97
11 United States Environmental Protection Agency (n.d.). Green vehicle guide: fast facts on transportation greenhouse gas emissions. Retrieved from: www.epa.gov/greenvehicles/fast-facts-transportation-greenhouse-gas-emissions

12 Ibid.
13 *Sun Metro* (2020). Transit fact sheet. Retrieved from: www.sunmetro.net/~/media/files/sunmetro/factsheet.ashx?la=en
14 Rodriguez, Ashlie (2015). Dyer Rapid Transit System to start construction around late 2017. *KVIA-TV*. Retrieved from: https://kvia.com/news/city-will-unveil-the-dyer-rapid-transit-system-design-tonight-at-6p/36881134
15 Merck, Amanda (2017). Artist's fake ads save historic streetcars in Border City. *Salud America*, October 11. Retrieved from: https://salud-america.org/artist-saves-historic-streetcar-in-border-city/
16 Centres for Disease Control and Prevention (n.d.). Retrieved from: https://ephtracking.cdc.gov/InfoByLocation/
17 Projected information. Retrieved from: https://epwater.org/cms/One.aspx?portalId=6843488&pageId=7416474

Conclusion

The Way Forward

I hope that this book helps to build a little more climate resolve by presenting success stories that almost weren't. And I hope it was helpful to hear about the process as well as the solutions. None of the stories in this book end with statements like: "And thanks to the actions we took the city's carbon pollution decreased by 25% every year since plan adoption." The stories are more nuanced. Victories were counted differently. This book describes a great many half-measures, because in many communities that's often the best we can achieve at this time. *Do what you can, with what you have, where you are*, encouraged Theodore Roosevelt. One day the scale of the solution may just match the scale of the problem, but, for now, we must count every small advancement.

Looking back, I see that the climate policies which have been implemented and the climate solutions which have been built rarely live up to the vision in the plan or rendering. However, I can also see that the plan's values were clearly evident in city decisions. The planning process helps inform decisions never envisioned by the plan. Something always comes of planning. Sometimes the effect is small or merely symbolic. Sometimes it is easy to overlook or it is eclipsed by what feels like a defeat. The 1971 book *The Lorax* (by Dr. Seuss) was close to having a downer ending, but it didn't. The Once-Ler gave the child the last Trufula seed. Tiny rays of hope emanate from every plan. Look for them.

There is no shortage of good ideas about how to mitigate and adapt to climate change but there is a shortage of leaders with the will to take action. City managers and elected officials are not trained to think about the future, and I suspect that they will learn to rely more on future-oriented urban planners as the climate worsens, the world's climate ethic builds, and more is demanded of local leadership. Urban planners have the power to educate elected leaders and the public and build systems that will reduce future damage. Government can't create consensus behind tough decisions unless it commands confidence that it knows what it is doing, however, and the field of urban planning will need to commit to climate planning and learn

DOI: 10.4324/9781003181514-19

316 ■ Conclusion: The Way Forward

Figure 13 The Farmhouse at Sandywoods Farm, Tiverton, Rhode Island

the difference between what works and what doesn't in order to stay relevant. We'll need evidence-based answers and success stories.

Climate planning is the new focus. The other goals remain, but climate must be first. The urgency of the other goals will begin to pale by comparison. Climate is the *cause célèbre* of the day, but it is more than that. You were students, urban planners, and citizen activists but soon you will be climate planners and climate activists. Refashion your tools, modify them, and invent new ones.

Begin with the proverbial "carrots" of the carrot-and-stick package that regulators have and add to those. This includes approvals, waivers, and expedited permitting. Next, turn optional guidelines into mandatory requirements. New regulations are more impactful than any incentive. Be bold. Recommend 15 requirements for new buildings, streets, and public spaces with each new plan and code update, and let the defenders of the status quo whittle your recommendations down to five or six. Every once in a while, urban planners should push the issue within an inch of their jobs. We're altruistically motivated people. We hear a call.

The field of urban planning is less about what should happen and more about what can happen. City planning is less an arena of good ideas than one of interests. Technocratic planners who conduct objective studies of problems and solutions, and then offer them without a consideration of limitations, are less effective than those who make political and financial assessments first, and then plan and act accordingly. We all know this instinctively. However, when it comes to climate planning, we will need to be bolder and more courageous because climate mitigation and adaptation happens at the local level and no less than the world is at stake. The problem with utopians is that they are not practical, it is true, but the problem with strict pragmatists is that they lack vision. Urban planners and local advocates will need to offer vision, and this means a new level purpose and meaning for those planners and for the communities they lead.

The climate problem is baffling, the opposition is committed (the opposition is often us, the people who love the world as it is too much to make any changes), and we each have a near infinite ability to take our world for granted. The results will be incrementable and often impossible to see. It will take a long time to reverse the course of this supertanker. But if you work on climate you will know that you are working to make the world a little better. And that's a lot.

Index

Note: Page numbers in *italics* indicate a figure on the corresponding page.

"2 degrees Celsius" climate goal 21
100 Resilient Cities Program 51, 248

accessory dwelling units 152, 154, 238
adapting buildings 62
affordable housing, provision of 59, 69–70, 93, 152, 168–169, 171, 176, 192, 259, 309
Agenda 21, 43–46, 233; *Agenda 21* (novel) 43; conspiracy theory 43, 45, 225; drafting of 43; principles of 43–44; proposals about wealth redistribution 43
agriculture/agricultural: loss of 138; preserves 174, 176; revolution 108
air-conditioning, proliferation of 285
air pollution 208; in heat islands 196; indoor 65
Alemán, Jon Elizabeth 158
algae blooms 36, 224
Al-Haqqani, Nazim 15
alternative energy 34, 107
American Coalition 4 Property Rights (AC4PR) 29, 31, 42, 45
American Dream of homeownership 169
American Institute of Architects (AIA) 112
American Institute of Certified Planner (AICP) 209
American Planning Association 71, 118, 194, 208–209, 277
American way of life 40
Anthropocene era 70, 98
anti-capitalism 109
anti-poverty programs 69
apartment buildings 30, 37, 82, 152–154, 311
aquifers 128; Hueco Bolson 136, 300; recharge zones 133, 138; Victorio Peak-Bone Springs 305
aridification: droughts caused due to 195; measurement of 195; process of 195

Art Deco Festival (1977) 119, 122
automobile ownership 166, 309
automotive industry, collapse of 164

backflow preventers 165
Barbican Wall, The 293
barrier islands 76, 78, 112–113, 116, 119–122, 237, 289–290, 293
Base Flood Elevation (BFE) 156
Baton Rouge, Louisiana 74, 78, 98, 107, 109
Bayou Fuel 81
beach-and-habitat-creation pumps 115
Beckles, Winter 92–93
bed taxes 293
Before the Flood (2016) 157
Bellamy, Edward 282
Bergh, Chris 117–118
bicycle-sharing system 10; *see also* car-sharing programs
bioswales 186, 198, 213
Birther Movement 45
Biscayne Bay 218, 221–223
Biscayne Canal 116
bleaching 101–102, 180, 228
Bliss, William Wallace Smith 300
block grant programs 69
blue and green: infrastructure 159; strategy for climate adaptation 159
blue-collar workforce 108
blue roof (water retaining roof) 104, 212
Borges, Renaldo 112
Boulder's Resilience Study 69
Bourgeois, Shaun 69
Boy Scout Eagle Badge projects 183
brainstorming 158, 259–260
Broome, Camille Manning 107
Brown Anole (*Anolis segrei*) 92

319

320 ■ *Index*

building codes 10, 12; in California 146; certification standards 61; hurricane building codes 32; LEED v4.1 BD+C guidelines 61; in Miami 112; regulation of 41
built environment 2, 266, 287
Burchell, Robert 47
Burnham, Daniel 255, 278–279
"business-as-usual" emissions scenario 283
Bus Rapid Transit (BRT) 38, 67, 166, 266

C40 Cities 92, 95, 105n10
California: building codes in 146; Camp Fire (2018) 146–147; fire hazards in 146; fire prevention requirements 146; Grand Jury report 146; home construction in fire-prone areas 146; Long-Term Recovery Plan 147; Paradise 147; zoning laws in 146
Camus, Albert 130
canyon effect 213
Capital Improvements Plans (CIPs) 5, 58, 65–67, 248, 267; Capital Planning Office 67; climate mitigation and adaptation projects 67; General Obligation (G.O.) bond referendum 66; involvement of people in 67–68; planning process 66
capital investments 66
carbon: action plan for cutting 275; capture mechanisms 193; carbon-driven capitalism 109; carbon-free zoning 32; cycle 172, 192; footprint 10, 60, 116, 138, 175, 213; pollution 10, 36, 43, 129, 192; reduction treaties 3; sequestering 171–172, 175–176, 186, 196; sinks 169, 171, 180, 201, 265, 308; soot 97; storage of 172; taxes 58, 279; vehicles 303
carbon dioxide (CO_2) 2, 91, 140, 179, 191; absorption of 59; in Anthropocene era 70; and the atmosphere 96–99; atmospheric concentrations of 71; *Carbon Dioxide and the Climate: A Scientific Assessment* (1979) 18; as greenhouse gas 97; in Holocene era 71; human-induced emission of 101; land use and transportation effecting emission of 99; in late Ordovician Period 97; polluting sources of 111; pollution in El Paso, Texas 307–308; in pre-Cambrian and Cambrian periods 71; savings of mass transit systems 103; time scales required for removal from the atmosphere 192
carbon emissions 36, 56, 95, 107, 166, 266, 293; China's pledge to eliminate 64; India's pledge to eliminate 65; net-zero emissions 312
carbon neutrality 63, 312; and adaptation goals 62; Carbon Neutral Pathways Assessment 62
CARES Act (2020) 55

Carpenter, Charles Chris 99–103
car-sharing programs 266
Casey Farm, Rhode Island 168, 172–173, 237
Casey, John L. 32, 37
catchpockets 306
Cave Man Flu 56
Center for Disease Control (CDC) 253, 266
Center for Planning Excellence (CPEX) 79, 107
charitable organizations 68, 184
charrettes 47, 68, 79, 81–82, 84, 122, 158, 244–245, 255
chemical run-off 172
Chernow, Ron 22
Chicago Climate Action Plan (CCAP) 58
Chihuahuan Desert 135, 299–300, 304, 306, 312
cholera outbreaks 110, 115
cigarette smoking: campaign to end 20; link with lung cancer 20; rates of 20; United States Surgeon General's report on 20
Ciraldo, Daniel 123
cityscape 196
city-wide resilience infrastructure 113
clean energy 94, 225, 302, 307
cleaner transit 259
clean technology 179
climate: Climate Protection Action Committee 12; Climate Smart Communities 247; Climate Vulnerability Forum 110; emergency 127, 130, 135, 256, 310; mega-project 116; resilience investment 38
Climate Action Plans (CAPs) 112, 243, 264, 303; *Climate Action Planning Guide* 247; for reducing greenhouse gas emissions 247; tax 58–59
climate change 1, 21, 156, 180, 206–207, 221, 231–232, 277; call to action 130; climate emergency 127; conference 94, 138; data gathering 16; denial and agnosticism 20–22; global awareness of 137; global commitment to fighting 99; as global problem 21; impacts of 10, 267–269; Intergovernmental Panel on Climate Change (IPCC) 2, 17–20; myth of 15–16; political implications of 103; propaganda on 22; relation with pandemic 56; science of 16–17; symptoms of 208–209; threat of 4; tipping point in 71; universal agreement among nations to tackle 94; Virginia Key Boulevard Levee 117
climate crisis conversation 2, 12, 15, 62, 129–130, 210–211, 213; community-character-*versus*-development dialogue 130; "save the trees" conversation 130

Index ■ **321**

climate mitigation and adaptation 65, 112, 118, 129, 169, 243; funding for 24, 57; initiatives in 10; projects on the CIP 67; water supply resiliency and 194

climate planning 1, 67, 129, 243; adaptation element of 244; assembling a Plan Advisory Committee 250–251; assembling the plan team 249; Big Five Ideas 263; Capital Improvements Program 267; Capital Planning Office 67; communicate publicly through interactive websites 253–254; community design element of 264–265; community facilities 267; Community Goals Statement 263–264; conduct of listening workshop 254–255; dealing with setbacks 275–280; determination of plan boundaries and their adoption 249–250; development of the preliminary draft 262–269; economic development and 264; emergency hazard plans 129; energy element of 266–267; growth framework element of 264; in Hammond, Louisiana 149–153; health element of 266; holding of project kick-off meeting 251; implementation and evaluating progress of 271–272; implementation strategy of 267; infrastructure element of 265; involvement of people in 67–68; kick-off and previous plan review 251–255; kinds of 243–245; living plan 272; Local Government Operations (LGOP) 256; mitigation element of 244, 252–253, 256, 258, 264; mobility element of 266; natural and cultural resources 265; plan direction and team creation 247–251; plan-making process 2; preparation for plan presentations and adoption 270–271; preparation of final draft and adoption 269–271; preparation of plan and report review 270; public design workshop for 244; public involvement on 2; public outreach and participation plan 251–252; reasons for U.S. to lead in 64–65; Request for Proposals for 68; review of previous plan and information gathering 252–253; stages of drafting 4; sustainability of 265–266; through forums and roundtables 66; visioning and galvanizing 255–262; vision plan component of 261

climate-related catastrophe 21

climate-related instability 304

coal-fired power station 64, 225

coast/coastal: drinking water, loss of 289; flooding 17; landforms, erosion of 17; municipalities, street plans of 50, 155; wetlands 266, 288

coastal armoring: annual maintenance of 49; disadvantage of 49; as flood protection tool 49; super levees 49

Coastal Protection and Restoration Authority of Louisiana 76

communal gardens 172

community: buildings 267; Community Involvement Session 256, 258; Community Redevelopment Agency (CRA) 58, 160; Community Supported Agriculture (CSA) programs 168, 173; design 264–265; facilities 267; image survey 257

community development 69, 248; Community Development Block Grant (CDBG) 68–69; Community Development Block Grant-Disaster Recovery (CDBG-DR) funds 68

Commuter Rail and Bus Rapid Transit 38

Compact of Mayors 62

Comprehensive Housing Act (2004) 169

Comprehensive Planning 252; and energy 111; *Practice of Local Government Planning, The* (2000) 248; process of 248; resilience elements 248; sustainability elements 248

compressed natural gas 302

Conaway, Marlene 91

Connecting El Paso project 303

constructive resilience 123

cooperative farming 173

coral bleaching *see* bleaching

Coral Gables, Florida 199, 201

coral reefs: bleaching of 101–102, 180; and coastal habitats 99–101; destruction of 102; fish populations in 102; Great Barrier Reef 102; impact of global warming on 102; life–death–life cycles of 102

corridor redevelopment 267

corruption, accusation of 92

COVID-19 pandemic 16, 55–56, 93, 127, 158, 248, 259

Co-Water Adequacy Rule (Colorado) 194

crop yields, decreasing of 179

Curtatone, Joseph 61–62

Dalbin, Frederic 138

Daquisto, David 188

DARA Group 110

Day After Tomorrow, The (2004) 127

dealing with setbacks, in climate planning 275–280; by keeping at it 279–280; by keeping the conversation going 278–279; by rebranding the effort 277; by seeking outside validation 277–278; settling down with long-term goals 275–276; working with the opposition 276

322 ■ Index

decision-making 207, 221–224, 278
deep injection wells 223
deforestation 168
Degrowth movement 109
Delphi mind control 40
demographic and density quotas 32
desalinization: in El Paso, Texas 300–301, 305;
  Kay Bailey Hutchison (KBH) Desalination
  Plant project 300–301, 305; solar-powered
  plants for 292; technology for 301
DeSantis, Ron 158
desert: cities, abandonment of 192, 307;
  settlements 300
development services 129, 211
Development Studies 248
dike-in-dune systems 113
Dircke, Piet 113, 115, 117
disaster planning, during Hurricane *Dorian*
  218–221
distortion of evidence and facts for money
  92–93
Dixon, Ralph Murray 112
Dougherty, James 80, 82, 183
Dover, Kohl & Partners 24, 79, 119, 174
downtown amenities 210
Downtown Master Plan (Missoula, Montana)
  129, 137–138
Downtown Plan and Development Code 206
drinking water 37, 138, 141, 160, 192,
  194–195, 208, 223, 268, 289, 304; effect of
  salination on 181; in El Paso, Texas
  305–307; Hueco Bolson aquifer 136; presence
  of mercury and lead in 110; rising cost of 128,
  163; in State of Florida 292
droughts: causes of 195; contingency plans 133;
  due to aridification 195; due to escalation
  of global warming 194; *Falling Dominoes:
  A Planner's Guide to Drought and Cascading
  Impacts* (2019) 194; Hazard Mitigation Plans
  195; impact on water resource management
  194; IPCC Special Report on 194; in
  Lubbock, Texas 205–212; mega-droughts
  194; mitigation assessment tools 195;
  mitigation requirements 194; problem of
  194–196; risk assessments 195; water resource
  inventories 195
Dr. Strangelove (1964) 221
Duany, Andres 41–43
Duany Plater-Zyberk (DPZ) 41
Dune (1965) 305
Dune Suit 305
Dustbowl Era 98
dust storms 306
Dutch solution, for urban planning 114–115

Earth Day (April 22, 2016) 56, 94
ecology, law of 102
economic development 28, 37–38, 58, 69–70,
  80, 93, 108, 129, 135–138, 183, 247, 254,
  263, 264, 299
economic resilience 134
Eco Pass (bus pass) subsidies 59
ecotourism 237
edible gardens 31
Egalond, Yan 182
electricity: de-carbonization of 63;
  generation of 109
electric vehicles: charging stations for 212;
  electrical vehicle supply equipment (EVSE)
  212; proliferation of 308; streetcars 67,
  302–303
Elevate Las Cruces Comprehensive Plan
  (2019) 95
El Nino (ENSO) 97
El Paso, Texas 136, 210, 282, 297–312; in
  2050 304–311; access to parks in 303–304;
  American El Pasoans 139; arts and culture
  development 299; automobile ownership
  309; Brio fleet 302; Burnham building
  298; Chamber of Commerce 132–134;
  City Council 302; Climate Adaptation Plan
  307, 308; climatological challenges 299;
  CO_2 pollution in 307–308; Coffee Box
  restaurant 299; Comprehensive Plan 302–303;
  Connecting El Paso project 303; construction of
  affordable housing in 309; County Economic
  Development Department 137; Day Zero
  304–305; desalinization in
  300–301; downtown resurgence in 134;
  drinking water in 305–307; drought
  contingency plans 133; *Dune Suit* 305;
  economic resilience 134; economy in
  309–310; *El Paso: 2050* model 140; energy
  in 311; flooding in 307; Fort Bliss (U.S.
  Army post) 300; Future Land Use Map
  133, 308; goal of reducing greenhouse gas
  (GHG) emissions 302; green economy 308;
  heat exposure in 310–311; high-speed rail
  308; household transportation costs 309;
  immigration to 300; Kay Bailey Hutchison
  (KBH) Desalination Plant 300–301, 305;
  La Ciudad Solar installation 307; land
  development regulations 134; land use and
  transportation in 308–309; looking forward
  from 2050 to 2100 312; mass-shooting in
  130; mass transit in 302–303; Open Space
  Advisory Board 131–134; *Plan El Paso*
  (2012) 302; *Plan El Paso* Comprehensive
  Plan Process 131, 133–134; population of

304–305; *quinceañera* celebration 298; rate of expansion of 308; renewable energy in 301–302; Rim Road 138–139; San Jacinto Plaza 134, 297; Shriner's Auditorium in 139; solar cell installations 301; Streetcar 302; Sun Metro 302; Sustainability Plans 308; unemployment, rate of 309; water conservation in 130–134; water recycling in 301; water resource management in 133; Water Utilities Public Service Board 133; Water Utilities treats and reclaims 301; wild land protection and reforesting 308; Works Progress Administration (WPA) project 139; *see also* Mission Valley of El Paso
emergency hazards plans 129
emergency management 67, 254
Emerson, Ralph Waldo 57, 171
emissions: sinks 59; sources 59
energy: conservation 300; efficiency 193, 212, 300, 311; generation 2, 111, 115, 302, 311; storage 193
Englander, John 113–114
enquiry by design 244
environment/environmental: crises 127; defense fund 92; justice 207; performance of buildings and transportation systems 57, 62; planning system 41; restoration 67; sensitive land 186, 259; sustainability 267
esprit de corps 245
European Renewable Energy Council (EREC) 193
evapotranspiration, process of 195
Everglades National Park 36, 288
Expanse, The (2015) 127

facadectomy 122
Fair Share Law 169
Falling Dominoes: A Planner's Guide to Drought and Cascading Impacts (2019) 194
famine 128, 304
farmhouse townhomes 170
farmland: consumption 38; loss of 168
Federal 3R Projects 50
Federal Emergency Management Agency (FEMA) 69, 83, 146, 290; Flood Insurance Rate Map (FIRM) 218; floodmaps 128; National Flood Hazard Layer Viewer 218
federalized living spaces 32
First Street Foundation 288
fishing industry 288
Flagler, Henry 285
flash floods 307
Flat Earth Movement 45
flooding: Base Flood Elevation (BFE) 156; decline in marine fisheries due to 293; due

to King Tides 155–156, 158; in El Paso, Texas 307; flash floods 307; hazards of 218; management in Miami Beach 155–160; risk of 25, 112, 277; stormwater 221; strategy to combat 185; Zone AH 219
flood insurance 219–220; Flood Insurance Rate Maps (FIRM) 128, 218; National Flood Insurance Program (NFIP) 162
floodplain management 146, 162
Florida Center for Investigative Reporting 225
Florida Department of Transportation (FDOT) 49–51, 232
Florida Keys: Area of Critical State Concern 187; Big Pine Key *Tier 1* 186; building permit 186; Comprehensive Plan for 180–182; hurricanes 182; King Tides 188; land conservation system 186; land suitable for development *Tier 3* 188; mangroves wetlands 186; National Marine Sanctuary 186; Pennekamp State Park in Key Largo 186; plan for a changing climate 180–182; sprawl reduction *Tier 2* 187; storm drains to block seawaters from surging 185; touring of 186–188; Upper Keys Planning Office 180
Florida Power & Light (FPL) 225–227
Florida State Road A1A (Fort Lauderdale): coastal armoring of 49; design of 48; multi-modal improvements for 48–52; reconstructing of 49–52; shoreline armoring of 49–52
forest: carbon absorption by 171; preservation of 168; protection of coastal regions from waves, erosion, and rising sea levels 186; *see also* wildfires
Forest Service Urban and Community Forestry Program (USDA) 198
Fort Bliss (U.S. Army post) 300–301, 310
Forty Years of Fabulous (1977) 119
fossil fuels 34, 36, 63–64, 92, 108–109, 116, 138, 172, 193, 213, 266, 283, 301, 307, 308, 311
Fourier, Joseph 18
freshwater wetlands 288
Futurama Exhibit of the 1939 World's Fair 73, 282
Future in Focus Summit, The (2013) 31
Future Land Use Map 133, 151, 153, 154, 264, 308

galabiyas 136
Gallinar, Carlos 132, 303
Game of Thrones (2019) 221
garden cities 174
Gelbert, Dan 160

324 ■ Index

Gemütlichkeit 98
gender liberation 282
Geographic Information System (GIS) 253, 282
George III, King 57
geothermal power 111
global capitalism 63
Global Climate Impacts in the United States
(2009) 267
global decarbonization 63
global economy, decarbonizing of 63
Global Energy Monitor 64
global heating 21, 103, 128, 186
global temperatures: Intergovernmental Panel on
Climate Change (IPCC) and 17–20; rise in
17, 179
global warming 3, 29, 36, 91, 98, 102, 128, 156,
282, 311; adapting to 63–64;
*Carbon Dioxide and the Climate: A Scientific
Assessment* (1979) 18; challenges of 65;
droughts due to escalation of 194; human
influence on 17, 20–21; impact of solar
fluctuations on 96; impact on coral reefs 102;
IPCC views on 65; negative impacts of 91
Godzilla (1954) 221
Gold Coast 285
Golden Gate Bridge *70*
Google Earth 219
Gore, Al 157, 161
granny flats 152, 154
Grapes of Wrath, The (1939) 148
Great Barrier Reef (Australia) 102
Greater Miami 285, 293
Great Plains 129, 145, 192, 206, 208, 213,
268–269
Great Recession (2008–2010) 73
Green Anoles lizards (*Anolis carolinensis*) 92
greenbelts 174, 308
green buildings 260, 264; framework for
construction of 61; LEED Platinum
certification 61–62; rating system 18; U.S.
Green Building Council 61
green economy 308
greener development, incentives for 212–213
greenhouse gas (GHG) emissions 5, 10, 12,
62, 91, 95, 98, 193, 210, 243–244, 264;
"business-as-usual" emissions scenario 283;
Climate Action Plans (CAPs) for reducing
247; daily tonnage of 30; in El Paso, Texas
302, 311; Greenhouse Gas (GHG) Inventory
62; impact of solar fluctuations on 96; Local
Greenhouse Gas Inventory Tool 253; net-zero
release of 62; offset by sinks 59; per person 30;
pillars of strategies for reducing 303; reduction
targets 21, 58, 110; in Southeast Florida 30

Green, Joseph Henry 96
Greenpeace 93
green roof (vegetated) 60, 111, 212–213, 266–267
green spaces 174, 259
groundwater, contamination of 133
Guardian, The (newspaper) 127

halocarbon emissions 97
Hammond, Louisiana: *200 Downtown* project
154; affordable housing in 152; Center
for Planning Excellence (CPEX) 151;
Comprehensive Plan 153–154; development
codes 154; Form-Based Code 153; granny flats
154; Hurricane *Katrina* 151, 153; Hurricane
Laura 153; land development regulations 154;
Main Street building *150*; mixed-use building
154; multi-family housing 152; planning for
climate change in-migration in 149–153;
population of 151; property tax revenue 153;
public investments 153; quality of life and
resilience goals 154; Queen Anne Revival
homes 152; *Square 71* project 154; threat to
coastal communities from rise in sea-level 150;
use of tax capture strategies 153
Hands-On Exercise 79, 256, 257–258
Hawaiian Electric Industries 193
hazards: climate-related 130; mitigation
programs 2; weather-related 130
heart of town, concept of 82–83, 85, 183, 291
heat island effects, plan to fight 196–204,
210, 266
heat-mitigation strategies 213
hedge funds 163
Herbert Hoover Dike 116
high-speed rail 47, 111, 266, 308
Holly and Smith Architects 154
home construction, in fire-prone areas 146
household transportation costs 309
Howard, Ebenezer 174
Hueco Bolson aquifer 136, 305
hurricanes: *Andrew* 151, 162; building codes 32;
Charley 182; cost of damage from 289; *Dennis*
182; *Dorian* 218–221; *Frances* 182; *Gustav*
77; *Harvey* 149; *Ike* 77; *Irma* 118, 150–151,
220; *Ivan* 182; *Jeanne* 182; *Katrina* 49, 77, 80,
146, 151, 182; *Laura* 153; *Lee* 77; *Maria* 220;
Matthew 220; *Michael* 207, 219, 220; *Rita*
77; *Sandy* 48, 114; storm surge protection 73;
Wilma 182; *Xu* 290; *Zeta* 290–291
hydropower 111

Ikiru (movie) 205
implementation and evaluating progress,
of climate plan: assistance in 271–272;

codification of 272; role of the Advisory Board in 272; tracking of 272
Inconvenient Sequel: Truth to Power (2017) 157, 161
industrial farming 172
industrial revolution 108, 174
industrial societies 36
industrial wastes 110
innovative technologies 59
interactive polling 256, 262
Intergovernmental Panel on Climate Change (IPCC) 2, 179, 180, 183; Comprehensive Assessment Reports 17–18; creation of 17; Fifth Assessment Report (AR5) 179, 282; Hockey Stick Graph 17–18; report on global warming 65, 102; Summary for Policymakers (2007) 191; and world temperatures 17–20
island community 182

Jacobs Engineering 160
Jacobs, Jane 243
Japan's National Route 1 system 50
Jean Lafitte, Louisiana: Bayou Fuel 81; Boulevard 83; coastal marsh 73; Comprehensive Plan project 73; Comprehensive Resilience 79; funding protective levees in 73–85; funds allocated for constructing levees 85; heart of town 82–83, 85; hurricane storm surge protection 73; *Jean Lafitte Tomorrow* project 79, 84–85; Lafitte Area Independent Levee District 83; New Orleans levee system 84; process of building levees 84; property tax 83; Safe House Emergency Operations Center 79; seafood industry 79; sea level rise in 73; Town Council 84
Jefferson, Thomas 19, 22, 29
job security 73
Jones, Jody 146

Kale Flato Architects 299
Kay Bailey Hutchison (KBH) Desalination Plant 300–301, 305
Kendig Keast 212
Kennedy, John F. 33
Kerner, Timmy 73–85
keypad polling 256–257
King Tides 155–156, 158, 188
Kiplinger's Personal Finance magazine 238
Kiwanis Club 183–184
Koch Industries 23, 30
Ko Tarutao Marine National Park, Thailand 99, 103
Krugman, Paul 65
Kunstler, James Howard 262

Kurosawa, Akira 205
Kyoto Protocol (1997) 94

Lago, Candidate 223–224
lakes: Maurepas 151; Okeechobee 37, 116; Pontchartrain 151
land conservation system 186
land development: code 51, 60, 192, 196, 199, 212–213; Land Development Regulations (LDRs) 5, 66, 111, 134, 154, 159, 279; laws 176; regulations and zoning 5
landfills 123; emissions 95; landfilling of wastes 265
land ice, melting of 283
land use 41, 145, 194; codes of 111, 146; in El Paso, Texas 308–309; Future Land Use Map 264, 308; for grazing and farming 171; zoning regulations 69
La Postada Hotel *197*
Laredo Builders Association 201–202
Laredo, Texas 196–204
Las Cruces, New Mexico 149; affordable housing in 60; arroyo and natural lands 60; building standards 60; carbon footprint 60; *Elevate Las Cruces* (Comprehensive Plan) 60; green roofs 60; land development code 60; requiring resilience in 60
Leadership in Energy and Environmental Design (LEED) 1, 18, 264; Gold certification 212; Platinum certification 61–62, 66, 212; standards in new construction 302
Ledru-Rollin, Alexander 276
Les' É cole des Beaux-Arts (architecture school in Paris) 244
Levine, Philip 156–159, 164
Leyden, Collin 92
light emitting diode (LED) bulbs 267
Listening Workshop 254–255
lithium-ion batteries 193
Little River 116
Liveable CommuniKeys Plan, The 180
livestocks 173
living with water, concept of 114, 117, 120
Local Government Operations (LGOP) 256
Local Greenhouse Gas Inventory Tool 253
Lomborg, Bjørn 65
Lonely Planet Texas travel guide 134
Long-Range Transportation Plans (LRTPs) 50–51, 167, 210
Look Ahead, Trend and Opportunities, A (2013) 31
Louisiana Flood Protection Authority 79, 84
low carbon mobility 62
low-income families 169

326 ■ Index

Lubbock, Texas: agricultural communities in 208; Climate Adaptation Plan 213; Comprehensive Plan 208–209, 211; Downtown Plan and Code (2021) 213–214; drought in 205–212; green code 212–213; green infrastructures in 213; incentives for greener development 212–213; jobs and economic empowerment 213; land development code 212; loop highway 210; mixed-use communities in 210; *Plan Lubbock 2040* 206, 211; *Strategic Water Supply Plan* (2018) 208

lung cancer, relation with smoking 20

Madoff, Bernie 163
malnutrition 65
mangroves wetlands 186
marine fisheries, decline in 293
Marshall, George 226
mass transit 30, 103, 266, 300, 302–303
Master Plans 77, 80, 121, 129, 137–138, 248, 275
McCarthy, Linda 138
Mead, Margaret 233
Mediterranean Revival condominium building 112
mega-cities 155
Metropolitan Transportation Plans (MTPs) 167
MetroQuest 37, 254
Mexican–American War (1846) 57
Miami Beach, Florida 83, 112, 117, 149; Art Deco District 122, 164; as America's Atlantis 156; Art Deco Festival (1977) 119; as barrier island 119–121; blue and green infrastructure 159; building codes 112; Capital Improvement Plan 275; *destructive versus constructive resiliency* 123; drinking water in 2050 292; economy of 293; energy in 2050 293–294; environment of 294; facadectomy 122; *Forty Years of Fabulous* (1977) 119; historic buildings 122; Hurricane *Andrew* 151; Hurricane *Irma* 118, 150–151; hurricanes in 2050 289–290; impact of rising seas in 2050 290–291; King Tides in 155–156, 158; land development regulations 159; levee and flood barrier system 113; looking forward from 2050 to 2100 294; mangrove forests 113; Miami-Dade County 291; Miami Modern (MiMo) buildings 122; migration in 291–292; natural islands 119; natural landscape to protect the city from rising sea 119; plan for North Miami Beach 122; *Plan NOBE* 122–123, 158; real estate roulette 123; real estate value of 161; risk analysis in 119–124;

sea walls, building of 158; shoreline and living shoreline breakwaters 113; South Beach 119; Southern Glades Trail 115; stormwater and flooding management in 155–160; Stormwater Master Plan 275; stormwater resilience project 160; Strategic Miami Area Rapid Transit (SMART) Plan 166; Sunset Harbour 160; temperatures in 2050 292; *Urbin Retreat* (condominium building) 156

Miami Beach Art Deco hotel *120*
Miami-Dade: 2045 Long Range Transportation Plan (2045 LRTP) 166; County Sea Level Rise Task Force 51
Miami-Dade Transportation Planning Organization: funds for the creation of the Southern Corridor 167; Strategic Miami Area Rapid Transit (SMART) Plan 166
Miami Design Preservation League's Art Deco Weekend 119, 123
Miami River 116
middle class, creation of 108
Mission Valley of El Paso: Comprehensive Plan 134, 136–137; discussion of climate with vulnerable population in 134–138; Hueco Bolson aquifer 136; impact of climate change in 136; San Elizario Chapel (1789) 135; Socorro Mission (1759) 135; Spanish missions in 135; tourism and tourism-based economies 136; UNESCO designation 136; Ysleta Mission (1682) 135
Missoula, Montana: Business Improvement District 137; Downtown Association 137; Downtown Master Plan 137–138; Downtown Partnership 137; threat of wildfires 138
Miyagi Prefecture (Japan) 118
Moken (sea people) 101
monsoon rainstorms 290
Montgomery, Alabama: Alabama Housing Finance Authority 59; investing in resilience in 59–60; provision of affordable housing 59; streets in flood zones 59; tree planting campaigns 59
Mowry, Bruce 159
multi-modal transportation networks 261
municipal sewer system 223

National Climate Assessment 17, 217
National Flood Insurance Program (NFIP) 162, 220
National Geodetic Vertical Datum (NGVD) 156
National Oceanic and Atmospheric Administration (NOAA) 19, 74, 185, 283; and global sea level rise 25; National Hurricane Center 217; Radar Map app 218

Index ■ **327**

National Register of Historic Places 122
National Weather Service 19
natural disasters 12, 77, 110, 145–146, 182
natural environment 2, 114, 168, 239
natural gas 108, 111, 302
natural gas-fired plants 225
natural islands 119
natural landscape 60, 265; management of 268; power to preserve 94; to protect the city from rising sea 119
natural parks 237
natural resource extraction 133
Nature Conservancy 117–118, 169
neighborhood parks 133, 157, 213
neighborhood planning: characteristic of 175, 248; prioritization plan 160
Nelessen, Anton 257
Nelson, Murray 187–188
Net-Zero Building 264
net-zero carbon emissions 312
Newfield, Martin County, Florida: planning compact urban Gorm and Knight Kiplinger's legacy at 235–239; quality of life 238
New Orleans: catastrophic weather events 146; Center for Planning Excellence (CPEX) 151; Hurricane *Katrina* (2005) 146, 148; levee system 84; plan for retreat after Hurricane *Katrina* 148; population of 146–147; school system 108
New Urbanism movement, in town planning 41, 173–175
New York City: BIG U protective system 117; Rebuild By Design project 117
non-fossil fuels 109
non-governmental organizations (NGOs) 68, 110
non-profit organizations 68, 202, 255
Northern Thailand 175
North Sea 116
north–south divide 27
Not In My Backyard (NIMBY) 41–42
nuclear energy 225
nuclear power stations 293
nuclear technologies, efficiencies of 193

ocean, acidification of 101
oceanfront real estate 113
offshore wind turbines 266
oil extraction 142, 212
O'Neal, Steve 211
optimized energy scenario 38
organic farms 168, 172
O'Rourke, Beto 6, 299
ownership of land 44

Pacific Descadal Oscillation (PDO) 97
Paine, Ken 168
palm trees, planting of 91, 199
Panama City, Florida 207–208
Parent Teacher Association 108
Paris Agreement (2015) 2–3, 94–95, 179, 307
Parks and Open Space Master Plans 248
Pavilion at Durbin Park, The 58
Pennekamp State Park, Key Largo 186
permafrost, melting of 179
Perry, Rick 133
photovoltaic farms 111
photovoltaic panels 225
Pineland Prairie 235
plague outbreaks 110
Plan Advisory Committee 250–251
Planet of the Apes (1968) 127
Plan for Chicago of 1909 278
Planned Urban Developments (PUDs) 196
Plan NOBE (Miami Beach, Florida) 122–123, 158
Plan Viva Laredo project 199
Plan website 253–254
political implications, of climate change 103
politics, on climate change 93–94
Poll Everywhere 256
Ponzi, Charles 163
Ponzi scheme 163
Portland, Oregon 95; climate solutions 63; local action plan for cutting carbon 275
power generation 65, 94, 96, 140, 193, 302
power grid, decarbonization of 95
Powers, Donald 174
Practice of Local Government Planning, The (2000) 248
predator habitats, restoration of 44
problem solving 115
Project Coordinator 249
property taxes 57–58, 69, 83
public buildings: LEED-rated design of 66; renovations of 66
public design workshop, for climate planning 244, 251–252, 255–262; community involvement session 256–258; on-site design studio 258–260; technical and stakeholder meetings 260; vision plan and policy plan framework 261; visualizations for plans, renderings, graphics, and photographs 260–261; work-in-progress presentation 261–262
public facilities, design of 267
public housing community 59
Public Infrastructure Fee (PIF) 58
public plazas, for recreation 159
public transportation 10, 165–166; Bus Rapid Transit (BRT) 67, 166; Long-Range

328 ■ *Index*

Transportation Plans (LRTPs) 50–51, 167; Strategic Miami Area Rapid Transit (SMART) Plan 166; Surface Transportation Assistance Act (1982) 50

quality of life 24, 134–135, 151, 153–154, 238–239, 261, 264, 271, 304, 306

raingardens 186, 198, 213
rainstorm 68, 290
rainwater management 61
Rapid Transit Corridors 166
real estate: development 93, 176; roulette 123
redevelopment trust fund 57–58
Red Menace 33
regional planning: Regional Planning Councils (RPCs) 24, 28, 46; threat posed by 40
Region in Motion scenario 38, 40
renewable powerplants 11
renewable technologies 193
renewable energy 10, 58, 61, 64, 94, 111; in El Paso, Texas 301–302, 311; power generation 193; *Re-Thinking 2050* plan for meeting energy needs 193; sources of 109, 193, 267; utility-scale 111
Representative Concentration Pathways (RCPs) 179, 282
Republican Liberty Caucus of Southeast Florida 29
Request for Proposal (RFP) 4, 68, 227
resilience grants 68–69; Community Development Block Grant-Disaster Recovery (CDBG-DR) funds 68–69; from Department of Local Affairs (DOLA) 68, 69; Federal Emergency Management Agency (FEMA) grants 69; for funding protective levees in Jean Lafitte, Louisiana 73–85; from Housing and Urban Development (HUD) 68
resilience: infrastructure 207; investing in 59–60; paying for 57–59; requirement of 60–62
Resilience Plans 248
Resilient305 Strategy 51
Resilient Redesign Workshop 112, 118
Re-Thinking 2050 plan 193
retreat to the heart of town, strategy of 83, 85, 183, 291
Rhode Island 90, 103, 163, 173–174, 182, 187, 237, 280, 301, 311; agri-art community in 167–171; climate change mitigation in 168; Comprehensive Housing Production and Rehabilitation Act (2004) 168–169; Comprehensive Permit projects 170; organic farms in 172; Red Rooster 170; University

of 121, 168, 171; *see also* Sandywoods Farm, Rhode Island
Right-of-Way Tree Planting Request Form 204
Right Tree Right Place campaign 198, 201, 205
Rio Grande 135–136, 139, 149, 192, 199, 300–301, 304–306, 308
roadmap 166
Roark, Howard 41
Rockefeller Foundation 51, 248
Rocky Mountain 129, 192
Rotary Club 132, 184
run-for-your-life storms, cycles of 291
rural landscape, preservation of 169
rural preservation and affordability 169
rural–urban divide 27

Safire, William 22
sales taxes 57–58, 69, 167
saltwater: intrusion 17, 77, 115, 268, 289; upwelling 184
Samaniego, Ricardo 135
sand motors 115
Sandywoods Farm, Rhode Island: affordable housing in 171; agri-art community in 167–171; Community Supported Agriculture (CSA) programs 168, 173; Comprehensive Permit 169; Donald Powers 174; fair housing laws 175; Fair Share Law 169; farm and communal garden 172; land reserved for a working farm and open space 169; land use policies 168; local food and energy production at 167–171; Meadow View Lane 171; Nature Conservancy 169; organic farms 172; preservation of natural environment 168; Rhode Island Comprehensive Housing Production and Rehabilitation Act (2004) 168–169; risk of wildfires 168; Senate Policy Council on design guidelines for Comprehensive Permit projects 170; State Housing Appeals Board (SHAB) 170; traditional architectures 171; Traditional Neighborhood Developments (TNDs) 172, 175; tree and shrub planting guides 172
San Elizario Chapel (1789) 135
San Francisco, climate issues in 69–73
Santa Monica, California 83, 226
"save the trees" conversation 130
Scott, Rick 156–158
seafood industry 79
sea ice and glaciers, decline in 17
sea level, rise in 10, 30, 40, 50, 91, 108, 116, 123, 148, 160, 164, 180, 192, 277, 282; 1-foot scenario 288; 3-foot rise scenario 288–289; committed sea level rise 283;

Index ▪ **329**

effect of 287–288; natural landscape to protect the city from 119; NOAA and 25; phenomenon of 25

sea people: *chao le* 101; Moken 101; Urak Lawoi 101

sea walls 10, 57–58, 158–159, 165, 186, 287, 290–291

self-contained living areas 152

self-preservation, sense of 277

septic tanks 6, 186, 221–224

Serenbe community 173

Seven50 ("seven counties, 50 years") plan 24, 28–29, 31–32, 36, 41–42, 122, 149, 183, 282; anti-*Seven50* cause 42; final summit (2014) 46–47; postscript 47–48; Region in Motion scenario 38, 40; scenario modeler 37–40; *Seven50 Blueprint for Regional Prosperity* 46; strategic upgrades 38; suburban expansion 38; summits two and three 31–37; trend 38

sewer system, improvements in 67

shade structures, over sidewalks 213

shapefiles 253

Sharia Law 29

shepherding development proposals 128

Sherwood, Carol 192

shoreline armoring 49–52, 58

Sierra Club 250

single-family homes 31, 35, 82, 152–153, 237

single-rider automobiles 58

Slabbers, Steven 112, 114

smart growth, notion of 30, 40, 134, 169, 264

social equity 114, 117, 247

social identities 3–4

social media 21, 253–254, 258, 270

social resilience 2, 79

social security 33, 282

socialist democracy 282

Socorro Mission (1759) 135

Solari, Bob 28–30, 32, 40, 41, 47

solar power 1, 109, 141, 193, 225, 227, 301, 308, 311; arrays 21, 67, 103, 142, 225, 294, 308, 311; cell installations 301; farms 61–62, 111, 301, 307, 310–311; fluctuations, impact on climate change 95–96; generators 66; panel installation 264; technologies 308

Solar United Neighbors 227

Somerville, Massachusetts: Assembly Square Neighborhood Plan 62–63; carbon neutral 62; Climate Forward Plan 63; climate solutions in 63; Grey Star Real Estate 61–62; LEED Platinum certification 61–62; life science buildings 61–62; net-zero release of GHG emissions 62; new zoning ordinance 61; requiring resilience in 60–62; Somerville Climate Change Vulnerability Assessment 62; Somerville Climate Forward Plan 62; stormwater management 63; sustainable buildings in 60; XMBLY Business Campus project 62

Southeast Florida: canals to drain stormwater into the ocean 288; climate adaptation effort 293; Climate Compact 148; climate mitigation and adaptation 24; climate-planning in 23–48; coral reefs in 294; daily tonnage of greenhouse gas emissions 30; drinking water in 2050 292; economy in 2050 293; environment in 2050 294; evacuation zones of 290; final summit (2014) 46–47; Flood Control Project 293; *Future in Focus Summit, The* (2013) 31; hurricanes in 2050 289–290; impact of rising seas in 2050 290–291; land development system in 163; *Look Ahead, Trend and Opportunities, A* (2013) 31; looking forward from 2050 to 2100 294; Miami-Dade County Sea Level Rise Task Force 51; migration in 291–292; mitigation efforts 157; National Flood Insurance Program 162; NOAA and global sea level rise 25; People's Transportation Plan 167; planning team in 41–42; Ponzi scheme 163; quality of life 24; reasons for growth of 162–163; regional effort in 25–31; *Resilient305 Strategy* 51; Rising Above Commission 291–292; Senate Bill 1094, signing of 158; *Seven50* ("seven counties, 50 years") plan 24, 28–29, 31–32, 36, 37–40; St. Lucie County Commission story 42–43; summits two and three 31–37; Sustainable Communities program 29; temperatures in 2050 292; threat posed by regional planning 40; transit infrastructure in 165–166; urban lifestyles for future generations 31; waterfront development 162; wetlands regulations 41

Southeast Florida Regional Climate Change Compact 24, 112, 148, 157

South Florida Resilient Redesign Workshop 112, 118

Spain's Colonial Empire 136

special assessment taxes 58

sprawl reduction 187

stack-and-pack high-rises 32

Standard Oil 285

Standard State Zoning Enabling Act (SZEA) 111

Statewide Transportation Improvement Plans (STIPs) 167

Steinbeck, John 35, 148

Stein, Isaac 119–124

330 ■ Index

Stoddard, Mayor 224–227
storm surges 26, 48, 73, 77, 113, 159, 181, 218–219, 287, 289–290, 293; defense against 265; wind-driven high tides 74
stormwater system: canals to drain stormwater into the ocean 288; flooding 221; gravity-fed 156, 288; management of 63, 197, 261; mechanized 165; in Miami Beach, Florida 155–160; resilience project 160; runoff 198
Strategic Miami Area Rapid Transit (SMART) Plan 166
Strategic Vision for Panama City's Historic Downtown and its Waterfront, A (2019) 207
street plans, of the coastal municipalities 50
street trees, loss of 47, 57, 93, 153, 170, 196–200, 202–204, 210, 224
suburbs/suburban 30, 174, 309; expansion 38, 152, 307; sprawl 168, 174, 265, 312
suicide-by-lifestyle 64
Sunshine State 225
super levees 49, 293
Surface Transportation Assistance Act (1982) 50
survivability, threshold of 91, 101
Sustainability Planning Toolkit 248
Sustainability Plans 29, 247–248
sustainable buildings 60, 207
Sustainable Communities Initiative 24, 29
sustainable development: defined 44; pillars of 247
Svarzbein, Peter 303
SWA Group 299
swing state 27

Tarutao Islands, Thailand 99–104; Adang-Rawi island group 101; *chao le* island 102; coral reefs and coastal habitats 99–101; fish species in 101; On Ko Adang island 99; Ko Tarutao Marine National Park 99, 103; Moken and Urak Lawoi sea people 101; political implications of climate change in 103
Tavernier Hotel *181*
tax credit 59, 154, 308
Tax Increment Financing (TIF) 160, 291
Taxpayer's Association of Indian River County 29
Taylor, Zachary 300
Tenet (2020) 127
Texas Department of Transportation 303
Thai boat *100*
Thoreau, Henry David 57, 108
Thunberg, Greta 137, 231
tiny homes 152
tipping point, concept of 70–71
town planning, New Urbanism movement in 41
Traditional Neighborhood Developments (TNDs) 172, 175

traffic congestion reductions 67
transit map 166
Transportation Improvement Program (TIP) 167
Transportation Investment Generating Economic Recovery (TIGER) grants 303
Transportation Planning Organization (TPO) 166–167
Transportation Plans 248, 251, 263; Long-Range Transportation Plans (LRTPs) 50; Metropolitan Transportation Plans (MTPs) 167
trees: campaigns for planting of 59; carbon absorption by 171; clearance of land 171; and the environment 171–173; as frozen carbon 172; as life support system 171; loss for spiritual reasons 171; oak tree 172; planting of 59, 172, 205, 224, 264; Right-of-Way Tree Planting Request Form 204; stewardship 199; wardens 198
Trump, Donald 141, 157, 211, 214, 238
Turkey Point Nuclear Generating Station 293
Turning Point˙ 256

unemployment, rate of 309
Union of Concerned Scientists 112
United in Science report 17
United Nations (UN): Climate Change Conference (2015) 94; Conference on Environment and Development (UNCED) 43; Educational, Scientific, and Cultural Organization (UNESCO) 135, 136–137; Environmental Programme (UNEP) 17; Framework Convention on Climate Change (UNFCCC) 3, 94; Global Tax 44
United States (U.S.): Army Corps of Engineers (USACE) 73, 116, 118, 185, 188, 283; Constitution of 162; Department of Energy 227; Department of Housing and Urban Development 68; Drought Monitor 194; Energy Information Administration 109; Environmental Protection Agency (EPA) 93, 110, 134, 252, 290; Global Change Research Program 267–269; *Global Climate Impacts in the United States* (2009) 267; Green Building Council 61; House of Representatives 299; Housing and Urban Development (HUD) 114, 117
University of Rhode Island 121, 168, 171
Urak Lawoi (sea people) 101
urban communities 32, 174
urban decay 165, 168
urban design 42, 93, 248, 255, 260, 263
urban estuary 119
urban lifestyles for future generations 31

Index ■ 331

urban renewal 73
urban tree canopy, loss of 2, 198–199, 292
urban water retention facilities 117
Urban Footprint program 206
Urban Land Institute (ULI) 118, 159
urban planning 2, 15, 27, 55, 129, 145, 169, 173, 233, 243, 276; America's tradition of 41; building codes 112; creation and update of 111; Dutch solution for 114–115; emergency hazard plans 129; importance of water adequacy in 194; municipal Comprehensive Plan 111; zoning as tool for 175
Utility Master Plans 248
utility-scale: renewable energy 111; solar 225, 266

vehicle miles travelled (VMT) 302–303
Victorio Peak-Bone Springs aquifer, in Dell City 305
Virginia Key Boulevard Levee: adaptation best practices 115; Alton Road study area 114; Army Corps' proposal for 118; climate action plan 112; climate adaptation infrastructure project 118; Climate Leadership Conference 117; concept of 119; elevating and floodproofing of homes 118; flood barrier system 113; idea of climate change 117; living with water, concept of 117; oceanfront real estate 113; reducing risk with 112–119; Rickenbacker Causeway 113; urban water retention facilities 117
virtual charrettes 248, 254–255, 258
virtual design workshops 255
virtual on-site design studio 258; virtual public design workshop 256
visual preference surveys 254, 257

Waggoner, David 74–75
Wakeem, Charlie 131
War of 1812 77
wastewater treatment 223
water: conservation of 95, 134, 196, 202, 208, 300–301, 306; efficiency 38, 194; harvesting, strategies of 133; quality 133–134, 158, 265; reclamation 306; resource inventories 195;

sanitation 65; shortages 192, 194, 300; squares 159; storage of 58, 67, 195; tower 219, *234*, 236–237; utility 67, 306
water recycling projects 10, 195; in El Paso, Texas 301; and water conservation ordinances 301
water resource management 133; Co-Water Adequacy Rule (Colorado) 194; impact of drought on 194
watershed protection 195, 265
water supply 134; in El Paso, Texas 305; "pipe-to-pipe" system 305
water-use technologies and policies 300
weather-related catastrophe 277
weather-related emergencies 129
wetlands 133; loss of 76; mangroves 186; regulations 41
white roofs 266
wildfires 17, 128–129, 138, 145, 168, 171, 195, 277
wild land protection and reforesting 308
wind: generators 66; power 1, 65, 111, 193, 266, 294, 311; turbines 67, 142, 169–170, 175, 193, 266; windfarms 21; windmills 142–143, 171, 208; windstorms 163, 201
wine-tastings and culinary competitions 173
Work-in-Progress Presentation 261–262
World Heritage Site List 135
World Meteorological Organization (WMO) 17, 56

Xcel Energy Windsource Program 58
xeriscaping 133, 197, 306
XMBLY Business Campus project 62

Y2K scare (1999) 15
Ysleta Mission (1682) 135

zero emissions technology 94
zero net energy consumption 264
zoning 145–146, 279; codes 196; for commercial development 152; Comprehensive Permits for 169; in favor of balanced communities 175; laws of 174; map 187; state-override of local zoning 168; as tool for urban planning 175; Zone AH 219

Printed in the United States
by Baker & Taylor Publisher Services